VOLUME 2

THE ALBERT OUTLER LIBRARY

Edited by Bob W. Parrott

THE CHURCHMAN

BRISTOL HOUSE

Anderson, Indiana

Albert Outler the Churchman

Published by Bristol Books, an imprint of Bristol House, Ltd.

First Edition, May 1995

ISBN: 1-885224-02-8

Printed in the United States of America

Bristol House, Ltd.
P.O. Box 4020
Anderson, Indiana 46013-4020

To order call : 1-800-451-READ

Table of Contents

Preface
Albert Outler the Churchman

Albert Outler the Churchman is the second book in a trilogy of sermons, addresses, and lectures that make up Part 1 of the Albert C. Outler Library. The first book of the trilogy, *Albert Outler the Preacher*, was composed of sermons given in local churches. This volume, *Albert Outler the Churchman*, includes addresses given on ecumenical, special, and conference occasions. These sermons on several occasions will be followed by a third volume titled *Albert Outler the University Professor*, a book of sermons given in chapels on university campuses. (Part 2 of the Albert C. Outler Library will be the efforts of five theologians to bring into focus Albert Outler's works in the areas of Christology, evangelism, pastoral psychology, ecumenism, and patristics).

Albert Outler the Churchman will in a special way excite the readers who heard some of these addresses, many of which were major commentaries and challenges at the crossroads of church history. Those who did not hear them will rejoice to find them preserved in these pages. While a Latin or Greek word or phrase may cause some readers to stumble, on the whole the messages are easy to follow. This was one mark of Albert Outler's genius—he could talk theology in a way that people understood.

Following the style of volume I of the trilogy, introductory comments will capture the thrust of each address while offering insights into the personality and character of the man. In this I shall point out, from what he says, unique dimensions of Albert Outler. Admittedly the exercise falls far short of the aloofness of "objectivity" (which he used to say was subjectivity pushed to its limits). Nothing more is intended than what the words say. They are "introductory comments."

These ecumenical, special, and conference occasions reveal a churchman in the broadest meaning. His audiences ranged from mourners at a memorial service to bishops, preachers, and priests in ecumenical settings. With this expanded audience Albert Outler's sphere of influence broadened considerably.

My thanks to Laura Randall, reference librarian at Bridwell Library, Perkins School of Theology, for her special talents in locating some of the more elusive note sources in these addresses. The noting of this book was a chore. I found myself doing with Dr. Outler's sermons what he did with John Wesley's sermons, looking in every nook and corner for his sources. This clearly indicates that when he gave these addresses and preached these sermons, he gave no thought to their publication. But in his last days he knew that they would be published and was pleased with that prospect.

My thanks also to Carla Outler, who gathered the material, my co-worker wife, Doris, and my secretary Mildred Zorn. And a sense of deep gratitude to God whose providence has now given this work to the church Albert Outler served and still serves through those who will read these words and get the message.

Bob W. Parrott

PART 1

Ecumenical Occasions

Introduction

This Lenten sermon for ministers was preached at the New Haven (Connecticut) Council of Churches on March 17 or 18, 1946.

The thesis: "Sacrifice . . . is a part of the process of reopening blocked communication, of reestablishing community where alienation was before, the escape from splendid isolation into a circle of belonging." The authority for this belief came from an experience of hearing Bach's *St. Matthew Passion*, whose text is taken from the Passion experience of Jesus as recorded in Scripture. The keen awareness of this scriptural thesis, reported Albert Outler, "did more than almost anything else to clarify and clinch my vocational decision."

This sense of sacrifice gave to his life's calling this threefold meaning: "surrender of self-regard and self-service; obedience to some higher obligation; and sharing in an ethically purposeful life." One observed that meaning worked out in Dr. Outler's community spirit. No isolationist was he. Name the cause and he was part of the cause of it.

Albert Outler was involved with Thanksgiving Square projects in Dallas, where he was instrumental in bringing together Christian, Jewish, Muslim, Buddhist, and Hindu leaders. When asked, "How did you fare as host for the Dalai Lama?", Professor Outler said, "No one has to be other than who he is."

SERMON 1

The Meaning of Sacrifice

The Methodists wheeze about Episcopalians in Lent.

Lent is a time when preachers step up their use of ancient and good Christian words and phrases, pointing toward Christ's passion and death, and looking on past them toward the glorious triumph of Easter morn. But what means this rhetorical revival? Is it more than an accommodation to the expectations of our acquiescence to the Christian year? Is it more than "seasonal conversion"? What do these old words mean and what do we mean by them? How close are we to the mind of the early Christians who were so deeply impressed by the events and implications of that last week and its climactic tragedy? Note well the emphasis upon the last week in all the Gospels.

A few years ago I went with a friend to hear Bach's *St. Matthew Passion*. This seems to me to be a quintessential union of great art and great truth—both ineffable—and I always feel emotion quite too deep for tears as the oratorio builds up, through its successive stages, to the climax of the *Passion Chorales* and then subsides to the benediction of the final double chorus: "In tears of grief here sit we weeping;" Hearts turned to Thee, O Savior blest."

As we went away, my friend (but lately emancipated from a fundamentalist theology and cultus and now the proud professor of a Socinian theology and a new fad for "the experimental enrichment of worship") turned to me and said: "That music is good but those words are awfully gruesome." I wondered sadly what Johann Sebastian Bach would have said to this divided judgment—this devout genius whose art and faith were reciprocals of any integral service to God.

Through the Gospel histories and the Lenten liturgies runs a scarlet thread of tragedy: sacrifice, ransom, atonement; Christ on the Cross, "who made there, by the sacrifice of himself once offered, a full, perfect and sufficient sacrifice for the sins of the whole world." Our prayers and our hymns will either echo or evade this ancient and elemental motif, and our sermons may essay to plumb its depths. What does it mean? What can we make out of it—we moderns who are persuaded by the prophets' denunciation of sub-ethical cultus?

I do not pretend to understand the "fullness of Christ's sacrifice" or the relation of human sacrifice to human redemption. But a beginning of understanding began for me many years ago as I listened to a sermon by a backwoods Georgia preacher on John 12:24. It was not a good sermon (I could tell for I was fresh out of college and I had heard good preaching). All I can remember of it now is that the preacher would repeat the text about every two or three minutes—and that, finally, the phrase "abideth alone" rose up and smote me "twixt the eyes of comprehension." Abideth *alone*—so that's it? The natural reward of self-preservation is to succeed—and to abide alone! Sacrifice is not, essentially, a technique for passing the buck or for bribing God. It is a part of the process of reopening blocked communication, of reestablishing community where alienation was before, the escape from splendid isolation into a circle of belonging.

It was, as I have said, a poor sermon, but that corny trick of banging away at the text for want of something more to say was a providential device for bringing me to see what I had never before imagined—and it became for me a moment of crucial meaning, which did more than almost anything else to clarify and clinch my vocational decision.

Then, again, years later, in the grim and shattering days of December 1940, I came across a book by a very sophisticated Frenchman, as different from my old backwoods preacher as you can imagine. The book was called *Pilote de Guerre*, and the man was Antione de St. Exupery. It was, and still is, one of the truly great books to have come out of this war. Amongst many others, one passage seemed to me to glow with an insight not wholly different from the one I had had in Claxton's chapel. Here is a summary of that penetrating thought: *Sacrifice is the essential act required to create or recreate true community.*

Divested of its magical and priestcraftly accretions, sacrifice is essentially the suffering entailed in establishing, maintaining, or recovering community: a family, a society, etc. It always has a threefold meaning: surrender of self-regard and self-service; obedience to some higher obligation; and sharing in an ethically purposeful life.

Now when we try to transpose this idea analogically to explain "the fullness of Christ's sacrifice," we have to remember the infinite qualitative distinction between God and man; between God's gracious love and man's greedy love. What would it take for the holy, sovereign God to reopen blocked communication with men? What does it cost to make communion where alienation was before? How can man's sins be forgiven without its being a travesty of the moral law?

Well, one thing is sure: What had to be done, God had to do. And notice that the New Testament never talks about God *being reconciled*, but rather about God reconciling himself to the world.

Our sacrifices partake of the quality of the divine sacrifice in that they, too, may be the means of serving community (*human* community). But we fall into a peculiar heresy when we cherish the notion that bearing our crosses is a replica of Christ on his. Not the Cross, but the Man on the Cross (the *middle* cross) is the reconciling agent. Not the idea of redemption but the *act* of redemption constitutes the quality of divine sacrifice.

This, or something like it, is part of our Lenten gospel. It matters a good deal whether or not we can find meaning in it so that our service of God in the liturgies of the season may not be awkward and perfunctory, but truly climactic and a ministry of grace. Let us not rush upon Easter and pass the Passion with averted eyes as the priest and the Levite did to the victim on the Jericho road. We are not entitled to the Easter triumph until we have fully shared the heartbreak of Good Friday.

> O dearly, dearly has he loved,
> And we must love him, too,
> And trust in his redeeming blood,
> And try his works to do.[1]

Introduction

In January 1960 the congregation of First Baptist church in Pasadena, California, heard in this sermon the basic Christology of Albert Outler. He preached more times on John 13:34-35 than any other. When he felt the need to express his deepest Christian beliefs, this text came rushing forth. What was new about this old love-God-and-neighbor commandment? "As I have loved you" was new. As you *are* loved, you love . . . that is the way Christ loved . . . the new way.

Albert Outler's journey along the ecumenical road was long and varied. He went to the World Council of Churches' Third World Conference on Faith and Order in 1952. Then he went to Lund. From there he went on to the Working Committee of Faith and Order and the chairmanship of the Theological Study Commission on Tradition and Traditions. He was a delegate to the Third Assembly of the World Council of Churches in New Delhi where he helped draft the New Delhi statement on the nature of the church. Meanwhile, he wrote *The Christian Tradition and the Unity We Seek*. After that he was appointed to the Consultation on Church Union (COCU) from 1964 to 1970. In 1962 he was invited to be one of the three regular delegates of the World Methodist Council to the Second Vatican Council. He became deeply involved in the complex revolution of Vatican II and its aftermath in the Roman Catholic Church.

In this sermon Outler was the informal ecumaniac preaching in a Baptist church. He once said, "'Spiritual unity' is easy enough—'we're one in the Spirit, one in the Lord; and they'll know we are Christians by our love.' That's pretty good when measured against the religious wars of the seventeenth century, but it's actually not very profound." Yet in this sermon Outler admitted that the subject of love is the most powerful and profound place to begin the dialogue.

SERMON 2

The Power to Love

There is often a wide gap between what we favor, and what we do. In our minds, most of us favor peace, patriotism, and the good life—yet our actions all too often obstruct peace, corrupt patriotism, and sabotage the good life. But the greatest of our favorite virtues and values is love. Everybody approves of love—especially in church. We know that love—unselfish love—is a good thing; that, without it, life is not really living or worth living. Nature Boy says, "The greatest thing you'll ever learn is to love and to be loved in return"; St. Paul says "The greatest of these is love." We know that we are commanded to love; that the Law of Love is the Law of Life, and the quality of any life depends upon the quality of that life's loving. Selfish love equals selfish life; fear-filled love equals fear-filled life, etc.

Yet we who favor love are not always loving; we know we ought to love, but all too often we lack the power and the wisdom to love—rightly, unselfishly, sacrificially, consistently, with utter trust in the power of love to redeem and triumph.

We have the power of love, yet we cannot summon or direct that power at will. We know the law of love, but we cannot love, wisely and unselfishly, just because we ought. We need—it is our greatest need—the power to love that wells up in the heart, that is guided by real intelligence and wisdom, that is expressed in faithful, fearless, and consistent action. Where is such power to love? Not in ourselves, by ourselves, surely. But yet in ourselves through the power and grace of God, insofar as we are really open and responsive to his power and grace. This is the gospel—that God in Christ gives us the power to love aright, and so to live rightly and so to come to eternal life through him who *is* life eternal. This is the central message of one of the most remarkable chapters in the New Testament: John 13.

It is worth noticing how this thirteenth chapter of John fits into the Gospel itself—and fits with the others. It is the pivot or hinge of the fourth Gospel, coming as it does at the close of the public ministry of Jesus and at the beginning of the Passion. Moreover, it occupies the same relative position in the fourth Gospel as the Last Supper does in the Synoptics. The symbolic act of Jesus washing the disciples' feet is John's equivalent of the Lord's Supper in the Synoptics, and one thinks foot washing should have been conserved in the church as a sacrament and ordinance (cf. 13:12-15).

But the climax of the chapter comes in verses 34-35. As if Jesus were leaving a will and testament and preparing his disciples for a future they could not fathom nor anticipate, he says, "I have a new commandment to give you . . ."

Imagine, if you will, how these men felt and what they were thinking in this dramatic moment. The memories of their first hopes when they had "left all and first followed" this Jesus; the shadow of the cross that was, even then, falling across that secluded Upper Room; and now their deeply stirred emotions as the result of Jesus' humble, yet dignified, act of menial service.

A new commandment. But what about the old ones? Their minds flashed back to Jesus' summary of the Law and the Prophets (Mark 12:29-33; Matthew 22:37-40; Luke 10:25-28; 39-40 derived from Deuteronomy 6:5 and Leviticus 19:18). The law of love—to God and neighbor: the quintessence of biblical ethics, the bone and marrow of biblical religion. A *new* commandment? What—and why? And so they listen with acute attention: "That ye love one another; even as I have loved you." We can almost see their attention sagging. Oh, that. Yes, that's right. But we already knew that. The new commandment turns out to be the old commandment. The Evangelist makes it plain that they had not caught the new twist that Jesus gave the old idea—even as I have loved you. And so he repeats the very same words in 15:12 and much, much later there is an echo of these words in 1 John 3:23 and 2 John 5.

The new commandment is the same as the old in ethical substance, but decisively different in motivation. What was—what still is—the old commandment? Thou shalt love the Lord thy God above all else and thy neighbor as one in whom you recognize an identity with yourself.

God above all else—above self and family, above all earthly powers and values, above anything and everything in my power or human power to manage and dispose of. To love God above all else and to love all else in God; this is the first and great commandment. If you ever give yourself over to meditation, this is the first great theme to dwell upon—the ultimate truth about ultimate reality.

But it has a corollary: If I love God, I must also love my neighbor as myself. But he is not myself. And I don't really love him if I imagine what *I* would like if I were in his situation and try to supply that. Early in our marriage, Mrs. Outler used to fix all sorts of delicious things for me that she would have liked if she had been me. I bought a chemistry set for my son who would have preferred a baseball outfit. Etc.

The command to love my neighbor as myself, as the Hebrew of Leviticus 19:18 shows, is the command to recognize, and act on the recognition, that behind and beneath the differences between me and my neighbor there is a basic identity: "The colonel's lady and Judy O'Grady are sisters under the skin."[1] My neighbor—next door, next precinct, next town, and next state, nation, planet, etc.—and I are creatures of God, and finally this is what makes us alike. Imagine what this would do to our pride and our humility, too. Pride of birth, pride of race, pride of power, pride of culture? Birth, race, culture are important but not basically important, and we foul things up when we treat them as if they were. But also we need to rearrange our humilities. Before whom do we bow and scrape? Why do we try to keep up with our neighbors? I knew Albert Einstein very slightly and held him in awe, but would have gone crazy trying to emulate him. Yet I could love him—or any other man—in dignity if I could recognize in him this identical humanity that God has created in us and by which he makes us neighbors.

This is the Law of Love and it is a good law, the law of life and salvation. But there's a hitch in it, as every sinner knows. You cannot love on order or just because you ought to. Neither God nor neighbor. I know I ought to love God. But if I'm afraid of him, or if I doubt his existence, or if I think I can get along without him except for emergency tow-ins—I won't love him, not really. I know I ought to love my neighbor, and I try, but if he's "different" or if it's inconvenient or costly, I'll switch over to other neighbors who are easier to love (because in loving them, I'm loving myself in and through them).

I know I don't like to be loved on order, and I think maybe God doesn't either. If I were underprivileged and some behemoth of benevolence moved in on me to love me in the mood of grim determination to do me good, I'd run or buck (and so would you and so do "they").

Where does the power to love come from? From the experience of being loved. We can love because we have been loved and our love takes on the quality of the love we have received. If we have been loved selfishly, neurotically, inconsistently, then our love to others tends to be the same. This is why we can favor love and not be loving, in love with love and actually be unloving. This is why impersonal living demoralizes life; it means to be treated as a thing, as a means, as an item in a column of statistics. And this robs us of being persons because we are not being so regarded.

So the new commandment: to love one another (our neighbors) as God has loved us in Jesus Christ. Love calls out love; we love him because he first loved us. God is love and he loved us, and Jesus Christ is the witness and proof and power of that love. But we don't get this power to love from him until we feel and know and respond to his love for us. We can and we do talk in shining abstractions about God's love in Jesus Christ. But instead we must know its power and force in our hearts, must feel ourselves caught up and upborne by its bedrock stability.

This is what the gospel means by faith—knowing and trusting God's love as we see it and feel it in the life and teachings, the death and resurrection of Jesus of Nazareth, the Messiah of God, our Lord and Savior.

When we have faith—and out of our faith we can love—the power to love is generated in our hearts and guides our heads and hands. It is then possible to love others as we have been loved, as we know ourselves loved, even now, even as we are.

For we know that Jesus' love for us was a costing love, an uncalculating love, a supremely confident love. Jesus loved his disciples (and us) past the point of safety and personal comfort—in the face of suffering, in the teeth of danger and the Cross. He loved them (and us), not because they were lovable and merited his love, but because they were his brothers and God's children. He loved them (and us) in the certain hope that his love would not fail or be fruitless, not because of the present hopeful prospects but because of his confidence that God can and will perfect his love and bring it to fruition. When the disciples (and we) realized how they had been loved, they gained the power to love others, like this! The power to love springs from the upwelling sense of gratitude in our hearts for the love we have received. We love our children in this way, not because it is convenient (it often isn't); not because they are lovable (sometimes they aren't); and not because we know how they are going to come out (we don't). We love them as the reflex of our gratitude to our parents. And if our parents didn't love us aright, it is proportionally difficult for us to love our children, and other people's children, aright! And so it goes.

The power to love comes from the power of faith to recognize and to trust the love of God in our lives and in the life of his creation. It is the power of God's grace transformed by the power of our gratefulness. We are just as loving as we are grateful—and just as unloving as we are ungrateful.

We have this power to love, in our hearts and lives, right here and now. If it is stifled or corrupted, it is because we have stifled or corrupted our sense of gratitude, gratitude to God and to our neighbors who have loved us. If we want to be loving, in action as well as in profession (not only with our lips but in our lives), we must open our eyes and hearts to the wonderful and gracious mystery of God's redemptive love of us—in Christ, in the church in the world.

> O dearly, dearly hath he loved,
> And we must love him, too,
> And trust in his redeeming blood,
> And try his works to do.[2]

> "A new commandment I give to you, that you love one another; even as I have loved you, that you also love one another. By this all men will know that you are my disciples, if you have love one for another" (John 13:34-35).

Introduction

The congregation at Preston Hollow Presbyterian Church in Dallas, Texas, on April 4, 1965, heard Albert Outler preach his favorite text: "A new commandment I give to you, that you love one another; even as I have loved you, that you love one another" (John 13:34). You love because you know you are loved. Jesus Christ showed the disciples God's love for them and the whole world. The commandment suggested that they reflect God's love for them outward toward others. This was more than the mere legalisms of the "old" commandments to love God and neighbor. This was an example lived out of gratitude to God for his love.

What does this sermon tell us about Albert Outler? It's not so much this particular sermon to this particular audience that signals something about the man. It is the text he uses. He talked about it more than about any other text. He talked about that Scripture in the same way that some people talk about their grandchildren. Except, in this case, people were never bored. When he preached the text, people were turned on. And the reason they are is easy to understand. They were receiving God's love for Albert Outler . . . and for themselves.

SERMON 3

The New Commandment

The thirteenth chapter of the Gospel according to St. John is a truly remarkable passage in the most profound book in the New Testament.

If you'll look at chapter thirteen carefully, you will see that the events described there fall precisely where the account of the Lord's Supper comes in the first three Gospels. Notice also that there is no reference in St. John to the institution of the Lord's Supper. The Upper Room experience comes after our Lord's public ministry, before the passion and death, on the night in which he was betrayed.

It was before the Passover festival. Jesus knew that his hour had come and he must leave this world and go to the Father. He had always loved his own who were in the world, and now he was to show the full extent of his love.

The devil had already put it into the mind of Judas, son of Simon Iscariot, to betray him. During supper, Jesus, well aware that the Father had entrusted everything to him, and that he had come from God and was going back to God, rose from the table, laid aside his garments, and taking a towel, tied it round him. Then he poured water into a basin, and began to wash his disciples' feet and to wipe them with a towel.

When it was Simon Peter's turn, Peter said to him, "You, Lord, washing my feet?"

Jesus replied, "You do not understand now what I am doing, but one day you will."

Peter said, "I will never let you wash my feet."

"If I do not wash you," Jesus replied, "you are not in fellowship with me."

"Then, Lord," said Simon Peter, "not my feet only; wash my hands and head as well!"

Jesus said, "A man who has bathed needs no further washing; he is altogether clean; and you are clean, though not every one of you." He added the words "not every one of you" because he knew who was going to betray him.

After washing their feet and taking his garments again, he sat down. "Do you understand what I have done for you?" he asked. "You call me 'Master' and 'Lord', and rightly so, for that is what I am. Then if I, your Lord and Master, have washed your feet, you also ought to wash one another's feet. I have set you an example: you are to do as I have done for you. In very truth I tell you, a servant is not greater than his master, nor a messenger than the one who sent him. If you know this, happy are you if you act upon it" (John 13:12-17, NEB).

This, then, is St. John's version of a dominical sacrament—a symbolic act that reveals the action of God's love; an outward and visible sign of an inward and invisible grace!

The tradition of footwashing as a sacrament dropped out of the church's practice—one might wish it had not, but that's scarcely the point. The story and its message are still there, for those who have eyes to see and ears to hear.

It is a story about the meaning of divine love, the ways of love, the implications of love, the relationships between love and morality. For it is not merely a drama of Christ's humbling himself. It is, rather, the dramatic setting for Christ's giving his disciples his "New Commandment." "A new commandment I give to you, that you love one another . . . as I have loved you." And this will be the world's sign that you are my disciples—Christians in the real and true sense!—if your love for one another resembles and represents my love for you as you've seen it expressed in a thousand ways over the past three years and as you've just seen it summed up before your very eyes!

This sacrament of footwashing is a sort of paradigm, or representative model, of Christian morality. Here is where Christian ethics could find its foundation, its fundamental motivation, its exemplary pattern of behavior. On the surface, and as a sort of threshold, it establishes humility and service—or humility-in-service—as the basic temper and posture of Christian discipleship and ethics. The Christian is the servant of the servants of God; dignity, when it is real, is not forfeited nor diminished when it stoops to menial service to others.

But this is more than a drama: it is the visualization of a profound and universal truth of Christian experience. The love we are commanded to show to others is a reflex of the love we have received from God through Christ.

When Jesus said, "a new commandment," every ear in the room picked up. New commandment. Why new? They remembered the old commandment—the summary of the Law and the Prophets: "You shall love the Lord your God . . . [and] your neighbor as yourself (Matthew 22:37, 39).

So what was new about this commandment to love one another? Was anything relaxed from the old or added to it? No.

What was new was its reference, its measure, and motive. You are to love one another as you have been loved—by me, by God. Your treatment of others is to be measured, not by their treatment of you, or by some timeless principle of justice nor even by your own preference on how to be treated. The Golden Rule is valid but minimal. Your treatment of others is to be guided by your treatment by God—by the pattern and model of God's outpoured love in Jesus Christ.

Now, what do we surely know about that love of God in Christ—wherewith we are to love one another?

1. It is a love none of us has earned or deserved. But this means that our love is not to be confined to those who have earned or deserved it.

2. It was a love that reached out to people in need—just because they were people and in need.

   Therefore—

3. It was a love that accepted pain and suffering, inconvenience, and betrayal—and death on a cross!—not because they are good and desirable, but because they happened to be the inescapable side-effects of costing love.

   Therefore—

4. It was a love that was not based on any calculations of imminent success or victory or frame and reward—but nevertheless an utterly confident love—since its final meaning and vindication are in the hands of God and within the certain compass of his sovereign grace!

   Therefore—

Christian morality is not a matter of rules—but also not a matter of abandoning and rejecting rules, in the celebration of moral chaos, in God's name.

It is the expression of gratitude—in life, in all of life, in everyday life, in the hollow and dreary stretches of life. Gratitude is the strongest and most nearly pure of all our moral energies.

Wherefore, little children, let us love one another as Christ has loved us.

Introduction

You can read the ebb and flow of ecumenism in these sermons preached on the subject. During the time of the preaching of this sermon at a community service in Thompson Memorial Chapel at Williams College in Williamstown, Massachusetts, on Sunday, April 30, 1967, Albert Outler was at his orbital ecumenical apogee. He was excited about the prospects of Christian unity. Sad to say, but there in the modern history of ecumenism is where the orbit headed toward the perigee, toward its lowest orbit of today.

But even then, back in 1967, Albert Outler had a hunch that things could go awry because of bureaucratic dig-ins as well as the wrong emphasis some were pushing for then. For example, "Tonight, COCU convenes in Cambridge with only one single topic under consideration—Structure. This is, of course, the central ganglion of the whole COCU scheme, since it deals with the thorny questions of the provisions for ministerial appointments and congregational programs, etc".

This statement sounded much like his more recent sermons that described an ecumenism in disarray. But the spirit of this sermon must not be watered down by interpretations of his more recent sermons. This sermon established Albert Outler as a thoroughgoing "ecumaniac," not of the ordinary garden variety, but of a thoroughbred stock. In fact a one-of-a-kind. As that grand army of ecumenical enthusiasts shrank back into the comfort of their denominational ranks, Albert Outler stood out front saying, "Our work is not to finish the job, but to get on with it!"

SERMON 4

The Ecumenical Road Ahead

Can you not see that while there is jealousy and strife among you, you are living on the purely human level of your lower nature? When one says, "I am Paul's man," and another, "I am for Apollos," are you not all too human?

After all, what is Apollos? What is Paul? We are simply God's agents in bringing you to the faith. Each of us performed the task which the Lord allotted to him: I planted the seed, and Apollos watered it; but God made it grow. Thus it is not the gardeners with their planting and watering who count, but God, who makes it grow. Whether they plant or water, they work as a team, though each will get his own pay for his own labor. We are God's fellow-workers; and you are God's garden.

Or again, you are God's building. I am like a skilled master builder who by God's grace laid the foundation, and someone else is putting up the building. Let each take care how he builds. There can be no other foundation beyond that which is already laid; I mean Jesus Christ himself (1 Corinthians 3:3b-11, NEB).

It is, of course, a great honor and a pleasure for me to have a share in this epoch-making service here in Williamstown and in this college. Such a gathering is impressive evidence that the ecumenical spirit continues to spread and deepen, now to the point where it really matters. The conventional pattern of services of ecumenical witness normally shunts them off onto marginal time: added "extras" on Sunday afternoon, or additions to the weekly calendar, etc. You have broken that stereotype. Here is a joint service in prime time, and this means that both congregations and ministers have forgone their most cherished hour in the week. No plainer proof could be asked of the fact that we stand in a new situation, that the ecumenical movement has moved far beyond its initial stage of cautious Christian cordiality, that many of us are beginning to feel ready for the upcoming next phase in the ongoing progress of the cause of Christian unity.

All of this is to say that ecumenism has finally become a popular cause after a half century of coterie service by a devoted but smallish group of professional "ecumaniacs." At the same time, its new-found popularity is also a sign of new crises looming up, new disenchantments for the impatient, as the road ahead gets rougher and more difficult. Ecumenism is usually a fun thing in its early stages—when you're making new friends out of old strangers, when you're discovering the riches and warmth of Christian fellowship across old boundary lines that used to seem sacrosanct but are so no longer. It's exciting to help make history—or at least to share in its being made—and to see the reversal of stereotypes that have finally come to be recognized as outworn.

And this is what's been happening in America and around the world for the past two or three decades, first among a smallish corps of grizzled veterans, then in an enlarged company of new-breed ecumenists, and now on a widening scale in local situations wherever there is enough imagination and initiative. There were, for example, the Oberlin and Montreal Conferences on Faith and Order, in 1957 and 1963, which involved more Americans and

Canadians than ever had been so before—and that saw Roman Catholic observers included, too. Then, since 1960 there has been Consultation on Church Union (COCU) with its crucial sixth annual session coming up this very week in Cambridge. COCU began, as you know, with four denominations and has now grown to ten. We have hammered out a rudimentary Plan of Union that bids fair to change the shape of American Protestantism past all recognition, even if the present projections don't come off quite as they are now envisaged. Concurrently with COCU, there was Vatican II and its unprecedented stimulus toward ecumenical activity between Roman Catholics and others. Vatican II has started a marvelous ferment and confusion inside the Roman Catholic fold itself, which climaxed just last Monday by a tremendous victory for academic freedom at Catholic University in Washington. That was an epochal event and a shot in the arm for all those who feared that the spirit of Vatican II was dying.

In short, the formal barricades against ecumenism are crumbling almost everywhere. Ecumenism is "in." Everybody who is anybody is "for" Christian unity. But it is just this formal acceptance of "unity in principle" that marks the point where the real work of ecumenical negotiation really begins. Now it begins to be in order to ask for definitions, for distinctions between essentials and nonessentials, for practical implications, for honest estimates of what unity will cost us in terms of order and organization.

"How beautiful it is for brethren to dwell together in unity!" Yeah! But on what terms and with what allowance for the prickly issues that have divided us, and still do? It is a hard and unavoidable fact that the recomposition of Christian unity means change—real change, radical change—in every one of the participating segments of the Christian community. It is also a fact that many of us tend to think of ecclesiastical progress in terms of minimum change, and our leaders are generally fearful of forfeiting our cherished traditions (chiefly those traditions of leadership that they bear for us so heroically!).

But here is where the crunch comes. On the one hand, Christian unity is not worth the sacrifice of real essentials in faith and order. Yet on the other hand, there's simply no hope at all for any real progress unless we can break up the old separatist patterns of denominational triumphalism. What then? How do we tackle the tangled issues in this paradoxical snarl of our ecumenical commitments, which mean change, and our traditional loyalties, which cling to continuity?

This is the nub of the whole ecumenical enterprise, and I must confess that after a lifetime's effort in preparatory work and then an exciting decade of one breakthrough after another (unbelievable giant strides that have brought us to our present situation), I find it a mite discouraging now to face the prospects of a slowdown and of the heavy slogging that lies ahead until the next great breakthrough. Most of the time, however, my morale is upborne by the comforting thought that the ecumenical movement has now gotten out of hand—out of the hands, that is, of the ecclesiastical managers and housekeepers. The ecumenical genie has been let out of the bottle and can't be stoppered up again.

This means that the ecumenical spirit has outrun the self-interest of the ecclesiastical leaders and their professional impulses to make haste slowly. It has also outrun the current centripetal patterns of ecumenical narcissism: "Why Can't They Be Like Us?" But we still haven't come up with an adequate theory of development that will allow for real change—mutation, metamorphosis, etc.—yet also conserve the legitimate core concerns of the various traditions for the preservation of their respective "distinctive witnesses."

It is, therefore, not surprising that an ominous slowdown is at the top of all of the current ecumenical ventures. For example, the Faith and Order Commission is heading toward its triennial session at Bristol this summer with a program that looks more respectable and routine than adventurous and daring. The World Council of Churches is in the throes of preparing for its Fourth Assembly in Uppsala in July of 1968, and as of now, the prospects are more ho-hum than whoopee! Tonight, COCU convenes in Cambridge with only one single topic under consideration—Structure. This is, of course, the central ganglion of the whole COCU scheme, since it deals with the thorny questions of the provisions for ministerial appointments and congregational programs. This year, the draft essay for our COCU sessions has been written in shockingly bland rhetoric—the handiwork of a committee who aren't bland at all. Why? Because the Episcopalians have to vote on the Plan in September and the Methodists the following April. Since the diehards in both groups are powerful and resistance is rising, it is important just now to ease back on the throttle a bit.

Or take the Roman Catholics and the visible retrenchment in their Reformation Roman Style, not only in Rome but also in many a diocesan chancery in this country and elsewhere. This in the face of the unprecedented crisis of authority and freedom throughout the church, which was generated by Vatican II and its summons to *aggiornamento*. Thus opens a new period in *their* postconciliar era—a highly critical one, too—in which the church decides whether Vatican II gets its second wind and continues to move ahead or whether the Roman Catholic Church slides back toward the *status quo ante*, with her rebels suppressed yet once again as in the grim days of the *Pascendi Gregis*.

Some observers read these various symptoms of reaction as evidence that the ecumenical movement has run up against a sort of ecclesiastical sound barrier, where it may have reached a point of diminishing returns. Others, and I am one, read the same signs as signifying that further and faster than any of us was quite prepared for, we've been moved ahead toward real decisions by the rising concern for unity amongst church folks generally. We are almost unexpectedly confronted by the hard practical issues that we never quite thought we would have to settle. This means that we're being hurried toward responsible decisions by rising tides of expectation and hope that are pressing against the unconfessed hypocrisies of those who have talked a big ecumenical game and yet who find themselves chickening out now that the time has come for the actual hazards of renewal and transfiguration.

Now, if something like this is so, those of us who have been caught up in the spirit and vision of Christian unity must realize that the responsibilities for the creative future of the ecumenical movement rest with us, here and now, at least as much as with the ecumenical jet set who may or may not represent the real commitments of their own constituencies. Services like this one, and their follow-ups, if you're really serious about this one, are coming to be as crucial for the ecumenical future as the committee meetings at Cambridge and Geneva and Rome. The very genius of ecumenism lies in the transformation of the loyalties of Christians in local communities—from denominational to ecumenical, from parochial to communal.

And always, in this or any other aspect of the ecumenical enterprise, what matters most of all is that we keep constantly clear about what it is we are doing, what we are after, what our goals are, and what constitutes appropriate means to such ends. We are not, I hope, concerned with church union for its own sake or on behalf of Christian coziness. If, by some miracle or fiat, we could get all or most of the denominations into some giant ecclesiastical merger (designed by corporation lawyers, God save us all!), we would have accomplished very little by way of church renewal or the reestablishment of the Christian presence in the modern world—not even much by way of practical economy, either, since the typical arrangements for such mergers take pains to retain all bureaucrats in the manner to which they so readily become accustomed and regard as sacrosanct. We Methodists know about this all too well in our proposed merger with the Evangelical United Brethren.

By the same token, though, there's no longer a future in merely spiritual ecumenism, with its bromide about "unity in the Spirit" being all we need to be one in Christ. Unity in the Spirit that does not proceed toward or aim at full communion is a chimera or worse: either a hypocrisy (a professed concern for unity while avoiding its risks) or else a dangerous self-deception (the delusion that Christians divided at their fonts, pulpits, and tables can really be "united in the Spirit"). The immediate aim of all authentic ecumenism is threefold: unity in membership, ministry, and communion (*communicatio in sacris*). And yet even these aims are instrumental to our ultimate ecumenical concern, which is for the renewal of faith: that men may hear God's Word in faith, that they may be turned from the ways of death to the way of life, that they may be confronted with the live option of a community of graced and graceful living.

Our real goal is not church union as such but Christian community and consensus—whence can then come the harvests of creative and diverse theologies, creative and diverse liturgies, creative and diverse common ventures in Christian witness and service. Christians acting in and from such a consensus would truly represent the people of God in the modern world, an available militia to act out the practical imperatives of the Christian community in local situations as the circumstances allowed or demanded. Christians acting under such imperatives, as ministers of the whole people of God, would then have to be reckoned with by the movers and shakers of the secular city.

Moreover, in place of our frantic efforts nowadays to come up with something new and outlandish in liturgy or in Christian ethical theory or in doctrine, we might find fully as much excitement in the quest to find appropriate ways to recapitulate and update the inexhaustible riches of the Christian heritage, which we have scarcely begun to rediscover and reappraise. Out of this could come Christians who believed what they said and understood what they believed, Christians whose professions had some palpable effect upon their behavior, Christians who could distinguish between God and man without disparaging either, who could identify themselves as men and women in Jesus Christ and each other as fellow creatures in the community of the Holy Spirit. One thing is clear: the old patterns of denominational particularism are over and done with as viable structures for the future. Even their advocates know that they are fighting a rearguard action, buying time before the other decision not yet made—whether the churches will disintegrate separately or pull themselves together for a new season of the Christian soul.

A few days ago a student dropped by to talk about his hopes and fears before the icy plunge into the parish next June. As he got up to go, I asked him what was the chief thing he was taking with him from his three years in seminary. He pondered this a full minute and said: "A sense of Methodism's legitimate place in the tradition of historic Christianity and a freedom to develop that heritage into something more truly catholic, evangelical, and reformed." This last phrase, of course, was an echo of his awareness of the slogan of COCU. Now, he's going to need a lot more than this insight when he turns up in Seattle five weeks hence, where he's going to have his new-found openness sorely tested by the parochial temper of his official board. He has a lot more, too. But what has stuck in my mind from the talk is that this young man is the sign of the church's future, a better future than we knew when I was young, a future in which a world perishing for the want of human community may find it in the Christian community of faith and grace and love.

The only hopeful and fruitful ecumenical program I can foresee, or have ever been interested in struggling for, is one in which the Roman Catholics will be seeking the fullness of their Catholic community and, in so doing, will discover that the fullness of catholicity contains the essence of the evangelical tradition for which the Protestants have stood trustee these past four centuries; in which the Orthodox will seek the fullness of their own Holy Tradition and will discover that the real fullness of Orthodoxy will allow for the Petrine primacy and for "the Protestant Principle" as well; in which the Protestants will be seeking the fullness of their commitment to Scripture, conscience, and reason; and will, in the process, find that the real fullness of the "Protestant Principle" calls for some sort of encompassing sacramental community and for rootage in the living tradition of Christ in his church. The way to Christian unity is not backward, to some erstwhile golden age, the "undivided church" and all that! There never was such a time long, long ago! But even more important, we know now that history's arrow (and God's providence) flies but one way—forward.

Nothing guarantees the future in such terms. But since it is painfully clear that the blind continuation of our old ways has no future at all, it ought surely to be obvious that the joint enterprise of a truly renewed Roman Catholicism, a newly vital and vigorous Orthodoxy, an actually reformed Protestantism—and all working toward convergence—that this sort of agenda holds the only promise worth working and praying and waiting for.

The cause of Christian unity and of Christian proclamation, which it serves, is long, difficult, wearying. It has its seasons: of planting and cultivation, of hurry and harvest, of fallow times and hibernation, of groping and root growth, of flowering and fruit. In any case and in any season, however, our work is not to finish the job but to get on with it, not to grasp the goal by dint of effort and human wisdom but to fill out the unity that we already have in Christ Jesus. This unity is not so much an achievement as a gift; it is the work of God in the hearts and minds of men and women who are willing to be re-made into one body even as we were originally baptized and confirmed into the one body of Christ by the seal of the one Spirit. Many hands and hearts have planted the seeds of ecumenism in this century. Some of them have sprouted and are growing, others just sprouting, others still dormant. Many hands and heads have watered and nurtured the growth of the ecumenical enterprise. But all faithful ecumenists rejoice in the truth that it is God who gives the increase, who sustains the growth process, who blesses the harvest of love. This is why we keep on at what is often a thankless job.

It does not exceed a devout imagination to suppose that the last quarter of this century may, in the providence of God, be a great season of harvest—a vindication of those who have planted and watered and hoped in God. It is not at all beyond the possibility of faith and love that God will fulfill the foretaste of fellowship that we are celebrating here today—if, in this present time, we dedicate ourselves to pray and work for that unity which is

> . . . made visible as all in each place, who are baptized into Jesus Christ and confess him as Lord and Savior, are brought by the Holy Spirit into one fully committed fellowship, holding the one apostolic faith, preaching the one Gospel, breaking the one bread, joining in common prayer and sharing a corporate life that reaches out in witness and service to all.[1]

There is, as I have said, no guarantee of such a future in a world tormented as sorely as ours and teetering as it is on the brink of global catastrophe. But in any future, it is surely the better part that we shall have done all that love and self-forgetfulness can contribute to the healing of "the sixth wound of Christ"—his sundered body. Only so can we who call and profess ourselves Christian be obedient in our time and circumstance to our Lord's imperative, that we love one another as he has loved us, that we give corporate witness to that love in communion and in service, to the end that the world that God so loved shall not perish but have everlasting life.

Introduction to Sermons 5 and 6

These two sermons on ecumenism are treated as one so that the reader may see *where* Albert Outler *was* in sermons on the same subject two years apart. The first sermon, which Dr. Outler preached at Wesley Methodist Church in Urbana, Illinois, on February 25, 1968, reflects excitement about the monumental breakthroughs on ecumenical frontiers, e.g., "Ecumenism has come finally to the grass roots, has spread from a spark to a blaze . . . the barriers are not all down—but they are falling." Then he spent over half of the sermon detailing dangers and ended with an expression of hope and faith.

Two years later, January 22, 1970, he preached at the Service for the Week of Prayer and Christian Unity at the University of Dallas. There he said, "We're in bad trouble . . . the scandal of disunity remains." But the major portion of this sermon was a rehearsal of the hope and faith he expressed in the first sermon. In spite of ecumenical setbacks, reverses, slowdowns, and stultifications, Outler ends by saying, "But who wants to bar a miracle? I don't; that's for sure . . . for the ones I've already seen have made all the difference in what I know about faith and hope and love."

When Albert Outler reached heaven and saw the harmony, the oneness, the loving as God loves (pure and undefiled by human perversions), he surely must have said, "I'm not complaining, Lord, but I wanted to see more of this on earth!"

SERMON 5

Buildup to a Letdown?

My own involvement in the ecumenical movement began in 1936, in the preparations for the 1937 Life and Work Conference at Oxford and the Faith and Order Conference at Edinburgh. Most of the time since, ecumenism has been an arduous, exciting, and lonely business—small committees and periodic conferences composed largely of the same people who kept on hopefully invoking the vision of "grass roots ecumenism" but who rarely saw any of it. Hundreds of meetings, thousands of miles, tons of mimeograph paper, widened horizons, deepened experiences of Christian *koinonia*—and very little else to show for it all. All of which is to say that until just yesterday, ecumenism was pretty much a coterie concern. We ecumaniacs worked at the job unwearyingly, with stubborn patience and a millennial spirit; maybe not in our lifetime but sometime surely.

And now all that is changed, with bewildering speed and vigor. Almost suddenly, all sorts and conditions of Christian folk have begun to seek and find each other, in a variety of modes and patterns: the discovery of mutual and common Christian commitments, mutual recognition, spiritual fellowship, Christian cooperation in community and social affairs, common prayer and dialogue, a fresh and rising hunger for full and genuine communion in sacred things—in mutually valid membership and ministries.

Ecumenism has come finally to the grass roots, has spread from a spark to a blaze. There cannot be many towns or campuses in America that have had no service of ecumenical witness in the past month; not many ministers who have not been in dialogue with colleagues in other churches whom they scarcely knew before; few laymen still unaware of the radical change of climate in the churches.

What lies behind these changes? At least five major factors:

1. The falling barriers that have separated mankind into races, classes, castes, cliques, sectarian and partisan groups of various sorts. The barriers are not all down—more's the pity and shame of it! But they are falling. The moral convictions that upheld them are crumbling. A new spirit of community is let loose in the world—even in a world tearing at its own vitals—for part of the horror we feel in the face of injustice, inhumanity, strife, and violence, at home and abroad, is that all war is civil war, all strife is *internecine*. This deepening of the conscience and sensitivity of modern man is both an effect and cause of this movement of Christians—long divided in bitterness or callousness—to seek reconciliation with each other and to serve the cause of reconciliation of their estranged human brothers and sisters everywhere.
2. The examples of the United Church of Canada and the Church of South India.
3. The Consultation on Church Union as a venture in the reform of mainstream American Protestantism.
4. The massive influx of the Orthodox into the World Council of Churches.
5. Vatican II and the distance between *Mortalium Animos* (1928) and *On Ecumenism* (1965).

The results are cumulative and exciting.

1. Christians at prayer and worship, across lines and barriers that had defied goodwill for centuries.
2. From diatribe and disputation amongst the theologians to

dialogue and ecumenical study. Dozens of ecumenical institutes of various sorts and levels, e.g., The Jerusalem Institute.

3. New initiatives in Christian cooperation in joint ventures in Christian social concern. New emphases on Christians in the social revolution as Christians and not as -ists, -ics, or -erians of this sort or that; on Christians in economics, politics and culture; on Christians as the salt of the earth. The Geneva Conference, 1966, on Church and Society; the National Council of Churches and the National Conference of Catholic Bishops' cooperative programs, the new working Groups co-sponsored by the World Council of Churches and the Council for the Study of Society, Culture, and Politics, etc.
4. Theological ferment and reconstruction.
5. Liturgical reform and experimentation.

One can see the point to the story heard across Rome these days about the priest from Bergamo who died and went to heaven, only to discover that the good Pope John had developed a thing about "open windows."

All of this, at least to a grizzled ecumenical veteran, is very strange and wonderful. There is something still deeply moving in the sight and experience of Christians being converted from strangers to friends, from aliens to brethren. The cynics can jibe at it all—that the Christians are huddling together like a dwindling herd before a mounting storm—but Christianity has been in bad trouble before and it didn't force hostile brethren together. What's happening in our midst is basic, epoch-making—and, by now, irreversible.

And yet, even in the flush of this new ecumenical dawn there are also dangers and they are equally imminent. The very success we are celebrating carries with it real threats; this ecumenical buildup could all too easily become the prelude to what could be a heart-rending letdown and a tragic demoralization. There are at least four reasons why this is all too probable:

1. Ecumenism has become fashionable—an "in" cause, attracting a sizable crop of fair weather enthusiasts eager to enjoy the first fruits of "togetherness," but unprepared for the

shocks and risks and demands of genuine ecumenical study and action, of lasting through to the end of the action. When the going gets rough, we shall lose a great many of our present comrades.

2. Deeper than this, however, is the fact that we still lack an adequate theoretical and theological framework in which to proceed from this moment of enthusiasm and expectation to further implied breakthroughs toward the pledged goal of *communicationes in sacris*. We've made enormous progress in doctrinal agreement or consensus—in the upper circles of Faith and Order—but we are still at loggerheads on the old dividers: membership, ministry, and sacraments. What is more, we are within sight of a minimal working consensus on the meaning of the sacraments and maybe membership. But we are still as nearly paralyzed as ever before the nettle of the ministry. Is there any conceivable way to reconcile and mingle the ministries of the churches that have now acknowledged each other as churches and that recognize each other's baptism—without rebaptism, reconfirmation, reordination? This is the crunch. Here is where the body's buried. Who shall deliver us from this body of death? In short, the tasks of ecumenical theology are very far from complete or successful, and on the one axial point around which the others turn, we are still groping and hoping and praying for a miracle.

3. But the spread of ecumenical interest means also a spread of ecumenical expectations—and this, in turn, is creating new pressures and confusions for the leaders of the churches and of the ecumenical councils. Here we've been going on and on, all these years, advocating and commending the cause of Christian unity and now—to our surprise—an increasing multitude says, "Okay, lead on, tallyho and all that!" But the fact is that ecclesiastics are deeply conservative and allergic to radical change. The actual recomposition of authentic Christian communion is bound to involve change—change in greater or lesser degree by all parties to the union. And now, much more swiftly than anybody had anticipated, the challenge of change looms up and is proving to be very

disconcerting indeed. Just as we have moved from diatribe to dialogue more quickly than was expected, so now we must move from dialogue to decision; and most of us are unprepared for that. It is as if the courtship were fun, but the prospects of marriage terrifying. And yet, if reasonable progress is not shortly forthcoming with promise of more, then the movement will quite shortly be in bad trouble. Hopes deferred do make the heart sick, and we're beginning to see multiplying signs of just that kind of sickness.

4. A subtler danger than any of these is looming up in the growing conviction of many newly recruited enthusiasts that the real genius of ecumenism lies in Christian cooperation—or Christians in prophetic and revolutionary action—with or without *communicatio in sacris*, or without any official sanction for mingled communions. In the face of the horrendous issues of war and peace, of ideological conflict that tears the world apart, of the struggles for civil rights and elemental humanity, etc., etc., some prophets and apostles find themselves violently impatient with the glacial anguish of doctrinal clarifications. Now that the old barriers of estrangement and repudiation are down, say they, we've got as much unity as we need to fare forth into the secular city and to move forward the cause of revolution. To wait up for, or even bother about, hangups in doctrine or at the Table of the Lord, is to mistake true Christian priorities and to miss the high tide of the present crisis. *Communicatio in sacris* is going to take too long; we cannot wait. And, in any case, who needs that? Here, veritably, is the heart of the matter: here is the new, antisacramental, anticlerical, antiecclesiological ecumenism and it has a growing host of advocates. Christian ecumenical action with or without sacramental union—or else sacramental union without authorized ministries for it.

The dilemma here is acute, and tragic. No one can contemplate the prospect of Christians who have newly found each other just standing there paralyzed while the theologians figure a way around or over the present dead ends, or chatting happily forever without ever solving the problem of memberships and ministries. Yet, Christian cooperation that ignores or sidetracks the question of full communion is self-deceiving and self-defeating. The world will see clearly enough that the Christians are divided and at the point they have professed to be most crucial, and the unsolved problem of basic schism will finally undermine all the brave show of united action.

The answer, such as it is, is twofold. First, we must, of course, press forward on any front in any good cause to manifest the Christian witness and ministry in and for the world: the message of love and human dignity, the message of grace and redemption. Cooperation by all means—but not as a substitute for real and full communion. Spiritual fellowship, of course, but, again, not as a substitute for "membership one with another" in the body of Christ.

The ecumenical venture has much to celebrate and be thankful for, here and throughout the world. But its very success has brought us to the brink of decision—real victory or real defeat. These are the only alternatives that partial victory has brought us to. One may hope and believe, as I do, that the same grace of God that has brought us thus far will lead and lift us further.

Now, in perspective, we can see that the first half of this century was a time of thawing and planting and cultivation, the thawing of the bitter chill of "Christians" in estrangement and separation from one another; of the planting of the seeds of ecumenism in a soil warmed by an aroused sense of mission; of the cultivation of the fresh growth of Christian fellowship, community, and service. Epochal as these developments have been, they are only harbingers and omens of what yet may come to pass. The cause of Christian unity has not yet come to have top priority in our denominations nor is it a prime value for the majority of Christians in those churches. But the tide rises and the spread of intelligent interest in ecumenical affairs widens.

It does not exceed a devout imagination to suppose that the last half of this century may, in the providence of God, be the season of harvest—of the culmination of the labors and hopes of those who

> died in [this] faith, not having received the promises,
> but having seen them afar off, and were persuaded of

> them, and embraced them. . . . And these all, having obtained a good report through faith, received not the promise: God having provided some better thing for us, that they without us should not be made perfect" (Hebrews 11:13, 39-40, KJV).

It cannot be beyond the possibilities of faith that God will give our children the fullness of what we can foretaste—if in this, our present, we dedicate ourselves to pray and work and hope for that unity that can be

> . . . made visible as all in each place, who are baptized into Jesus Christ and confess Him as Lord and Savior, are brought by the Holy Spirit into one fully committed fellowship, holding the one apostolic faith, preaching the one Gospel, breaking the one bread, joining in common prayer, and having a corporate life reaching out in witness and service to all . . .[1]

There is, of course, no guaranteeing that this will come to pass, or even a guarantee that our human history on this planet has that much of a future. But whatever the future, it will be the better if we have done all that love and self-forgetfulness can do to heal "the sixth wound of Christ"—his sundered body. Only in this way can we who call and profess ourselves Christian be truly obedient, in our own times and places, to the manifest petition of our Lord: that we love one another as we have been loved by God in Christ and give witness to that love in service to all our neighbors to the end that the world that Christ died to save may truly believe—and so be saved!

SERMON 6

Christians in the Waiting Room

This liturgy in which we have shared is a tough act to follow. Multimedia is more exciting nowadays than monologue—and sermons are monologues, in form if not always in spirit. And it has made two or three points that I also want to make in this sermon—the three points that constitute the essence of all Christian visions of the future:

Point One: For the moment, we're in bad trouble.

Point Two: In the long run, God's sovereign grace will triumph—since already he is Lord of all, despite all appearances.

Point Three: *Ad interim,* Christians have their work cut out for them.

This is the gist of Daniel's message to a demoralized community of the literally alienated: exiles, refugees, disowned. It is likewise the message of John's *Apocalypse* to underground Christians persecuted for their illegal religion. More and more it is a meaningful message to us, or at least to those of us who have begun to doubt whether some of our cherished causes have any chance of succeeding in the foreseeable future.

On point one, there is no doubt (is there?) that, for the moment, we're in trouble, serious trouble—in the church, in the academy, in the world. The churches are wracked up with concurrent crises: of faith, of authority, of commitment to mission. All the conventional indices of ecclesiastical health point downward; ministerial morale is at a new low; conflicts and tension are at a new high; the ecumenical movement is in a slump after a boom time of high hopes and great expectations; the militants and the diehards have us polarized with the middle in between the shrinking and the mutinous.

We have delighted in the foretastes of Christian unity and are prepared for the main course. We've worshiped and worked and dialogued, some of us for thirty years or more—but to what end? The scandal of disunity remains: we are still barred from the central sacrament of God's incarnate love and Christ's mystical body, the Eucharist. And none of the rash defiances of the new ecumenical underground and none of the claims of the new guerrilla ecumenists (that we already have all the unity we need to get on with our Christian mission in the world today) will quite conceal the tragic fact that Christians who cannot commune with each other at the Lord's Table cannot fully represent him in any other capacity—however worthwhile.

And yet the official leadership in the churches moves toward the risks of ecumenical decision with such glacial slowness as to suggest the need for an apocalyptic miracle for anything more to happen. Given the will to unite, the basic theological premises of authentic unity are within our grasp—in any case I know—and cover a lifetime of negotiations over the world and among all Christian groups. The liturgical barriers are difficult, but not at all insuperable; there's not much more prospective trouble here than within some of the churches now. Presently, the Catholics will add the doxology to the Lord's Prayer; will that be a cue for some Protestants to drop it? But the problem of the reconciliation and mingling of ministries is a sunken rock that has wrecked many ecumenical barks, and the problems of polity and structure remain insoluble.

Meanwhile, the ecumenical veterans feel their hopes waning: the new recruits find the old patient timetables intolerable, and the mob of ecumenical summer soldiers turns away from Christian unity as a cause to something more exciting and imminent. Or so they think: disruptions, contestations, new targets for their superabundant sanctimonious outrage. This pitiful assemblage tonight is a commentary on that text in Judges about Gideon and his band.

The academy is in trouble, too, but you need no details about that from me. Every educator has his own biopsy, some more alarming than others. But as a friend of mine, hounded from the presidency of a great university to take refuge in a great industrial complex, wrote on his Christmas card, "What a relief to move into the peaceful groves of business from the jungle of Academe!" The young are alienated from their elders, and now the elders feel alienated by the current versions of an ancient anti-intellectualism.

And "the world," the blessed *saeculum*, is in trouble, bad trouble, by any measure you care to use. For all the outcry against war and for peace, there is no rosy dawn of peace on *any* strife-torn front in the world—not even in Biafra. For all the burning ghettos, the cause of black dignity has not been well served by black militancy. For all our newly sensitized horror over man's inhumanity to man, the blight of poverty in the world remains and grows. And for all the zeal of *United We Stand,* we remain a nation divided—deeply, tragically divided (and with an election year coming up).

Anyway you take it, then, the Christian cause is on the wane, under pressure—served badly by its rebels, served worse by its *immobilisti*. And so it is that the corny virtues of fortitude and hope become more and more relevant, even for survival. And this brings us back to Daniel and John, with their game plan for the fourth quarter, with our side trailing by three touchdowns.

What impresses me most about them is their rock solid confidence in God's eventual victory—the triumph of his gracious purpose, in this world and the next. God's will that men and women shall learn to live together in justice, love, and peace cannot finally be thwarted. And so the prophet in the lion's den and the seer on Patmos get sneak previews (apocalypses, literally), of the drama of the triumph of grace. They sound a bit bizarre to us today, as if for TV (if the *Exodus* made a popular movie, why has *Revelation* been ignored?). Cosmic convulsions, successive kingdoms, beasts, arcane numbers and names, angelic visitations, seals, trumpets—and that final heart-lifting, heart-healing vision of a new heaven and a new earth coming down from heaven. Like—Wow!

All this has, of course, been variously interpreted. Some eager souls have probed these texts as if they were an almanac for the future—like Jeanne Dixon's forecasts last Sunday, or "the World Tomorrow" with Garner Ted Armstrong! Actually, mainstream churches have been moved to counter all this with warnings to the uninstructed not to pry too far into these divine mysteries. Others, more sophisticated, have turned apocalypse and eschatology into new categories of existential interpretation: insights of faith into the immanence of the transcendent—that bit about *life in the Here and Now* as the moment of crisis and Christian responsibility.

All of life should be understood eschatologically; all causes can be cherished and served in the certainty that God's gracious sovereignty is not only eventual, but truly present. And some theologians have lately taken to italicizing "hope" as if it could be separated out from St. Paul's trio of virtues all by itself, a sure sign that things are worse than we had feared. Whenever faith or hope or even love is exalted above the other two, the Christian whole is lost.

But the messages of Daniel and John still have a common import for us in our liturgy here tonight. This much, at least: if you have lost heart because your cause is lagging, you're a "dropout"; if you give up or goof off in your crucial commitments, it's bad faith and bad judgment.

I've devoted a lifetime to the cause of Christian unity (some days it seems longer than that). For the greater part of it, I've been buoyed up by my hopes, nourished by visible signs of progress. I blanch at the memory of the reams of paper I've used, the time and labor invested, the heartaches and scar tissue from it all. I'll cherish some of it forever, no matter.

But what about my goals and my hopes? They are, in fact, in jeopardy. And this is part of what we mean when we say that Christian unity is eschatological! It will take a miracle to bring Christians together in joyous, glorious communion, and right now the odds against that are overwhelming. But I've seen miracles, even been involved in a few! John XXIII's pontificate was one—and Vatican II—and, back of that, less-heralded turning points like Lund and New Delhi. There's a quiet miracle going on right now in Palestine (and Father Hesburgh will be in town next week to talk about it): an ecumenical institute started by Roman Catholics, managed by an ecumenical Academic Council with Roman Catholics in the minority, rising steadily on a hill halfway between Jerusalem and Bethlehem, almost literally under fire.

All of which is to say that I'm prepared to take the apocalyptic vision, to work my head off for it. Not that silly business about "God's in his heaven; all's right with the world" but, rather "God's involved with his faithful children here on earth and nothing can finally go wrong!" This means that I can't ease up or goof off in my own commitments, even when my battered spirit is bottoming with every bump. In God's hands, all my offerings are hallowed by his grace. I must, therefore, be about my Father's business "while life and breath shall last"! Something like this, however you might wish to state it, is the essence of Christian hope and confidence.

Meanwhile, we've got our work cut out for us in the here and now! Biding our time until God brings off the victory by himself is faithless, hopeless, loveless—these three, but the worst of these is hopeless! There are, as you well know, plenty of feasible things to be doing now and urgently—not by ourselves or on our own, but in the confidence that God wills it (the ancient crusader's cry!) and that he is working his will in the *arcanun* of unfolding history.

Christians are in God's waiting room, working like crazy to be ready for God's eventualities. Our agenda is endless and infinitely varied: each item is every man's choice of how he must go about his heavenly Father's business. I have less to tell you about what to do exactly than about the requisite spirit and self-understanding in any and all the jobs and projects. And first here, surely, is the daily task of the deepening and enriching of one's Christian identity and growth in grace.

It is all too easy to fire off in one well-intentioned way or another and call that Christian—when the life of communion (with God or Christ through the Spirit, with one's self in your inner depths of prayer and devotion, with each other in worship and service) goes malnourished. Every new fad lures us on to this. Most of the dropouts I have known had already dropped out in spirit—in their habits of spiritual renewal and upbuilding. Prayer may not be a Christian's only business or even his chief business, but is his first business—*sine qua non.*

Yet another paramount need in God's "waiting room" is the settled habit of critical calculation of means and ends. In all too many of the current fracases, in the church and out, one sees the extremists preoccupied with the end in view or with the means, the utopian who disregards the requisite means, and bigot who argues that good ends justify evil means. Here, surely, is the tragedy of the activist: he intends one thing and, more often than not, achieves something quite different and usually worse.

This leads one to wonder about the future of the NOW generation when it becomes the next THEN generation; when people educated in today's politicized universities have to function in tomorrow's technologized world. Has anybody heard lately from Mario Savio?

By the same token, however, unless while we're waiting for the new heaven and the new earth—and for a common Eucharist from which to go forth in joyous witness and service—unless meanwhile we are bent on real risk and radical change, on real reform instead of slogans and evasions, we're in for a heart-dulling wait.

Here, rather most especially, the leadership of the churches stands indicted for a simple, tragic reason: the good (and the familiar) is the enemy of the best, and leadership is dedicated to the ears to the good (and the familiar). There are, I have come to believe, more men of goodwill in the Establishment than in the Opposition—and if this be treason, I couldn't care less. But these good men are so overwhelmed with doing "pretty well" that their imaginations are hobbled and sublimated into rhetoric. Their vision? The new heaven and the new earth—what else? But their operating principle—the first law of motion: a body remaining at rest or in motion unless *acted upon*, etc. The other technical term for this same administrative ideal is inertia. And so we have to ask and demand answers to many basic questions. For example,

1. Is Christian unity desirable? Who will deny it?
2. Is it possible? Who will deny that—and on what grounds?
3. Can we hope for it? In the new heaven, perhaps?
4. Now? Who will give us ground for any such hope?

The fluctuating line of Christian hope and confidence runs between the two extremes of endless patience with well-meant inertia and pious impatience with any interim between vision and reality—between fruitless reflection and fruitless action. I myself have erred on the side of patience; I'm pleased to see others err in the opposite direction—so long as they don't strip the gears! The main thing for us all is the full mix of apocalyptic faith and hope and love!

The decade of the '70s is bound to be difficult—the somber '70's—a baffling rash of insurgency, counter-insurgency, and inadequate reform! Barring a miracle, it will most probably end with those of you still around then, still talking and hoping for Christian unity, radical concord, love and justice, world peace—the same old bag. Alternatively, the extremists may have brought it off—to the left or the right: a revolution without its promised reward! And always there's the chance of a literal end of it all: a bang, a whimper, or a cough!

But who wants to bar a miracle? I don't, that's for sure. For the ones I've already seen have made all the difference in what I know about faith and hope and love. And so may it be with you and all God's people: from the miracles of God's grace already vouchsafed us to the miracles of God's grace still to be anticipated and prepared for with all our powers!

> And I saw a new heaven and a new earth . . . And night shall be no more; they need no light of lamp or sun, for the Lord God will be their light and they shall reign for ever and ever . . . . Even so, come quickly, Lord Jesus. The grace of the Lord Jesus be with all the saints. Amen! (Revelation 21:1, 22:5, 20-21).

Introduction

The thesis for this sermon, preached at the Lutheran Theological Southern Seminary on October 20, 1968, is the first sentence: "The Christian style of life is not so much preoccupied with 'the life of the world to come' as it is with the reflex significance of the Christian hope for life in and for this world."

Albert Outler was keenly aware that his end could come at any moment. He made no big deal of this awareness; it is simply a fact of life that he accepted. Once, when the essay of his life via the editing of his sermons was mentioned, he said, "You know that this life's end could come at any moment, and I may never see the end of what you are doing." And then hastened to say, "That would be just as well!" You could take that last statement seriously or humorously and it would be all right—because on the one hand he was glad to let you meditate on his thoughts, and on the other hand he did not want to see one word that stretched out of proportion the truth about who he was.

What stood out in this sense of his own self-understanding was this: Death was his constant companion. Death had "taken" his mother, father, a sister, a brother, et al., and a deep sense of his personal losses remained with him along with a sense of his own "end," which was coming at any moment. But he lived by God's sovereign power of grace with this knowledge, and experienced by grace through faith victory over death. The final victory came as no surprise.

SERMON 7

The Christian Style of Life

The Christian style of life is not so much preoccupied with "the life of the world to come" as it is with the reflex significance of the Christian hope for life in and for this world. The chief New Testament passages that deal with death and resurrection are climaxed by comments on Christian morale here and now in this life. After a long section on death and the Christian hope in his first letter to the Corinthian Christians—quite "modern" for the mid-first century—St. Paul finally draws his "secular" conclusion:

> Therefore, brothers beloved, continue steadfast and secure, always abounding in the Lord's work [in *this* world!], knowing that whatever you do is never in vain, in the Lord (1 Corinthians 15:58).

It belongs to the Christian style of life to confess God's providential responsibility for the ambiance of human existence and its meanings—creation, preservation, consummation. His faith in providence amounts to a confidence that God knows his business and is about it. The "demonstration" of this—sufficient for the hazards of faith—comes from our *memoriae* of what he has already done in the history of Incarnate Love and in the pilgrim history of the people of God.

And yet it is of equal moment for any Christian humanism to confess that God has made us responsible for our share in human history, past and future. We were put on this earth to tend it, to turn it to the use and service of the human cause. This means careful stewardship of wit and reason, of life, time, and talents—all under the disciplines of love and community. Christian humanism is a summons, for God's sake and ours, to bring sanity and love and sacrificial service as oblations in the tasks of rescuing human life from indignity and in promoting the fullest achievement of the human possibility. Man is the maker of culture; he is also the corrupter of the cultures he makes. God provides for both and holds his judgment firm against man's abuse of what would have been proper. He does not prevent man's inhumanity; he only vetoes its ever being vindicated as truly human. And this means, for all who live under such a providence, a high-hearted acceptance of their shares in both the world's work and its weeping.

If something like this is true, it would really amount to an earnest affirmation of the human enterprise because of our faith in God's provident purpose for it. It would affirm that life finds its meanings and values within a matrix of givens that are themselves gifts and means of grace. And it asserts that man's invested powers of rational self-understanding, moral self-direction, and spiritual self-fulfillment are sustained by the selfsame love that holds the world in being. It affirms that righteousness and love are not merely divine imperatives. They are, in truth, the preconditions of man's true sanity and wholeness.

The question of where man's real hope lies gets more urgent by the hour. The world is shrinking; the human family is spawning; the resources of technology are doing scarcely more than breaking even; the pace and pressures of modern living are steadily mounting. None of the problems of becoming human, of being human, or of staying human is being solved for good and all—molecular biology and planetary emigration to the contrary notwithstanding.

We would, therefore, do better to learn to live in the atmosphere of God's grace with the courage provided by his love—the courage to face death daily and to react to disaster without hitting either the panic or the destruct buttons; to labor and love with the confidence that counts on grace as the fulcrum for the levers we have to push and pull to get the world's work done.

Instead of reading our fear-reactions as clues to an idiot world, we could learn to decode them as reminders of our radical and ungrudging dependence. Faith is not a falling back on God when all else has failed or is failing. It is, rather, accepting our lives from God's hands; it is having and enjoying and taking leave of the whole round of human life in community as beloved children of God, "in knowledge of whom standeth our eternal life, whose service is our perfect freedom." Is there any other final ground, any other imaginable security?

Introduction

In this clergy-breakfast sermon in Oklahoma City on April 11, 1975, Albert Outler interpreted new ecumenical directions wrought by God's Spirit. Those directions, as he saw them, were mingled sacraments, mingled memberships, mingled ventures in Christian social action—along with cherished diversities in traditions, liturgical forms, organizational styles—all open to development and change.

Dr. Outler was saying that these new directions should have been, in fact the old directions. This was the historian in him talking. He was looking back and seeing himself as one who "played a minor role in some of ecumenism's greatest scenes"; as one who played out with the old-style ecumenism: "The modes of ecumenical dialogue and experimentation to which I have given my life are by way of being played out, even before I am (though some may think it is nip and tuck!)." To Albert Outler the cause of Christian unity in Christian witness, Christian service, and Christian comradeship could neither "be lost nor stayed"—because it is God's will.

"To which I have given my life"—Albert Outler gave himself so completely to the cause of ecumenism that the denomination he was visiting or addressing at the time often claimed him. When he was with Presbyterians, they claimed him. It was the same with the Baptists, Pentecostals, Episcopalians, et al.

Eastern Orthodox professor, George Florovsky, once said that he didn't know how it happened, but somehow Albert Outler had turned into a "Byzantine Methodist"!

SERMON 8

Ecumenism Today: New Directions

It has been thrilling in my lifetime to watch the ecumenical cause emerge from the ancient forms of denominational rivalry and triumphalism and rise to its splendid crescendo—what William Temple called "the greatest reality in modern church history"—and to have played a minor role in some of its greatest scenes. But on this score I've lived too long, for in the last four to six years the cause has been faltering; and the blunt truth is that we are in an ecumenical slump.

The fact is plain and undeniable—whether you are sad or glad about it—but its explanations are multiple and a mite confusing:

a. The passing of the pioneers and the reduced stature and charisma of current ecumenical leadership.

b. The radical shift in Christian concerns—from ecumenism either to social action as the norm and form of true ecumenism or to charismatic renewal and new modes of religiosity, which for various reasons, are typically indifferent to organic unity.

c. The unexpected entrance of Roman Catholicism into the ecumenical situation. This posed new difficulties for traditional ecumenical problems and a spiritual challenge to Protestantism and Orthodoxy, which they were simply unprepared to respond to with any degree of zest, imagination, and daring. Historians will rank this as a great tragedy.

d. The foot-dragging of bureaucrats. This was the most obvious and most disheartening reason. In America for example (and Britain, too), when the ecumenical leaders took the churches up to the brink of union, the bureaucrats looked over the edge and drew back. (They'd never been more than nominally in favor of Christian unity at any stage of the process; they were the ones who stood to lose. Despite all their pious dodges, their foot-dragging was self-interested.) Everybody knows that structure was the partially submerged rock on which the Consultation on Church Union tore out its bottom, and everybody knows that all the mainstream churches in America have turned to one or another exercise in structural overhaul as if in that lay salvation and the coming kingdom. I don't know a single instance where this obsession with reorganization has resulted in genuine gains in the missional effectiveness of any of the churches, save in the unintended sense that in the United Methodist Church, for example, narcissistic preoccupations in our reorganized boards and agencies have left local congregations freer than ever before to do their own thing—if, that is, they had something of their own thing to do.

e. American phobias of ecclesiastical monopoly and the pigheaded obsession of American ecumenists—especially the practical people (administrators and the like)—with merger as the only model of Christian unity they could envisage or imagine.

So, ecumenism isn't going anywhere fast. Right? Wrong! Like all other good causes that God's Spirit is trying to lead us to, dead ends can be turned into new ways to the same eventual goal. And if it really is God's will that all Christ's brothers and sisters be one, to the end that the world may believe, then their ineptitudes and foot-draggings become obstacles but not final barriers.

And so it is with us today, even in a country whose sectarian and denominational traditions are as triumphalist and self-righteous as America's. What we had was *coterie ecumenism*—the ecumenical cause led by a smallish cadre of ecumenical pioneers, visionaries, enthusiasts. Now, the ecumaniacs (of which I am still one, without apology and despite my relegation to the sidelines in my own church) have been thwarted by the bureaucrats (who never really wanted union) and by church members (who fear loss of identity in merger or further burdens from more bureaucracy as their probable dividends from any united church they can conceive).

But this lost battle is not the end of the crusade by any means. For the old denominational lines, as we knew them once, are no longer decisive or permanent boundaries for the church life of many truly committed Christians (not to mention the nominal ones who couldn't care less, save for the wrong reasons). People move about the country now as a matter of course, and they move their church membership for other reasons than blind denominational loyalties. They neither know much nor care much about the issues that once stiffened the pride and consciences of their forefathers.

Biblical interpretation has come to be ecumenical (or nondenominational at least) and so has church history. Theologians within any given denomination are often as widely divergent amongst themselves as across denominational lines. Cherished denominational traditions (especially the triumphalist one) no longer grab the youth. Christians without much well-remembered history are newly interested in the Christian tradition itself ("our common history as Christians"), and traditionalist Christians are more interested in getting with it in the contemporary scene than ever before. There's nothing denominational about civil rights, liberation theology, or Christian social action—and nothing much denominational about experimental liturgies or mass-media religious programming. Only the denominational structures remain and those who live and die by them.

In short, ecumenism and our laggard progress toward the unity that God wills, and to which we profess to be committed, has shifted from the leadership of the churches to the people in those churches. We used to be warned not to outrun the cherished loyalties of the layfolk (the backward layfolk, it was implied). Now the layfolk are ahead of their clerical and curial leadership in both their ecumenical experience and vision.

And what this means, crucially, is that the rectification and validation of ministerial or clerical ordination (one of the top priorities in the old ecumenism) is now no longer front and center. The reason is simple. We have no intelligible formula by which this can be achieved, except by some sort of "leap"— from our various historical discontinuities into some sort of reconstituted and reconciled common ministry based on "spiritual gifts, graces and fruits."

But the mingling of our memberships is possible—on doctrinal and practical grounds. The doctrinal basis is our mutual recognition of our respective baptisms and (theoretically) our confirmations as members—in some true sense—of the people of God and the body of Christ. If you deny that I am a Christian and a church member in some sort of good standing, then obviously we are not in ecumenical dialogue in any serious sense. Your job, then, is to proselyte me if you can. But if you and I are Christians (again in some sense of valid church membership), then we are already eligible for the mingling or sharing of our memberships without having to choose one and abjure the other. The only way to rule this out, theoretically, is for you to deny my baptism or my confirmation or my status as member of the body of Christ. And it is an ecumenical fact of crucial importance that there are fewer Christians prepared to make such denials than ever before.

This is why, in the Consultation on Church Union, for example, the new line is neither merger nor mutual reconciliation of ministerial orders, but the mingling of the memberships of the constituent churches on the basis of renewed profession of their baptismal vows and renewed commitments to the Christian *koinonia*, sacraments, and disciplines. This was, in fact, proposed at Cincinnati this past autumn after having first been broached in Cambridge in 1968. The Methodist delegation in Cincinnati opposed the actual resolution but not, I would want to insist, on Methodist principles. The idea itself was approved by a large majority, and now becomes the new horizon of ecumenical concern and debate, and a very hopeful one in my view.

For it promises unity without merger, it allows for the continuities of existing plural traditions without continuing efforts to sanctify our separations, and above all it allows for the realities of grassroots ecumenism to affect the further evolution of institutional and organic relationships and forms. When a Methodist becomes an Episcopalian or Presbyterian, he has had, up to now, to leave off being a Methodist (either happily, unhappily, or indifferently). Now, the idea is that membership in any one church on some agreed basis of common vows and commitments—and most rituals of reception are into "the Church of Christ" and not into the United Methodist Church or the United Presbyterian Church in the United States of America, etc.

And what, then, of reconciled orders? That will follow in due course, if it is true that ordination is a representation of church membership and not church membership as a support system for the ordained ministry (if, that is, the *laos* is the church visible in the world and the *cleros* is its ordained servants and representatives). How would *you* stand on that "if"?

Ecumenism is in the doldrums nowadays—true enough. Particularly and specifically, ecumenism as we have known it (the ecumenism in which I was bred and to which I have devoted a lifetime). But God moves in mysterious ways his wonders to perform. And one of his current wonders is the way in which he is moving among his people to lead them out of their older nestings and clans and thus into new experiences of discovery of our mutual Christian reality (and defects). Another wonder is the way he is bypassing his chosen curial characters and their knee-jerk impulses to foot-dragging! Mingled memberships and mingled sacraments, mingled ventures in Christian social action—along with cherished differentiations and diversities in traditions, liturgical forms, organizational styles, all open to development and change. This is not "federation"; it is, rather, organic union in the only sense that organic union ought ever to have been used: mutual recognition of our Christian confessions and commitments, mingled memberships, mutual access to our common Christian *koinonia* (which is to say, sacraments and service). "One Lord, one faith, one baptism, one Eucharist (though not necessarily in one rite!)—nothing was said in Ephesians (or even the Pastorals) about one polity, one hierarchy. This is all the unity we need or could do with. Anything less is ecumenical game-playing, if not hypocrisy!

The modes of ecumenical dialogue and experimentation to which I have given my life are by way of being played out, even before I am (though some may think it is nip and tuck). But the cause of Christian unity in Christian witness, Christian service, and Christian comradeship can neither be lost nor stayed. It is God's will; it is the precondition of any truly Christian witness in a raddled and disbelieving world; it is the only kind of relationship that fulfills the New Testament metaphors about the body of Christ. And it is, in fact, being wrought out partially, piecemeal, and against scandalous resistance from those who ought to be its pioneers and leaders. It remains for us to decide whether we would prefer, in good conscience and clear vision, to be a part of the problem of Christian schism and unity or part of its solution.

Introduction

This Palm Sunday sermon was preached in March 1980 at Davidson College Presbyterian Church, Davidson, North Carolina. Beyond the gospel writers' memories of that first Palm Sunday, Albert Outler was grasped by a truth that those stories told: "Palm Sunday is the day for a Christian to rise up and deny that Murphy's laws have any final validity for us. Realists we are and had better be; cynics and pessimists, *no*—never! . . . These are darkly shadowed days in our world's history. All our easy optimisms have been shattered, or will be . . . . And this is what Palm Sundays may still be good for. For we know now that this Palm Sunday will be followed by yet another Maundy Thursday, with its renewal of Christ's new commandment: that we love one another as he has loved us . . . Then will come Good Friday . . . . Then will come Easter . . . and the rising hopes of Pentecost." Albert Outler sees the storm clouds coming (if they are not here, they are on the way). Our Palm Sundays give us hope amidst it all. You will notice that Dr. Outler used the personal pronoun *we*. These were *his* observations out of Scripture—out of life.

Why is it that we look at the rich and assume that everything is in order in their lives (e.g., "They don't need anything. Nothing can go wrong"). We tend to do the same with supremely intelligent, fine folks like Albert Outler, who have made a niche for themselves in this life (e.g., "They've got it all together. Nothing can go wrong"). Wrong! When Albert Outler mentioned Murphy's law (if anything *can* go wrong, it *will* go wrong), he knew first hand how that dismal spirit had slowed the ecumenical movement to a walk (and in some instances to a stagger!). And he knew that his Presbyterian audience that day knew it (though in the sermon he never mentioned it). It was enough to say, "Our hope is in God—literally the only hope worth hoping."

SERMON 9

The Paths of Glory

The memories of that first Palm Sunday experience must have become blurred with the passage of time before they were written down. In all four Gospel accounts of it, there is no mistaking the fact that it was a rousing occasion, but no two of the evangelists recall its details in quite the same way.

Matthew's version (21:1-17) makes it a very full day, complete with the Triumphal Entry, the cleansing of the temple precincts, plus a series of healings within the temple proper.

Mark's typically brusque memoir (11:1-11) recalls only the Triumphal Entry and a quick look around the temple, leaving the cleansing as an order of business for the day following.

Luke's is a variant of the Matthean account, but the variations are significant; he adds the lament over the Holy City and sets the cleansing inside the temple, which suggests that he did not know the actual temple area well enough to realize that the money changing and sales of sacrificial animals would have taken place in the spacious temple precincts outside.

John makes it out as mostly an affair of the great throng of pilgrims from abroad rather than either the people of Jerusalem, as Matthew has it, or, as in the Lucan account, only the whole company of the disciples singing aloud their joy with hosannas and the *benedictus qui venit in nomine Domini.* In a retrospective note, John adds that at that time Jesus' disciples did not understand this, but after Jesus had been glorified they remembered that the Scripture prophecy had been written about him and how it had been fulfilled by him (John 2:22).

The common core in all four memoirs is that Jesus' final challenge to the Jerusalem establishment had started out bravely. At the time, it must have been exciting for the disciples and very promising (something like that Iowa caucus for the partisans of George Bush).

Leaving all questions about his divine foreknowledge to one side for the moment, this much is clear: Jesus had already realized that his decision to go to Jerusalem to prophesy in the citadel of tradition was a risky business. He had already dismissed the temple and the temple cult as nonessential; he had already announced the at-handedness of the kingdom of heaven. He was about to drive the money changers and the purveyors of sacrificial animals out of their accustomed places—and all this was deeply offensive to all sorts of people. Jesus was, in short, taking his life in his hands—against all opposition, open-eyed, and unafraid.

Luke's memoir of the lament over the city has a faintly despairing note in it. Yet once the procession had started, the hosannas and the *Benedictus* were full-throated and excited—whether it was as public as some remembered or whether it was a demonstration of the already committed.

Actually, one may suppose that the whole affair had begun modestly enough. Clearly, it was to be a symbolic reenactment of Zechariah's prophecy, a bit of consciousness raising, a confrontation with the Sadducees that might just possibly win over some of the Pharisees, who also cherished their own hopes of the Messiah.

But the shadow of the cross falls darkly over the celebration. The cleansing of the temple (ignored by John) and Jesus' derogatory predictions of its destruction, stirred a deep resentment among the Sadducees (who controlled the temple cult) and also the Pharisees (who supported that cult as a means of integrating temple and Torah). Humanly speaking, Jesus' doom was sealed before the echoes of the hosannas had died away or the palm branches had withered.

Now, the traditional theme of Palm Sunday homilies since St. Augustine's time, at least, has been the fickleness of people, who will shout, "Hosanna in excelsis," on one day and then cry, "Crucify him," five days later. Thus passes the glory of the world; thus the plaudits and curses of the crowd swing back and forth. So it had been and so it still continues: upon the pinnacle today, down in the pits in a few weeks or months or years, at the most.

The older ones here will know about this pious melancholy from a poem most of us memorized in high school, back in the days when such things were done. It is, of course, Thomas Gray's "Elegy Written in a Country Church Yard." It was immensely popular in its time, along with other lugubrious exercises, such as with Edward Young's "Night Thoughts" and James Hervey's "Meditations Among the Tombs." One of the elegy's most familiar stanzas runs like this:

> The boast of heraldry, the pomp of pow'r,
> And all that beauty, all that wealth e'er gave,
> Await alike th' inevitable hour.
> The paths of glory lead but to the grave.[1]

One might think that Gray had Palm Sunday and Good Friday in mind, but not Easter and Pentecost.

Now, I do not wish to disparage any part of this ancient wisdom. I have no apologies for any fickle mob, and I would hope that none of us imagines that we in our time are very different from those who cried "hosanna" when their hopes were raised and then switched to "crucify him" when their cherished prejudices were offended. The Palm Sunday story can still stand as a parable of all shallow-rooted loyalties, all ephemeral hopes. It has a touch of irony to remind us of all our very good intentions that have already paved over a large tract of you-know-where.

Most of us have never had our confessions of faith sorely tested; none of us is entitled to feel smug about those people who were so easily swayed to equal enthusiasms in opposite directions. Even the disciples, even the Twelve, were caught up in the ebb and flow of these tumultuous feelings. Some of them, Judas most of all, felt a surge of hope and expectation as they came within sight of Jerusalem, crested that famous ridge to the east of the Holy City and saw that magnificent panorama spread out across the Kidron Valley. I have done it myself many times and have never yet felt blasé about it. But come Good Friday and where would they be in the crunch? Not only Peter, but all the rest? Who was there at the end, on Calvary? *Stabat mater dolorosa*—and very few others besides her.

Even so, there must be something to be said for hosannas and the *Benedictus*—whenever hope springs up in our hearts, whenever a glimpse of the providential future, in God's hands, is vouchsafed to us; whenever our side scores, even for the nonce. It is no accident that the hosanna and the *Benedictus* have inspired some of the best in all of sacred music; it is, for example, by far the most lyric and reverent moment in Beethoven's *Missa Solemnis*.

In the providence of God, as Matthew saw clearly, it was wholly fitting that the tragic drama of the Passion and the Cross and the Resurrection should begin with this symbolic fulfillment of one of the most hopeful of the older prophetic visions. How else could a human tragedy like this ever have been transformed into a "divine comedy" (i.e., where the end is triumphant)? When we see Palm Sunday in retrospect, as we do, then its succeeding climaxes—Maundy Thursday, Good Friday, Easter and Pentecost—are recognizable as successive peaks in an ever-rising *massif*.

I hope it will not sound too irreverent to suppose that God was not so cynical about Palm Sunday as some Christians have been; surely he must by now be used to brave beginnings basely aborted. And so one way to understand his providence is to realize how patiently and compassionately he has dealt with us, and all the generations before us, even when we have been as ebullient as the disciples were on Palm Sunday—yet also as craven as they on Good Friday. How many Christian causes have we begun with great enthusiasm and then either let them slide or maybe even have abandoned them? How many fresh crucifixions have we set up by not staying the course in our own commitments—commitments to the righteous rule of God in human lives, to human liberation, to some good cause that we approved of more heartily than we actually supported?

But this can mean only that each new Palm Sunday is yet one more invitation to still another try at welcoming Jesus Christ into our world and into our own lives as Lord and Savior, Lord of history, and still the herald of God's kingdom—that kingdom that even now is so near at hand and yet still so frustratingly far away. Rather than the world-weary pessimism that says, "Forget it," to any good cause (because we already know that its final results won't match our first enthusiasms), Palm Sunday is the day for a Christian to rise up and deny that Murphy's laws have any final validity for us. Realists we are and had better be; cynics and pessimists, *no*—never!

Our hosannas and our "Blessed is he who comes in the name of the Lord" need not bespeak a selfish enthusiasm for any private advantage of our own. They may, instead, express our bolstered confidence in God's good providence, our faith that his righteous rule is no mere fantasy. They might even renew our commitments to that rule and our expectations of it as our most intense loyalty, our most joyous imperative.

These are darkly shadowed days in our world's history. All our easy optimisms have been shattered, or will be. There is not a sizable spot anywhere in the world where life is going really well for any sizable fraction of humanity. Any one of us can identify a dozen detonation points for disaster, for global catastrophe. If our faith and staying power haven't yet been tested to the brink of apostasy, they will be. It was so in Zechariah's time; it was so in Jesus' time. Now, God help us all, it is our turn.

And this is what Palm Sundays may still be good for. For we know now that this Palm Sunday will be followed by yet another Maundy Thursday, with its renewal of Christ's new commandment: that we love one another as he has loved us. Then will come Good Friday, that gaunt skyline with its three crosses, those callous soldiers, those weeping women—yet also that strange business of a man from the Establishment letting Jesus have the first use of his own freshly hewn tomb. Then will come Easter, but even that will not be enough by itself—just as it was not enough for the first disciples, until the descending flames and rising hopes of Pentecost. And from all these mighty acts of grace together will come fresh credentials for our faith and hope and love, even in this grim present and in our shadowed future.

Thus it is that our hosannas and the *Benedictus* are not only for now but for all that God has done, all that he is doing and all that he will do to bring in his kingdom, to set the captives free, give sight to the blind and justice to the oppressed and a new order of peace on earth.

This hope and our help is not in ourselves alone—even though without a real desire to help turn our best hopes into human realities, we ourselves could turn up, come Good Friday, in the mob that cries out once again, "Crucify him," as Christ is being crucified in so many places in the world, some of them with our complicity. Our hope is in God—literally the only hope worth hoping. And this is what I would hope that we mean when we say, "Blessed is he who comes in the name of the Lord" (Matthew 21:9).

Wherefore, hosanna—even in these times—hosanna in the highest!

A Prayer for Illumination

> Almighty God, who hast given us all Holy Scriptures to be read, marked, learned, and inwardly digested, so now by the inspiration of thy Holy Spirit, who inspired those same Scriptures, illumine our minds and dispose our hearts to the end that we may attend upon what is read and expounded here this day, to our profit and edification and to thy greater glory, through Jesus Christ our Lord. Amen.

And now may the grace of our Lord Jesus Christ, the love of God, and the fellowship of the Holy Spirit be with us and remain among us, this day and all the days of this Holy Week to come. Amen.

Introduction

On April 1, 1980, Albert Outler told the Davidson College Presbyterian Church in Davidson, North Carolina, that "the essence of Pilate's plight was his not knowing when and how far to go with the flow, and when and why to take a stand against a popular outcry when it was cruel. . . . It comes down, in Pilate's case (and ours!), to the sin of omission."

Professor Outler would have been the first to pray that his sins of omission be forgiven, and being the human that he was, those moments in the human predicament would inevitably come. But there was one less sin of omission for him than there would have been when you recall how he worked back in the 1950s, store by store, business by business, to get black students accepted in the Southern Methodist University community. Quietly, yet persistently, he helped to right some grave human injustices.

The business community with which he worked in Dallas for the cause of integration was made up of Methodists, Baptists, Episcopalians, Roman Catholics, Jews, Presbyterians, etc. There was a church union already working where existed injustices of all sorts. The overt sins of the world—sins of commission—point to the covert sins of the church—sins of omission. He urged those in his Presbyterian audience, who avoided dealing with the overt sins of the world, to become one in Christ by permitting "this Holy Week to be a time for a resensitizing our consciences to that sort of repentance that will make us aware of how much we can do—to the least of Christ's brethren (and the greatest) and so to *him*."

SERMON 10

Pilate's Plight

Send out thy light and truth, O Lord; let them lead us, so that our ears are open to thy Word and our wills are disposed to the service of thy Kingdom, through Jesus Christ, our Lord. Amen.

The most that can be said for Pontius Pilate was that he was an undistinguished Roman civil servant, whose mediocrity and insensitivity had earned him a ten-year exile in one of the marginal jobs in the Roman Empire: a thankless task of trying to keep some semblance of law and order in the tiny, turbulent territory of Judea and Samaria. Philo tells us that he was a brute; Josephus explains how he finally lost even this poor job because of his bungling a later riot in Samaria. For all his importance as the human judge in the great drama of Holy Week, the Gospel writers leave his character largely unexplored and attribute his motives to nothing better than political expediency.

It was in the apocryphal literature that Pilate really came into his own—with more help from pious imagination than any empirical facts. We have an apocryphal Gospel of Nicodemus in which he is a central figure, and Tertullian professes to have seen a book containing the official report that Pilate had submitted to his superiors explaining the Jesus affair. There is even a legend of his later conversion to Christianity, along with his wife, Procula. And in the Coptic church to this day they are both enrolled as saints!

In the canonical Gospels, Pilate appears, naturally enough, in a harsh light. Each Gospel account has its own twist, depending on the respective special audiences, but they are all agreed that Pilate could have prevented Jesus' death, if only he had been willing to stand up to the religious establishment and to the Jerusalem mob. They all agree that the decisive consideration in his final decision was Pilate's persuasion that Jesus was some sort of political insurgent. What is stressed in each account is the agitation of the crowd and Pilate's dread of a riot. It puts one in mind of those TV scenes from Teheran—with the mullahs and the militants shouting their slogans, waving their fists, shaping history by sheer force of hysteria.

Matthew has a tradition about the intervention of Pilate's wife on Jesus' behalf; he also has an explanation for the fatal choice between Jesus Barabbas and "Jesus called Messiah." The whole business, according to Matthew, was a demonstration instigated by the Jewish leaders on behalf of a political prisoner in preference over a religious visionary.

Mark's explanation would have made good sense in Rome (where practical politics were readily understood): "So Pilate, in his desire to placate the mob, released Barabbas to them—and then proceeded to have Jesus flogged and handed over to the soldiers to be crucified" (Mark 15:15).

Luke lays more stress on Pilate's vacillations—how he had tried to pass the buck over to Herod Antipas and had it passed right back to him.

John focuses on the main point—what sort of a "king" was this man Jesus and just how dangerous has he to the Roman peace? Rome was generally tolerant of the splatter of religious movements throughout the empire—except where any one of them raised the banner of revolt or a rival kingship to Caesar's. There can be no doubt that the essence of Jesus' preaching was the kingdom of God, and it would certainly seem that the essence of his own self-understanding was that of herald and agent of that kingdom. But Pilate was too dim-witted and too political an animal to understand Jesus' assurance that his kingdom was not of this world.

All the Gospels agree that Pilate was more concerned about the charges of subversion than of blasphemy, that he was not fully convinced of Jesus' guilt but that prudence seemed the greater part of valor under the circumstances. This is the point of Matthew's report about that symbolic washing of Pilate's hands, as if he could rid himself of the whole affair.

There is no question of appealing for any special sympathy for Pilate. He stood at one of history's turning points and never knew it; he actually tilted history's scales and never realized what he was doing; he wrought a horrid cruelty simply as part of his job. This, of course, is the basis for Anatole France's short story in which the aged Pilate is confronted by a Christian convert. As it turns out, Pilate had long since forgotten the episode of Jesus' death entirely.

None of us is likely to identify with Pilate, even in times of uneasy consciences. So what then have we to learn from this stolid, unimaginative, heavy-handed sergeant-major who just happened to be at history's knife-edge at a crucial moment and so got himself forever enshrined in the creeds? Well, maybe more than might appear at first glance.

For example, the essence of Pilate's plight was his not knowing when and how far to go with the flow and when and why to take a stand against a popular outcry when it was cruel. Most of us, I should think, deplore the rise of violence and the demoralizations of contemporary society in which every index of social and spiritual health is tilted downward. But what did we do that might have helped stem the flood of permissiveness and disorder when it would have made a difference? Besides, of course, deploring it and washing our hands of any complicity in it? The success of evil, as Edmund Burke reminded us long ago, is not due so much to its intrinsic power as it is to the apathy and tolerance of good men and women like you and me.

We are a society with a whole repertory of addictions: drugs, alcohol, sex, narcissism, self-indulgence with a thousand faces.

None of us is responsible for this maybe, as direct agents, yet we are all responsible for it as passive observers who have failed to take a stand somewhere along the line against the hue and cry of the multitude ("peer pressure" is the current jargon for it). Pilate's plight was that he felt he could not afford to antagonize this particular mob. How different is that, really, from our fear of appearing to the mob as blue-nosed Puritans? It is to our credit when we have supported the good causes of liberty denied. But what about our track record in the cases all around us of liberty abused?

Crucifixion is long since outmoded as a physical penalty for subversion or rebellion. But character assassination has not been outlawed; it often goes under the unglamorous rubric of "gossip" or the glamorous rubric of "investigative reporting."

In our town, this past winter, some carelessness was discovered in the financial affairs of one of the social agencies of the city government, and the TV people jumped on it with all four feet, putting one of the men who was allegedly involved on a series of programs. It was easy for them to convict him of looking like a fool and then to disavow all responsibility when he thereupon committed suicide. Now, who really pulled that trigger and which of us in the TV audience was wholly innocent?

Pilate's plight was that he was unwillingly involved in a theological dispute and tried to settle it by a political act. How different was that from the way in which, in our time, our governments and our courts are now settling theological issues of great moment by means of arbitrary judicial and legislative decisions? And many other acts that result in unintended crucifixions still occur, and they follow from some moral lapse of the conscience and courage on the part of this man or that woman. More of us are caught up in the same sort of plight as Pilate's than we may quite realize.

We, too, have his tendency to pass the buck, to expect help from somebody or somewhere else. Thus, we may be able to see ourselves in Pilate's sandals in some degree: with the same tendencies to excuse ourselves from complicity in injustice, oppression, and so much of the incidental misery in the world. Here are parents complaining of the quality of public education, who have not done all they could to educate their own children and their friends. Here are students complaining of their teachers and not accepting their own responsibilities for an inadequate education. Here we all are, complaining of inflation and still stoking its fires by our own conspicuous expenditure, comforted by the allegation that it is the government and not we that is chiefly responsible for this challenge to our nation and our way of life.

If we prescind from Philo's obviously prejudiced charge, we could conclude that Pilate may not have been an especially cruel man by nature or by habit. The Gospel stories agree that he went further than most bureaucrats and military men would have gone in trying to let Jesus off. But in the end, he bowed to popular pressure and became an accomplice in a hideous cruelty—even as perhaps an unwilling accomplice. Yet he had the duty and power to resist popular clamor and he failed to do it.

Our plight is far more subtle and yet still fully as serious. Think of the human cruelties we are involved in, almost unaware of—the cruelties of racism, sexism, ageism, and the cruelties of world hunger and underdevelopment in countries around the world, in which we as Americans have been incriminated without quite meaning to be. We are aware of the mindless resentment against us in many parts of the world, just as Pilate was aware of the Jews' hysterical hatred of the Romans.

But since we are so serenely convinced of our own lack of malice and any evil intent, we are less sensitive than we might be to the reasons why the wretched of the earth have turned against us. Remember, the pax Romana was, on the whole, a very great advance in the ancient world over anything that had ever gone before. The Augustan vision of a stable, peaceful world, based on Roman law and justice, was a noble conception—one of the grandest in human history. And Pilate was the responsible agent of that *Pax Romana* in Judea and Samaria.

It was one of the most dramatic moments in history, the local official of the world's greatest empire passing judgment on the herald and agent of the kingdom of God. This was the point to Pilate's question: are you a king (or what kind of king are you?)—and of Jesus' equivocal answer to the effect that a Roman procurator would not be able to understand even the bare notion of the kingdom of God on earth. But, for that matter, do we understand it? The coercive powers of this world are still unable to comprehend a kingdom of persuasion, a kingdom of love and righteousness that, in the end, will be mightier than any other power on earth!

So what would you have done if you had been Pilate? Would you have risked a riot in order to save an innocent man from being lynched? It will not do (though some have tried it) to see in Pilate a sort of marionette of Providence (as if, since God was intent on Jesus' death as an essential part of his scheme of salvation, there had to be somebody to sentence him to the cross). This is no better than the theory that there had to be a Judas since the scenario of salvation called for a betrayal. Pilate, and Judas, and you and I have our respective roles in history's drama, but not in any history that has been all that prescripted, else it would not be history, which is nothing if not a texture of human decisions that represent humanity at its best, its worst, and its ordinary muddle.

It comes down, in Pilate's case (and ours!) to the sin of omission, and here is where we are acutely vulnerable to judgment. In a congregation and a community like this (more than most), there seems to be a decent minimum of deliberate sins, of intended commissions of sin, flagrant and defiant sins against morality and humanity. Actually, I might say the same things about the people I know in Dallas, though you'll never believe me if you've been watching that TV horror about our town. But what about our sins of omission, what about that multitude of things undone that we should have done if the circumstances had been just right?

One of the saintliest and most learned of all the Anglican bishops was Archbishop James Ussher (who has had the great misfortune to be remembered for his acceptance of the then generally acknowledged date of Creation, as 4004 B.C.; actually, he did not invent that date and he was a great theologian, a truly godly man). On his deathbed, so his eyewitness biographer tells us, his final prayer was: "O God, as thou hast dealt mercifully with my sins of commission, so be thou doubly merciful in the matter of my sins of omission, since they were so many more."[1]

I hope that it goes without saying that we cannot escape our part in Pilate's plight simply by choosing, or resolving, to be more conscientious and more resolute in standing against the wrong. Such resolutions are pitifully weak against the torrent of custom and the encrusted evils of an inhumane society. What a man or woman does in a moral crisis does not depend, really, upon his or her good resolutions but rather on the sort of faith and trust and conscience and loyalties to God's kingdom and his righteousness that faith and hope and love have generated. Christian courage is a rather different thing from the common run of good resolutions. When the aged Polycarp was asked by the governor of Smyrna to revile Christ and so save his life (actually, almost pleaded with), his answer was: "Eighty and six years have I served my Lord and he has never failed me; why should I fail him now?"[2] Real courage comes from our loyalties, which is to say, from our deepest faith and truest trust.

The harshest question that we shall have to answer at the Judgment, which is also to say the question about our ultimate concerns here and now will be: Did you do all in your power to stand for humanity and justice? Did you do all you could have done, even to the point of suffering, to stand against inhumanity and cruelty, even when you were not a direct accomplice?

> "For when the Son of Man comes in his glory . . . he will say to those on his left and [and that will include the Pilates of this world]: 'There is a curse upon you . . . for when I was hungry, you gave me nothing to eat; when I was thirsty, nothing to drink; when I was a stranger, you gave me no home; when naked, no clothes to wear; when I was ill and in prison, you did not help me.' And they will reply, 'Lord when in the world did we ever see you hungry or thirsty or a stranger or naked or ill or in prison and did nothing for you?' And he will answer, 'Anything you left undone for any of my brethren, however humble, you did not do for me.' " (Matthew 25:31, 41-45, NEB).

This was God's judgment against Pilate—not because his sin of omission was unforgivable but because he was so insensitive about it all, so utterly unrepentant.

God forbid that anything like this should ever be the final judgment on any one of us. So may this Holy Week be a time for resensitizing our consciences to that sort of repentance that will make us aware of how much we can do—to the least of Christ's brethren (and the greatest) and so to *him*.

Let us pray:

> Almighty God, save us from any complacency in our judgments of Pontius Pilate; help us to see how nearly we have come to his insensitivity—to his standing aside and letting intolerable things happen. So make this Holy Week a time of fresh discoveries about ourselves and about thy grace—to the end that we may enter more fully into the true joys of Easter and Pentecost. Through Jesus Christ, our Lord—and Lord of all. Amen.

Introduction

In addressing the "dogmatism versus indifferentism" doctrinal controversy (March 1, 1981) Albert Outler revealed as much about himself as he did about the subject—*he* was immersed in his subject! To those who avoid a rigorous analysis of doctrine he threw in a bit of humor at himself: "Sometimes I get such doubtful compliments as 'you don't sound like a theologian' (e.g., the DePauw coed: 'That's the best lecture I ever heard in a grits and gravy accent')."

As an answer to the indifferentism versus dogmatism approaches to doctrine, John Wesley worked out a distinction between "the heart of Christian faith" and the "opinions" that grew up in reflection and debate about this inner core of heart religion. Albert Outler carried that same approach into the arena of the 1972 United Methodist General Conference, where he plowed through the doctrinal pluralisms of opinions with the transcending Spirit of universal love to the core of heartfelt experiences of grace. This transcending experience in no way prevented Dr. Outler from continuing to press his point following the debate. About one participant he said, "We still fall easily into serious and heated arguments in any given fifteen-minute conversation."

This self-disclosure accounted for a phenomenon often witnessed in Albert Outler—the drop of a word could start an argument that, if copied, would present an essay worthy of publishing in the best academic journal. He called it "heated"; some called it "hyper"; or "righteous indignation." Whatever you called it, you knew that beyond the "heat" was a warm heart—a grace.

SERMON 11

Methodist Pluralism

Some people are born Methodists, some become Methodists, and others have Methodism thrust upon them. But there are two or three strange things about us that puzzle other people, and would trouble us more if we were more self-conscious about what it means to be a Methodist. One is the Methodist success story of the past 200 years. Another is our preoccupation with organization—"methods." But a third thing that puzzles people from the older churches is our relative lack of a strong sense of tradition and heritage, accompanied by a fuzzy view of Christian doctrine and what Christians do believe, or ought to believe, if they are to bear Christ's name in his church or in his world.

A piece on Methodists in the old *Life* magazine many years ago emphasized that we were heavy on muscle and good works, light on theology and heritage. One can hear it said that Methodists can believe almost anything at all, or next to nothing. People reared in the tradition of the great confessions have something to point to—Augustana, Westminster, Trent—and wonder why the Methodists don't have such a heritage. Some Methodists wonder, too, and have even tried to manufacture the image at times. Note that the Commission on Doctrine and Doctrinal Standards had this original nickname, "the Creedal Commission"!

Here are some results, from 1968 to 1972 and since then: The Judicial Council's decision that doctrine is merely an administrative matter, subject to simple majority rule. We may be the only mainline church in the world with an official rule that truth can be decided by 50% plus 1! In the United Methodist Church we actually have not one but two "confessions"—neither of which is "confessional" in the traditional sense.

It is, therefore, not surprising that in the United Methodist Church we have the problem of pluralism, of doctrinal diversity, of dogmatism versus indifferentism, and an unhappy tendency to settle for simplistic ad hoc solutions.

The result is the reinforcement of yet another tendency: to regard doctrine, theology, and rigorous analysis as excrescences (warts!) on the Christian life—and to be avoided where possible. "I am not a theologian . . ." is often a proud boast—too often by clergy. Sometimes I get such doubtful compliments as "You don't sound like a theologian" (e.g., the DePauw coed: "That's the best lecture I ever heard in a grits and gravy accent").

But the fact is that our success story is not being updated any more; simplistic solutions are not working so well (not ours, at least), and more and more we have to become more self-conscious about what we as Methodist Christians believe and why and to what ends—in terms of personal fulfillment and social transformation.

We need to understand in what sense we come by this pluralistic tradition honestly. It began with John Wesley himself. He was a very strong-minded man, son of two strong-minded parents. He lived in a time of clashing, harsh polarities—dogmatisms and bitter controversies and a rising indifference sustained by disgust over ill-tempered religion. Blood and ink had been spilled over controversies about vestments, prelacy, doctrines, Sabbath observance, freedom of speech and of religion. It was, for example, illegal merely to be a Roman Catholic in Wesley's lifetime, and even he was convinced that if the Puritans had their way, another king would be beheaded, or, if the Roman Catholics had their way, Great Britain would be delivered back to the pope!

He himself was heir to many different traditions: Anglican,

Puritan, "the radicals," Lutheran-Moravian, and deism. So also were his allies and disciples: Howell Harris, George Whitefield, Vincent and Edward Perronet, et al. He came gradually to believe that their differences were not focused in the essential core of Christian faith—in one God, the Trinity (in some sense), the Atonement, a vital experience of Christian faith, good works as the fruits of faith, a vision of Christian existence grounded in grace. Everybody agreed to some such essential core, so long as it was not conceptualized and formulated into forensic propositions (lawyer-like language to be taken literally and enforced by some sort of inquisitor). This essential core was rooted in Scripture, enriched by centuries of Christian experiences of grace and worship, refereed by reason and common sense, and emotionally anchored in the heart by Christian experience (the assurance of God's unmerited mercy for Christ's sake).

All the rest of Christian reflection was reflection on all parts of this core. And everywhere Wesley saw the tendency to take one or another doctrine or opinion or interpretation as if it, too, were essential core: a shibboleth that justified controversy and intolerance toward all who differed, toward all who said, "shibboleth." Moreover, they were as intolerant of those who differed in these doctrinal interpretations—predestination or free will, irresistible or free grace, episcopal or presbyterial polity, moralism or antinomianism, etc., etc.—as of those who denied the basic core itself. Nowadays, we see such controversies in economics, politics, and the merits or demerits of jogging, smoking, or caffeine!

And so Wesley began to work out a working distinction between "the heart of Christian faith" and the doctrines and "opinions" that grew up in reflection and debate about this inner core of heart religion. Almost ruefully, he concluded that true religion does not consist in orthodoxy, or right opinions:

> . . . neither does religion consist in orthodoxy or right opinions; which . . . are not in the heart but in the understanding. A man may be orthodox in every point; he may not only espouse right opinions, but zealously defend them against all opposers; he may think justly concerning the incarnation of our Lord, concerning the ever blessed Trinity, and every other doctrine con-

> tained in the oracles of God. He may assent to all the three Creeds—that called the Apostles', the Nicene and the Athanasian—and yet 'tis possible he may have no [heart] religion at all. . . . He may be almost as orthodox as the devil [who understands orthodoxy perfectly] . . . and may all the while be as great a stranger as he to the religion of the heart.
>
> This alone is religion, truly so called. . . , the Apostle sums it all up in three particulars—"righteousness, and peace, and joy in the Holy Ghost."[1]

Essential Christianity is the faith (from God in Christ through the Holy Spirit) that works by love and issues in righteousness and peace and joy in the Holy Ghost. Indeed, "orthodoxy"—when it is dogmatically maintained in the spirit of intolerance—is a hindrance to holiness.

Thus, in a sermon entitled "Catholic Spirit" (Sermon 39) he proposed his own doctrine of pluralism. His text, from 2 Kings 10:15, is mostly a pretext. It connects with what follows at the point that Jehu was not a bland amiable middle-roader, hence no likely candidate for the charge of being wishy-washy in his opinions. So if Jehu could show "Catholic Spirit," the rest of us can, too.

Wesley then concludes that, although all Christians must belong to some church, no one denomination is the true church in the sense that all others are false. Again, although all Christians must worship God corporately, decently and in order, no one liturgy is the true one, in the sense that all others are false.

He then comes to his sketch of the essential core:

1. Belief in God and in his sovereign wisdom, power, grace, and providence;
2. Belief in the Lord Jesus Christ, as Savior and indwelling Spirit; belief in salvation as "submitting ourselves unto the righteousness of God which is by faith in Christ Jesus";
3. Experience of the faith that enacts itself in and by love;
4. Love of God with heart, mind, soul, and strength in wholehearted commitment;
5. A commitment to God's will above one's own so that the

love of God directs one's behavior;

6. Love to neighbor—"all mankind, without exception"; and
7. Showing one's love by one's works.

Given this doctrinal and ethical core, speculative opinions in theology are bound to be diverse, but they must not annul one's life commitment to God in Christ. Predestination is allowable but it is not a part of the core. The same is true of all explanations and interpretations of Scripture and traditional dogma. So also are all our choices in liturgy, polity, and social and economic theory.

This brings him to an emphatic comment on what "catholic spirit"is not. First, it is not "speculative latitudinarianism." "It is not an indifference to all opinions" or "unsettledness of thought." It is not an unformed "judgment concerning the main branches of Christian doctrine" or "a lack of interest in theological discussion." "It is not anti-intellectualism."

It is not even "practical latitudinarianism." It takes worship and the question of better and worse ways to worship seriously, seeking always to be "both scriptural and rational."

What is catholic spirit then? It is love, "universal love," that takes all the plural options in doctrine, liturgy, and polity and transcends them all. Catholic spirit means respect for those with whom we differ, and genuine love and goodwill toward them.

Here, then, is a different attitude toward this whole problem of doctrinal consensus. It rejects bigotry and intolerance as heartily as it rejects indifferentism and lack of considered or reflective Christian truth. It is concerned with the most careful and thoughtful Christian reflection: Christians are to think through their experience and are honor-bound to be able to give an account (a credible account) of the faith that is in them. But no false pride of mind that what I have thought through and believe to be true is true in the sense that all other formulations of the same problems are wholly false. The same goes for bigotry, excommunications, contempt for others who are not yet in the truth as we are, and holier-than-thou self-righteousness.

This sermon, and other similar views on pluralism, were the base line that guided the Commission on Doctrine and Doctrinal Standards, but not at the outset of our work. First off, someone proposed that we draw up a new creed to replace the antiquated ones we had in the 1968 *Discipline*. And then we discovered that we could write a dozen "creeds" more readily than one. We had some indifferentists and some dogmatists (the liberals, it might as well be told, were more intolerant of the conservatives than the other way around).

The outcome was something of a miracle of a group of 40 people growing together in love and understanding that transcended our opinions. John Cobb and I are no closer together on theological method and ideology than when we began. But we came to realize how much more important our mutual respect and love meant than our differing speculative views. This is not indifferentism; we still fall easily into serious and heated arguments in any given fifteen-minute conversation. But the "statement" that came out of the Commission—the twelfth full draft (after dozens of subcommittee statements)—represented real consensus.

We hoped that the Judicial Council would have had the wit to see that it was a constitutional matter—for we wanted it to go down through the Annual Conferences and congregations for debate. The Council ruled otherwise, so we fell back on Plan B: to see whether the General Conference vote would be the equivalent needed for a constitutional amendment. If not, I was authorized to withdraw the whole business from the Conference floor—and move for another quadrennium of work on it. The vote was a shade above 97% for, less than 3% against. Incidentally, we have the signed ballots for this vote in our archives, and I am still surprised at some of the 27 people who voted against it.

It is an interesting section of our *Discipline*[2], and I have had some interesting comments on it from people who recognize in it an alternative to dogmatism and to indifferentism. The far right has denounced it as indifferentist; the more moderate among the conservatives recognize it as including them within the Methodist theological ballpark. It is worth reading, studying, and referring to your friends who ask "Do Methodists really believe anything definite?" There is a common core. There is a distinctive Methodist emphasis. It is called the Fourfold Guidelines of "The Methodist Quadrilateral": Scripture, tradition, experience, and reason.

Introduction

You will not be misreading when you read the following: this sermon was preached at the "Conference on the Restoration Ideal in American Christianity" on the campus of Abilene Christian University (July 15-18, 1985) to an audience of Church of Christ scriptural enthusiasts, who were eggheads of that special bent. Yes—*Church of Christ*!

In this sermon Albert Outler related Methodism's many historical and traditional variants with the one theme that keeps the Church of Christ in existence, and that is "apostolic Christianity."

Whenever in the sermon Albert Outler hit at Methodism's lack of tradition at any given time in its history, the Church of Christ audience surely must have flinched (they seldom refer to "tradition"). For them it is "all Scripture," which, in effect, makes for them a well-grounded tradition.

In this sermon/lecture Albert Outler piled on the words, which called to Outler's mind what Merrimon Cuninggim said about him at a Kent Fellowship meeting, where they met and shared papers. One evening they had a party where everybody did something or other. Outler recalled, "Meri's part was to do an impressionist imitation of me. He started out with a perfectly clear first clause and went on. It was all, I thought, rather interesting. He went on and on and finally he said, 'If anybody here knows where this sentence is going to end, they are a better man than I am!' " (Note here Outler's humor-at-self, which, incidentally, is not to be found in Wesley.)

SERMON 12

Biblical Primitivism in Early American Methodism

Several stereotypical ways may be followed to misunderstand early Methodism in America that have, nonetheless, continued to seem credible to Methodists and non-Methodists alike, even until now. One is to connect its first century in America too closely with its Wesleyan antecedents in eighteenth-century Britain. Despite the Anglican filiation of John Wesley, Thomas Coke, Joseph Pilmoor and others, Francis Asbury and the bulk of American Methodists in the early decades understood themselves in terms of a modified "nonconformity" that set them apart from the Episcopalians on the one side and other American Protestants on the other. Their Arminian theology set them off from the Reformed traditions generally, and their societal polity (with its connectionalism, itinerancy, and monarchial episcopacy, etc.) distinguished them from all the congregationalist and Presbyterian traditions. Moreover, they were well content with these "Methodist distinctives," as they called them.

Another misleading stereotype is the supposition that American Methodism in its recent second century (1884-1984) amounted to a simple extension of that first one. Sweeping social changes and drastic doctrinal reorientations (noted in Robert Chiles, *Theo-*

logical Transitions in American Methodism, 1790-1935) altered the ethos and outlook of mainline Methodism in ways that require a reformulation of almost all generalizations about the early decades, or, at the least, nuanced differently. Nor will generalizations that are sound enough for "United" Methodism (since 1968) hold without important revision for the other Methodist bodies in America (e.g., The African Methodist Episcopal Church, the African Methodist Episcopal Zion Church, The Christian Methodist Episcopal Church, the Wesleyan Church, the Free Methodist Church, the Church of the Nazarenes and—much less—the various Pentecostal churches, who also have a "Wesleyan" provenance).

Indeed, the Methodist heritage itself has a more shadowy lineage than one would guess from the myths about John Wesley as its founder, *de nihilo*. It goes back at least to the seventeenth-century negations of "High Calvinism" (as distilled in Dort, 1619), gathered under the misleading umbrella term "Arminian." Its alternative doctrines stressed grace and free will, along with a variety of notions about "double justification" (as with Martin Bucer and the so-called "School of Saumur," e.g., Amyraldus, LeBlanc, Cameron, Peter Baro, et al.).

We know about this still-obscure tradition largely through its critics, e.g., the French Protestant Jean Daille in his *La foi fondée sur Les Saintes Scriptures, Contre les Nouveau Methodistes* (1634), the English Nonconformist Theophilus Gail, *The Court of the Gentiles* (1672), the Lutheran Johannes Vlach, *Dissertationes Trias* (1680) (one of those dissertations deplores the doctrines of *Nostri novi Methodistae*). An English Puritan critique of this "new method in divinity," aimed actually at John Goodwin and Richard Baxter(!), appeared in an anonymous pamphlet in 1696: *A war Among the Angels of the Churches: Wherein is Showed the Principles of the New Methodists in the Great Point of Justification*. Its author, "A Country Professor of Jesus Christ," was especially incensed by what seemed to him as their "neonomianism," their false doctrines of imparted righteousness in justification, and their preference for the doctrine of Christ's atoning death as the "meritorious cause" of salvation, in contrast to the Reformed doctrine of the atonement as justification's "formal cause."

Thus, when the brothers Wesley and their friends formed a semi-monastic society in Oxford in 1729 and labeled it "The Holy Club," they were bound to remind some of their Anglican critics of those old "new Methodists"; and this was the nickname (appearing first in 1732) that stuck. Nor is it unimportant that Wesley treated the appellation as a nickname (and preferred to speak of his disciples as "the people called Methodists").

It was natural enough, therefore, that when the Methodist movement began to spread as a religious society within the Church of England (in 1739 and thereafter), it would appear as an ecclesiastical anomaly: neither Anglican nor Nonconformist. As friendly a critic as Josiah Tucker (afterward, Dean of Gloucester) could admonish the Methodists against doctrinal confusion and warn them against the dangers of separation and schism. (Cf. his *Brief History of the Principles of Methodism: Wherein the Rise and Progress, together with the Causes of the several Variations, Divisions and Present Inconsistencies of this Sect are attempted to be traced out and accounted for*, 1742).

John Wesley, however, was all the more convinced that the times called for an evangelical alternative to the sacerdotalism of "the Church as by law established" and the Calvinism of Nonconformity. He saw his revival as a providential corrective to the formalism and moralism of the national church; he sincerely believed that the Methodist gospel of grace ("repentance, faith, and holiness") was a recovery of "apostolic doctrine"—still another reform of the Reformation. The Methodists recoiled in horror from the "wars of religion" that had followed the sixteenth-century disruptions, and their memories of religious anarchy in Cromwell's Commonwealth left them suspicious of what they saw as theocratic visions both in Calvinism and in "radical Protestantism."

In America, the Methodists were latecomers (our earliest firm date is 1766), who had blithely lightened their inherited baggage from the Old World. To begin with, many of the first Methodists in the colonies were Irish (some of them Palatine Germans who had first migrated to Ireland and become Methodists there before their further transplantation to the New World). Their "primitivism" consisted largely in their zeal for Scripture as "the sole rule of faith and practice" and their sense of "the Apostolic Church" as a perpetual charter rather than as an imitable model.

Once their colonial ties with Britain and the Church of England had been severed, American Methodists were torn between their tenuous loyalties to John Wesley and their need of a ministry of their own. Inevitably, there were initiatives on behalf of a self-constituted "restoration" (as in the "Fluvanna Schism" of 1782-1783).

Francis Asbury (the only English Methodist appointed by Wesley who had remained in America throughout the Revolution), held out for some link of legitimation with Wesley and the British Conference. Wesley, in turn, was prepared to reverse his erstwhile negative views of "American independence," and moved quickly on several fronts to provide the Americans with the makings of a church, independent, but still linked with their British heritage. It was Wesley the churchman who dared to act as "a scriptural *episkopos*" (with what he thought was patristic precedent) and to ordain two "elders" (Thomas Vasey and Richard Whatcoat), and to "ordain" his assistant, Dr. Thomas Coke (LL.D.) as "general superintendent" for America.

This trio was to proceed forthwith to the new country and provide a ministry of "Word, Sacrament, and Order" for the Methodist people. With them, he sent along a curious abridgment of the *Book of Common Prayer*, which he had prepared for the new church, along with an anti-Calvinist abridgment of the Thirty-nine Articles. Its title was *The Sunday Service of the Methodists in North America*, 1784. As a personal blessing and as an official warrant for all these protocols of continuity, he drafted an open letter "To Our Brethren in America," reflecting his sense of tradition as taprooted in Scripture and developed in his church history:

> As our American brethren are now totally disentangled both from the State [the new USA] and from the English hierarchy, we dare not entangle them again either with the one or the other [note this affirmation of the separation of church and state six years before the First Amendment]. They are now at full liberty

> simply to follow the Scriptures and the Primitive Church. And we judge it best that they should stand fast in that liberty wherewith God has so strangely made them free.[1]

This is the same man who had, a decade earlier, "submitted" his Collected Works (1771-1774) "to the judgment of Holy Scripture, right reason, and Christian Antiquity."

There can be no doubt that, for Wesley, "apostolic Christianity" was normative or that its restoration continued as an ideal for him and his people. But he was also immersed in church history; he took some sort of continuity of ministries for granted. Was Wesley, then, a "restorationist"? The answer here hinges on one's understanding of "tradition," "continuity," and "development" in church history since the end of the apostolic age.

Even the American Methodists, with a far less vivid or rich sense of tradition, understood themselves as reforming a debilitated church rather than reconstituting one, *de novo*. With remarkable self-reliance, therefore, they constituted themselves into the first independent denomination in the new American nation with a title connoting their polity, "The Methodist Episcopal Church" (1784). Coke and Asbury were elected as their general superintendents (and promptly took on the title "bishop"). They arranged for an itinerant ministry tightly "connected" from Maine to Georgia, which then was dominated entirely by Francis Asbury, who reigned without a peer for a full quarter century (he died in 1816).

Wesley had supposed that his "brethren in America" would wish to continue under his spiritual direction and theological tutelage, as British Methodism had done so willingly for the preceding two generations. He also assumed that Dr. Coke, as his delegated *locum tenens*, would be cordially received as the head of the new church, or at the least as Asbury's senior partner. All these assumptions were miscalculations—both of the American temper and of Asbury's temperament.

The Americans were prepared to acknowledge Wesley as their eponymous patriarch, but they were equally resolved upon maintaining their new independence. Asbury assumed the mantle of leadership, quietly eased Coke out of the picture, allowed *The*

Sunday Service to fall into disuse, and proceeded to set as distinctive a mark on American Methodism as Wesley had done in Britain.

His "primitivism" had no speculative theological basis. He had next to no sense of tradition, but also no strong convictions about a church in apostasy since the end of the apostolic age. It was, rather, that the Bible served him sufficiently in his personal spiritual hungers and in his passion for awakening and converting souls. In typical Methodist fashion, he added the *Book of Discipline* and the *Hymnal* to "the iron ration" of his preachers. What he had learned from John Wesley (from slight acquaintance and only a brief career in the English Conference) was twofold: That the church is best defined by its commitment to mission and that a religious society is best directed by a single head.

In America, he came to see how the talents of the preachers could be multiplied by frequent rotation (itinerancy). The Methodists were quick to adopt the patterns of revivals and camp meetings and put them to good use. On their own, they invented the circuit rider—a Christian militiaman, traveling light, meshed into a network of "conferences" (from local charge, to district, annual and general), subject to appointment and frequent reassignment. Until recent times, Methodist preachers were never "called"; they were sent—never "elected" by a congregation; they were "received."

It was a strange combination, a focus on Scripture and "experience" as the fonts of authority, together with a monarchial polity within an egalitarian society. What is more, since this unique polity seemed to work so well, not merely on the frontier but in the towns and cities, the Methodists came readily to believe that they had rediscovered the most adequate contemporary analog to polity in the apostolic church.

The Methodists resisted all ideas of "the invisible church" (this they associated with Reformed notions of *numerus electorum*, "the secret number of the elect"). They did, however, insist on probationary church membership, plus a strict discipline within the church membership. Their "article of religion," *Of the Church*, Article XIII, adopted from Article XIX of the Thirty-Nine Articles (itself derived from Article VIII of the Augsburg Confession) was suitably ecumenical:

> XIII. The visible Church of Christ is a congregation of faithful men in which the pure Word of God is preached, and the Sacraments duly administered according to Christ's ordinance, in all those things that of necessity are requisite to the same.[2]

In his sermon, "Of the Church" (number 74, 1785), Wesley expanded the same definition:

> The catholic or universal church is all the persons in the universe whom God hath so called out of the world as to entitle them to the [character of Christians], united by "one spirit"; having "one faith, one hope, one baptism. . . . [Then follows a comment on "national and local churches"]. A particular church may therefore consist of any number of members, whether two or three, or two or three millions. But still, whether it be larger or smaller, the same idea is to be preserved. They are one body, and have one Spirit, one Lord, one hope, one faith, one baptism, one God and Father of all.[3]

Among American Methodists, this view was focused on "the church of the converted," with constant stress on regeneration and assurance (with frequent allusions to Acts 2:41-47). In Wesley, Scripture and tradition had been integrated as the mutual interdependence of revelation and interpretation. No one among the American Methodists knew enough about tradition to appropriate such an integration. Thus, Wesley's concept of fourfold authority—of Scripture (as base and font), tradition, and critical reason as hermeneutical pillars, and of experience as confirmation—was drastically altered. Scripture was kept as base and font, but tradition was ignored, and reason turned into rationalization (*fides quaerens-argumentum*!). "Experience" was enlarged beyond its original denotation of "assurance," into emotive concerns of all sorts, with an authority of their own (because they were emotive). After all, what is there polite to say to a patently sincere assertion: "Deep in my heart, I know that . . ."?

Classical Restorationism, especially in America, felt bound by "the silences of the New Testament." Methodist primitivism tended to take those silences as concessions to true believers to follow the leadings of their consciences and common sense— within the canons of faith, hope, and love. Methodist ministers were largely self-educated, with biblical perspectives of salvation that discouraged critical study of church history on the one hand and speculative theology on the other. They were bound into a close-knit fellowship in which "membership in full connection" in an Annual Conference was distinguished from ordination—and meant a good deal more in practical terms. And this distinction persists in the Methodist ethos still.

Besides the Articles of Religion supplied by Wesley, the Americans produced one of their own (Article XXIII "Of the Rulers of the United States of America"), but they declined to attempt any other statements of official orthodoxy.

They stoutly rejected "formalism" (as they saw it among the Episcopalians and Roman Catholics). Their eucharistic theology varied from memorialism to the sort of "spiritual realism" reflected in Charles Wesley's "Hymns for the Lord's Supper." They retained The Apostles' Creed as an optional usage, but quietly dropped the phrase, "descended into hell," from their version of it. Some congregations used "the Creed commonly called Nicene" for Holy Communion.

In 1808, the General Conference adopted a "Restrictive Rule" that forbade the revocation, alteration, or change in The Articles of Religion as well as the establishment of any "new standards or rules of doctrine contrary to our present and established standards of doctrine"—and then resisted all motions designed to specify what those "present and established standards" were.

Indeed, this ambiguity still persists. The doctrinal Rule has never been challenged, constitutionally, but this has not prevented Methodist theologians from continuing their theological developments in bewildering variety, with little or no regard to their official "Rule."

In 1968, when the Evangelical United Brethren brought their Confession of Faith into the United Methodist Church, it was declared "consonant with the Methodist Articles of Religion" by vote of the General Conference—and a second Restrictive Rule was added that the text of that Confession was unalterable. One might think that this would have made for a stable theological tradition (even a static one!). Everyone knows, of course, that the opposite has actually been the case. In 1972, the United Methodist General Conference approved Wesley's fourfold guidelines as authoritative; in 1984 the Conference mandated a "doctrinal commission" to produce "a new statement of United Methodist standards of doctrine."

One can, therefore, see in American Methodism a distinctive mingling of primitivism and churchliness. This has generated an ethos all its own: Methodism had been a sect that became a church without ceasing to be a sect, professing a biblical base. Throughout the nineteenth century, Methodists in general accepted Richard Watson's dictum that Holy Scripture is unique "in its power to communicate divine truths on all subjects connected with our moral state."[4] This impulse to improvisation supported the conviction dearest to Methodist hearts: the church defined as mission. Their enthusiasm and zeal for converts attracted enough adherents so that the Methodist growth rate outpaced the population curve for the first half century; thereafter it led the other Protestant denominations, until an unrecorded day in 1924 when the Baptists edged ahead and have continued on the rise ever since. Earlier on, Methodists took their cheerful statistics as proof of their recovery of the original power of apostolic Christianity. Since the reversal of our growth curves, we have had to seek other grounds for self-congratulations.

Given their Anglican origins, Methodists have been especially sensitive to the outright rejection of their ministerial orders by Protestant Episcopalians, their open scorn of the pretensions of a Methodist episcopate, and, therefore, the validity of their sacraments. This generated a large literature, best represented by Nathan Bangs in his major treatise, *An Original Church of Christ: Or, a Scriptural Vindication of the Orders & Powers of the Ministry of the Methodist Episcopal Church* (1837). It is chiefly an argument with the Episcopalians, but its triumphalism is generalized. Banks was a primitivist of sorts; his claim is that the Scriptures provide the church more with a charter than with a blueprint:

> In the course of this investigation, we hope to derive some assistance from the early history of the church,

reminding ourselves, in the meantime, of the fallibility of ecclesiastical writers . . . . When we take our leave of the inspired writers, we no longer have an infallible guide.[5]

He distinguishes between Scripture itself as revelation and "the primitive church as a privileged witness" as chief aid in the business of valid interpretation. Given this distinction he can stake out the Methodist claim to a biblical authority for their doctrine and polity:

> Without presuming to condemn others, we [Methodists] think that we have sufficient authority from the Scriptures as to the truth of our doctrine—and from the primitive church as to the efficacy of our polity—so as to do what we have done and as we will continue to do.[6]

What is unmistakably clear in the New Testament (to Bangs) is the gospel: the revelation of God's grace in Jesus Christ and of the church's mission to provide witnesses to that gospel in all places and times.

> To the Scriptures, therefore, we must make our ultimate appeal . . . . So far as they lend us their infallible light, and we suffer ourselves to be ordered by it, we shall not be led astray.[7]

But note the different nuance here from the similar sentiments of the Puritan Thomas Brooks (1608-1680): "Where the Scripture is silent, there I love to be silent and where the Scripture hath no tongue, there I have no ears."[8]

Bangs is, therefore, convinced that Asbury and Coke had been justified "in organizing a church according to the apostolic model." It was a church with a classic trinitarian theology, Christology, soteriology. Yet it was also a church in continuity with the church through the ages. It had itinerant ministers and local elders, and class meetings led by layfolk. Ministers served under annual appointment without appeal, and the bishops shared the same bursary with the other circuit riders. Bangs sees Methodism as a leaven among the denominations, "to review pure and primitive Christianity" (a favorite phrase).

Bangs takes pluralism and a sort or "spiritual ecumenism" for granted:

> It is possible to cleave to our own institutions and yet exercise a catholic spirit toward all who love our Lord Jesus Christ in sincerity. There are superficial differences between Christian communities, but these cannot be felt at the heights which are above the accidental forms which are created and destroyed, by time.[9]

A generation later, this same tradition is reformulated by a disciple of Bangs, Richard Abbey, in *An Inquiry into the Ecclesiastical Constitution, the Origin, and the Character of the Church of Christ and the Gospel Ministry* (1860):

> The Methodist church, for instance, is not apostolic because of her confederate character [nor, by implication, would she be if she were congregational in polity]. It is apostolic because, and only because, of her conformity, in faith and practice, to the religious doctrines which the Apostles held and taught. This is the test, and the only test, of a CHURCH OF CHRIST[10]
>
> . . . A church is a *society* of Christians, preaching the Gospel, administering the sacraments and otherwise following Christ[11]
>
> . . . We conclude, then, that the character of the primitive church is to be sought for in the principles of the true religion and not in the mode of ecclesiastical association [i.e., polity] into which Christians form themselves.[12]

Both the strengths and weaknesses of American Methodist theology in the nineteenth century may be measured in Richard Watson's *Theological Institutes*, for this single book taught more Methodists what little school theology they know than any other (including Wesley's *Sermons* and *Notes*). Its first edition stretched from 1823 to 1829; it then went through five revisions and thirty printings before the century was out.

Arminian in substance, Calvinist in form, Watson sought to provide the Methodists with what Wesley had chosen not to: a systematic theology. His ecclesiology was heavily influenced by William Cave, *Apostolici* (1677), one of Wesley's favorites. Watson's premise, that "the primitive Christians owed much to what they had learned in the Jewish synagogues," allowed him to argue that

> In all those particulars in which they were left free by the Scriptures, primitive Christians adopted those arrangements for the government which promised to render it most efficient in the maintenance of truth and piety.[13]

These samplings (since there were no influential "correctives") may be taken as representative of American Methodist ecclesiology down through the century until "the liberal transitions" toward its end. They reflect a special brand of primitivism that was neither magisterial nor restorationist in their typical forms. Its distinctive emphasis was on development: the adaptation of efficient means to serve the perennial end of the apostolic mission. It served the Methodists in justification of their ministerial orders (against the Episcopalians), of their connectional polity (against all congregationalists), of their gospel of universal redemption (against the Calvinists). Not at all incidentally, this sense of a biblical taprootage remained with the Methodists (sometimes in strangely altered forms) throughout the three transmutations that altered mainline Methodism in the twentieth century out of all comparison with its origins:

1. Its eager, if also belated, embrace of the Enlightenment and its theological spinoffs in liberal Protestantism.
2. Methodist enthusiasm for the Social Gospel; the *Social Creed of the Churches* (adopted by the new Federal Council of Churches in 1908) was a Methodist product.
3. The tragic immoderations of the late nineteenth-century controversies between the liberals and partisans of holiness.

There is a sad irony in the fact that all Methodists in their bitter differences (always to God's greater glory!) have appealed to the same biblical vision of a peaceable kingdom of God on earth for their authority and vindication, even as they have differed hopelessly in their appeals to the Bible for their rival programs.

After a brief interim of cooperation in the early stages of The Second Great Awakening, the Methodist primitivists and the Reformed restorationists (both well portrayed in Arthur Piepkorn's *Profiles in Belief*, Vol. II) tended to go their separate ways. Rice Haggard began as a comrade of James O'Kelly (the first American Methodist openly to rebel against Asbury's pious tyrannies) and ended up as loyal ally of Barton W. Stone. For all their differences, these two disparate traditions have shared the conviction that the essence of the true *koinonia tou Christou* is its visible manifestation of faith in Christ and its imperative to be witness to God's self-disclosure in him. This shared tradition is reflected in Thomas Campbell's *Declaration and Address* of 1809, which can have had no direct connection with Wesley's earlier definition of the church (see note 3). Here (as if it were not already more familiar to an audience like this than to me) is Campbell's definition:

> The Church of Christ upon earth is essentially, intentionally, and constitutionally one—consisting of all those in every place who profess their faith in Christ and offer their obedience to Him in all things, according to the Scriptures, and who manifest the same by their tempers and conduct . . .[14]

What is to be learned from all this, beyond commonplaces about the ironic discrepancies that have always existed between the professions and performances of religious movements? Is it instructive to recall that the restorationists began by eschewing denominationalism and then fell victim to its virus? What is the moral to the fact that mainline Methodism began by professing its distinctive aim the "spreading of scriptural holiness over these lands" and then fell into a preoccupation with organization that has put a premium upon maintenance and then confounded that with mission?

This much at least is clear from almost any reading of this

history: that both restoration and holiness are ideals so fructifying that even when tarnished by the kinds of entropy with which we are so familiar as church historians, they still retain their regenerative power as ideals so that, like the Holy Spirit who inspires them, they defy domestication and continue in their power to spark off new insights and new vitalities in later generations. For, always, there is a remnant who look beyond old formulae to their still-living powers of refreshment. It is this vision of apostolic Christianity recast in later ages (less by replication than reappropriation) that can always find new relevance in new times and circumstances. And if such an ideal of a vital community of "new creatures in Christ" still defines God's will for the unity of Christians in time and space, then it also continues as an urgent, however baffling, task for his obedient children in whatever history that may still unfold.

Introduction

Albert Outler preached this sermon to the Greater Dallas Community of Churches in November 1985. In it he wrapped his threefold life-long emphases—Ecumenism, the Rule of Grace, and John Wesley (by implication in the use of his prevenient grace)—by calling attention to Wesley's call to "catholic spirit." While acknowledging that divisions still exist, Outler went on to what ought to be and can be.

In this gathering were Methodists (United, Free, etc.) Baptists (of many varieties), Roman Catholics, Assemblies of God, Pentecostals, Nazarenes, Wesleyans, Presbyterians, Anglicans and even a few Church of Christ people. If the world could have witnessed the occasion, it would have said, "What is going on here? We have never seen Christians together before." The world has never seen the One True Church, Apostolic, and Universal. And Jesus Christ lived and died and lives again in his Holy Spirit that the church might be. These facts bothered Outler, and as long as he lived he kept on keeping on bothering the divisions about the problem—while offering a solution: God's Rule of Grace.

SERMON 13

The Ecumenical Experience

This is a great occasion and I feel greatly honored to be a part of it. Monsignor Rehkemper's introduction, for all its exaggerations, is more deeply appreciated than he or you can realize, for he has been one of the ecumenical stalwarts in this community for a quarter of a century, and his contributions have been quite literally extraordinary.

When I first agreed to this assignment for your Thirty-Fifth Assembly, I think I did not realize how aptly my title would fit the occasion or be exemplified by it. This is an ecumenical experience of the first order, a demonstration of it more impressive than anything I can think to say of it. What a splendid mosaic of festival and fun, of business and worship, of ho-hum and wow!—all the more significant because it is a facet of a wonderfully complicated network of caring and concern that animates this community of churches, year 'round and years long.

I take great pride and satisfaction that this sort of thing is happening in my home town, but it must be seen in the larger context of grass-roots ecumenism that is now where the cause of Christianity is finding its liveliest manifestations. For events like this are taking place all over—in Dallas and Des Moines; in

Chicago and Charleston; in Melbourne, Seoul, and Vancouver—all in different styles and format but all in the same spirit of Christian fellowship that has moved beyond our old separations and isolations. Here, in many ways, is the ecumenical experience in microcosm.

As your charter puts it, this community of churches exists "to express and celebrate the unity of the church" even before that unity is achieved. You exist "to respond to human need, suffering, and injustice" despite the fact that such needs and sufferings and injustice continue almost undiminished. You exist "to provide opportunities for understanding and cooperation between the diverse ethnic cultures and religious groups represented in our community," on the heroic assumption that Dallas (and Greater Dallas to boot) is "a community" or even liable to be.

What is more, such an event as this is happening as if it were right and fitting, a part of the ecumenical network, without much thought or wonderment about how strange and hopeful it is tonight, or how unthinkable it would have been four centuries ago, or even one. The church to which I belong had its first centennial in 1884, and one of the themes of that year was how God loved denominationalism (partly because he had encouraged so many different ones), but that he had a particular favorite (and it was evident which one that was). I recall a rousing sermon thirty years ago (by a then-leading Dallas minister) to the effect that denominationalism is to religion what free enterprise is to business: God's chosen way of weeding out the weak and keeping the others on their toes.

We ought not to forget that it used to be a bit more grim—and dangerous. In many years of wandering over Europe, I have yet to find a place where there are not reminders and memories of those horrid "wars of religion" that devastated the Continent and Britain and Ireland. But I also know many places where the ecumenical experience has wrought healing miracles—as at Dinkelsbuehl (near Ulm) where, on the anniversary of the end of one of the wars, the Protestant minority have an early service and then go to the larger Roman Catholic church to share their worship (and sing together *Ein Feste Burg Ist Unser Gott*). For there has been a slow and unsteady progress from bitter enmity to toleration, and from toleration to mutual recognition, and thence to events like this one tonight where the reality of Christians in community is palpable, even if Christians in full communion is not possible.

Back in 1772, however, the French *lumiere*, who wrote the article on Japan for the *Encyclopedie*, explained to an imaginary Japanese reader that Christianity had begun as "a benign, gentle, patient religion" but had since become "a sanguinary, murderous religion which had become hardened to the shedding of blood . . . ." The pity of this misleading characterization is that it was not altogether wrong—as our Jewish brothers and sisters know all too well, and as the multitude of religious martyrs make plain, Protestants and Catholics, depending on who had the upper hand, when, and where.

Even in America, where the new nation began with a resolve to separate church and state and not to prohibit the free exercise of religion, the spirit of contentions lived on. We progressed from violent deeds to violent words (and cartoons), in ways so ugly and unchristian that it ought still to be remembered to our shame. Nor are we free of religious prejudice and discrimination even yet.

This tragic history gave doctrine and theological debate a bad name, as if such things cannot be civil and open-minded. How often have you heard a portentous utterance prefaced by a disclaimer: "I am not a theologian, but . . ."? Allied with this was a feeling that, since our doctrinal and sacramental divisions are so touchy and intractable, it is better to ignore them. The motto of one of the ecumenical conferences in the 1920s was: "Doctrine divides; service unites. Let us, therefore concentrate on service and thus avoid unseemly disputes."

This is why my heart is gladdened by so obviously an inspirited event as this one. Here is a grass-roots ecumenical experience that goes far beyond the stage of toleration and presses toward effective cooperation in all sort of cooperative endeavors. Here are Christians hand in hand, heart with heart, in all sorts of God's good causes in the world, coming closer to the Christ-like spirit than ever we could if we were in jut-jawed dispute, even if also in what we thought was to God's greater glory! It means that we can both work and dialogue together, seeking both to find ways to proclaim "the faith once for all delivered to the saints" and join in all manner of good works. Who cares nowadays whether one's partners in the service of God's kingdom and his righteousness are Presbyterian, Lutheran, Episcopalian, Methodist, Baptist, or Catholic?

In the meantime, old-order ecumenism (from the top downward) has lost its momentum, partly because it has been outrun by the unexpected progress made by the theological pioneers toward a consensus in doctrine and ethical vision. The self-professed ecumenists in my generation supposed that it would take forever to get even close to doctrinal consensus and, therefore, they would not have to deal with the difficult problems of a radical shake-up of the denominational status quo, which would be threatening to their own accustomed loyalties and positions! But Faith and Order (the doctrinal arm of the ecumenical movement) has taken on new life and found new constituencies among Christians generally; this can be seen in the unprecedented response to its consensus pamphlet, *Baptism, Eucharist and Ministry*, where the enthusiasm among grass-roots Christians has been greater than among church officials! New-order ecumenism will have to depend more on the Christian community generally than on those who already feel more at home with the situation as it stands.

It is still possible to say the proper things about Christian unity in ideal terms while doing next to nothing to get past the scandals of denominationalism, or to conceive of Christian unity in organic terms, which is to say, consensus in biblical and apostolic doctrine, shared sacraments, and unity-in-diversity. They seem bound to some false vision of organic unity as a radical homogenization of all the different Christian traditions, an ecclesiastical multinational organization. And so they frighten Christian folk to death with images of a superchurch with a top-heavy bureaucracy and a lock-step conformity in the church at large. This is a perverse misunderstanding of true catholicity, historically and essentially, for even from the beginning, "catholicity" meant unity-in-diversity.

Moreover, denominationalism, as we have known it, is a scandal before God and in the world. It is what John Wesley called a hindrance to "catholic spirit," to the conversion of the unchurched; it is a denial of the *koinonia* of Christ. And on the other side,

Christian unity does not require homogenization nor rigid structures. What it does require is a broad and flexible consensus in the faith (not the systematic theology) once and for all delivered to the saints, mutually accepted baptisms in the name of the Triune God, holy Eucharists for spiritually hungry believers who may thereby be reconciled, again and again, to God in Christ and fed by God the Holy Spirit—where the priestly ministry of the church is truly representative of the church as a whole (which is the literal root meaning of the term "catholic"), from God's people for God's people by God's people. This may sound utopian and out of reach; I believe it is within reach of the first generation of Christians who can divest themselves of the tragic history of irreconcilable conflict and of the delusions of an ecclesiastical pecking order. Something like this is the essence of the ecumenical experience.

But even at the grass roots two new worrisome tendencies have appeared. The first is to rest content with overleaping denominational barriers in good causes without a comparable conscience about the barriers themselves. Christians of different races and ethnic diversifiers work together even as racism persists within the denominations and between them. And so on and on—discrimination, poverty, hunger, injustices of all sorts.

The other, an equal danger, is the all-too-easy willingness to turn the biblical doctrine of faith and good works on its head in favor of high-flown words about justice and peace and social change that all too often skirt the precipice of hypocrisy. For Christians to work at what is called Christian social action, without immense self-sacrifice on their part and without being able to share in the common sign of Christ's broken body and shed blood, is to corrupt in subtle but deep-reaching ways the essential meaning of the Cross of Christ and of cross-bearing. Which is to say, Christians bear witness to the means of grace by which the despoiled image of God may be restored in the lives of his human children so that they can be Christ's living witnesses in all the world and in all of God's good causes in the world.

Yet many Christians who have discovered how good it is for brothers and sisters to dwell together in unity are strangely apathetic toward their lack of consensus in doctrine and to their stubborn separations in baptism, Eucharist, and ministry. The old fear of Christian contentiousness still haunts our tribal memories. Don't rock the boat. Don't mess with the status quo. Stick to what we know best, viz., good works, or what we take to be good works, and leave the hard questions of shared communion till later. This is not the ecumenical experience or vision.

What this amounts to, though, is a strange reversal of the biblical doctrine of faith and good works. There faith in God comes first, and good works of whatever kind come out of grateful response to God's initiatives. Anything else (including good works and good intentions) is, as St. Paul says, doomed to futility in the long run. This is what his epistle to the Romans is all about. And whenever Christians have tried to put good works before faith (or instead of gospel faith), the paradox of good intentions turning into baffling frustrations shows up. Faith without works *is* dead, and good works *are* to be undertaken. But good works that spring from any other motive than faith in God's saving grace and God's gracious, sustaining Providence are misdirected. They lead us into high-minded efforts that fail to satisfy ourselves or the good causes to which we devote ourselves.

First, they mistake words for deeds and good intentions for finished accomplishments. Many Christians, and most humanitarians, have raised the art of the *rhetoric* of peace and justice to the fine art of illusion, of taking words and resolutions and symbolic gestures as real accomplishments that tend to satisfy our impulses to do good, short of real Christian martyrdom. We are great hands at trendy rhetoric, at bold resolutions, brave banners, noisy protests. Good cause follows upon good cause in our assemblies and debates. We are bemused by tokens. In my church, for example, one has to use inclusivist language, but both our ethnics (whatever that means, since we are all ethnics) and the women know that we are not inclusive in any complete sense. A third of our seminarians are women; we are not even remotely prepared for our representative churches to have women pastors in the foreseeable future. We speak, feelingly and smugly, about God's preferential option for the poor—and, therefore, his preferential option against the non-poor (namely, us). When was the last sermon you heard on the rich young ruler (the equivalent of our yuppies!) "going away sorrowful" because of Jesus' demands for divestment (not only in South Africa but also in North

Dallas)? We speak in pacifist terms and concepts without renouncing the rights of property and self-defense and without a clear distinction between the legitimate and illegitimate uses of force.

There is a radical spiritual priority in the Christian life. Seek *first* the kingdom of God and his righteousness (on this earth and in the service of his works of love and mercy) and let all else follow as consequences and implications. Ideals of national or denominational pride and triumphalism, motives of self-interest and free enterprise, fundamentalist notions of legislated morality enforced by governmental edicts—all these are masks for what are, at bottom, self-defeating strategies.

The early Christians did not even try to overthrow the most brutally efficient system of law and order that this world has ever known, the Roman Empire, but neither did they accept it on its own terms and go along with its inhumanities. They set out instead to reject idolatry, to worship God in Christ, to walk in the Spirit, in unity before the world, and to live by Christ's code of self-giving love. Their baptisms, their Eucharists, their holy festivals—these were their ways of resignifying their sense of being citizens, first and last, of a different kingdom or commonwealth than that of Caesar or Mammon, or any of the pagan gods and goddesses!

The kingdom of Christ, the domain of the Spirit, the fellowship of the redeemed: these do not sound like revolutionary slogans or a revolutionary outlook. But they enabled Christianity to survive persecution, fire, and sword—and to change the world. Mithraism tried to capture the switches of power in the Roman Empire, and then lost itself and the world to which it had wedded itself when the empire fell into anarchy.

The love of God and of neighbor out of gratitude to God for his love of us—this is the biblical order of faith and good works. Love of God and neighbor: this is the vital order of Christian social activism. This is the Christian safeguard against ideology and moralism, against politicization, against moral disillusionment, from crusades that promise a human panacea if only the right men and women with the right opinions are in power and if the right laws are enacted. Almost all ideologies profess love of neighbor and propose programs for neighborly help. Some few also profess faith in God or in transcendent values. The crucial difference is in their priorities: love of neighbor, with love of God as an option, is the ideological priority. Love of God above all and love of neighbor as of consequence is the Christian order. And one of the great discoveries of the ecumenical experience has been just this: God's kingdom and *his* righteousness—above and before all other considerations—transcends divisiveness and alters history.

The trouble here, of course, is the implied either/or, as if to love God more is to love the neighbor less, or vice versa. The biblical order is clear: Love of God *and* of neighbor—in that order and with one's motives for the love of neighbor springing from the fruits of the love of God. We love him, not from sentimentality, but from gratitude (we love him because he first loved *us*). He has loved us in our need—God was in Christ, reconciling the world. And so we love our neighbor in his or her need (and we must define "neighbor" in universal terms as any and all of God's children) out of our sense of being reconciled by God to God in Christ, without whose grace our lives are poor and pitiful.

On the other side, it is tragic that professed Christians should suppose that it is ever enough to love God and to worship him without self-giving. St. John is clear here: He who does not love and serve his brother and sister does not love God, for how can we love God whom we have not seen (save in the face of Jesus Christ) unless we love our brothers and sisters whose needs are visible before our eyes?

The cause of Christian unity is, therefore, a seamless robe and falters when its proper order of priorities and motivations is tampered with. Love of God that neglects love of neighbor is a debilitated love of God—and false worship. Love of neighbor not taprooted in love of God is altruism and finally self-defeating. Love of God and neighbor together—this is the Law and the Prophets and the gospel! And it is the substance and heart of every authentic ecumenical experience.

But together in yet another sense, also. The world may welcome the love of Christians but not be convinced of the love of God if Christian witness and service do not flow from Christian unity. And so the ecumenical imperative remains. Love one another as I have loved you (Jesus tells us) *in order that the world may believe*—so that the world , so loved by God that he gave his only Son to save it, may come not only to welcome our witness and service but be brought to faith by our unity.

The ecumenical experience at the local level and on the largest global scale is more than Christians being civil to each other and helpful to those in need. It is the outward sign of a divine command and promise: that Christians shall be one and united in their witness and service. A divided set of rival Christian denominations is as great a scandal before God and the world as a superchurch would be—and God forbid that we should settle for either! A community of Christians, taprooted in faith, united at their fonts and holy tables and in their pulpits, with a basic biblical consensus on essential truth, living in the Spirit, witnessing in life and death to Jesus Christ—this is the ecumenical ideal. And it is still a live option in our time if we, who have been rescued from our isolation from each other, are able to inspire (and pressure) our leaders and help them to see that what we have discovered in our own place and time can become their pattern for Christian community all over the country and world.

The ecumenical experience of unity with others who name the holy name of Christ must work up from below—and then go outward and upward and forward. For nothing less than the future of the church herself is at stake. And that future begins here and now with us, who ought not rest content until the scandal of disunity is transformed into that love and communion that attracts the whole human family to that peace of Christ that the world cannot give and cannot take away! God speed the day and bless us in the way!

PART 2

Special Occasions

Introduction

This speech ("sermon" in the sense that Albert Outler preached when he spoke), on the role that liberal education played in the lives of women in the setting of World War II was given at Sweet Briar, a women's college in Sweet Briar, Virginia. They were challenged to see education not as a luxury but as a necessity. "It is one of the treasures we are fighting for. To lose it would be an appalling defeat for all the moral issues at stake in this war. When you work at the job of authentic education, of mastering, exhibiting, and transmitting our cultural and spiritual heritage, you are serving your country just as surely as those gallant brothers and sweethearts of yours who fly the planes or man the guns."

Dr. Outler preached education with as much certainty as he preached grace. Indeed, it was grace that laid a liberal education out for them to "study, think, contemplate, analyze, weigh and balance, see and listen, synthesize and evaluate."

In many ways Outler was a man before his time. This sermon challenged that all-woman audience: "Open your books—keep them open—and what is more, use those books and the minds of your teachers and friends as portals to a larger and clearer view of life, a new and more creative personal distinction and freedom . . . ." No male chauvinism in this sermon. He preached then what women are experiencing now. One wonders who in the audience that day heard his challenge and began to move in the direction of the greater freedoms that women know today. Yes, he was a person before his time.

SERMON 14

Women, War, and Liberal Education

When a professor talks to students about the joy and value of the life of learning and of liberal education, the average student suspects him, and often quite rightly, of subtle self-glorification, of the vanity implicit in a pep talk. Even so, and in the face of rightful suspicion, I have come to talk to you about your main job in college, about the business of a liberal education and the crucial significance of this kind of education for these days in which we live and the years in which our lives are set.

The kind of speech I would like to make has already been made and far more effectively than I could ever do it. It was an address delivered by Wendell Willkie at Duke University on January 14 of this year [1943]. If you have not already done so, it would certainly be worth your while to look up the speech in the files of the *New York Times* or *Vital Speeches* and read it for yourself. For Mr. Willkie was concerned with what we, too, are concerned: the fate of liberal education in our time and the value of genuine intellectual life and work.

There can be no doubt that we stand on the threshold of far-reaching changes in the character of American education, not only for the duration of the war but also beyond. For the duration, it may be necessary to interrupt the education of the majority of young men and some women. But unless the continuity of education is carried on unbroken, unless the citadels of liberal education are preserved in their essential core, we shall come upon a great disaster, a new triumph of barbarism.

In any case, and in the meantime, the opportunities and obligations of women's colleges and young women themselves are clear: to maintain and improve the standard of intellectual, moral, and spiritual culture, which is the fruit of liberal education conceived in its best and most vital sense. Let me quote Mr. Willkie on this point:

> Now it is clear that we cannot solve our manpower problem without putting women to work. Yet the fact is that there are millions of women above college age, not needed in their homes or for the care of their children, who are still available. Until these older women are all employed there is no need whatever to drag young women out of the colleges and to deprive them of their one great opportunity for a liberal education. On the contrary, it is a very harmful thing to do. For just now millions of our young men are being deprived of this opportunity, and the per capita percentage of college attendance in the United States is going to fall to a record low for our time. At least, therefore, let us preserve, through the women of America, the continuity of the liberal arts.[1]

Now if all of this is so, it plainly means that we in the colleges must think again and think deeply about the meaning of liberal education. We must consider its object if we would see why its failure would be an irreparable calamity for us and our generation. The object of a liberal education is the acquiring or achieving of a way of life (a "philosophy of life," if you like), based on intelligence and character, a composite of sound learning, critical thinking, personal integrity, and good will. This way of living, the fruit of liberal education, is creative and adaptable—it is relevant and can be effectual even in an unexpectedly different or radically altered future. This is in contrast to the general result of vocational education, which tends to "date" or "type" a person with a few special skills that are then often outmoded by technological advances.

The word "liberal" in the phrase "liberal education" shows that it is concerned with the liberation of the human mind and spirit. A liberal education is a liberating education. What it seeks to do is to free the mind from contented ignorance, from naïve and unexamined prejudices (prejudgments) and illusions and their sinister cousin, superstition. The value of such an education is that it elevates the entire understanding, and guides from a broader perspective the hands and heart in the work and decisions of life. A truly educated person is one whose spirit has been freed from the stifling grip of race and class and national prejudices and antipathies, whose civic loyalties are above that narrow partisanship that exalts class and group and vested interest above the general good, and whose life is delivered from fanaticism of every kind.

The sort of education that will serve us in our uncertain and difficult future is one that has disciplined the intellect and the will, broadened our human sympathies, and that has made us citizens of the world and lovers of mankind. Some such vision as this and a faith that it is possible for you, even in these days, here at this college, must constitute your badge of intellectual and spiritual pilgrimage.

All of us are distraught and bemused by the tremendous events that are shaking our world and remolding the shape of things to come. A sensitive or curious person nowadays lives in a state of almost perpetual excitement or tension. It is difficult to study in such an atmosphere, to concentrate, to think objectively and clearly. And yet it must be done.

For the free mind and free spirit are always hard won; they come by study and thought, and they entail an awful lot of drudgery of uninspired and uninspiring spadework. There is absolutely no substitute for it. The reason for this is quite simple but compressive. First judgments, first impressions, intuitions, or what have you, are often accurate (i.e., as far as they go), but they are seldom adequate. What you see the first time may truly be there but it is unlikely that the first time you will see all that is there for you to see. A great painting seen once or twice, a great symphony heard for the first time, a profound philosophical idea or ethical ideal first presented—all of these yield meager harvests compared to what is really there for us.

To pass from these unripe fruits of snap judgment, of first impressions, of easy intuitions, to the mellower fruits of wisdom and maturity we simply must needs study, think, contemplate, analyze, weigh and balance, seek and listen, synthesize and evaluate. Study enlarges our span of comprehension. Wisdom is neither snatched nor bought; it comes and grows and we must accept its ways and seek it as it may be found. Despite all the distractions of our days, we must fight to find the time to work at this, our main job.

Education of the sort of which I have been speaking is not a luxury; it is a necessity. It is one of the treasures we are fighting for. To lose it would be an appalling defeat for all the moral issues at stake in this war. When you work at the job of authentic education, of mastering, exhibiting, and transmitting our cultural and spiritual heritage, you are serving your country just as surely as those gallant brothers and sweethearts of yours who fly the planes or man the guns.

This, then, is our present task and opportunity. "Burn your books," says Willkie, "—or, what amounts to the same thing, neglect your books—and you will lose freedom, as surely as if you were to invite Hitler and his henchmen to rule over you."[2]

Open your books—keep them open—and what is more, use those books and the minds of your teachers and friends as portals to a larger and clearer view of life, a new and more creative personal distinction and freedom, a new skill and wisdom in communal living. It is not given us to choose the days of our living; it is given us to determine, in part at least, the living of our days. For this we shall need trained minds, free spirits, intelligent good will, and the grace of God. Happily, all these resources are ours for the having; let us lay hold upon them; let us look well to their use.

Introduction

This sermon was preached on May 21, 1954, to the National Council of the YMCA at Pittsburgh, Pennsylvania. While this sermon would fit almost any worship occasion, it is made for Mother's Day. Mothers illustrate his thesis that "the . . . highest source of all for human courage is love. . . . In the good mother we see weakness made strong, responsibility without glamour, loyalty without rational reflections—a fearlessness that begets courage and security in others—and that is begotten of love."

Outler's mother was all that, and more, as she was a companion to her preacher-husband and mother to two daughters and three sons. Albert was the youngest child in the family. He knew the truth of the text: "There is no fear in love, for perfect love casts out fear." He experienced that truth through a mother who knew a courage that even his best words could not adequately express. From the comments he made about his mother,
viz, "feisty and had a sense of worth and dignity," there is validity in the following conclusion: If perfect love casts out fear, as Scripture indicates, she had plenty of love . . . because, without a doubt, she was fearless.

SERMON 15

The Source of Christian Courage

In this is love, not that we loved God but that he loved us and sent his Son to be the expiation for our sins. Beloved, if God so loved us, we also ought to love one another. . . . if we so love, then God abides in us and his love is perfected in us. . . . God is love, and he who abides in love abides in God, and God abides in him. In this is love perfected with us, that we may have confidence for the day of judgment, because as he is so are we in this world. There is no fear in love, for perfect love casts out fear. . . . By this we know that we abide in him and he in us, because he has given us of his own Spirit. And we have seen and testify that the Father has sent his Son as the Savior of the world. Whoever confesses that Jesus is the Son of God, God abides in him and he in God. So we know and believe the love God has for us (1 John 4:10-12, 16b-18a, 13-16a).

Courage is a fascinating human virtue. From the most ancient time it has been cherished and celebrated. The courage and fortitude of primitive man must have been extraordinary. Homer makes of it one of the most highly prized of all man's powers, as he projects what must have been not much more than a rustler's war into a great epic of human adventure and divine destiny. The heroic figure towers above the mob—as in the *Chanson de Rolande* and the saga *Beowulf*.

The heroic image is still with us in the celluloid courage of Gary Cooper or the heart-lifting, heartbreaking valor of General de Castries and Mademoiselle de Galard. We thrill to epic tales—and when we have no heroes, we invent them to serve an unquenched need. There is Superman and there was Oliver J. Warbuck (or maybe still is) and there is Terry Lee—just to sample a few of the purest types in our modern folk mythologies. There are also other types, somewhat more mixed, such as Fearless Fosdick and also certain fearless patriots who acknowledge no other patriotism than their own.

But our heroes stand a little apart from us. We ourselves are not heroes, except in some of our daydreams and fancies. That's why we laugh so wryly at the "secret life of Walter Mitty" and why some of us feel more at home in Pogofenokee or with Dennis the Menace, where both our friends and enemies are still a bit timorous inside when you come right down to it!

But we need courage; we yearn for it. We seek to bolster up what we have of it. And we are never proud of our lack of it. Essential cowardice is a mortal sin! It takes courage to stand up to the dangers of life, to the risks and threats and fears that disturb and frighten our pilgrim way. It takes courage to face the tragic certainties of transience and death, not to cringe and not to turn morbid or maudlin. It takes courage to be, as Paul Tillich has reminded us; and it take courage not to be, as Hamlet discovered. Incidentally, the bookstore at Union Theological Seminary, where Professor Tillich teaches, recently received an order phrased as follows: "Please send me *The Courage to Be Paul Tillich*—and charge to my account!" When Tillich heard of it, he is reported to have muttered: "Ach, that someone else should want it, too!"

Something deep inside calls us to stand up and stand steady (even at personal risk); something close to the heart deplores self-maintaining weakness. This is more than our deep unconscious memories of how the aggressive and fearless buck got the best women and knocked off the old man of the tribe. It is more than the excitement of hair-raising deeds of derring-do. Courage is a moral virtue. At bottom, it is an affirmation of life, a positive act on behalf of being. Cowardice is its opposite; it is the denial of the transcendent meaning of life. To be or not to be? That *is* the question. Courage is the will to be—the will that our existence be meaningful. Cowardice is the failure of that will. Courage says yes to life; faint heart says no or maybe.

Now, whence does our courage come, what we have of it? What are the different kinds of courage, and what difference does it make which kind we have or seek? Without any pretension at being exhaustive or pontifical, I would suggest that there are four main fonts of courage, each with its characteristic quality. They are:

1. Fury
2. Glory
3. Loyalty
4. Love

We have doubtless all seen men do incredibly brave deeds in fierce or cold rage. I have a friend with the Congressional Medal of Honor who modestly deprecates his courage. "I wasn't brave," he says (and I omit his adjectives!), "I was just so mad that I didn't quite know what I was doing." There is courage that rises in the fury of battle, in the wild excitement of combat and struggle. This is an authentic form of ecstacy—so frequently celebrated in the sagas and the epics. This sort of courage is regularly linked with comradeship-in-arms, and it leaves glistening memories for many a brave reunion. However, its phony imitations provide the program for such soggy affairs as American Legion conventions and the post-war absurdities of Colonel Blimp and his American opposite numbers.

Fury is a source of courage; but the courage born of fury, even when it is powerful and exalted, is still a barbarous and essentially an amoral expression of the will to be. The furious man, in the ecstasy of violence and exaltation, is not really superman after all, as the primitive myths would have it, but rather subman. He is man now back in the jungle and forest, where fang and claw and supercharged adrenals carry the premiums in the struggle for self-assertion and self-maintenance, where cunning is more effective than reflective intelligence. The furious hero has a sort of affirmative courage to be, all right, but not quite and not really the courage to be a man!

Most folk who come to a lovely church like this know this courage of fury only at a distance. We are mild-mannered members of the peaceable kingdom here. But a cynical psychiatrist might guess that in sweet-tempered and restrained civilized folk, there is a fearful lot of pent-up fury that gives us, not courage, but heart trouble! Medical men generally are puzzling about the correlations between unmanaged rage and hostility and degenerative disease in modern society. All too many modern heroes have the courage to beard lions and their fellow tycoons, but not the courage to live wisely and well.

There is a second source of courage—or courage on a slightly higher level—that has always been a powerful motive in pushing men out into the thick of things. This is the thirst for glory.

This has been quite a cult in Western society, as for example, in feudalism and the Renaissance. Or it can be a code, as it became in English society in the seventeenth and eighteenth centuries. Last summer I spent a whole day wandering around Blenheim Palace in Oxfordshire, wondering at the peerless courage of the first Duke of Marlborough and matching the monuments of his courage and his zeal for glory.

I've finished reading two very different stories of the same thirst for glory and the courage it inspires. One is Mrs. Cecil Woodham-Smith's *The Reason Why*, an incredible account of the splendid and silly courage of Lord Cardigan, Lord Lucan, and the Light Brigade. The other was Bruce Catton's *Stillness at Appomattox*, with its vivid vignettes of Sheridan and McClellan.

The courage that comes from the drive for glory and honor, pomp and circumstance is truly a form of the will to be, the will to be known, to be acknowledged, to be significant to others. It is a cut above fury, but it is still defective. For it is the will to be—superior! This is the courage of vanity and it is all too readily corrupted when the rewards and joys of glory have to be shared by an equal, or a successful rival!

A third and still higher source of courage is loyalty to an authentic cause. Actually, this is the classical concept of courage. In the *Laches* Socrates forces a bluff old soldier to recognize that courage requires wisdom, that courage is indeed a form of wisdom. Loyalty to truth, loyalty to a high and demanding cause, patriotism and religious loyalty—all of these inspire courage to risk one's private convenience or security for a collective good that draws our allegiance. Courage of this sort rises above animal passion and human vanity to a vision of the good, the good for which a devoted man will face danger and death itself. This is the courage of the valiant mind and spirit. It is a high and lofty temper of life.

It is, if anything, too lofty for us humans. This is why such courage has so often overreached itself and fallen into resignation and the fortitude of despair. Socrates drinking the hemlock, and Marcus Aurelius in his winter camp on the Danube, and many of the silent heroes in the current fight for freedom are always in danger of the retreat into privacy, of self-containment, self-sufficiency. Why does the word "stoic" mean something stolid and negative in common parlance, and why is it usually linked in the pat phrase "stoic endurance"? The philosophers of spiritual courage all too often abandon their assault on the world's wrongs and concentrate on self-maintenance. Spiritual courage is high; it is hard to attain unto. As fury drags man back toward the subhuman, the courage of the mind tempts him to the false endeavor to be superhuman.

The fourth and highest source of all for human courage is love. The readiest illustration that courage at its best is neither furious nor glory-struck nor even primarily rational wisdom is, of course, to be seen in the mothers of the world. In the good mother we see weakness made strong, responsibility without glamour, loyalty without rational reflections—a fearlessness that begets courage and security in others—and that is begotten of love. When we are acting with and for those we love, and who love us, we find a new kind of courage rising in our heart, a new power to cast out our fears and timidity, a new daring to risk and endure.

"Perfect love casts out fear." We know this, at least with the top of our heads, for both Holy Writ and our best psychological wisdom speak with the same voice here. The best courage comes from the best love. To those who love and know themselves loved, threats and dangers may excite and frighten, but they do not dismay. In their love they find the courage to be—and not to be; the bravery to acknowledge and affirm the good in existence over and beyond themselves—at the hands of God.

In the human life of our Lord, we see this sort of courage in its singular and pure form. Here is steadfast devotion to God; here is courage capable of anger but never degenerating into fury; courage that acknowledges the power of public favor and disfavor but that is never dependent on it; it is a courage deeply rooted in ancient loyalties to land and folk, and deeply versed in the wisdom of God's people. But much more than all of this, here is the courage that flows from Jesus' utter and authentic certainty of God's love and invincible grace in his life—and death. Here is love so utter and so deep, so reciprocal and absolute that Christian faith recognizes and confesses that here in this truly human life there is also something even more than human life. Here is love incarnate, Immanuel, God with us!

In his summary of the Hebraic teaching of God's claims on human life, Jesus enunciated the double imperative that we are to love God supremely and our neighbor as ourselves. This is the law and the prophets, this is the basic rule of faith and righteousness. This is also the pattern of Christian loyalty: God above all and neighbor as ourselves. The love of God empowers our love of neighbor, which, in this turn, gives a Christian the courage to stand up to the dangers that threaten his neighbor—as heartily as he himself stands up to life. This mutual love is the central spring of Christian social ethics; it is the motivation for the continuing Christian revolution, the ground for the typical Christian discontent with any human status quo. For Christians must be as concerned to make a good world for their neighbors as for themselves. This is why any authentic Christian experience involves the constant and radical criticism of all the conventional values in economics, politics, society, and in culture.

But the commands to love God and our neighbor do not supply their own motive power. You tell me I should love God and my neighbor and I agree. But does this mean that I do love God and my neighbor just because I know I ought to? Love, as we all know, cannot be commanded; it must be called out from the inner depths of our being, as a response to the loving and the lovable.

This is why Jesus gave us a *new* commandment, a really new one, and this new commandment, which is not a law at all, is the truly unique source of Christian courage. "A new commandment I give you—that you love one another as I have loved you" (John 13:34). To love our neighbor as ourselves makes a lot depend on how we love ourselves. To love each other as we have already been loved by Christ is the spontaneous expression of love as it has been awakened and purified by Christ's love, which has been freely given for us all.

And how has Christ loved us? With a love that did not calculate our worth or merit but that went out in unmeasured concern for the concrete human beings before him. Thus we are to love each other with a careful calculation of his prospective worth to us. It was a costing love that did not seek suffering and death, but that accepted them as the price of love. Thus we are to love each other with a willingness to suffer, if need be, to make good our loving concern. It was an utterly confident love that left to God the issues of destiny and contented itself with the tasks and the gifts of love here and now.

> O dearly, dearly has he loved,
> And we must love him, too. . . .

So runs one of the simplest and loveliest of the passion hymns, "There is a Green Hill Far Away."

> And trust in his redeeming blood,
> And try his works to do.

To know ourselves loved by a love that does not and will not let our lives fall into blank unmeaning, but that never ratifies our selfish and unfaithful living to stand as God's meaning for our lives—this is the source of Christian courage and cheerfulness, and confidence. Such a love casts out our deepest and direct fears—of meaninglessness, of transience, of death. And such love stirs up in us the courage to love our fellowmen as Christ has loved us.

The roster of the heroes is long and never more luminous than in these very days of ours. Men who knew themselves beloved of Christ in unmerited, costing, confident love have kept their sanity in concentration camps, have fought against tyranny and for justice, have made the witness and triumph in martyrdom. In the ordeal of our times, when men wilt under the tremendous and unrelenting pressure of the vast and confusing conflicts into which we are flung, we need more than ever the kind of courage that comes from Christian fearlessness in a fear-filled world so that we may use and risk our best gifts and powers to serve mankind and God's kingdom!

> What then shall we say to this? If God is for us, who is against us? He who did not spare his own Son but gave him up for us all, will he not also give us all things with him? Who shall bring any charge against God's elect? It is God who justifies. Who is to condemn? It is Christ Jesus who died, yes, who was raised from the dead, who is at the right hand of God, who indeed intercedes for us. Who shall separate us from the love of Christ? Shall tribulation or distress, or persecution, or famine, or nakedness, or peril, or sword? . . . No, in all these things we are more than conquerors through him who loved us. For I am sure that neither death, nor life, nor angels, nor principalities, nor things present, nor things to come, nor powers, nor height, nor depth, nor anything else in all creation, will be able to separate us from the love of God in Christ Jesus our Lord (Romans 8:31-35, 37-39).

Let us pray:

O God of grace and glory, thou hast set us to our callings in a fateful hour of tremendous responsibility and magnificent opportunity. We thank thee for the invigorating sense that all things are being made new, and that it is given to us to share in the titanic events passing over the world. Grant us, O Lord, so to live in these fear-filled times that we may be cleansed from vainglory and self-seeking; that we may be endued with the gallant and undaunted courage of our Master and, in his love, love each other without fear and greed.

Thus may we seek first thy kingdom and share richly in thy grace—through the spirit and love of Jesus Christ our Lord. Amen.

Introduction

Albert Outler told the Methodists at the Aldersgate Festival at the University of Chicago (May 18, 1958) that "it is meet, right and our bounden duty that we should celebrate Aldersgate," but that "Aldersgate cannot be organized. If Wesley couldn't, nobody can." But we can learn from his experience. We learn from Wesley's Aldersgate experience that the pole of "faith is primitive and that (the pole of) works are derivative." Outler further said, "Once we understand—really understand—this dynamic synthesis between faith and work, we have a key to the interpretation of those conjoined motifs that are so distinctive of Wesley's whole enterprise—justification and sanctification, personal and social religion, grace and growth, gospel and law, faith and nurture, revelation and reason."

With this dialectic in mind Outler set out to show that once the mysteries of incarnation and creation are accepted by faith, "the Christian mind is both free and enabled in its search for an intelligible account of existence in the world. . . . You cannot begin with creation and pass directly to incarnation, as a logical implication or a straight-line development in religious ideology. It is only in the light of the Incarnation that creation is really and fully and finally credible—rather than the other way around." Outler concluded his address with this challenge: "We will not have had our Aldersgate until we can, on the one hand, confess with incredible joy that Christ has taken away our sins, and then, on the other hand, plunge into the work of his kingdom (which includes the imperative to inquiry) with all our might. Then we shall know our hearts strangely warmed, our minds strangely invigorated."

In this sermon Outler did more than preach. He had an experience—an Aldersgate experience. And was passing it on.

SERMON 16

"Unite the Pair So Long Disjoined"

O Lord, how manifold are Thy works!
In wisdom Thou hast made them all;
The earth is full of Thy creatures.
I will sing to the Lord as long as I live;
I will sing praise to my God while I have being.
May my "thoughts" be pleasing to him,
for I rejoice in the Lord (Psalm 104:24, 33-34).

This idea of an Aldersgate Festival is an inspired one, I think. Here we are, most of us Methodists, assembled in the great chapel of a great university, recalling a decisive spiritual event in the life of our founder and asking ourselves how this memory should illuminate and empower our living in the present moment.

Still and all, when Methodists get together to celebrate John Wesley's Aldersgate experience, a job of demythologizing is in order. We need to remind ourselves that Aldersgate was not the time when John Wesley became a "real Christian." Nor was it the event that made him a Methodist. He was a Christian long before Aldersgate; and he had, in a certain sense, been a Methodist since childhood—that is, if by "Methodist" you take it in its eighteenth-century meaning (i.e., an obsessional-compulsive psychological character). The strangest thing about the Aldersgate experience is that it was unorganized, a most untypical thing for John Wesley up to that moment, and not the standard pattern for his performance in the decades that followed. He is careful to point out, in the Journal account, how self-conscious and self-managing he had been in his efforts to reproduce in himself the Moravian model of self-conscious faith. But he also makes it plain that in the actual moment of fulfillment, he went unwillingly, he heard perfunctorily, and his heart was warmed spontaneously! That's what made it so strange.

This would seem to suggest a generality: Aldersgate cannot be organized. If Wesley couldn't, nobody can. It is meet, right, and our bounden duty that we should celebrate Aldersgate. We do well to cherish it as a vivid symbol of the crucial moment when striving faith is turned into trusting faith, but we must be very clear that we cannot and are not even intending to put Aldersgate on the production line.

The most important thing for us to see is that at Aldersgate Wesley's deep-seated tensions—between faith and works, between God's gift and man's response, between God's part and man's part—were finally and fruitfully resolved. He had been an earnest, faithful, practicing Christian since 1725 and had been trying with grim and desperate conscientiousness to do his part in the business of salvation, hoping (sometimes rather against hope) that God was doing or would do his share in return. Then came his contacts with the Moravians, and from them a new anxiety that he was following a wrong-headed order. The initial primitive action in salvation, they taught him, is faith; and faith means the abandoning of man's initiative, the willingness merely to receive, to respond. Only as a second, consequent action may the man of faith "seek the constant use of all the means of grace." The means of grace must always be subordinated to its course and to its end. Aldersgate was the time when the vital truth of this dialectic struck home to Wesley's heart. It turned a grim neurotic into an effective evangelist.

Wesley takes pains to locate the two poles within the dialectic of faith and works. The pole of faith is indicated in the words that every devout Methodist knows by heart: "In the evening I went very unwillingly . . . about a quarter before nine [notice this clinical touch!] . . . I felt my heart strangely warmed. I felt I did trust in Christ, Christ alone for salvation; and an assurance was given me that he had taken away *my* sins, even *mine*, and had saved *me* from the law of sin and death."[1]

Thus far, this could be *any* pietist. This is where the pietist's climax usually falls and where his testimony usually closes. But Wesley goes straight on to the other pole of the dialectic: "I began to pray with all my might."[2] He realized that he was still striving under grace ("yea, fighting with all my might"—notice the same phrase twice in successive paragraphs), just as he had been doing before the heartwarming, but now he was conscious of victory.

Both before and after Aldersgate, Wesley was a strenuous Christian. But after Aldersgate he never quite forgot that faith is primitive and that works are derivative. This became, I think, the most distinctive thing in the Wesleyan pattern: radical faith that prompts the believer to earnest, strenuous endeavor. This endeavor takes the form of witnessing to the faith. Wesley closes his account of the Aldersgate experience with the record: "I then testified openly to all."[3]

Once we understand—really understand—this dynamic synthesis between faith and work, we have a key to the interpretation of those conjoined motifs that are so distinctive of Wesley's whole enterprise—justification and sanctification, personal and social religion, grace and growth, gospel and law, faith and nurture, revelation and reason. The Christian life is always both a gift and a task. Grace is its ground; upwelling gratitude is its energy. By "nature," Wesley actually linked sharp distinctions and tended to press them as far as possible. But Aldersgate made of him what we might call a conjunctive theologian, this despite his "double-or-nothing" temperament.

In a place like this and on an occasion like this, it is especially fitting that we take notice of that one Wesleyan conjunction that bears most directly on the vocation and the motives of a Christian scholar: faith and reason, piety and learning, the surrendered heart and the enfranchised intelligence. Wesley was a scholar, a rather good one for his own day. He never forgot and never lost his pride in having been a Fellow of Lincoln. He aspired to a scholarly conception of the ministry, and his formula for the proper academic qualifications of a well-furnished minister, if seriously applied, would evacuate our Conferences forthwith. But if the Methodist movement began at Oxford, it was soon in the fields, and it has never really returned to the university, except to bear witness—and this more often to the conflict between piety and envious curiosity than to the conjunction of faith and inquiry.

Many Methodists are both learned and wise. Some are more learned than wise; many more are more wise than learned. But let's face it. We simply have not supplied our quota of Christian scholars to the Christian family in the past two centuries, if by scholarship we mean the highest level of disciplined curiosity and critical inquiry. It is often said with pride among us, "I'd rather have a warm heart than an over-stuffed head!" Even those who are not actually threatened by either one still know where their choice between them should fall. We could amply endow a great university if we had a dollar for every Methodist boast of indifference toward rigorous scholarship and abstract theory. Recently I heard a Methodist university president eulogized by a Methodist bishop. The high point of the episcopal encomium was the assertion that although the educator was an egghead, he had learned to wear a wool hat over his egg head so successfully that he had thus avoided giving any offense to the anti-egghead.

This anti-intellectualism, which we know so well amongst us, is an inheritance of a long tradition—from Tertullian to à Kempis to the radical Protestants to the pietists. Wesley was aware of it as a threat from the very beginning. It was to him an antinomianism of the mind, and Wesley was against antinomianism of every sort.

The revival had hardly begun before both John and Charles were aware of the threat of complacent ignorance amongst the Methodist people. Without shifting the center of their concern from the faith that prompted men and women "to flee from the wrath to come and to be saved from their sins," they were also concerned that the Methodists should be able really to read their Bibles and honestly to understand their religion. So the Wesleys began with a school at Kingswood, and then went on to many different sorts of projects in adult education. For the dedication service at Kingswood Charles wrote a hymn, which, although not one of his better poems, is a typical expression of the basic Wesleyan concept of faith *and* learning and therefore of the Christian scholar:

> Come, Father, Son, and Holy Ghost,
> To whom we for our children cry;
> The good desired and wanted most
> Out of Thy richest grace supply;
> The sacred discipline be given
> To train and bring them up for heaven.
> . . . .
> Error and ignorance remove,
> Their blindness both of heart and mind;
> Give them the wisdom from above,
> Spotless, and peaceable, and kind;
> In knowledge pure their mind renew,
> And store with thoughts divinely true.
> . . . .
> Unite the pair so long disjoined
> Knowledge and vital piety:
> Learning and holiness combined,
> And truth and love, let all men see
> In these, whom up to thee we give,
> Thine, wholly Thine, to die and live.[4]

Notice this trio of linked phrases: Knowledge and vital piety, learning and holiness, truth and love. They bespeak a synthesis of head and heart that is profoundly biblical. They acknowledge the gospel's primacy, but they welcome the heritage of culture. They denote a distinction between God's revelation of himself to the eyes of faith (forgiveness of sin through his justifying grace) and God's revelation of his creation to the eye of the mind (via scientific discoveries). They enforce the distinction between the domain of faith and of inquiry, but point beyond this distinction toward the higher unity between the two domains. Indirectly, they remind us that if such a distinction is ignored or misconceived, then faith and inquiry fall into deadly conflict with each other.

In holding together "knowledge and vital piety," the Wesleys were intent on keeping faith at the center without driving reason outside the circumference. As men who supposed that biblical faith and classical culture had been synthesized already in patristic Christianity, they could distinguish between what is given in revelation as the sum of all revelation and what is given in revelation as the domain of inquiry and discovery. Thus, they point to the revelation of God in Christ as the domain of faith and the revelation of God in creation as the domain of inquiry. It should go without saying that the aim of such distinctions is a fuller, richer knowledge of God that issues in a life in which learning and holiness are combined.

This is the point at which the Christian faith differs sharply and unavoidably with Hellenism or with any other world view that does not root its primary assumptions in the mysteries of incarnation and creation. The intellectual perspectives of the classical world, or of the modern world, for that matter, have no natural place in them for the doctrine of an unhistorical revelation of redemption and no place for a doctrine of *creatio de nihilo*. And yet everything in the Christian faith begins with these two mysteries. Given these, the Christian mind is both free and enabled in its search for an intelligible account of existence in the world. This is the real meaning behind the familiar theological mottoes: *nisi crederitis, no intelligetis; credo ut intelligam; fides quaerens intellectum*. For in each what is to be believed is not anything and everything, whether in Scripture or in tradition, but is the two essential and ultimate mysteries: incarnation and creation. Faith in these mysteries supplies the primitive outlook for all rational inquiry within the Christian perspective. Given these primordial *articuli credendi*, the Christian intellectual can investigate any and all questions; he can appropriate all the treasures of human wisdom with real appreciation and discrimination. Samples of how this has been done in the history of Christian thought may be seen in Augustine's conversion of Platonism and in Aquinas' subtle but radical transformation of Aristotle.

Now, in Christian theology, you cannot begin with creation and pass directly to incarnation, as a logical implication or a straight-line development in religious ideology. It is only in the light of the Incarnation that creation is really and fully and finally credible—rather than the other way around. It is only in Christ that creation ceases to be a cosmological riddle and becomes the doctrine of God's sovereign grace and goodness in the world and in human existence. Only in Christ is our faith in the goodness of the created world secured. Only in Christ is our faith (that nothing in all creation can separate us from the love of God) turned into a triumphant conviction; only in this conviction can inquiry proceed without agonizing and crippling doubt.

But once we have faith in Christ, we can then look at God's creation with a curious eye and an eager question, as an intelligent child in his father's household feels the impulse and the permission to investigate. This is my Father's world—a home to live in and enjoy so long as I do not absolutize it. Creation is a laboratory, a clinic, a museum, a vast, exciting theater of discovery so long as I do not try to infinitize the discoverer, the discovery, or the process of discovering. Faith comes first but learning follows after faith. And the kind of faith that narrows its concern to the question of salvation and neglects the tasks of inquiry and judgment is a faith that stultifies the mind and finally impoverishes faith itself.

Saving faith, in its specific and proper sense, rests on the revelation of God in Christ. But by the same taken, Christian learning, or the task of Christian inquiry, rests in its most basic sense on the revelation of the world as God's creation. The response of faith to the revelation of God in Christ makes a man a Christian; the call to explore and understand God's creation makes him a Christian scholar. And the more surely a man believes the tragedy of existence is finally overcome by God's redemptive power, the more confidently and rigorously can he thereupon pursue any "intelligible field" of learning he may elect.

The Christian scholar must begin with faith—and not just faith in any and every bold assertion, but faith in the validity and finality of God's redemptive action in Jesus Christ and in his sovereign grace in and for his world. But with his faithful response to God as the ground and end of existence, the Christian scholar then proceeds by the method of critical inquiry to try to understand nature and history and human experience. This task of critical understanding becomes his special and principal occupation. It is the scholar's unique way of exercising his Christian vocation.

Rightly understood, then, the act of faith prompts the thrust of the mind toward inquiry. From God's self-disclosure we pass to his creation and to his purpose which is our intelligent participation. This involvement with God provides both the motives and the methods of Christian inquiry in any field or discipline. The mystery of creation gives us our valid motive for inquiry: wonder, love and praise—"to glorify God in all his works" and to enjoy him in and through them. This is the chief end of the academic man! And his methods must be appropriate to his goals. Meaning must be read off the data and not imposed on it. But this is impossible unless there is meaning in the data, and this requires an assumption of faith.

Behind the Christian *credo ut intelligam* there are two hidden, and sometimes forgotten, presuppositions: (1) God's creation is intelligible and (2) we discover its meaning rather than create it. This being so, the Christian scholar is then free to find and choose his field of intelligible inquiry, to dig into it with what may seem irreverent curiosity (but which is nevertheless a higher seriousness), to follow the evidence where it leads, and to proclaim his findings without the faintest fear that real truth will ever destroy real faith or that real faith will stultify this sensitivity and obedience to truth.

The Christian community, with its zeal for faith and its fear that learning corrupts intellectual curiosity into intellectual pride, has not encouraged this kind of scholarship so much as it might have and should. We have been generally too content with the knowledge of salvation and not enough drawn into the sustained probings, into the rational mysteries of this created world in which the drama of redemption is being wrought out. We have tended to suppose that there was a Christian predetermination of empirical inquiry or rational analysis: a Christian biology, a Christian historiography, or a Christian psychiatry, a Christian logic, a Christian economic. Sometimes, and this is equally bad, Christians have supposed that faith and learning must be kept in separate compartments for separate contexts, days and occasions. Most of us profess a belief in academic freedom; most of us profess our support of the mission of the university. But as a Methodist people, we have yet to match our faith with appropriate works.

In this time of crisis, both in culture and in education, the Christian scholar and the Christian community face a most unprecedented challenge and opportunity. It is, in sum, to call and train and cherish the intellectuals in our midst, and to engage the intellectual strangers within our gates in fruitful dialogue and inquiry. We must, if we are to be adequate to our age, persuade thoughtful men that the proper study of mankind is not man and his existential context but man as God's creature and the child of God's redemptive grace. We can do this only if we really understand the biblical distinction between God's responsibility for our creation and salvation and our responsibility (under God) for our history, our culture, our technology, our answer to God's call and claim upon our lives. When men believe that they are responsible for their creation and salvation, they become titans and fools! When they believe that God is in direct and unmediated control of their history and technology, they become superstitious and irrational. It is the business of the Christian scholar to show men what God can do with those who love him with their entire powers, thought, and understanding and whose joy is to praise him in the work of his hands.

The Methodist Church is currently engaged in a quadrennial emphasis upon higher education, which is in effect an effort to respond to the challenge of the Kingswood hymn: to unite the pair so long disjoined, knowledge and vital piety. But in this concern for higher education, the most important thing is our own share in it. More important than our promotional campaigns, than our increased support of higher education and the campus ministry (which is still so slight as to be scandalous) is the recovery of the Wesleyan synthesis in faith and worship. We greatly need a revival and reshaping of Christian curiosity, of Christian delight in discovery, of Christian joy in sharing the truth and the means of coming to the truth. We will not really come into our own or into our share in the Christian community until we come truly to hold our faith and works together.

We will not have had *our* Aldersgate until we can, on the one hand, confess with incredible joy that Christ has taken away our sins, and then, on the other hand, plunge into the work of his kingdom (which includes the imperative to inquiry) with all our might. Then we shall know our hearts strangely warmed, our minds strangely invigorated. Then, we can pray and work with all our might, faithing and thinking and openly testifying to all.

Introduction

On March 17, 1961, Albert Outler spoke to the American Institute of Decorators. While he divorced himself from any notion that he was an interior designer, he challenged the designers to recognize that their role, like his, was life-giving and God-given. He said, "Any learned person can ask of any other learned person this question: What does your learning contribute to the sum of human wisdom, human joy, human happiness, dignity, fulfillment—personal and social? Any professional person has to answer this question—he does answer it, one way or another (thoughtfully or carelessly)." He was talking about himself when he said, "In a university, this is the most relevant and universal question that should be asked or kept in the background of an egghead's working consciousness. Without it . . . he tends to compensate for his lack of a whole purpose, an integral vocation, a humane and humanizing concern."

Following the address Taylor Robinson wrote Dr. Outler, "I'm afraid I have an impossible talk . . . that of making you even remotely aware of the commotion you occasioned by your address. The response was so overwhelming, so genuine, I can only say you made a far deeper impression on this audience than even they thought possible. They were obviously hungry for this kind of inspiration and stimulation. So much so that there was a unanimous request that I get from you a printed copy of your précis to be distributed to the members."

They never heard his disclaimer. One address on their subject and he became in their minds an authority on decorating. Strange how that happened to other audiences on other subjects. Why this reaction? Part of the answer would be: he presented the case so well for the Authority of all vocations!

SERMON 17

Designing Life

If any of you think it strange for a professor of theology to be speaking to a group of decorators and designers, let me assure you of a similar feeling. Yet it may be that we do have a common concern, a common cause, and that some of my comments may be pertinent and relevant to your interest—above all, to your sense of vocation and purpose in life.

I know, of course, that interior design is a business, a big business in contemporary America. I know, also, that for a business to succeed it must render a needed service in ways acceptable to those able to pay for it. This means solvency for the businessman and satisfaction for the customer. At this basic level of your work, I am the merest amateur and have nothing to say that would justify my appearance here on this occasion.

But interior design is, or ought to be, a profession—in the older sense of a vocation dedicated to the enhancement and enrichment of human life enlisted in the never-ending struggle between barbarism and civilization, grossness and culture, caprice and order, the private good and the general good. This is the notion of a profession as it came to be applied to the ministry, the law, medicine, and teaching. The work of the true professional is not his special competence or technical skill, but his interest in the quality of life of those with whom he deals—and the contribution that his "know-how" can make to the common good. The real pro in any field is one whose professional dignity and discipline help the profit motive in second or third place. A minister whose chief interest is in his salary is an unworthy minister; so for a doctor or a lawyer. A teacher who is in his profession chiefly for the money is actually disqualified for the joy (insofar as stupidity is a disqualification in my profession).

Now, as I see it, the interior designer is a missionary for culture, a tastebringer to the philistines, an *arbiter elegantarium*. You are men and women with a superior sense of civilized taste, style, and manners as this applies to the environment and atmosphere in which people live and work. You know that the style and atmosphere of a room affects what goes into that room, affects the people in that room and the web and network of relationships into which it fits (or fails to fit).

An ugly room, a bleak room, a garish room, a clamant room, a cluttered room—be it a living room (aren't all rooms living rooms?) or office—stultify at least some of the possibilities of living in that room. The relation of different rooms makes a difference, too. For when we pass from one atmosphere into another (from Victorian to Cecil Beaton, from gingerbread to Swedish modern), there is a clash that can be reconciled only by an interior standard of taste and quality and human values.

The point is that what you are doing deeply affects the quality of human life, the standards and value scales of young people, the images and symbols by which people identify themselves, understand themselves, and form priority judgments about values, about life, even about death and destiny. You have more to do with the texture and taste of our culture than you know, and your responsibility is fully as great as your influence. An America engrossed in materialism, dedicated first of all to a pampered, sybaritic, epicurean existence—thing-minded, gadget-minded, enervated and soft—cannot survive the stern realities of a world at war; and, far worse, does not deserve to survive (will be no more lamented or recalled then the glory that was Greece and the grandeur that was Rome). The challenge before us all is that challenge of building, supporting, and defending a civilization that is in fact, civilized, humane, authentic. The Greeks conquered their Roman conquerors by the sheer power of their superior taste and culture. The Romans gave the world its first great vision of society based on law. The Judeo-Christian tradition brought into such a world the dimension of faith and righteousness, based on God's sovereignty in the world.

The barbarians overran the Greco-Roman world, and naturally tried to take over the material values of civilization: palaces, beds, water supply. But they had no technical know-how (and couldn't repair the water system), and not much taste (and so ruined the palaces they had confiscated). We are seeing this today in Cuba and the Congo. But it is nearer home than that. It takes two or three generations from barbarism to breed a civilized man; it takes only one generation to slip back from civilization to barbarism (i.e., to the state of preferring tribal or racial peer-group values to rational or universal norms of beauty, truth, and goodness).

Every profession stands in the breach against the pounding seas of barbarism: the doctor against quackery, the lawyer against anarchy or tyranny, the minister against idolatry, the teacher against willful ignorance, the artist against tastelessness. The first premise of taste, therefore, is that it goes far deeper than what people like and will pay for (or won't), what's fashionable (or isn't); it is rooted in the cause of civilization itself and has to do with what people ought to like, with the common and constant themes that persist in the wild vicissitudes of fashion.

In this respect, you and I are custodians, trustees, guardians of the best in the legacy of the past, and pioneers and prophets of what may yet be brought for the enhancement of blessing of human life and society.

It is true, of course, that your taste, your prestige as a civilized person, your technical competence may simply be hired—*quid pro quo* (bookshelves with uniform bindings, etc.), or you may design living and working interiors for people you'll never meet and some of whose characteristic functions you do not understand (e.g., the interior design of academic buildings, etc.). This happens, too often, to all professional people: doctors hired for pills or surgery, lawyers to win a case, ministers to pray or "officiate," teachers to pass out information, etc. But this is obviously and perilously close to prostituting one's vocation, to forfeiting one's ordination to enhance and bless human life with one's contribution to the improvement of the wisdom of men and women. Our job is never done until we have engaged people in their part of self-improvement. You may design a tasteful, efficient interior (and this will upgrade the taste and culture of the people who live and work in it). The Duke University chapel is an example. But you have to establish your right to resist or overcome bad taste, the various forms of crudity, ostentation, and the myriad cuds that human vanity feeds upon. The second premise of taste, then, is that it must be acquired; it cannot just be hired.

There is an interesting distinction in the New Testament that goes back to classical Greek itself and that is difficult to bring into English—a distinction between *bios* = life and *zoē* = life. *Bios* means the wherewithal of life; *zoē* means life itself at its best, life lived at its highest level. We have our own ways of pointing to something like this. We say this man is making a good living; that man is living a good life. See the difference. We speak of "living it up" and of "living up to one's ideals."

This distinction is of especial importance to people in your profession, for you inevitably straddle both sides of it. All of us realize that *zoē* depends on *bios*; that there has to be adequate wherewithal to support the aesthetic, moral, or spiritual dimensions or levels of human existence. But the problem is one of primacy and dominance . . . where the stuff of life is confused with life itself, where status symbols are mistaken for status-reality, where comfort is prized above creativity. Those who have to do with the material means to aesthetic ends must work harder than ever to escape the blandishments and tyranny of things or the delusion that the abundant life consists in the abundance of the things that we possess. This third premise of taste is that it is dominated by a passion for quality above stuff and façade. That his environment exists for man and not man for his environment!

There are other premises of taste that have to do with defining what it is. What is beautiful and why? What is restful or efficient or impressive (or whatever) and why? What makes this room elegant and that room overdone? Why does this setting really suit these people but that one seems faintly absurd (a mink coat with beatnik leotards, an Alfa-Romeo driven by a priest)? These questions push us back into the basic philosophical issues of human existence. Whenever you begin to consider the problem of taste and culture seriously, it always confronts you with an unavoidable (and maybe insoluble) query about the nature of man and the meaning of the human condition. What is life about and what gives it meaning, dignity, joy?

But this is the basic problem of what, in our civilization, has been traditionally called "the humanities" as contrasted with the so-called physical or natural sciences. Every profession has its proper technical area of theoretical know-how—inquiry, experimentation, disciplined imagination, research, and new frontiers of learning. Without such learning, one cannot really judge the standards and practices of a specialist but must rely on his authority in his field (as judged by his peers). But any learned person can ask of any other learned person this question: What does your learning contribute to the sum of human wisdom, human joy, human happiness, dignity, fulfillment—personal and social? Any professional person has to answer this question—he does answer it, one way or another (thoughtfully or carelessly).

In a university, this is the most relevant and universal question that should be asked or kept in the background of an egghead's working consciousness. Without it he tends to lapse into specialism, commercialism, or some other mode of half-life that tends to compensate for his lack of a whole purpose, an integral vocation, a humane and humanizing concern.

At Southern Methodist University, we are in the early and groping stages of an experiment in getting this question posed in a more dramatic or visible form than it is in the normal round of our commonplace activities. It is called the Graduate Council of the Humanities. It promotes such programs as The Festival of Learning and Wisdom, public programs of various sorts, and events that emphasize the cultural revolution in America and your part in it. The crux of the present moment and the future is whether the basic motivation of the revolution is truly human, humane, and humanizing. The tremendous imbalance between the two cultures in our society and the dreadful struggle between free men and totalitarians confronts us with the challenge of man's capacity to lift his life to the level of meaning. One of these capacities is the power to elevate the quality of life by conscious endeavor. What you and I can do to serve and support these endeavors may be more important than anything else we can do to serve the present age, our callings to fulfill; may it all our powers engage to do our Master's will.

Introduction

This sermon for the World Fellowship Service of the YWCA was preached on Sunday, November 13, 1966, in the National Cathedral at Washington, D.C. Albert Outler said, "Peace is made, if at all, by persuasion and service, by holding to the frail reeds of reason and dialogue, by deeds of compassion and self-sacrifice, by being deeply human and truly spiritual, by rejecting the extremes of the hot-eyed crusaders (left or right), by preparing for peace in time of war, by being on the ready for either doom or dawn." He also said, "Peacemaking is the enterprise, carried through suffering to a cross if necessary, to overcome evil in the world and estrangement between people, by love. Peacemakers are those who place themselves by choice in the midst of human conflict—to do and to speak the truth in love at the cost of a cross, with their vindication expected, not from their worldly success, but from God's blessing and unconquerable providence."

Those who observed Albert Outler through the years know that he, by choice, placed himself in the midst of human conflict, e.g., racial, sexist, political (secular and church), etc. In these conflicts he never joined sides. He spoke to all sides. About the time you thought you had him lined up with you, he attacked your argument. He did this with studied carefulness. He respected your position until you cemented it in dogmatism, self-righteousness (condescension), etc. This accounted to a great degree why Albert Outler did not join organizations that took a solid I-won't-budge-an-inch attitude. His ventures were of the searching varieties. His approach also accounted for many of the crosses he had to bear. About the time he got off one, he was being nailed to another. If being nailed to a cross amid conflict makes for peace, Outler qualified for the title "peacemaker."

SERMON 18

Blessed Are the Peacemakers

It would be a commonplace to say how impressive a group of this size in a cathedral like this on an occasion like this really is.

It is, of course, an honor and a privilege to be with you. Yet, actually, the sermon this day is being preached, and the text obviously dictated, by the occasion itself. What I should like to do is to put our theme-beatitude in a larger context within the cluster of the last three beatitudes in the opening section of Jesus' Sermon on the Mount:

> Blessed are the peacemakers; God shall call them his children.
>
> Blessed are those who suffer persecution in the cause of righteousness; the kingdom of heaven shall be theirs.
>
> Blessed are you when you endure insults, persecution and calumny for my sake [for Christ's sake]; your reward in heaven is right; yours is the same lot as the prophets who were before you (Matthew 5:9-11).

Blessed are the peacemakers. Yes, of course—how nice.

But how bland can you get? For almost everybody is, or calls himself, a peacemaker—including the warmongers. We love peace; we have pacifists and peace movements (rival peace movements, in fact). Diplomats are peacemakers and so are the politicians. In short, who isn't? It is hard to know, in all this double-talk, who is conning whom. But one thing is clear: The cause of peace is popular and we can be ruefully grateful for that. But it does tend to bleach out the original beatitude; it casts doubt on the notion that peacemakers rightly belong among the blessed; that is, among those whose lives are meaningful, who know it and are gladdened by that fact.

But if the world is full of self-professed peacemakers, why is it also at war, in the throes of violent social revolution, full of people in misery in their poverty, full of people unhappy in their affluence? Evidently the old text needs a second, closer look. To suggest how this might be done is the purpose of this sermon.

The first thing to notice is that this peacemaker bit comes along with two references to suffering—for righteousness' sake and for Christ's sake. Peacemaking, real peacemaking that is, has something to do with deep involvement in unpopular causes, not because they are unpopular, but because they are right. It has something to do with a willingness to suffer insult and persecution, not because one is a masochist, but in Christ's name and for his sake.

Now, this clue that peacemaking involves something more than platitudes is confirmed when you realize that the word "peacemaking" ("peacemaker") occurs only twice in the whole New Testament: here and in Colossians—where the redemptive work of Christ is described in cosmic terms and related directly to the Cross:

> In Christ, the full reality of God, by God's deliberate action, came to dwell in human flesh. Through him God was working to reconcile the whole creation to himself—making peace through the shedding of his blood on the cross, reconciling all things, through him. Formerly you yourselves were estranged from God, and your deeds were evil. Now by Christ's human suffering and death God has reconciled you to himself.

> Be sure therefore that you continue in this faith (that God's love is your life's foundation) and never falter in your hopes as they are lodged in the gospel (Colossians 1:19-23).

To the early Christian who wrote Colossians—and who obviously had our Lord's beatitude in mind—peacemaking is a risky business. Jesus Christ is the model peacemaker, and Christians are peacemakers as they share in his self-giving ministry of reconciliation. Peacemaking is the enterprise, carried through suffering to a cross if necessary, to overcome evil in the world and estrangement between people, by love. Peacemakers are those who place themselves by choice in the midst of human conflict—to do and to speak the truth in love at the cost of a cross, with their vindication expected, not from their worldly success, but from God's blessing and unconquerable providence. Peacemakers are those whose lives are offered for peace—not by polarizing the good guys from the bad guys, but by trying to convert the bad guys (which is an unwelcome task) and by admonishing the good guys against self-righteousness (which will get you chewed up by them self-righteously!).

And so our bland little bromide turns out to be a booby trap for the sentimentalists and the hypocrites. Everybody talking peace ain't making it! Instead of a pleasantry, our beatitude is actually an ethical program: the way of love as a way of life, love that does not seek but may earn insults, love that does not aim at a cross but may well lead to one. Peacemaking is one's agonizing commitment to the resolution of destructive conflicts in one's time, place, and circumstances—a humble awareness of how little we can do to change things and a startled pride in the discovery of how vitally important that little can be, in the providence of God. Peacemaking is the resolute rejection of hate as a policy, as one's motivating force for reform. It is the willingness to suffer injustice rather than commit it, to be crucified sooner than to crucify others. And this, said Jesus, is the truly meaningful life; such people really are God's favorite children.

Sounds square, doesn't it? But not dull, I can assure you. In Jesus' case, it got him caught in the middle of a three-cornered fight among the political establishment (the Sadducees), the ecclesiastical establishment (the Pharisees), and the main protest movement of the time (the Zealots, who went storming around raising rebellion against Rome that would, when it came, destroy not Rome but Jerusalem and Jewry). It is often like that—zealots achieving a very different end from the one they had in mind, like the Berkeley beatniks helping to elect Ronald Reagan.

It is not said, "Blessed are the peace lovers and the peace praisers." "Peace" is all too often a glib abstraction, readily extolled by those who take small risks in its behalf. Real peacemaking is always a doing. It begins at home, in one's neighborhood and city, and thence around the world, in the conflicts that you can reach or that have reached you.

Nor is it said, "Blessed are the peacekeepers": the quiet, retiring souls that lie low while conflict rages, that wait until righteousness begins to win and then cheer from their hideaways. One may keep the peace oneself and still contribute to the conflict by one's implicit and maybe even unconscious role in the moral anomalies of the situation.

Nor is it said, "Blessed are the pious hell-raisers in behalf of peace." "Burn, baby, burn" may be ever so fervent, and we should try to understand its horrid provocation, but it is not an effective peace slogan. The one thing that would have made Jesus a popular hero overnight would have been for him to raise the standard of revolt against Rome. He was constantly pressured to do so, and no one could deny it would have been a just cause. Instead, he chose a different way, the way of peacemaking that turned into a *via dolorosa* that has been endlessly redemptive. The Zealots went on their blind self-righteous way, first to covert sabotage and then to open violence, all of which let to endlessly destructive consequences.

Peace is made, if at all, by persuasion and service, by holding to the frail reeds of reason and dialogue, by deeds of compassion and by self-sacrifice, by being deeply human and truly spiritual, by rejecting the extremes of the hot-eyed crusaders (left or right), by preparing for peace in time of war, by being on the ready for either doom or dawn.

And what are the odds for such peacemaking and such peacemakers? Let's face it—they are poor, as they were in Jesus' day and have been ever since. The world, like a tired and spastic acrobat, reels on the razor's edge of danger most of the time. Humanity manages mainly by the skin of our teeth. This has certainly been proved to the hilt for all of us here. Some of us have survived two and a half world wars, a decade of reckless optimism, a decade of ruthless depression, and two decades of cold war with terrifying episodes of brinksmanship. And now in these cold war decades we have seen Freud's grim diagnosis of human society—in *Civilization and Its Discontents*—demonstrated with horrifying realism: That the constraints of civilization are too feeble for the barbarian in us all.

Now, we are in a war in Vietnam in which surrender is unthinkable, negotiation unpromising, escalation disastrous. In Europe, the Western Alliance is falling apart. The Communist community, outside Red China, is turning revisionist in a big way. Last summer in Russia, I saw a proletarian society in a determined push to become as bourgeois as anything I have seen in the decadent West. In Asia, a new apocalypse of terror has come with the fireball over Lop Nor two weeks ago—for who doubts where they will aim their first operational ICBM, and who believes that they will hesitate about "first strike"?

In the so-called Third World are the heartbreaking paradoxes of liberty gloriously gained and ingloriously abused, where progress comes too slowly to abate the fury of those who couldn't care less about real, long-range consequences.

Here in America we have handled our power and responsibility so ineptly that we have drawn down on ourselves a universal enmity that is only partially undeserved. But worst of all, we have begun to abandon the American dream of a truly open society, and are developing extremes that flourish because the consensus of the moderates has become clamorous and confused.

From all this comes the rising tide of misbelief and unbelief that we hear so much about, the disenchantment of those who were enchanted by their false expectations of what history has to offer. All this talk about religionless, secular Christianity comes out of the disillusionment of those whose illusions have now turned to what man can make of himself by human effort. And so comes on the new crop of crusaders with their programs and panaceas and their fierce contempt for all who fail to fall in line.

The prospects of peace are poor in the situation where "moderate" has become a dirty word, where the radical left rejects its old alliance with the liberals and the radical right heaps scorn and contempt on honest conservatives.

It is a great tragedy, these secessions from the American mainstream, from the complex consensus required for the minimal functioning of democratic institutions. For this rising intolerance from left and right has finally triggered an equal and opposite reaction by the badgered and bedeviled men in the middle. You may remember that revivalism once was effective in America because it could exploit the Puritan conscience of the average man. But revivalism overplayed its hand by unloving denunciations, and with it went the Puritan conscience of America. *Mutatis mutandis*, the civil rights cause was moving ahead at a steady rate, largely because of the bad conscience of WASPS (White Anglo-Saxon Protestants)—a bad conscience we had earned and that should have been exploited. But when nonviolence turned to violence, whatever the provocation, the white man took it as a justification of his biases. The discovery that he was hated gave him an excuse for lapsing into his unredeemed prejudices with a self-righteousness to match the self-righteousness of the Negro racists. This is the saddest lesson to be learned from last week's elections. And a bad conscience, once lost, is very hard to resensitize.

What is there then to save us from cynicism? Why should we suppose that we could be peacemakers in these days with any chance to affect our history and destiny? I can think of two answers that are still impressive. The one is that, though the powers of evil seem always to have the upper hand, they are forever being thwarted from final victory. This is not for want of trying and not for any lack of human ineptitude or blindness. Sometimes, force itself has had to be resorted to in order to save mankind from a greater evil—as in 1914-18, in 1939-45 and in 1950-51. The world of the Versailles Treaty was a mess, but not so bad as the one that would otherwise have been shaped from Potsdam. World War II did not make peace, but it prevented a Hitler victory.

But war cannot make peace; only self-sacrificial love can do that. And this, in fact, is what has held the world together—the kind, fair-minded, dedicated servants of peace. Your own heroines in the YWCA have blazoned the way and have left you a shining path to follow. The servants of peace, in the churches, the synagogues, the schools and colleges—these are the people who have made it possible for the statesmen to keep the seams of international society from fraying too badly. And so there is proof that the Spirit of God, who is the Spirit of peace, is working in this same parlous world of which otherwise we speak in doleful tones. The peacemakers have God going for them!

The other warrant for believing that peacemaking is for real and promising is the abundant evidence, if seen in the right perspective, that the power and grace of God are still effectively at work in human hearts and lives, at deeper levels than conscious professions of formal religious belief, and yet also in and through those who serve him by name and who serve their sisters and brothers in his name. There are more men and women of goodwill in the world than you'd ever know from reading the papers or staring at the boob tube.

For one thing, we've survived two decades of nuclear terror; for two decades nuclear holocaust has been staved off. How? I don't quite know and Dr. Strangelove didn't know at all. But the question is still worth pondering, for it has been something of a miracle, a miracle of peacemaking that might well come within the scope of our beatitude. It cannot be taken for granted, however, and we should ourselves seek to find all conceivable ways to strengthen the hands of those who have access to the "panic" and "destruct" buttons.

Again, in the uprush of political freedom over the world, we have seen a fearful turmoil and progress bought at a frightful cost in many places. What needs to be noticed, however, even as we deplore disorder, is the fact that these new nations are actually managing—almost never by the towering genius of statecraft—by the peacemaking of many people, mostly unknown, viz., missionaries, medical people, engineers, civil servants, merchants, and homemakers. These last two, incidentally, have always been the world's greatest peacemakers, partly because they need peace for their vocations.

For all the horrors of modern man's inhumanity to man, there is a new passion among men of humanity, new standards of meaning and value for human life unknown in earlier ages. The winds of the Spirit are blowing in our midst; the grace of the living God is at work in the hearts and minds of men who do not always realize that it is this same Spirit who has made their hearts anxious until they find life's real serenity in peacemaking love.

From all this, and much else that gets ignored or scorned by the bigots and the radicals, one can conclude modestly, but hopefully, that human existence really is, as Jesus said it was, in the hands of God: that our being is from God in God and to God. It was the essence of Christ's revelation that caring love may entail frustration and a cross, but

> . . . that scaffold sways the future,
> And, behind the dim unknown,
> Standeth God within the shadows
> Keeping watch above his own.[1]

If this is so, then the vision and vocation of peacemaker has all the meaning and hope Jesus says it has; and in our time it has taken on new dimensions of significance. It is, indeed, the only calling a person can have that is not already ticketed to futility. The gospel of God's love in Christ and Christ's love shed abroad in and through our lives is the only alternative I know to raw cynicism, to real despair.

For it was into just a world as this one, and to just such men and women as we are that God sent his son Jesus, his Word of Love, his Deed of Invincible Goodness to open to us and to all men the ways of life and death. These ways are still open, and God still holds us thus in his judgment and mercy at one and the same time.

The way of life—life here and now and anywhere as well as life hereafter and in the world to come—is the way of love: love of God, of neighbor, of self, love of God's good world and of his wayward children in that world, love that suffers but that also delights in the gifts and blessings of God in creation, love that is dedicated to righteousness but that seeks redemption from self-righteousness as from damnation.

The way of costing, caring love is the way of the peacemakers. Those who walk in it really are the children of God, the real children of God—blessed in their own lives and an unmerited blessing to all the rest of us. It is to this way that you and I are called by God's calling and with God's promise: the promise that for our sufferings for love and humanity we shall know the comfort of his grace and an eternal weight of glory. Can you think of a more authentic mode of existence, a better way to make a gift of the life that you have yourself received as a gift from God?

Let us pray:

> Almighty God, our heavenly Father, in whose peace is our peace and in whose service is our perfect freedom, grant us peace in heart and mind and will and the wisdom and courage to serve thee in peacemaking as thy children, through Jesus Christ our Lord. Amen.

Introduction

"It is the love of Christ that constraints me" (2 Corinthians 5:14).

Albert Outler described this text as "St. Paul's recipe for *self*-control under the constraints of Christ's love," and used it in a baccalaureate sermon preached at Queens College in Charlotte, North Carolina, on Sunday, May 17, 1970. It was adapted from a sermon preached for the Chicago Evening Club on April 5, 1970. Paul was saying, "The love of Christ . . . gives me a new sense of purpose, a new agenda for living, no longer for self, but in faith and hope and love—a new sort of moral authority, noncoercive but imperative. It affirms our freedom and yet commands our voluntary obedience to God in trying to realize his loving purposes in the world." Outler added, "this love commands us to love others out of our gratitude to God."

We live in a world where "sanity and madness can no longer be clearly differentiated. What is sorely needed is constraint—'the constraints of love.'"

One thing you noticed about Albert Outler . . . he sometimes "lost his cool" when someone expressed self above God. He never denied that nature endowed him with the temperament of a personalized gauntlet—to be thrown into the fray where someone was trying to play like God. He preached grace, argued grace, fought for grace —while living in grace, while knowing that God loved him *anyhow*. His purpose was to get them to love him the same way—*anyhow*. It was his smartest move—if he could do that; then all (including himself) would have calmer spirits.

SERMON 19

The Constraints of Love

"It is the love of Christ that constrains me" (2 Corinthians 5:14).

Here, embedded in a long passage on Christian morale, we run on a brief formula for Christian morality, St. Paul's recipe for self-control under the constraints of Christ's love. The word "constrains" is crucial. It's a special term in Greek, used to refer to a special kind of leadership: the captain of a company of troops, the director of a chorus, etc. We would use it of the conductor of a symphony orchestra, or a coxswain of a crew, or a coach moving his team about the field. It suggests the guidance of a group by one man, but direction without coercion; it means authority that serves the corporate self-discipline of the group. The members of a symphony orchestra are gifted and temperamental persons. We recognize this in their individual noodlings before the conductor appears and lifts his baton. But since they want to make music together, they all obey the conductor—they accept his "constraints"—and they do this freely out of respect for him and their own pride of artistry. He leads and they follow, and both they and the world are better for it.

St. Paul, as we know from Romans 7, understood the human

heart as a sort of cockpit of warring impulses. No amount of simple sincerity or good intentions ever quite manages to fend off frustration or assure harmony. Here in our text he is reporting that he has found a new mode of guidance and self-direction so marvelous that he can talk about being a new man: His natural inner chaos has been eased; a new inner harmony is being experienced. "The love of Christ *constrains* me," gives me a new sense of purpose, a new agenda for living, no longer chiefly for self, but in faith and hope and love, a new sort of moral authority, noncoercive but imperative. It affirms our freedom and yet commands our voluntary obedience to God in trying to realize his loving purposes in the world.

This constraining love of Christ has a double reference. Christ was God's love incarnate, divine love seeking out each man's full potential, his potential for self-disciplined freedom. Christ's love calls us to love God in grateful response, but also we are to understand our lives as lived out in every moment immersed in God's love. This love commands us to love others out of our gratitude to God! This is the essence of the Christian ethic.

This love of God that constrained Paul to love others had wrought harmony in the jangle of his tumultuous spirits. It had raised his natural pessimism to a new pitch of self-confidence; it had curbed his native aggressiveness without curtailing his fierce impulse to be free. He had found the Christian way: To be freed by Christ's love from sin and selfishness, to be bound by Christ's love to all our human kin, to be inspired by Christ's love to a cheerful, intelligent service in the world. This is the promise and hope of the gospel.

For St. Paul knew long ago, as we know now, that the human predicament is focused in the tragic fact that our human aspirations are out of proportion to our human capabilities, that to be human is to court frustration on a cosmic scale. Our reach does exceed our grasp, and from this flows our grandeur and our misery. Of all God's creatures, we are the least continent and least content; we live in a perilous balance between appetite and inhibition. Left to our devices, our behavior is inordinate; our best intentions go awry; our self-restraints are sadly insufficient. Now Paul had found himself constrained by Christ's indwelling love and he realized how remarkable it was: Any force that could bridle that unruly heart without stifling its thirst for glory could do at least as much for others. And so he defines the Christian life as an experiment in love to others constrained by God's love for us in Christ.

To be human at all, we must be free. But this radical need for freedom is two-faced: it is a hunger without a natural limit, that is never sated by more freedom. Every emancipation opens up new vistas and new limitations; the most free man who breathes is still finite and death-doomed. Thus the freedom that makes us human is all too easily abused, and freedom abused leads into new modes of slavery. "You are free to do your own thing" is a liberating gospel to men and women and young people who have been bound and gagged by conventional and external restraints of fear, shame, or moral bribery. But it is also a snare and a delusion when it leads us once again into new tyrannies, tyrannies of passion and unbridled appetites, tyrannies of drug addiction, tyrannies of new tribal and peer-group pieties.

By the same token, our human aspirations drive us in an effort at intellectual mastery. The hungers of our minds for the knowledge that is power and for the wisdom that is peace are as distinctively human as the will to freedom. But their temptations are equally dangerous. The greater our knowledge, the greater our power: power over nature, over other men, over the domains of science, the arts, and industry. And yet our intellectual ambition is foredoomed; always there is more to know than we can ever master. The mystery of self-knowledge and the mystery of the ultimate exceed our furthest intellectual outreach. Moreover, when we let our curiosity run wild or lend our intelligence to evil intent, the result is always inhuman (not just subhuman). Self-serving knowledge is a fatal corruption of the very same aspirations to authentic self-understanding that have lifted us out of our animal matrix.

Then, too, there is our inordinate hunger for love itself. Our humanity hungers and thirsts for love, and always inordinately, for we are never loved enough to last forever. Always there is our need for more assurance that we are cared for, no matter what; we have to have some evidence that our offerings of love and devotion to others are accepted and acceptable. But love is the easiest of all sentiments to corrupt. Love unrequited easily passes over into self-pity, self-indulgence, bitterness. The same energy that protects and comforts a frightened child fuels the rampages of sex-maniacs and bomb-throwers. And so love requires the constraints of love: the self-chosen subordination of appetite to the imperatives of unselfish service of others, the actual total welfare of all mankind. But it is just precisely this that is lacking in contemporary society whether in the cultic vanguard of the Age of Aquarius or amongst those whose half-comfortable, half-secure world is being tumbled in over their heads.

For ours is a time of breakdown of the old patterns of constraint that held society together for centuries. We are witnessing—and sharing in—the passing of knee-jerk obedience, the withering of old taboos, the weakening of the sense of shame and bad conscience in the face of social disapproval. The most oft-quoted couplet I hear nowadays—or that comes to mind after every depressing bout with the daily paper is that bit from Yeats's "Second Coming" which he wrote in 1920!:

> Things fall apart, the centre cannot hold . . .[1]

This is all too true. What we call civilization has always been a fragile affair of tacit agreements not to overburden each other with our incontinent impulses. Human culture lives by limits. Artists and sages know when and where and why to stop. Animals or men herding and mating without reticence, veil, or shame may create many animal effects but none that warrants the term "culture." There have been times when, comparatively speaking, the restraining power of customary morality (fear, shame, and greed) has given human society interludes of stability and comparative decency.

But it is also obvious that our most recent interlude of conventional morality and social restraint (now easily sneered at as "Puritan" or "Victorian") is passing or past. There are also those who speak of the passing of the Age of Reason. The human animal, whose instinctual controls have never been adequate in and of themselves, is currently courting chaos. More men have more freedom today than in any age since Eden—and are more radically discontented with the consequences. Our curiosity has generated a technology that has conquered earth and space, and is also in process of rendering the planet uninhabitable. Love knits man in community and makes him fully human; its counterculture, rage, is turning the secular city into an asphalt jungle. I know psychiatrists who are seriously suggesting that sanity and madness can no longer be clearly differentiated. What is sorely needed is constraint—"the constraints of love." But what hope is there for that in our present climate of outrage and contestation?

The horrifying rise and spread of violence is only the most obvious symptom of a deeper social agony—of men, women, and youth lacking assurance of their own dignity and being denied it by others, of permissiveness run riot, of recklessness as a style of life, of reason prostituted to the uses of self-justification. Riots in the streets or in the courtroom are the new theater of the absurd for those who have despaired of re-forming society to their own sweet wills. These are the first fruits of their wildfire gospel of utopia *now*—and this reign of terror has just begun.

On the other side, over against this welling tide of anarchy, stands the obtuse morality of the Establishment, the mutinous partisans of order by repression. There still remains in our society a heavy overlay of the old restraints of force and fear—force against force, propaganda against propaganda, the obstinate deadlock of the activists and the immobilists. Our society is caught between revolution and backlash, and is being macerated thereby.

We hear talk of a crisis of morality: the rise and spread of brazen crime and shameless experimentation—sex, drugs, herd behavior, and what have you. But what is this crisis except the absence of internal controls in the lives of persons who have lost their fears of external authority or any real hope for a better long future that might compensate for self-denial now? The new morality speaks of love, but usually in terms of romantic sentiment, rarely in terms of constraint, much less the constraints of Christ's love.

We hear talk of crisis of belief: the loss of old verities and convictions, the decline of conventional religiousness, a new godlessness, a new self-confidence in human self-sufficiency. We see the dabblers in secular religion and exotic cults of one sort and another. But what is this but the absence of inner beliefs, of nominal religious observances, of the widening chasms between profession and performance? There will be no new age of faith until we recover an inner sense of the transcendent mystery in which we live and whose name is Love—and in the moral constraints of that love. Man's hope hangs, not on what he can make of himself, but on what God has done, and can do, with and for us.

We hear talk of a crisis of authority: of the disappearance of the old modes of constraint, the old arbiters of disputed issues. What is this but the disappearance of any substantial consensus as to our mutual social interests and goals, an agreement as to the appropriate means to agreed ends? Violence and rebellion are pathological signs of a desperate rejection of the civilized processes of persuasion and progress.

In a society as nearly out of control as ours, with vast issues hanging on the twists and turns of passion and unreason, the prospects for real freedom (even for the rebels) are dim indeed. Suppose, for example, the young were to succeed in "liberating" their universities, could they educate themselves or could they coerce free men to teach them what they think they want to know, and call that education? On the other hand, there is no brighter prospect for a return to "the good old days," the reimposition of external controls by repressive or arbitrary authority. And so we are being whipsawed between the utopian visions of the "New Left," the counterrevolution of the "New Right" and the newly roused distemper of middle America. The standing order cannot stand, yet it is increasingly clear that the vaunted counterculture of the Aquarians is a tragic illusion and will remain so.

It is therefore high time to speak, more emphatically than most of us have for some time past, of the Christian alternative to chaos: The pattern of a life fueled by the same hungers for freedom, self-understanding, and love as all other human projects and yet guided and controlled by the constraints of love—not fear, not greed, not illusion—but the love of Christ himself. Jesus came preaching man's access to the kingdom of God, the imminent prospect of God's righteous rule in human hearts and lives in freedom and reason and loving self-discipline.

What the world needs now
Is love, sweet love.[2]

But love without manners and self-control will leave the world a wreck. Stewart Alsop tells of a young hippie reporting his recent conversion to "the revolution" that had been sparked by a side remark from a Students for a Democratic Society revivalist: "What we need is a society in which people love each other. This," the young man said to Alsop, "was a mind-blowing experience, a moment of real truth." But why hadn't he heard that before in its original Christian context? This is a stern reproach to the church and its failure to witness to its own essential message and experience: a world in which free and knowledgeable men love each other freely and intelligently. Has any revolutionary vision ever surpassed that? And yet the vision is a naïve and romantic will-o-the-wisp unless the love that liberates and binds such men is love of a higher order: God's love in Christ, God's sacrificial, costing love that satisfies our highest aspirations within and because of our finite limits.

We have too long been dominated by the regal image of leadership: of restraints at the cost of freedom. The king on his throne, the boss at his desk, the little Caesar in the family or the college—the ethics of the carrot and the stick—this is what many of us supposed was "natural." And now a new generation is prepared to revolt against any and all constraints of this sort—but under the tragic illusion that justice always replaces tyranny overthrown.

Leadership in the Christian pattern goes by a different style, and this is what our text is driving at. Our leader was a man of God's own choosing who chose for himself the way of unselfish service, the way of universal charity and brotherhood, the way of the Cross and Resurrection—and who calls us to follow him. This is the kind of love that prods us and guides us to love others in responsible freedom and in intelligent self-restraint. Love like this saves us from the dismal prospects of depending on ourselves for the ultimate sustenance of our hopes and aspirations. But it is also the chief imperative of our moral behavior: "Love so amazing, so divine, demands my soul, my life, my all."

The essence of Christian faith, hope, and love—and of Christian social ethics—is not our love for God but his love for us let loose in the world in and through the life, example and mystery of Jesus Christ. As we recognize this love and accept it, the whole of existence becomes grace-filled and all of life is rendered grace-full. This purges and ennobles our human love. It turns our freedom from servitude into freedom for service. It becomes a constraining, shaping influence in all our human endeavors. This way lies the deepest satisfaction we can ever know, the highest exaltation that we can experience and sustain.

Our world is perishing, literally, for the want of love and peace and community. Its hungers will never be fed or even assuaged by ballads or bombs. The self-demanding, self-righteous prophets of self-interest are finally self-defeating. But when will men come to realize this? When will we reawaken to the marvel of God's love and so be reconciled to him—and constrained by him? Is there any other hope and promise of a new and better world?

"The love of Christ constrains me," for it was Christ's mission—in his life and death and subsequent history—that men should learn to abandon their selfishness and to accept their new freedom to live and die in the atmosphere of grace.

It was because Paul had learned this secret and had proved it out in a strife-torn and dedicated life that he could raise so serene and hopeful a doxology as that which brackets our text:

> No wonder then that we do not lose heart! Though our outward humanity is in decay, yet day by day we are inwardly renewed . . . We come therefore as Christ's ambassadors. It is as if God were appealing to you through us: in Christ's name, we implore you, be reconciled to God! . . . Sharing in God's work, we urge this appeal upon you: You have received the grace of God; do not let it go for nothing (2 Corinthians 4:16; 5:20; 6:1).

Introduction

In this sermon preached at Hockaday School on January 30, 1967, and at the Cum Laude ceremony at St. Mark's School of Texas in 1971 (both located in Dallas), Albert Outler said, "We love [God] . . . because he first loved us! Our only hope of learning to speak the truth in love rests on our grateful awareness that we have been and are loved in truth. Thus, the love of God is our chief support and aid in growing up."

By that definition of maturity we are still "growing up" when we die. For God loves us up to, and through, the end of this existence. On the other hand, when you speak the truth in love (without telling people that this is what you are doing), you have in that moment revealed "human maturity."

In this sermon Outler spoke the truth . . . in love. And in so doing maintained that lad-of-a-boy spirit, excited about the present, curious about the future, and hopeful to the end.

SERMON 20

The Measure of Maturity

'So shall we all at last attain to the unity inherent in our faith and our knowledge of the Son of God—to mature manhood, measured by nothing less than the full stature of Christ. We are no longer to be children, tossed by the waves and whirled about by every fresh gust of teaching, dupes of crafty rogues and their deceitful schemes. No, let us speak the truth in love; so shall we fully grow up into Christ' (Ephesians 4:13-15).

As our text this morning, I call your attention to the striking phrase, "speaking the truth in love, we are to grow up!"

Growing up, how do you measure maturity?

Nowadays, everybody knows or knows about Trafalgar Square. There it is, a veritable hub of London life, with its swirl of traffic ceaselessly circling it—(the wrong way, too)—with its towering monument, its splashing fountains and those veddy, veddy British lions, staring off down Whitehall or over toward St. Martin-in-the-Fields or, with a slightly upraised glance, at the National Gallery across the road. I have seen it more than once, jam-packed (this summer when the ban-the-bomb marchers filled it with their violent advocacy of peace at any price), and then also in its more normal aspects with a wonderful motley of the old and the young strolling about or just sitting on the benches or the fountain's rim. And almost always there has been the fond father with a camera and his child perched up between the paws of one of the lions, ready for the inevitable album shot.

But this past summer I "discovered" something in Trafalgar Square that I had not known before, had not noticed in my guide book. Over on the northwest wall, across from the National Gallery, is a set of bronze markers, registering the standard British measurements of length. They were put there by the Board of Trade in 1886, and they register the inch, foot, yard, ell, link, pole, etc., etc. There, in the place that was once near the heart of empire—in all of the clatter of the city and the indifference of the normal denizens of the Square—are the signs and symbols of objective public measurement, against which all other linear computation can be checked, if, that is, they are within the system of inches, feet, and yards. The whole business, of course, gets complicated now that Britain is moving toward the metric scale, in which case the standard measurement will be the platinum meter-bar in the Bureau of Weights and Measures at Sèvres. This is not a really serious complication, for computation in either system can be transferred to the other or to any other linear system, like any other of the newer linear systems.

The point is that length can be measured at a very high level of precision. And so can mass and velocity. Nor does it matter so much as it seems to some, that our measures of length, mass, and velocity are not absolute, that all are relative to the correlative situations of what is measured and who is measuring them. Relativity is not equivalent to subjectivity, and nothing but confusion can come from any such misidentification.

But as everybody knows, the case is radically different when we come to personal and ethical values: to the business of the quality, worth, and meaning of human existence. The throngs in Trafalgar Square could be measured for height and beam by those bronze standards there, but this would not tell us much about the quality of their lives, their maturity or lack of it, the worth and meaning of their existence. Yet this is what matters most of all to all of us, to the vacuous as well as the thoughtful, to the frustrated as well as the fulfilled. The differences between maturity and immaturity, between responsibility and irresponsibility, between effectual and ineffectual behavior, between blessedness and doom—these are the real differences, the decisive differences, the fateful differences.

But how are these degrees of maturity or immaturity to be measured, or even understood? It is ironic that we do "measure" such difference, naturally and unavoidably, even when we pretend not to. Every existential judgment we make, of ourselves or of anybody else, includes in it some measurement of maturity. Most of us have had experience on some sort of selection committee where we have had to make a comparative estimate as to the maturity of the people under review. And thus we know how important, in such cases, is some such verdict as "gifted but immature." No wonder, then, that our Lord warned us against overconfident judgment of others, since in the very nature of the case, all our judgments are partial, imprecise, and unreliable. Yet he also realized that we are forever measuring and being measured, that we can hardly avoid the process even by trying to bow out of it.

Here then is our predicament, and it dogs us all: we are forever judging each other and ourselves by some measure of maturity, the accuracy and adequacy of which we are bound to doubt, but the necessity of which we are bound to admit. With what judgments we judge, we are judged; we are the victims as well as the agents in this bewildering process.

Two time-honored ways for improving our batting average in this game of measuring and being measured are, first, the delineation of some ideal concept of maturity; second, the identification of some exemplar of maturity: a hero, a sage, or a saint. These two methods can be mixed, of course, and often are. Both of them rest on the same assumption, that the root of immaturity is ignorance of what real maturity is or would be like in action.

A fair amount of classical ethical theory has been built around these ideal conceptions of human maturity: Plato's prescription for power and wisdom; Aristotle's golden mean, the Enlightenment's idea of pure reason and/or pure feeling. All these notions, together with their modern psychological counterparts, are based on the premise that maturity becomes a live option to the human mind and will, when it is adequately defined. But in the strange domain of personal and interpersonal affairs, abstractions are singularly insufficient for insight and understanding. Hence, a far more nearly universal measure of maturity has been sought in human examples of it, persons who manifest in their lives and influence those qualities of meaningful living that the rest of us could recognize and wish to emulate. Mature persons—the wise, the good, the heroic, the movers and shakers, the creative mutants who change the level or direction of human development—these are the paradigms of human character that impress us, at least to the extent of showing us the difference between humdrum and vital experience, between authentic and inauthentic existence. But even here, the crucial thing is the type or pattern of our human heroes.

And here we come upon one of the really ominous symptoms of the sickness of contemporary man. He has no heroes or heroines who are heroic. Our discovery of the radical ambivalence of all human virtue has made it plain that the bravest of the brave are still frail flesh, that sages are fallible, that martyrs are often narcissists, that the good guys have mixed motives, that the bad guys and dolls are somewhat more victim than villain. If ever we suffered from the myopia of uncritical, sentimental adulation of the unworthy—what I call the Little Orphan Annie complex—we have now come 180 degrees away from that danger and have plunged into its blasé opposite, what one could call the Bedrock mind, the Pogo-Peanuts worldview, the cult of the sick funster. The contemporary novel is not only a literature without heroes; its common *kerygma* is that the very notions of heroism and virtue are fatuous.

This goes along with other ironic and tragic symptoms of a demoralized society (literally demoralized!). When educators and educational instructions (as at Vassar or Cornell) take a dim view of promiscuity as not being the maturest mode of human sexuality (as distinguished from most animals), there is a great hue and cry about freedom, as if private morality or immorality have nothing to do with human maturity and public morale. The denial of human absolutes, the exposure of the poseurs of perfection—all of this is valid. Indeed, it is a contribution to maturity itself since one form of childishness (old style childishness, that is) is the idolization of the ordinary. But it does not follow that the opposite is any better: the bored contempt for virtue and the pathological devotion to the gospel of *nil admirari*. Actually, this is another form of childishness (new-style), the leveling tendency of peer-group behaviors, the determination to cut everybody down to size. This is a false democratization of human virtue, yet it goes on even in the citadels of the egghead and the snob.

The saint and sage who wrote the so-called Epistle to the Ephesians for the upcoming members of the second generation of Christians, was vividly aware of the challenge of maturity, as it was confronting this new and unstable Christian community in its historical development. The Christians in Asia Minor, to whom he was writing, were not converts from Judaism. Instead, they had grown up in a highly sensate, relativistic culture in which they had been slaves, as our author says, to the gods and rulers of this world, slaves of passion and herd-running. Now they have been rescued from this swamp, just as the Jewish Christians had been delivered from their grim desert of legalism. Their common task now was the business of exemplifying a pattern of mature life in an immature world, of developing their responsible vocations, of transcending their past childishness and inconstancy, of growing up into Jesus Christ, who is "the measure of the stature of the mature man."

Our author propounds a formula for this process: "Speaking the truth in love." If it didn't sound so awkward, we might translate the phrase "truthing in love," since the verb "to truth" is as common (to be truthful) as the noun "truth." The man is obviously talking about the habit of manifesting the truth or letting the truth be manifested in the spirit and temper of *agape*, the love that attends to the good of the loved one, the love concerned with well-being; love that is outgoing, upbuilding, and unselfish. The rule, then, is that by speaking the truth in love men and women, who have accepted God's love and have come to rest the weight of their lives in his care, will grow toward maturity, maturity measured by the personality of Christ Jesus, who is God's two-fold revelation of human existence—and of God himself!

Thus we have here a combination of an abstract definition of maturity and a dynamic example of maturity: The human existence of Jesus Christ in whom God has identified himself with us in our history so that we might be rightly related to him in and through our identification with Jesus Christ as disciples. The link between the abstraction and the example is the injunction to speak the truth in love.

Now, the obvious difficulty in such an appeal to the example of Jesus Christ as the human paradigm of mature and meaningful life comes from the difficulty of knowing how an example turned into an ideal may then be transposed to some other age and context as an exemplification of the *same* ideal. The exemplary is always slipping off into the realm of the ideal and vice versa. In the Middle Ages the imitation of Christ was a specific program of Christian asceticism and devotion. In the nineteenth century the quest for the historical Jesus was motivated in large part by the assumption that in this way we could reenter the presence of a great and good man, a religious hero, an ethical genius whose life and teachings (and religious faith) were uniquely exemplary for morals and for faith as well.

When I was young, people were still reading Sheldon's *In His Steps*, equivalent in that day to today's *The Power of Positive Thinking* or *Calories Don't Count*. It had a wonderfully simple thesis: The Christian should model his ethical behavior on what he judges Jesus would do if he were here and in a similar situation. This procedure left too much to the subjective imagination of disciples with their various prejudices and presuppositions. And it allowed, even if it did not actually encourage, the identification of one's own highest ideals, however formed, with the teachings of Jesus and the charter of the kingdom of God. For example, it allowed many people in my part of the world to make Jesus out to have been a WASP (White Anglo-Saxon Protestant). Nevertheless, it had a real advantage; it put the Christian up against a higher measure of maturity than his own, and so forced him to a crisis of self-encounter with an actual human counterpart to himself.

The critical study of the New Testament has sharply shrunk the image of the historical Jesus. Nobody seriously denies some sort of historical existence, but many question our knowledge of Jesus' personality—his self-conscious feelings, images, etc. Thus, we have had the older liberal norm of the religion of Jesus supplanted by a newer pattern of the *kerygma* about Jesus as the Christ. Whatever the advantages of this *kerygma*-centered interpretation of the Christian faith (and it has some), it leaves us with little help in the matter of a human examplar of maturity. Indeed, it is inclined to sniff at the whole thing as moralistic, Pelagian, and not fully consonant with the gospel that exhorts us to accept our being accepted by God in our unacceptability—immature and faintly proud of it. *Felix culpa!*

This clash of views as to the quality of our understanding of Jesus as an example drives us to the point where we can see the wisdom of our text; our business as Christians is to grow up (i.e., mature) into Jesus Christ, who is the measure of our maturity, by learning to speak the truth in love.

The power of significant speech belongs to the very essence of human beingness. The Greeks spoke of man as *ho zoon logon echon*, the animal with the capacity for discourse. It is in dialogue that we express ourselves, expose ourselves, become ourselves. Like it or no, we are judged by our communications, by our conversation and colloquy, for these are slices of ourselves by which we are known and must be willing to be known.

But this means that our speaking must express the truth as we are given to know the truth, else we condemn ourselves for lying, which is a strangely disastrous mode of immaturity. We can bear to deceive, said Augustine, but not to be deceived. Once a man is known to be reckless with the truth, to be a deliberate and stylish liar, he loses the right to be heard speaking the truth, even if in some particular instance or other he may actually be speaking the truth.

But there is always the agonizing question of a jesting Pilate who asked, "What is truth?"—and would not stay for an answer [a reference to Francis Bacon's *c.* 1625 essay "Of Truth"]. Truth, in most instances, is more approximate than absolute, more a matter of balanced probabilities than of partially dogmatic conclusions. Just here we come to the really primary, unique business of academia: to help people mature, and to stay mature, by developing in them the tastes, the habits, and the moral conscience of critical inquiry so that they come to love the truth, desire to speak the truth in spite of a severely disciplined conscience as to the limits of their claims to possess or manage the truth in absolute terms.

But unless we add to this loyalty to truth the phrase "in love," the results are cruelly inhumane, and not even the whole truth. No human being knows enough or has truth so firmly in his grasp that he can always speak of it objectively in bare, stern, unconcerned justice. This is why, for people concerned with the truth and also concerned for persons, there is almost always a tension between conscience and compassion. Loveless truth cuts and cripples; it is the venom in the snappish brood of oral-biting wits that often make a snake pit in the halls of ivy. But love that ignores the demands of truth and evidence will stultify the human spirit, which finally lives and dies in the context of what is real no matter what sort of theories or wishful thinking we may indulge in. The truth that matters is the truth that abides in love, the love of the truth and the love of those for whom the truth is a means of grace and an agency of freedom. In short, the most valid measure of human maturity, of significant existence, is one's disposition and endeavor to speak the truth (critical, weighed, tested truth) as far as we know it, in love (self-investing, donative love).

This would be another abstraction, another exhortation, another "Be good, sweet miss, and let who will be careful," except for one thing: we cannot love on order nor will our way into a benevolent frame of mind. We love, not because we choose to love, but because we are attracted by the lovely. We love because we are loved, first and most of all by God, "who loved us and gave himself for us." We love him, says St. John, because he first loved us! Our only hope of learning to speak the truth in love rests on our grateful awareness that we have been and are loved in truth. Thus, the love of God is our chief support and aid in growing up. It is as we learn to love as we have been loved by God that we find the wisdom to order our lesser loves in some right and due proportion, without a Puritan fear of love or a pagan antinomianism.

If our hearts were open to the manifold ways in which we ourselves have been loved by our fellow men and by God, we might also realize how rich our lives have been made by the love of truth and of truth in love. We might then finally understand what it is to speak the truth in love, what it is to be mature: To speak all the truth we know as graciously (and as gracefully) as we can, with all the gratitude and responsibility we can muster, with a thoughtful concern for the well-being of our neighbor, i.e., the whole company of our fellowmen.

As we get the hang of speaking the truth in love, we begin to get glimpses of the saving truth about our share in the determination of our destiny. It is our part to use our powers as far as we can, yet at the same time to cast our essential anxieties on the grace and love of God. Beyond this, there is no other major responsibility in existence that we can manage or need to worry about: neither reputation nor status, fame nor fortune, neither self-complacence nor self-reproach. And this renunciation and commitment will constitute our maturity, the pattern of life in which we can live and work (and en*joy* our life and work) at the top of our powers, with both fortitude and faith, serving the twin causes of inquiry and reverence, joining as they should be joined the two highest values of human experience: tested knowledge and vital piety.

> Let us therefore no longer be children tossed to and fro and carried about with every wind of doctrine, by the cunning of men, by their craftiness and deceitful wiles. Rather, speaking the truth in love, we are to grow up in every way into him who is our head, even Christ (Ephesians 4:14-15).

Let us pray.

> Eternal God, light of the minds that know thee, joy of the hearts that love thee, strength of the wills that serve thee; grant us so to know thee that we may truly love thee and thus to love thee so that we may truly serve thee, through Jesus Christ, our Lord, who is thy love in deed. Amen.

Introduction

On his return to the chapel of Duke University for the Founders' Day celebration on December 8, 1967, Albert Outler jumped into the task at hand, remembering the founders of Duke in a meaningful and respectful manner. Referring to Jesus' aphorism, "To whom much is given, from him shall much be required" (Luke 12:48), he said, "And who will further deny that it was one of the ordering principles of those forebears whom we rejoice to honor here today." The tendency was to say to them, "And so, what have you done for me lately?" Expressing this feeling he said, "What, then, can Founders' Day mean in such a climate, when it is also true that what our founders did for us is so plainly insufficient that we have to keep on building and rebuilding and developing and planning." Then he dropped this challenge: "We are as responsible for making the utmost of our unmerited gifts as they did with theirs." Later in his sermon he said, "The enduring significance of a man's life lies in what he does with his abundance, whatever that is." He added, "What a man does with what he does not really need for mere survival defines his true humanity and writes his real epitaph."

Those who knew Albert Outler sometimes wondered if he had not been too careful in shedding any surplus that might come his way. He wore that same gray/black slip-on sweater for years; his old car, "George," very nearly bounced him into pain. But at the sight of a prize volume in a back-alley, dusty, old book store in London he was willing to plunk down a $100 bill, or maybe even more if the book were published by Wesley. But then that was not splurging. That was an investment through his scholarship for others. That is his real epitaph.

SERMON 21

And So What Have You Done for Me Lately?

There was no resisting Chaplain Wilkinson's invitation to return to Duke University for this Founders' Day celebration, not merely because of the great honor of such an assignment, but much more because of the vivid, warm memories I have of the best seven years of my life invested in this place, away back when. I first came to Duke in 1938, the year of the Centennial, and I still remember being bemused by the paradox of a school so obviously new, having a hundred years of history behind it. I have a host of other memories, too—of President Few (so gentle and modest that it was never clear just how he brought it all off); of Shelton Smith and Harvie Branscomb (who continued my theological education after the Yale faculty had cried quits); of an unbeaten, untied football season; of the mustering service in this chapel on the day after Pearl Harbor, 26 years ago today.

I have, however, come to the age when reminiscing gets out of hand all too easily and I must forego its selfish pleasures. It is enough if you can realize that all those cherished experiences help me to feel very much at home on this campus, a living relic of a part of that past we are gathered to commemorate.

Over the years, whenever I have thought of the men and women who are enrolled as the "Founders" of this university, two Scripture passages come readily to mind and say essentially the same thing. One is Jesus' parable about the so-called "talents" (Matthew 25:14-30)—about two men who made the most of what they were given and one who goofed off and then excused himself with a brave show of self-righteousness. The other passage is Luke 12:48—this one not a parable but an aphorism: "To whom much is given, from him much shall be required."

Here is an obviously square, uptight moral maxim—God's rightful expectation of us is that we put our human freedom to reconstructive use. Moreover, this maxim comes from the mouth of Jesus; he evidently took it seriously. The notion that a man's life may be measured by his response to his opportunities sounds dreadfully moralistic, but who will deny that Jesus understood it as integral to a fully human style of life. And who will further deny that it was one of the ordering principles of those forebears whom we rejoice to honor here today.

And yet it strikes a discord in our modern ears, and this is itself a clue to the climate of our age. These are the days of the NOW generation (there is a soft drink that makes a pitch about its "NOW taste" and a new university that advertises itself as "the NOW university"). The past goes unremembered and the future is dreaded. Change is the only constant in the relentless flux of continuing social revolution. Mutations come so fast we cannot assimilate them and so slowly that the discontented go unsatisfied. Ours is an epoch that mingles idealism and outrage, when disintegrating value systems pose dangers as dire as the specter of disintegrating atoms.

All this has been given trenchant commentary by Eric Hoffer, our wonderful modern Montaigne. It is in his book *The Temper of Our Times* that "the presence of a global population of juveniles [his irreverent term for young folks] spells trouble for everybody. No country is a good country for its juveniles . . . even in normal times every society is in the grip of a crisis when a new generation passes from boyhood to manhood."[1] But ours are not normal times. Our "social chemistry has gone awry; no matter what ingredients are placed in the retort, the end product is more often than not an explosive. . . . The chief trait which characterizes the temper of our time is impatience. Tomorrow has become a dirty word. The future is now, and hope has turned into desire. The adolescent cannot see why he should wait to become a man before he has a say in the ordering of domestic and foreign affairs." He is "panting to . . . act as a pathfinder in the van of mankind . . . Rudeness has become a substitute for power, for faith, and for achievement."[2]

One of the obvious side effects of such a mood is that, in it, the past is readily dismissed, by common consent, as more of an incubus than a blessing. "The Past is Prologue"—so runs the motto on the portal of our National Archives (with a nod to Shakespeare's *Tempest*)—but most of my young friends feel strongly that their prologue was a flawed affair, which they would rather shed than celebrate. God knows, they say, the world we have had foisted on us is in a pluperfect mess (or stronger words to the same effect). It is so grimly unsatisfactory that many are trying to opt out of it. Others turn to destructive protest, fiercely self-righteous. There are those who really do believe that they can "grasp the sorry scheme of things entire, shatter it to bits and then remold it—nearer to their hearts' desire."[3] And so they turn away from their past in conscientious ingratitude. They know that they are heirs of a legacy once called great, but they scorn to be beholden to it. They are like the wheeler-dealer in the old wheeze, who came to foreclose on an old family friend. The victim's plea for mercy was a recital of what he had done for his tormentor in times past: given him his first job, introduced him to his wife, bailed him out of bankruptcy, etc., etc. At the end, the entrepreneur brushed it all aside with a scornful question: "And so, what have you done for me lately?"

What, then, can Founders' Day mean in such a climate, when it is also true that what our founders did for us is so plainly insufficient that we have to keep on building and rebuilding and developing and planning—when, for example, the financial goal of your Fifth Decade Program is nearly thrice the sum of your original endowment? What word is there from this particular past that remains worth hearing in the present and for the future? This much at least, in the spirit of our parable: that we are as responsible for making the utmost of our unmerited gifts as they did with theirs. This may sound trite but to accept and affirm it is the purest honor in our power to offer to their memory today.

I am as willing as Antony was to bury the past and not to praise it, but not without a word of witness about its achievements and their present import. As an emerited member of more successive "Now Generations" than I care to remember, I claim the right to call attention to those convictions and passions that fueled and guided our forefathers—not merely in their praise, but in solemn testimony that their best convictions and passions are still urgently relevant for us, here and now. The founders that I knew, or knew about, didn't spend a great deal of time looking back, either—only enough to gain and keep perspective—but what they would ask of us is that we review the past for its insights, that we plot the future with hopeful plans for real action.

In such a testimony, my first point is that history has a striking way of confounding contemporary judgments as to who the real swingers and the real squares really are. Frederic Morton has spoken recently of the current *nouveau avant*, the frenzied and failing struggle of "moderns" to keep pace with modernity, to stay "in," to make the changing scene. Naturally enough it's more than flesh and blood can manage, hence the desperate recourse to drugs and herd behavior in lieu of self-reliance. And then there was the pathetic story in the *Times* two weeks ago of how ex-professor Timothy Leary has now become the ex-guru of the League for Spiritual Discovery. I've no quarrel with the League's message that "you are free to do your own thing," but it is always fair to ask if a given "thing" is a real doing or a disastrous self-deception. And it comes to mind that the now bedraggled motto, "Tune in, turn on, drop out," is a fairly close paraphrase of the alibi of the "unprofitable servant" in our parable: "I took your money, wrapped it in a sock, and left it be while I went about my tripping. See here it is!"

For all their faults and shortcomings, our founders saw life with clearer eyes than this. They were, for the most part, compulsive types who were enchanted by goals and dreams that seemed unreal to most of their contemporaries. They sometimes drove themselves and others to tasks that we might wish had been conceived in other terms. They were nonconformists, but in a different style than nowadays— when nonconformity has to run in packs and wear uniforms in order to sustain itself.

It is not that they were heroes or saints nor that they ever saw the fullness of their dreams come true. The men who led the way from the Union Institute to Trinity College to Duke University were constantly engaged in an unequal struggle between need and resources, with inadequate support, in a climate where the correlation of *eruditio et religio* was suspect by the pious, as indeed it still is, though now for quite opposite reasons, by the non-pious! When I came to Duke in '38, it could still be said that the buildings were more imposing than the academic community that dwelt therein. And yet it was that first century, and most especially its last two decades, that created the exciting and demanding future that lies beyond you now. You are heirs not only of a tradition of great philanthropy but of a lifestyle, a gospel of opportunity and duty that is still more relevant and valid than most of its alternatives.

Its gist was this: that this enduring significance of a man's life lies in what he does with his abundance, whatever that is. It is, I take it, a truism that human culture in all its higher reaches is the product of the use or abuse of surplus accumulations of various sorts in a given population—food, wealth, invention, creative intelligence, etc. When human energy is absorbed in the prime necessities of self-maintenance, only a meager margin is left for being really and fully human. On the other hand, when there is ample food and shelter and fun and games, but no passion to surpass, society stagnates and calcifies. It is with surpluses and the concern for their creative use that the agony of culture begins—and it is an agony. For the "haves" can oppress the "have-nots" and the wise and good can create those values that mark off civilization from savagery. What a man does with what he does not really need for mere survival defines his true humanity and writes his real epitaph.

In amassing and managing one of the great American fortunes, the Dukes and their associates were conspicuous for both their energy and enterprise and yet also for their humane concern and their effective generosity. There are not many comparable cases to match the results they achieved, relative to their means and potential, in American education and in their contributions to church and society. They were children of their age, and their clay feet were baldly exposed. But they were creative men: visionaries, architects, builders. They were disciplined men, desiring to be judged by results and not merely by good intentions. They were men of character and a code—self-accepted, self-administered, self-assessed. Their kind has been shrewdly analyzed by Leon Harris in his superb recent biography of a kindred soul in this same tribe—Godfrey Lowell Cabot.

> He was a hero not in the Greek sense, but in the only sense in which we have heroes left: a man who performs over and above his duty by normal standards, who marches to his own drums and is willing to take risks in doing so; who is dedicated, in the literal sense of self-placement without stint; not driven to a position but self-given and whose life is ordered by such presently unfashionable words as duty, probity, integrity and character.[4]

But surplus money, even in quantity and without strings, cannot build a university without yet another surplus fruitfully managed: leisure time. Too many of us have forgotten, or never knew, that the Greek original for our word scholar, *schole*, means "leisure time" or, by extension, "a man with time to think and the disposition to do so." Your predecessors here-—faculty and students-—had far less leisure than they needed or than would now be thought minimal for academic excellence. My first teaching load was twice what would be normal now. Moreover, our amassed capital from the leisure of other men—which, being interpreted, is the library—was still comparatively meager, even in my time. The status of eggheads in the environing society of this region was only barely respectable, and their influence in practical affairs was negligible. Yet it was these men and women who rooted the scholarly tradition here, who cultivated the arts and sciences of critical inquiry and taught others to do so, who blazed a trail that has not yet been followed to its end.

And so the story goes—of men who wrought well with their abundances and who have earned the right to ask us how well we are doing, or propose to do, with ours. It is just here that our salute to the founders become an arresting challenge to our own self-examination and self-dedication. For there never was a generation so immersed in abundance as our own. There is, indeed, a sort of surfeit of it—as the flower children are trying to tell us in their garish ways. And, as all the prophets prophesy, there will be more leisure and more gadgets and more affluence. There will be more people with more time and at least the technical means to manage larger surpluses more creatively than ever before since Eden.

Yet we already know, and the knowledge strikes panic in our hearts, that our equivalents of the achievements and contributions of our forebears will demand of us a discipline and dedication—of heart and mind and will—that we are loathe to impose upon ourselves and that cannot be imposed on us by others. It is closed to us to replicate the feats and the failures of the founders. It is, however, open to us to receive from them our heritage, gratefully to renew its imperatives of *noblesse oblige* in our own time and circumstances, to stretch out our vision of NOW to include our duty to the future, to make the most of change and not merely to endure its happenings. There is the challenge of poverty in an affluent society; there is the challenge of human equality and harmony in a morbidly race-conscious society; there is the challenge of license and violence in a free and ordered society; there is the anguished hope of peace in a war-torn world, haunted by the terrors or incineration and irradiation. But, most of all, there is the challenge of being truly human ourselves, of finding the wisdom and the will to distinguish license from liberty, outrage from moral indignation, tantrums from significant witness and real results.

It will not do to plead the enormity of the issues and tasks before us. By any fair comparison, our forebears underwent as much as ever we must face. And if they bequeathed us a world in agony, let us beware lest we insure that the agony will never end—or else end in some final flash of meaningless destruction. They were men who hated to lose on their investments. *We* are their *chief* investments and they would happily forego all our eulogies of them in exchange for evidence that we had caught something of their spirit and faith.

And thus we come at last to the heart of the matter. The vision of the good society is fatally blurred by men who suppose that it is no more than a human task, a human achievement. "The secular city" is finally unfit for human habitation without the reconciling forces of love and hope and faith. The parable of the talents makes sense only in the context of the kingdom of God, the righteous rule of God in the hearts and lives of men. Humanity will never experience the fruition of its hopes and expectations apart from the acknowledged lordship of Jesus Christ, the man who makes our manhood actual and real, through God's sovereign love incarnate in him.

It was no mere whim of Mr. Duke's that placed this chapel in the center of the campus, and it has been no accident that its influence in this community, both symbolic and actual, has made an enormous difference in the life of this university and the region—which can be measured merely by imagining how it would be here now if there had never been such a symbol of *religio* here to match the omnipresent tokens of *eruditio*.

Founders' Day is a day for remembrance, for reverence, for gratitude, for renewed perspective. It is also a day of resolution and dedication. "It is for us, the living". . . and all that! This, then, is no mere ritual episode, no merely routine ceremonial. For on our response, to what is here remembered and portended, hangs the verity of our faith and the sincerity of our confessions that (as we shall hear again, in a moment in the Hallelujah Chorus) the Lord God omnipotent does, indeed, reign and shall reign, forever and forever.

Let us Pray:

> Almighty God, who has given us a goodly heritage beyond our deserving and has set us to tasks and goals beyond our powers of full achievement, forgive us our failures of nerve, hope and vision. Strengthen our hearts and wills to make the utmost of our futures—in faith and love—and so enable us honestly to honor the memory and the purposes of those we gratefully name as our founders in this place. Let our heritage from the past inspire us, let the good in the present give us courage, let the challenge of the future beckon us, through the grace and love leading of Jesus Christ our Lord and Savior. Amen.

Introduction

Albert Outler preached this memorial sermon in the Perkins Chapel on the campus of Southern Methodist University, 10:00 a.m., June 24, 1974. His opening sentence lifted up the three reasons for the occasion and went on to elaborate their significances. They were ". . . to celebrate a young life, to moum an untimely death, and to witness to our faith that in life and death and in life beyond death we are neither alone nor bereft."

When Outler's secretary, Wanda Smith, lost her son Lanny in an accidental electrocution, she was obliterated. She felt her faith was not strong enough to carry her through the grief. But Dr. Outler helped her to see that what she had been typing for him all along was really true, that she was in God's keeping no matter what happens, from the worst imaginable to the best imaginable. Outler witnessed to her the stark truth that "the joy [Lanny] gave his mother and the love she gave him . . . was a sign and sample of authentic grace, a human expression of God's grace, joy, and peace. . . ."

Wanda Smith knew that the Holy Spirit was the Comforter, but she also knew whom in her life the Holy Spirit used to get that message across to her.

SERMON 22

Landgrave Willard Smith Memorial Service

Dearly Beloved, we're gathered here this morning to celebrate a young life, to mourn an untimely death, and to witness to our faith that in life and death and in life beyond death we are neither alone nor bereft. We are God's children; his grace and mercy are always with us, even in grief, even when we cannot see the way ahead and cannot feel the full assurance of that grace and mercy.

We're here to grapple with the mystery of a stark and stunning tragedy. No easy words soften our grief; no glib phrases wipe away our tears. Here we are, up against an acid test of our Christian faith, our deathless hope in Christ, our obedient commitments to God's overarching providence, our professed willingness to live and to die in the sustaining power of his love.

What is called for now is not so much an explanation as an opening of our hearts to God's holy, healing Spirit. Not speculation so much as the inner witness of his love. Not resignation so much as a willing obedience to accept our loss and to weave it into the fabric of life as we go on our own several pilgrimages toward that heavenly home to which Lanny has preceded us.

Our hearts are wounded and thus we're driven to seek out

the final ground on which we stand, by which we live . . . the faith by which we face the actualities of life and death, Lanny's and our own. Which is to say: the bedrock certainty that the eternal God is our refuge and also Lanny's, and that underneath our sorrows and weakness are the everlasting arms of God's healing and enabling grace. Lanny's life was short; his death untimely. And it already has and will always have real and lasting significance and meaning. Each of you who knew him will have your own special memories to cherish, your own share in that special sort of happiness that he knew and that he shared so generously with all around him. For my own part, what stands out most clearly over the past decade was the joy he gave his mother and the love she gave him. This to me was a sign and sample of authentic grace, a human expression of God's grace, joy, and peace shed abroad in our hearts by the Holy Spirit. Joy and love, given and received—is there anything more real, anything more precious, anything more truly eternal in all our lives?

And in a moment like this we also know as we may always have known in a way, but never quite so poignantly, that life is not a possession but a gift—not to be clutched at but to be cherished—yet also offered up. Not to be hoarded nor to be thrown away, but to be put to its best use in gratitude and dedication. Death is the proof that we are not our own, that we are bought with a price, that in the midst of life we are always on death's threshold, which opens into that true fullness of life that is God's gracious provision for those who love him and seek to do his will.

But blessed be God; death's harsh word is not life's final word. God is not remote from nor indifferent to our sufferings. Rather, he is truly Emmanuel—God with us. This is the meaning of his gift of his own Son to us, to all mankind. His Son, who came not to be ministered unto but to minister, and to give his life as a loving offertory for others. And even in that life with us he shared our griefs; he bore our sorrows as his own. Thus it was that he became and forever is our High Priest, as the epistle to the Hebrews tells us. Not one who was unable to sympathize with our weaknesses, but one who has been tested by death's challenge to faith and hope. And this is why in this particular hour of need—in the hours that will follow this one—we can always approach the throne of the heavenly grace, confident of God's help and caring love.

And so we mourn, but not as those disconsolate without faith or hope or love. Lanny's life was a lovely, precious gift to all of us, to each of us in different ways, and it is our part now to cherish what he meant to us and will continue to mean even as we resign his life with us to a happier life with his heavenly Father. The weight of our grief comes from our fear that death somehow writes life's final word. The lifting, healing power of faith comes from an assurance that God's grace continues to write out the full and final chapter of our lives and our lives beyond our death. This was the faith of the prophet Isaiah and of the apostle Paul. Death is swallowed up in victory. It shall have no more dominion. And if this be so, then God be praised who giveth us the victory over death's dominion even now, in the time of our lives, through Jesus Christ our Lord and Savior.

There's a practical conclusion that St. Paul adds to this triumphal of faith: "Therefore beloved, let us, ourselves, stand steadfast and firm, always abounding in the work of the Lord, for as much as we know that none of our labors in the Lord is ever actually in vain." Herein stands our peace and joy and gladness. And so today, but not just for today, we celebrate Lanny's life. Loving and lovely as it was; joyous and joy-giving as it was. We mourn his death, yet not in despair or bitterness, as we reaffirm our faith and hope and love that outlasts the changes and chances of this mortal life. We also rededicate ourselves to all the works of love and mercy that can translate faith and hope and love into gracious living and serenity. "For all the saints, young and old, who from their labors rest, thy name, O Jesus, be forever blest." Hallelujah. Let us pray.

> Almighty God, the fountain of all life, who art our refuge and strength in times of trouble and need, enable us, we pray, to put our trust in thee and thee alone, that we may find comfort and healing and peace through Christ our Lord.
>
> O heavenly Father, Father of all spirits, we thank thee more especially at this time for one life that thou gavest us as gift and blessing. We thank thee for all

our happy memories and all our living hope; for the sacred ties that bind us to the unseen world; for the dear and holy dead who encompass us as a cloud of witnesses and make a heaven, a home for our hearts even now. In this fellowship and communion help us to learn to live and work and hope, through Christ our Lord.

Almighty God, who art leading us through the changes of time to the peace and joy of eternity, be near to comfort and uphold us now; help us to realize how precious in thy sight are all thy children, that they live with thee evermore, that thy mercy endureth forever. We are grateful for the life of Lanny Smith that thou hast given us for a season, and we pray thy help in offering it back to thee in obedient faith. Assist us now to return to the scenes and tasks of our daily lives; to bear our griefs and trials with patience, courage, and hope. And when our summons comes may we be found faithful and may we, too, find our peace and joy with thee forever, through Jesus Christ our Lord. Amen

Benediction:

The peace of God which passeth all understanding keep your hearts and minds in the knowledge and the love of God and of his Son, Jesus Christ. And the blessings of God the Father, the Son, and the Holy Spirit be with each of you and remain with you all always. Amen.

Introduction

On Tuesday afternoon, June 1, 1976, Albert Outler preached this Memorial Sermon at the North Texas Annual Conference. He explained what is meant by the word "saints." That obviously put the audience at ease, and helped them be more like the saints they were (a term they normally consigned to somebody "worthy". Then he expressed a deeply personal emotion. E.g., he said, "Such an act of remembrance of this particular group of cherished comrades in the faith has greater significance for me this year than ever. I knew them all and some of them very well. It also means that death strikes closer and closer home, to each of us, with every passing comrade-in-Christ." Then he witnessed to himself and the congregation when he described how with active endurance (patience) you run the race *with* the cloud of witnesses (the saints). And concluded with three challenges: ". . . let us go with a renewed consciousness . . . of accrued wisdom, that we might learn from those who have gone before us"; ". . . go hand in hand in a renewed sense of fellowship"; and ". . . go in a corporate act of praise for what has been and what is yet to be."

The striking thing about this message is that he delivered it with the sense that he was receiving it. Those with him when his sister Frances died in February 1984, said that "he took it hard." He had lost his tutor—he was her protégé—and he mourned. And should. But his grief was not disconsolate. He mourned his losing and rejoiced in happy memories of her life and work and her fellowship with him in days gone by . . . a further sign that he listened well to what this sermon had to say for him in any time and place.

SERMON 23

For All the Saints—Including Us

The concluding clause in the Apostles' Creed sounds like a laundry list of miscellaneous items of Christian belief strung together: "the Holy Spirit, the holy catholic church, the communion of saints, the forgiveness of sins, the resurrection of the body and the life everlasting. Amen." As a matter of fact, however, these tremendous phrases grew up with the creed in the course of a couple of centuries as implications of the church's faith in the Holy Spirit and their experience of his work in their midst.

The earliest version of this creed (135-140?) ended with a bafflingly simple affirmation: "I believe in the Holy Spirit." Period. This helps us to understand how the early church took for granted that the All-Governing Father was the source of human creation and redemption, that the Lord Jesus was the agent of that redemption, but that the Holy Spirit was God at work in human hearts and human history, garnering in the harvest of redemption.

But what does it mean to believe in "God at work in human hearts and human history"? Well, this much at least: That our life in and by the power of the Holy Spirit is a life together in a holy, universal, sacral community, whose most distinctive feature is its being a communion of saints (thankfully remembered saints and thankfully acknowledged saints); further, that this fellowship in the Spirit includes the special experience of "the forgiveness of sins" (God's forgiveness of our sins against him, without merit, and our forgiveness of those who offend us without our seeking revenge or compensation); finally that this community of saints lives by its hopes of the resurrection and of life everlasting, rooted in Christ's triumph already achieved and in the church's organic relationship with him—i.e., as his body, which means that we are truly "members one of another."

Christians, as Christians, do nothing alone or in protracted privacy. "Christianity," said Wesley, "is not a solitary religion" and he might have added that it is not a religion for solitaries. Withdrawals for rest, for study, for prayer, for renewal—yes—but only by way of preparation for a richer life together, for communal worship, remembrance, resolution, action. All Christian action is "social action"— either in preparation or in performance.

The oddest sounding phrase in this sad paragraph, to many, is that one about "the communion of saints." For we tend to suppose that this must refer to a smallish, select company, a class with few members, and clearly not including us! Who, me, a saint? You've got to be kidding! And, in some cases maybe I am! Actually, however, this is a sad commentary on the way we've spoiled a great New Testament term, a great Wesleyan term. The saints with whom we are in communion are not the guys and gals with halos (intolerably sweet and good). They are all those faithful people, living and dead, whose main intention was and is to love God above all else and all else in God's Spirit.

Not to be a saint, therefore, is not just to be imperfect (or to be "human," as we like to say, in one of our favorite moral copouts). It is, rather, intentionally to love something other than God (to love ourselves or to love some other creature, i.e., some idol) more than we love God, and to love that other in terms of our own self-interest. The choice is startlingly stark: Are you a saint (by intention and aspiration) or are you an idolater? You *pays* your money and you *takes* your choice, even if it makes you uneasy to profess that you or your standard-brand acquaintances are "saints" or would want to be called "saints." But that's what "saints" means in the phrase "the communion of saints."

And there's something more there, too. The communion of such saints includes the living and the dead—those who have died in the Lord, who have rested from their labors, but whose works still follow them, and those who are still striving on toward God's high calling and glorious hope in Christ Jesus our Lord. Christianity is the most extended family in all God's creation. We belong to all those who have lived and died in sure and certain faith; we belong to that encompassing great cloud of witnesses before whom we run our race, fight our good fight, keep the faith—or betray it. And they belong to us. They are our heritage; we are their hope. And it falls to us to demonstrate that their lives and labors were not in vain. This is the church catholic: this immense host of Christians who have lived and died in communion (shared faith, hope, and love) and all those, of every race, nation, sex, and mind-set around the globe today who still live in Christian community.

This, to me, is an inspiring vision: this grand succession back through the generations, to Pentecost; this immense outreach of Christian fellowship around the world and back again.

But it is also too big, too vague—like trying to pick out friendly faces in the stands of a crowded stadium. And so, the communion of saints has also a human-scale dimension: memories of "our own saints," those men and women whom we ourselves have known and loved and lost awhile. And it is our continuing fellowship with our fellow saints in our own time and provenance.

This is what any proper memorial service is all about. We are here assembled to gather into one time and ceremony all our scattered thoughts and griefs and gratitudes; all our thanksgivings and praise to God for these particular people of our own company and friendship who have crossed over the divide from faith to sight, from hope to fulfillment in the years since our last Conference session. It is a small sampling from a much larger one, but it is our sampling. Since God has given us the blessing of these particular ties of friendship, love, marriage, family, and the bonds of common memories of good and faithful servants in the Christian ministry, we praised his name and give him thanks.

Such an act of remembrance of this particular group of cherished comrades in the faith has greater significance for me this year than ever. I knew them all and some of them very well. It also means that death strikes closer and closer home, to each of us, with every passing comrade-in-Christ.

And so we mourn their passing—and we do well to mourn. Christians are not Stoics and the notion that our griefs should be suppressed (as if inappropriate) is more Stoic than Christian. What is Christian, however, is that our grief is not, and never need be, disconsolate. We mourn and we rejoice. We mourn our losing; we rejoice in a host of happy memories of their lives and work and their fellowship with us in days gone by.

Each of us has his or her own memories to cherish: some not much more than casual, some informal and episodic, some intimate and rich. But there is one common note in all our memories: These were dedicated people. They had heard and answered a call that led them outside and beyond themselves—into lives of witness and service, in the ministries of Christ's church and in his name. Now they have joined that "cloud of witnesses" in that crowded stadium of "all the saints who from their labors rest"; they have become our heritage; they have left us as their heirs. And for this we are truly grateful to God; for this we are all richer in our lives. For each one of them we give thanks and praise, and, what is equally important and appropriate, we rededicate ourselves to our high calling in the ongoing communion of saints here on earth—those whose love of God is the true love of their lives.

For the main point to that metaphor in Hebrews 12:1-2 is that since we are surrounded by this great crowd of witnesses (who are not just spectators, but participants), it is our part to run life's race as it is set before us with undiminished zeal and with even greater patience—looking unto Jesus and his example in this same race, with even starker trials and suffering.

It's easy to be misled by that word "patience," for in our common usage it comes closer to some notion of passive endurance than it ever did in the original Greek (or Latin). There, and especially in this text in Hebrews, it means active endurance: That we should run life's race—and run to win God's favor and praise—not just because we must, but because we are both called and driven by Christ's love and grace: called by compassion, driven by zeal. Patience, in this setting, means the willingness to "pay the price," whatever that price may be, that comes with the ordeal and adventure of Christian witness and service—to endure as well as to enjoy all that is involved in fulfilling our own Christian vocation.

This Memorial Service is, therefore, a time of honest grieving, of grateful remembrance, but also of clear-eyed rededication—a sort of "catching our second wind," as they say in cross-country racing.

> All praise to our redeeming Lord,
> Who joins us by his grace,
> And bids us, each to each restored,
> Together seek his face.
>
> The gift which he on one bestows,
> We all delight to prove,
> The grace through every vessel flows
> In purest streams of love.
>
> He bids us build each other up;
> And, gathered into one,
> To our high calling's glorious hope,
> We hand in hand go on.
>
> *Charles Wesley*

And how shall "we hand in hand go on"? Let me tick off three ways without elaborating. First, let us go with a renewed consciousness of heritage, of good example, of accrued wisdom, that we might learn from those who have gone before us.

At Portland, a shrewd sociologist, fascinated and baffled by the unwieldy and dicey procedures of the General Conference, commented to me, "There's a danger in so much inexperience so confident of its instant wisdom." The Christian church has had a lot of experience; we are the losers when we ignore it.

Second, let us go on hand in hand in a renewed sense of fellowship, of really belonging to one another, in life and death. None of us can say to any other, "I have no need of you," or, "It does not matter to me how life goes with you."

Third, let us go in a corporate act of praise for what has been and what is yet to be.

One of the truly great hymns of the church is William How's "For All the Saints Who from Their Labors Rest." It's a hymn with a backward look, not in nostalgia but gratitude. Verse 2 is a recollection of God's providence, then and now. But its attitude is forward-looking: That we may be "faithful, true and bold," that our share in that "blest communion, fellowship divine" may be worthy and fruitful; that our hearts may be brave for the conflicts ahead, our arms strengthened for the struggles ahead. And even if verse 6 sounds quaint to some ears, its note is catholic and joyful—including all whom we remember and memorialize this day—and including ourselves, and our confidence and joy in the Lord.

> From earth's wide bounds, from ocean's farthest coast,
> Through gates of pearl streams in the countless host,
> Singing to the Father, Son and Holy Ghost,
> Alleluia, Alleluia. Amen.

Introduction

Albert Outler did it again in this Mission Fair sermon at Nebraska Wesleyan University. He was addressing the Lincoln District of the United Methodist Church. The date was March 1, 1981. The social activists were unhappy because he did not come down on their side as any liberationist knew he ought; the tight-fisted, self-styled evangelicals (a minority in that particular audience) went away wailing, "He had his chance and missed it!" And, again, Albert Outler held on tight to his patron St. Sebastian (the saint with arrows sticking him from all sides).

Here is his non-crowd-pleasing statement: "But in this either/or process—'saving souls' or 'liberation'—what has gotten short shrift is the original impulse to, and authority for, missions: the heralding of God's kingdom and the effort to understand and live by the parabolic mysteries of the Rule of Grace . . . . If 'evangelicals' understood the real meaning of grace and of the Rule of Grace, their soteriology would not be so narrow and otherworldly. If 'liberals' understood the meaning of grace and of the Rule of Grace, they would not put so much of their hopes on secular aims and strategies."

How could Outler get by with such totally unpopular, alienating statements? Only because of who he *was*. He *was* one led by the Rule of Grace. He spoke the truth in love (definitely not self-serving) and thus gained the respect of some "enemies" from all sides, which in itself was a result of the unexplainable mysteries of the Rule of Grace.

SERMON 24

The Mission Fair

Jesus did not gather his disciples as a social club or "an encounter group" or as a representative cross-section of Palestinian society (although they were a close-knit group, interacting and representative). He gathered them in to send them out—not to promote an institution but to be witnesses to, and to be examples and heralds of, God's Kingdom.

Notice how Jesus' teachings focus on the phrase kingdom of God or kingdom of heaven. Notice his patience and care in trying to explain what God's righteous and gracious rule in human life means, is designed to mean, will mean as men and women come to understand, to respond, to live in and by the Rule of Grace, rather than the rule of self-interest, the rule of power and pomp, the rule of pride.

This is what the Sermon on the Mount is all about: it hinges on the admonition "Seek, as your first habitual priority, the Rule of Grace; and whatever power you need to get things done, whatever pomp you need for decency and order, whatever self-realization you need to find peace and joy in grace-full living—all these things will come along as the fruit of grace."

The meaning of grace and of the Rule of Grace constitute the theme of the parables, as if an undefinable reality were being pointed to in so many different ways that you finally begin to understand and respond in ways that are different from definition and moralistic self-direction.

Jesus did not collect a group of men and label them disciples. He enlisted them as comrades in his mission: to herald and usher in the kingdom, the Rule of Grace, as the essence of God's design for his human family.

The Gospels and the rest of the New Testament tell us how difficult it was for men and women to understand what it would mean to live in and by the Rule of Grace, instead of the rule of law, or of power, or of pride. And the yo-yo history of Christianity is the mixed-up, glorious, tragic story—impressive in some ways, depressing in others—of men and women affirming and professing the validity of the Rule of race, even as they were trying to hang on to as much of the rule of pride and self-esteem as they could.

"The kingdom of God" sounds like a political phrase and is easily supposed to be the rule of God's power over men and women, in place of the power over men and women exercised by political figures like kings, presidents, IRS agents, police, etc. And so we have tried to politicize the church, as well as everything else in life, since politics is the art and process of harmonizing a given number of self-serving persons in a given *polis* or *civitas* or community. The Rule of Grace is different, and it gives us all kinds of trouble in trying to respond to it as a radical alternative.

Jesus left his disciples (and us) with a cosmic extension of their original mission in Palestine: all the world, discipling all *ethnoi*, and initiating them into the alternative *civitas* in which humans may live, the *civitas Dei*, the Rule of Grace, the community of grace. The Great Commandment, the extension of Jesus' mission into history, from then till now and "to the end of the age."

But what is grace? It is love of a special sort. Where most loves reach out to gather in, grace reaches out to give, to share, to enhance. Grace is unmerited love, more concerned with the well-being of the beloved than of the loving one. It is, to use an awkward phrase, other-oriented rather than self-serving or self-centered. It is respect for and interest in the other(s). It is the sharing of gifts with less thought of return or reward than of hope and expectation that the other(s) will be blessed or fulfilled or enhanced.

Something like this has been at the heart of "the expansion of Christianity" through the centuries. It is an ambivalent story of great faith and egregious blunders, of heroism and timid compromise with the world, great visions and appalling blind spots, e.g., the Crusades; the nineteenth century and its evangelism of the world—and the ambivalent consequences.

Even so, the survival of Christianity through the ages is an impressive one but authentic always and only to the extent that it retained its sense of MISSION, and to the extent that it remembered that the essence of mission is the GIFT OF GRACE, the outreach and ingathering of grace, the promotion and support of the RULE OF GRACE in the hearts and lives of human beings, human community, human societies, the human potential on this earth.

But two tempting alternatives have distorted the Christian community in its long course of outreach and ingathering. On the one hand, there has been the temptation to other worldliness, to grace as an escape from the frustrations, sufferings, disappointments of this life, to "heaven as our happy home," "pie in the sky by and by." Thus, more passion to save men's/women's souls than to change their material circumstances. This was the basis for the Marxist charge that "religion is an opiate for the people," which seems less true to Polish workers today than it did to Engels and Marx.

But Christianity did expand "from Greenland's icy mountains, from India's coral strand,"[1] and the missionary impulse has always been the chief agency in and behind that expansion. Even so, human hope and compassion were crucial to the expansion; the chief bar to missions among Protestants was the doctrine that it is God who works our salvation and human means and agencies are not necessary, e.g., William Carey, Thomas Coke, et al.

What happened, though, especially among Methodists (in England and later in America), was a lurch to the opposite extreme—into Pelagianism. The essence of Pelagianism is that men and women who know what is good and right and are exhorted to do the good and right they know will, as a matter of their inherent moral disposition, do the good and the right. Thus, the main concern of Christian mission came to be seen as teaching the people what was and was not good and right, and exhorting them to do it.

Stage by stage, the vision of the kingdom of God on earth was turned into a utopian vision—here "at home" and for humankind at large.

> The day of dawning brotherhood
> Breaks our eager eyes,
> And human hatreds flee before
> The radiant eastern skies.[2]

But with the new post-colonial consciousness, a new wave of guilt began to wash over Western Christians, and a new focus on missions, evangelism, Christian social action, began to take shape. We were told to be ashamed of the old-style missions, which tried to save souls and also to westernize people who were doing very well in their "native ways." Besides, there were all these "nice Christians" and all these missionaries who acted out a certain sort of "white supremacy" when they were affirming that

> In Christ there is no east or west,
> In him no south or north;
> But one great fellowship of love
> Throughout the whole wide earth.[3]

Moreover, other religions had their validity too, and they were as good for their believers as Christianity was for us. What these people really needed, and still need, is justice and liberation from oppression, poverty, and war (and hunger and disease, the miserable children of all these evils). And who can deny such needs?

So missions came, especially in our church, to be more and more associated with social "missional priorities" than with saving souls, and more and more this dreadful false disjunction came to be accepted as the choice we must make. We have "evangelicals" on the right who propose to fund and sponsor their own mission projects, and we have the mainline mission agencies that appeal to church loyalty and "connectionalism" as bulwarks against such schismatics. We have seen the specter of "selective giving" raised, and we have seen the rites of exorcism against such a demon.

Since 1976 we have had a splendid vision of missional priorities: the crusade for peace, the war on poverty and world hunger, the crusade for ethnic equality and enablement. These are Christian causes, every one of them, as are most of the missional resolutions in our *Book of Resolutions*, where most of the good causes in the world were advocated by at least a majority of the General Conference delegates in 1980 (many of them without debate and some without serious consideration by the delegates).

But in this either/or process—"saving souls" or "liberation"—what has gotten short shrift is the original impulse to, and authority for, missions: the heralding of God's kingdom and the effort to understand and live by the parabolic mysteries of the Rule of Grace. And in this process, we have lost a great deal—indeed, the heart of the matter. If "evangelicals" understood the real meaning of grace and of the Rule of Grace, their soteriology would not be so narrow and otherworldly. If "liberals" understood the meaning of grace and of the Rule of Grace, they would not pin so much of their hopes on secular aims and strategies.

I take it that what you are interested in here is not merely reacting reflexively to our Board of Global Ministries or to the evangelical schismatics either. The great cause in the United Methodist Church today is to recover and renew the original sense of mission—the heralding by word and lifestyle the kingdom of God on earth, the Rule of Grace and righteousness; the proclamation of God's unmerited gifts of pardon, reconciliation, assurance, and dedication; and the transformation of persons and societies by the means of God's gifts and fruits more than human achievements, however nobly intended!

But this means that missions is, first of all, evangelism; and that evangelism aims at social action through the saving faith that works by love; and that the Rule of Grace is global in its outreach and divine in its source, activation, and ends. This means an end to Pelagianism and all notions of self-salvation or saving others by human effort. It also means the end of any concept of missions that is content with snatching lost souls one by one from some human quagmire. It calls for an integral sense of mission to the whole person and the whole of humanity.

In the Gospel that is the most intensely missionary in its

emphasis, Jesus began his ministry by quoting a set of missional priorities from an old prophet:

> The Spirit of the Lord is upon me, because he has anointed me; he has sent me to herald the good news of grace to the poor; to proclaim release for prisoners [liberation] and recovery of sight for the blind; to let the broken victims [of sin and of human oppression] go free, to proclaim the opening future of God's special favor (Luke 4:18-19).

Today, said he, this text has come true in your very sight and hearing.

Luke goes on to comment that the people were "surprised that words of such grace should fall from his lips" (v. 22). But he spoke the words . . . words that defined both the missional priorities of the Rule of Grace for that time and for all time. For to those of us who are called into that rule and gifted by such grace, it is still our calling and sending to do whatever we can, wherever we are, to whomever our outreach can stretch, with grateful hearts for God's gracious gifts to him who has anointed us (and we have all been anointed, haven't we?):

> to have some good news to announce to the poor;
> to seek liberation for all victims of man's inhumanity to man;
> to seek healing for all who suffer—physically or spiritually,
> and to emphasize that the NOW is the beginning of a season of God's special favor.

What would some such sense of grace and dedication and participation in the rule of grace mean for us—in our lives, in our local church and ministry, in our denomination, in the Christian world, in the human community?

The ascending Lord said to the first disciples:

> Your business from now on is to be witnesses to me, where you are now, and nearby and then in widening

circles to the ends of the earth (Acts 1:8).

Do you and I have any other business, as children of his grace—even now?

Introduction

The congregation was Presbyterian (First Presbyterian Church, Dallas, Texas, April 30, 1981). The occasion: the Eighth Annual Urban Consultation. The Presbyterians "elected" Albert Outler to bring the following Wesleyan interpretation (prevenient grace) of the New Testament book of Hebrews: "But if we have no abiding city hereabouts, as Hebrews told us long ago, we do have an abiding altar. It is a movable altar; it does not require a permanent locus within any particular holy city. It is the altar of sacrifice—of Jesus' sacrifice (and ours)."

The Presbyterians listened attentively to Outler's presentation of Wesley's prevenient grace, a grace without a tinge of favoritism for any, without anyone deserving it, without a predetermination of good for some and bad for others. But a grace that is in itself predetermined by the very nature of God's Being. God cannot help but be loving because that is who he is. Thus grace is there before you arrive, stays with you, and remains in the memorable events of redemption.

The Presbyterians continued to invite Albert Outler back to preach. The "predestined" sermon they heard on grace had been preached there before. Each time Albert Outler got there, he reminded them that grace was there before he arrived, before the church was born, or even the world created.

Maybe if ecumaniacs would talk more about grace and less about structure we could have a church united. We seem to be united in wanting to hear that good news— and were united when Albert Outler had something to say about it.

SERMON 25

No Abiding City

It is an honor and pleasure to be with you here tonight in this Eighth Annual Urban Consultation, however strange it may seem to some for a Methodist to be talking to Presbyterians or for a theologian to be invited to be talking to practical churchfolk. My presence here is at the behest of John Anderson, a cherished friend and longtime stalwart leader, not only here in Dallas but also in the farther reaches of the Lord's several vineyards.

When he called to say that he thought I could be of some service to you in your gathering, there was no use pleading that I am no authority on urban problems (actually, I am rather more like a victim of them). Nor was there any use pleading that I am only a professor (an emerited professor at that); or that I have no inner leading nor outward authority to lay any godly admonitions upon a gathering of Presbyterians! John's answer was merely that I had been elected to the task. And as it turned out, so I was, since my affection for and indebtedness to him, made this particular initiative of grace (if that is what it proves to be) irresistible!

The rest of you will have to judge how valid an instance this is of your doctrine of election or of irresistible grace. In any case, you must not judge John too harshly. His ministry in this church stands in the eyes of many of us hereabouts as exemplary of what you will be reflecting upon in your discussions of Christian ministries in an urban setting.

It has been a long-time impression that one can at least get off to a safe start with Presbyterians if one begins with a biblical text. Wherefore, to be doubly safe, I have chosen two of them, both from that wonderful but strange little essay, so arbitrarily attached to the Pauline corpus by the canon makers: the so-called "Epistle of Paul to the Hebrews" (an apt enough entitlement if one remembers that it is not an epistle, nor by Paul, nor to the "Hebrews"). But the canon makers had a very good reason for placing this early Christian reflection on the person and work of Jesus Christ exactly where it now stands, since it rounds off the Pauline center section of the New Testament with a fresh reminder of the centrality of the historic Jesus, as over against the Pauline stress on "the Christ of faith" and the contrasting stress in the Pastoral Epistles on the church as institution. My very distinguished friend, Samuel Sandmel, used to speak of Hebrews as "the fifth gospel" and I think he had a useful point.

In the epilogue to this essay in soteriology (13:1-16), there is a tricky and obscure passage reflecting both the conflicts and the emerging stabilities of second generation Christianity. It begins with an exhortation to *philadelphia* (brotherly and sisterly love), and goes on to a real identification of Christians with the unliberated and oppressed (as distinguished from having endless conferences about "them"). There is a fine Puritan word in favor of the undefiled marriage bed; another Puritan word against the love of money, together with an assurance of God's sustaining grace in all the dangers of this life (in a time when Christian existence was actually dangerous). There is even a ringing Christological slogan, struck off in mid-paragraph without a proper syntactical connection—"Jesus Christ the same, yesterday, today and forever" (v. 8). This is followed by a stern warning against strange (or new) doctrines (which must have an odd sound in our modern ears, since doctrines seem more interesting nowadays if they do sound "strange" than if they sound old-fashioned and familiar).

Finally (v. 15-16), there is that crucial and obscure analysis of the difference between the older sacrificial system in Judaism and a new meaning and function for the idea of sacrifice among Christians. "We Christians have an altar" (Jesus' atonement) (v.10), but it has no physical locus in the Holy City. Here (in Jerusalem) we have no abiding city (*ou . . . menousan polin*); we are still seeking one that lies somewhere out there down the road ahead. *Ad interim,* however, we must fully involve ourselves in our sharing in Jesus' mission, viz., in the unbloody sacrifice of praises to God, the sacrifice of good works and the sacrifice of active participation in the ongoing mission of the church in the world. "For with sacrifices like these God is well-pleased." This, of course, is an updating of an old theme: as in Micah 6:6-8 ("What shall I bring when I approach the Lord") and in Psalm 51:17 ("A broken and a contrite heart, O God, thou wilt not despise").

Notice the various notes of sadness, defiance, and hope here. Obviously, the destruction of the Holy City (in 70 A.D.) was still a horrifying (maybe even a recent) memory. And with Jerusalem in ruins, there was no alternative prospect of the Christians ever having a more abiding city (not Rome nor Geneva nor even Atlanta or Nashville). Remember, an early end of history was still imminent in Christian expectations, but the time was drawing on when Christians (Hellenistic Christians at that) would simply have to haul down their hopes of a quick ending of the world's business, and would have to accommodate themselves to the far more difficult tasks of living in a history that would go on and on unconscionably—a history that would be all the more wearing because all their earlier hopes for a final solution to the church's problems were fading. Even we, nineteen hundred years later, are still searching for that imminent, final solution. If we knew, given so and so or this and that, that all our problems of man's inhumanity to man would soon be solved, most of us could undertake a lot more and endure a lot more than we can now, given our present uncertainties. By now we know that there are no final solutions to the troubles of the world, and so there is less comfort for us than was intended in these old words: "Here we have no abiding city" (v. 14). Our business as Christians is to keep on seeking one. Especially for the liberated (and Pelagians) amongst us who have a whiff of "pie in the sky bye and bye."

Any careful reader of Hebrews would already have linked our text with an earlier one, 11:9-10: "By faith, Abraham sojourned in a land of promise as an outsider [*allotrian*] . . . because he was on the lookout [on the prowl] for a *polis* with foundations, foundations girt by God"—viz., a human habitation that would be permanent and truly human and humane.

But the fact is that Abraham was a sojourner, and all his sons and daughters are still sojourning in a world in which there is no resting place for long. The history of such sojourners is long, uneven, and often tedious. We have here no abiding city (and never have had), but still we continue in our quest, generation after generation—always to be blessed with the sight of that heavenly city glittering on some horizon. "Thine alabaster cities gleam. Undimmed by human tears."[1] (How long have we been singing that sort of thing in our pilgrimage, through smog and hydrocarbons and worse?)

But if we have no abiding city hereabouts, as Hebrews told us long ago, we do have an abiding altar. It is a movable altar; it does not require a permanent locus within any particular holy city. It is the altar of sacrifice—of Jesus' sacrifice (and ours)—an altar of celebration of the forgiveness of sins, an altar of service to the victims of sin and of inhumanity, an altar on which our good works, our participations in the grace of Christ, are offered up as sacrifices, well-pleasing to God.

There are, therefore, at least two things that we modern Christians have to learn from this second-generation Christian who wrote Hebrews. The first is that urban renewal (as then understood or even as we think we understand it) may be a good work and still prove no final solution in the Christian quest for "that city whose foundations are designed and sustained by God" (Hebrews 11:10).

This is a hard saying for our utopians to swallow—the visionaries of Acrosanti, of New Harmony, of the Plaza of the Americas—but there it is. How many cities (from Ebla to Dallas) have been built and then rebuilt, and still never turn out to be quite fit as a truly human habitation for all their people, or even for most of them?

Yet, and this would be point two, the Christian quest for the God-girt city we seek must go forward within the cities of this world. The Christian presence in and mission to the earthly city is where the Christian mission is going to win, lose, or draw—then and now. Our ministerial vocations, ordinations, and commissions are always to a provisional program, whose design and end lie in God's hands, not ours. To flee the city or to repudiate our mission in it just because we have never quite succeeded, nor are likely to in any foreseeable future, is both to misunderstand the Christian cause and to betray a great number of God's people.

Christianity began in the cities of the Graeco-Roman empire (the "People of the Way" were first called "Christians" in Antioch). Most of our continuing history has been a tale of many different cities: Jerusalem, Antioch, Ephesus, Rome, Alexandria, Constantinople, Aachen, Paris, London, Berlin, Moscow, Bombay, Boston, Philadelphia and on and on.

Even with the rise of monasticism, it was the city that defined the monk's choice of solitude. Indeed, in Eastern monasticism, the monks were often street gangs who lived in the cities themselves! That is how Theodosius got into trouble with Ambrose (when he herded those unruly monks of Thessalonica into the coliseum there and massacred them).

The term "pagan" comes from *paganus*, which originally meant "rural" or "agrarian." "Heathen" is a made word from "heath-dwellers" (i.e., country folk). The American myth that rural (or small-town) life is the natural setting for pure and undefiled religion has few counterparts in earlier church history or in the rest of the world. Bad as urban Christianity is (and always has been), peasant Christianity is either no better or maybe even worse (what with its long association with unsanctified folkways of various sorts).

But Christianity's associations with the cities of this world (from that early underground house church beneath San Clemente in Rome to Bob Schuller's crystal palace of light in Los Angeles) has always been ambivalent.

Christianity went into the cities and stayed in them because that was where the people were. This has been truly a strange and fascinating demographic phenomenon. Bad as cities are for human habitation, they have served, from antiquity, as magnets both to the adventurous and to the uprooted and discontent. People have piled into the cities and multiplied within the cities, and when they could not get "inside the gates" they have huddled around the cities' walls in slums, ghettos, barrios, suburbs, exurbs.

There is a city character (what else would the term "urbane" signify?). The urbane person prefers the noise and grime and excitement of city streets to the relative peace of the woods and parklands (I say relative peace and quiet, since all too often nowadays the peace of the woods and parklands is shattered by the splutter of motorbikes, outboards and chain saws). Even so, our escapes to these outdoor refuges are usually for the time being. If all the professed ecologists in Dallas would move permanently out to where they could truly be "at one with nature" (but would do it "cold turkey"—no off-the-road vehicles, no frequent traipsing into town for supplies, etc.), it would relieve our congestion by a good deal, and would reduce our level of self-righteousness by even more.

The success of the Christian mission in the cities has never been better than partial and sadly ambivalent. At first, they had the problem of being a *religio illicita*, whose members could blend in with the Roman urban underclass as they could not out in the countryside. Then in Constantinople there came the exciting prospect of Christians getting their hands on the switches of political power. This constantinian vision of a Christian theocracy has persisted in a hundred different forms to our own day, when our own social-action folks are still convinced that if we could capture city hall, or CETA, or HUD, or the legislature, or the governor's mansion, or the Congress, or the White House, the kingdom of God could be ushered in forthwith.

But for Christianity, history in the cities has been checkered with patterns of development and decline so variegated as to defy all neat generalizations. On Sundays, when the libraries were closed, I have walked the streets of London counting the churches that, once upon a time, were bustling and full. The ones that remain are mostly monuments to a fading past, save for tourists and antiquarians like me. I have seen Notre Dame de Paris full only twice in all my life, and now the Sainte Chapelle is not used for religious services at all. And something like this is the case in all the older cities in "the Christian world."

As for the impact of the urban church on the "urbs," this, too, has been a mixed record: a composite of soaring visions, heroic efforts, and modest results. Rome has more churches and religious houses and schools and missions per square mile than any other city in the world; it is, and always has been, a profoundly secular city. Byzantium came close to being an exception, for nearly a thousand years, but it was only a partial exception; and the cost to human rights is hard to justify, certainly nowadays.

In their history in human culture, cities have played many

roles, with many different reasons for being. Their original purpose, in most instances, was mutual self-defense against marauders, invaders, besieging armies. To this was mixed the economic advantages of city life, compared to the cycles of feast and famine that go with gathering, hunting and agrarian lifestyles. And always, also, a city means excitement—people to foregather with, spectacles of various sorts and always the possibilities of "bread and circuses," including the occasional excitements of mob violence.

But cities are also the garbage dumps of shattered hopes, broken dreams, disappointed expectations. Nobody came to Dallas in order to live in the squalor of our slums, or even in the sordid unhappiness of North Dallas and of "Southfork." The secular city is, as Isaiah said of Jerusalem, a sort of harlot. She promises pleasures that disappoint even when "satisfying," but even more often deceiving as to what pleasures are available and at what cost. Cities are engines of progress—technological, economic, cultural (and even spiritual)—but they are also black holes that suck up human aspirations. And Christians are as strongly lured to the cities as other people, with dreams and visions that also are as vulnerable to self-deception.

What is more, cities have to be built (more often than not) with human sweat and tears (and blood, too). But even as they are being built they are already on their way to blight. And always with physical blight there comes human blight, and, as we know too well, human blight accelerates physical blight even when it does not cause it directly. The Goths and Vandals did not destroy Rome; they simply could not cope with its technology and so let it sink into uninhabitable decay.

Harvey Cox caught the imagination of liberal Christians everywhere with his thesis that the secular city has a whole array of human virtues all on its own, fit to be celebrated for their own sake. A longer and closer look gives us a different impression today. Save for quite exceptional human beings (who manage their comfort and equanimity very largely at others' expense), the urban condition is very far below anything that could be called a human optimum.

In most cities this deficiency begins with housing and goes on to transportation, to circumstances in the work place, to living standards and lifestyles, to political discontents, to cultural impoverishment (sometimes because of media deprivations; sometimes because of media distortions—not just by faking but by their uncomprehending selectivity and biases). In most cities the fraction of people below the poverty level is scandalous, but the spiritual and moral poverty of the rest of us is almost as disgraceful and dehumanizing. We live in justifiable fear of violence and of civil disorder, but not in enough fear of the poverty of soul and community spirit. In the ancient world the most pervasive and devastating human crisis came with the transition from the small, human-sized cities (or communities) to the larger and larger cosmopolies. In a human-size community, everybody is identified and meshed into the communal life. Much as this life-in-a-fishbowl may be put down, it has some qualities that sustain the human spirit that are missing in our anonymous existence in the modern cosmopolis or in the split-level existence of suburban residence and urban employment.

Meanwhile, the urban family is under desperate siege: the divorce rates soar; the lifestyles of singles and singles again evolve into unaccustomed forms; child abuse and child neglect go almost unchecked; public education goes from bad to worse; and urban politics become more and more partisan. All this has happened in this city in the past three decades, before my very own eyes, and I can scarcely be very proud of my strenuous and yet unavailing efforts to counteract this whelming flood of dehumanization.

And still our churches stand—a few in the inner city, a few on the blighted fringes, still more in the satellite belts and suburbs. And together they raise the question of the Christian presence in the city. This, too, is an old story. If you had asked a Roman in the third century about the Christian presence, you would have gotten a blank look from the average citizen. In fifth-century Byzantium, there would have been no need to ask about the Christian presence, but rather about the Christian influence.

When Rome fell in 410 A.D. (it was actually a sort of massive sit-in by Alaric's Visigoths), the civilized world trembled. But a Christian bishop in North Africa was stirred to reflection about what looked to so many other Christians as if it were a mortal setback to the Christian cause. He turned, as if by instinct, to our theme in Hebrews—that here on earth, not as separate and sacralized communes, but as a special people (*populus*) within the "city of earth" (*civitas terrena*).

Cities are not defined by their physical circumstances so decisively as by their moral and spiritual climates. The City of God, on earth and in heaven, is defined by its love of God above all else and all else in God. This means a city on the earth and in the world, but not of the earth and not beholden to any of the political virtues of self-defense, self-aggrandizement, dominance in a pecking order, or pomp and circumstance. A people who love God must also love God's creatures—human and otherwise—and must, therefore, seek justice and equity and fair play for them all. The *civitas terrena* is the *populus* (in the same demographic area) whose prime love is self-interest, which is to say, dominance for some and survival for the rest. In the city of earth, human rights and values are controlled by political means or else explode into violence when political means fail to serve their self-interested ends.

The modern city is a far cry from anything Augustine could have imagined, but the issues are strangely alike and still remain. The trouble was that the Western world went on to identify the *Civitas Dei* with the Roman Catholic Church, and then went on to confound the secular and the sacred. Thus, they came to define Christian presence not so much by the action and influence of sacrificial, sharing love as by the various signs of ecclesiastical status and influence. The rise of the urban middle class in Western society brought stability and vast new economic strength, but dug a chasm between the bourgeois church and the church of the workers and the church of the poor.

In the nineteenth century the European intelligentsia, by and large, made common cause with the proletariat against the bourgeoisie. And then in our century, many liberal Protestant clergy have sought to identify themselves with the intelligentsia against that same bourgeoisie whose they are and whom they are supposed to serve. The result is that the "gathering storm over the churches," predicted by Jeffrey Hadden a dozen years ago, has now broken upon us even as, during that same period, the Western bourgeoisie has been cruelly macerated by inflation and taxation and is no longer our captive fat golden goose.

This leaves us with the appallingly difficult problem as to whether urban churches can be multigenerational, multiracial, multiclass (which is to say, whether we can ignore the siren songs of the church-growth movement, which seems to sanctify homogeneous, not to say homogenized, congregations). The urban church, seeking that heavenly city that God hath wrought for us, must become all things to all men, women, and children so that, by God's unfailing grace, we may save some for life in a "city" whose love of God and neighbor identifies men and women as Christians, i.e., brothers and sisters in a good family.

Cities are forever changing, for better or for worse; they improve or they deteriorate. They suffer from growing pains or from decline; they lurch toward bankruptcy or they grind down the faces of the poor and the middle-class taxpayer. They give themselves up to ego trips and to collective seizures of social pathology. They provide incomparable resources for human development, yet also irresistible pressures toward depersonalization. Here we have no abiding cities. Rome is still forever where it was, but it is not the same human place it was two hundred years ago—or twenty, for that matter. And so it goes.

Yet the earthly city is the Christian mission's greatest challenge and greatest opportunity. The city is the test case of what it takes to transform a huge collective into a human community, in which very large populations may coexist humanely! But more, cities are the places where God's bewildered multitudes abide, where decisions are made, where human tensions are most creative or most destructive. Cities are the womb of human history; they also are history's dumps. They are, to lapse into the vernacular, "where the action is"—and more people want to be there than is good for them.

When Jesus had to put his mission to its final test, he set his face to go to Jerusalem, not because it was so attractive but because it was so crucial in so many ways. When he was about to enter it, he wept, not from dread nor sentimentality but from a divine grief that this city whose very name means "peace" was so stubbornly insensitive to the things that could bring it peace. And his worst times during that week of testing came during his hours in the "downtown church"!

We will have misread our text, therefore, if we conclude from its undeniable truth that our cities do not abide, that we can either abandon them to their fate or that we can capture and convert them to our own ideal ends. Our mission in the city is crucial and imperative; the church's future is linked with the city's future. What matters is our realism and our commitment. To flee to the desert (or the suburbs) seems an easy answer, but it is not a valid one. To think of hauling the heavenly city down from the skies and setting it up here on the banks of the Trinity, or the Hudson, or the Chattahoochee is the fatuous dream of the Enlightenment, which now seems uncommonly absurd in retrospect. Even reading Carl Becker's once famous *Heavenly City of the Eighteenth Century Philosophers* is a curious experience now—although one that every Christian idealist should set for himself as an exercise in penance.

Our mission is in the city, but we must not define that mission chiefly in secular and mundane terms. We have no warrant for settling on our lees, or for making a bold bid for a theocracy, either. We are sent to stir things up, to turn the world upside down (or right side up), but not to exaggerate our own importance. Our mission in the city is to set up the altar of Christian sacrifice in her midst, and to understand the nature and manner of that sacrifice.

For if here we have no abiding city, we still have an altar in every city and town and wherever. It is not a marble slab but the movable locus of the Christ Event re-presented, a reproducible reenactment of Christ's sacrificial priesthood for us. This is the main point to the argument in Hebrews about Christ's great High Priesthood. At this Christian altar we become sacrificing and sacrificial priests for others, offering up our sacrifices of praise to God and to his children, in Christ's name.

And in the gratitude thus generated we are prompted by grace to sacrificial good works (*eupoi-ias*) and sacrificial sharing (*koinonia*). It is with these sacrifices that God is well pleased (*euaresteitai*). This, as I hope you will remember, is the argument that brings the author of Hebrews to his great benediction, a special blessing for all those pilgrims who have no abiding city here but who still seek for one, a *civitas* with the abiding foundations that only God can give. If so, then it may become our benediction, too, for our time together here:

> May the God of Shalom, who brought again from the dead our Lord Jesus, that great shepherd of God's sheep, through the blood of the everlasting covenant, make you perfect in all goodness so that you may joyfully do his will—and may he make of us what he

would have us to be, through Jesus Christ, to whom be glory forever and ever. Amen.

Introduction

On this special Sunday night occasion where Albert Outler preached prior to "a Festival of Wesleyan Hymns" at First United Methodist Church, Ashland, Virginia (March 17, 1985), those present heard him speak on one of his favorite themes: Discovering Wesley as a "theologian in the great tradition of historic Christianity from whom plain people could learn what the Christian life is all about."

When Outler said to the Council of Bishops that "given our present theological drift and confusion, the United Methodist Church has a dim future," some railed about how his "negative" stand could hurt the denomination. He acknowledged that what he said would sound negative to those bent on defending the status quo (as Truth always sounds when it differs with opinions).

He said further, "I was invited to do the opening sermon in the Uniting Conference. Before the conference met I let off that balloon about monarchical bishops, that they ought to be real leaders or they ought not have so much power as they have. That upset a whole bunch of them. I then went to Miami Beach, and all the bishops were there. When I walked through the crowd (of bishops), it just parted like the Red Sea. So I wrote the committee and said that if there were the slightest bit of embarrassment, I'd be happy not to do the sermon. So I got invited the second time to do the sermon."

Outler once said: "I would not have made a good bishop." And he would not if by "bishop" you mean "caretaker of the cathedral."

SERMON 26

Why Wesley?

Here we are, a goodly gathering of people called Methodists, (American Methodists, and Virginia Methodists at that) launched out into our third century and still celebrating our heritage, our identity, our mission. Moreover, we are doing what true Methodists love to do and often do well: sing Charles Wesley's hymns and join our hearts in corporate prayer and praise.

My assignment, on such a festive occasion, is to speak (briefly, they said) to an interesting question that often comes my way: "Why all this blow and go about John Wesley? Where does he fit into the Methodist picture, save as our Founder, sort of?" Sometimes, my non-Methodist friends (and Methodists, too) put it like this: "Why would an old man invest his last quarter century with a man like John Wesley, on the grounds that he is still an interesting and fruitful theologian and also a significant ecumenical resource?" These are fair questions, and they have two rather different answers: one obvious and not very important; the other not so obvious and actually quite important.

The obvious answer, of course, is that John is the Methodist patriarch and we Methodists need often to recall "our Father in God," as Asbury called him occasionally. He was not, of course, the very first person to go by that nickname "Methodist," for there were people in the seventeenth century, with different versions of the doctrine of double justification, and they had been called Methodists, too. But John Wesley gave the nickname a movement to go with it, and we still stand in that tradition, in a manner of speaking.

Wesley has been a sort of cult hero, who stood tall at 5'2", with a constant weight (around 125 lbs.) that never varied by much over 70 years; a great evangelist and a prodigious traveler, preacher, journalist, a man with a wonderful mother and a genius poet for a brother, who grew up in a national church sodden with apathy, who, then, on the strength of a marvelous conversion, brought Christianity back to life in Britain and left behind the Methodist church as his best-known legacy.

In the course of his fabulous career, he came to be associated with a network of shrines that have drawn admiring Methodist tourists to them ever since. To the Epworth parsonage in which he was not born (but where he lived a short while); to that suite in Lincoln College (it is the wrong set of rooms, but the right college); to a church at South Leigh where he is said to have preached his first sermon (where he did preach his "first sermon" after he had already preached it elsewhere); to the site of the Aldersgate experience; to the site of the Foundery; to the New Room in Bristol (the nearest to the real thing among all the Wesley shrines); to the chapel and house on City Road, etc. I do not mean to disparage Methodist sentimentality about Wesley and the Wesley shrines nor the Methodist habit of collecting Wesleyan memorabilia and relics. I mean only to raise the question of how far these things go in the proper appraisal of John Wesley's importance, for his time or ours.

Another possible answer to our question, "Why should we be interested in John Wesley?" is that he was an interesting man on his own terms, a real overachiever. Dr. Samuel Johnson found him an enchanting conversationalist, and a wide range of other people (high born and low) found him impressive. He was an erstwhile don who lived in a slum; he was the most effective evangelist in his century; the most familiar "private" person in eighteenth-century England. And yet we do not have a biography of Wesley that is even close to being adequate (Robert Southey's is still the best). The hero worshipers have not been able to see him critically, warts and all. The others, like Stanley Ayling, have not bothered to get their facts right or to probe them at a proper depth.

And so we come down finally to the bare possibility that Wesley is worth knowing for what he still has to teach us about the gospel, about Christian existence and the Christian life, about nonviolent reform and social change, about the history of Christian thought, about the possibilities of an ecumenical Christianity.

This is important, for despite his image, even in America, as patriarch and founder, the fact remains that American Methodists, from the beginning, were more interested in him as "patriarch" than as "doctor." Asbury rejected Wesley's authority quite decisively—and offended Wesley so deeply that they died unreconciled to each other. What is worse, Asbury was never deeply influenced by Wesley's theology and never sought to ensconce Mr. Wesley as chief doctor in American Methodism.

Much more research is needed on this generally unexamined point, but this much we know already: Wesley's Sunday Service was quickly marginalized in American Methodism, and when in 1808 a motion was made in the General Conference to stipulate Wesley's *Sermons* and *Notes* as our standards of doctrine, it was defeated. This did not mean, I think, that they were repudiating Wesley altogether. I believe (as my colleague Richard Heitzenrater does not) that the *Sermons* and *Notes* are included by implication in the phrase of the First Restrictive Rule, "our present existing and established standards of doctrine," which is what they were concerned with in 1808. But Adam Clarke and Richard Watson were more influential than Wesley as theological tutors in the first half of the nineteenth century. And, in the century and a half since then we have had very few Methodist exegetes and theologians who were so deeply indebted to Wesley as their theological mentor as they were to others.

The result has been a denomination with a patriarch to reverence, but not a doctor to learn from, which is quite different from the Lutherans, the Calvinists, the Anglicans, the Romans, or the Orthodox. Methodist professors and preachers have their various mentors, depending on what schools they went to and when, and all sorts of similar, quite accidental factors. But Wesley is rarely their chief mentor, and when he is, it is often not first hand, but from secondary and tertiary and legendary sources.

Among the influential Methodist theologians listed in Professor Langford's *Practical Divinity*, not a single one of them was trained as a Wesley specialist and the number of Wesley specialists (as compared to Luther and Calvin and Hooker specialists) is, and always has been, miniscule.

Last December a Methodist biblical scholar delivered a paper at the Society of Biblical Literature that "explained" John Wesley's biblical scholarship as having had some interesting features looking toward "modernity" (for all its archaisms), but that he cannot now be taken so seriously as, say, Walter Kummel.

One of the most interesting features of our time, in all the churches, is a wide-ranging fresh new interest in doctrinal consensus or convergence. It is happening in the World Council of Churches, in the uniting churches, in the Lutheran and Reformed traditions, in the Consultation On Church Union, and now in the United Methodist Church. We have a new doctrinal commission, with a General Conference mandate to write a new doctrinal statement. It has two Wesley specialists on it. But what will the majority come up with and what reception will the result receive throughout the denomination at large (especially if it triggers debate in the General Conference and in the annual conferences thereafter) over either or both of the first two Restrictive Rules? Who is prepared for that now, and how could you get yourselves prepared?

All of which is to say that, as meaningful as John Wesley has been to us Methodists as patriarch, founder, great saint of God, evangelist par excellence, preacher and pastor, indefatigable social reformer of a very special sort—and all that—he still remains to be discovered as a rich and fruitful teacher of Christian truth, as theologian in the great tradition of historic Christianity from whom plain people could learn what the Christian life is all about, and from whom theologians of all the denominations could learn what folk-theology is all about—competent and fruitful theology, historically contexted, yet also and equally a theology to preach to plain folks inoculated against technical analysis!

For Wesley was, and still is, a great Christian theologian in the great tradition of historic Christian faith, rooted (if not to say immersed) in the Holy Scriptures, which he not only knew so well that they were for him a second language, but acquainted at first hand with those grand themes he thought about in scriptural perspectives (as contrasted with the way most of us think about particular Scripture texts). He was a biblical theologian who never was concerned to produce a "system" of "biblical theology."

Wesley was a theologian who lived in the long tradition of Christian experience and thought—in time, space, and variety; an ecumenical theologian, a theologian with truly "catholic spirit"; firm on the essentials (which, for him, were very few) and open-minded with respect to the multiple options of theological opinion. He understood the Christian heritage more clearly than most of our contemporary professors and preachers, and we and they could learn more from him than we have yet realized.

Most of all, he was a theologian of God's sovereign grace, manifest and communicated in Christ, sustained and kept perennially vital by the Holy Spirit among us. The converse of sovereign grace and God's offer of universal redemption was a doctrine of human freedom, responsibility, and self-determination. It was neither Pelagian nor Augustinian, neither deist nor predestinarian. The human will is neither free and open nor fully prescripted by divine or natural influences. The human part is always reactive—to the initiatives of the Holy Spirit to which we may respond positively (and are led further into the light) or from which we recoil (and sink deeper into alienation). Grace is God's unmerited love and favor, revealed in Christ, and energized in us by the indwelling Spirit of God—prevenient, accompanying, justifying, regenerating, sanctifying, and the like.

This grace calls forth faith, faith that really trusts in God's presence in Christ to reconcile the world to himself, and not just the world, but us; and not just us, but you and you and me. But it also calls forth love and gratitude (the human reflex of grace) and calls us into a new life in Christ, a life of spiritual communion and discipline and also a life of love to God (above all) and love to neighbor (i.e., every child of God to whom we can be of any service). The fullness of this love to God and neighbor is what Wesley called "scriptural holiness," and it was for the purpose of spreading such scriptural holiness over these lands that God had raised up the Methodists as a special people.

Why Wesley, then? Because we have so much to learn from him —as a person, as a saint, as an evangelist, and as a teacher of the Christian message for us and our time. Given our present theological drift and confusion, the United Methodist Church has a dim future. We are notoriously long on organization, propaganda, muscular Christianity; pitiably short on theological competence, evangelical excitement, relevant social and cultural influence. Given a rediscovery of Wesley (or a *dis*covery, if that would be what it was) we would have, not a panacea, but at least a new and rich and exciting additional resource for understanding the Christian life, for comprehending the order of salvation, a powerful Christian ethic of virtue that is neither legalistic nor antinomian. And all of this would have come from a man whose life was an incarnate demonstration of his message.

Christian churches need a whole faculty of doctors—teachers—not one but several, and none need be regarded as infallible or a substitute for the primary source of all our Christian learning: the Holy Spirit in the Scriptures and the Holy Spirit in our hearts. Thus, in our Methodist faculty of teachers, John Wesley deserves inclusion, not as a cult hero but as a saintly teacher from whom we can learn, from whom we can learn what he learned: the Scriptures, the Christian tradition, a reliance upon right reason and common sense along with openness to vital Christian experience of God's reconciling, empowering love. This would give us all a new future, as Christians and as a church, and this is at least a partial answer to the question "Why Wesley?"

Why Wesley, indeed? We now turn to the Wesley hymns to see the substance of the hymns answer the question, "Why Wesley?"

Introduction

This sermon preached to the Wesleyan Society of the Virginia Conference, March 1985, said some things unheard of by many Methodists, e.g., "That Christianity would be in genuine dialogue with the wisdom of the world, i.e., science, culture, technology—Christianity in dialogue with other religions, with Hindus, Moslems, Buddhists, and the like. Getting Wesley a hearing is not a Methodist project so much as it is an ecumenical project."

It is a comforting thought to think that the editing and publishing of these sermons will give a wider hearing of Albert Outler's insights into the ecumenical contributions of John Wesley—that Wesley's Rule of Grace is worthy of the most serious theological consideration.

Outler said in 1985 over dinner: "Is there really something to Wesley as a theologian to be taken seriously by the whole church? Or am I just an old man imagining things? If he is not, then I have wasted the better part of thirty years of my life." Could you ever have looked Albert Outler in the eyes and told him *he* was imagining *anything* other than reality?

SERMON 27

Wesleyan Spirituality

One of the ironies of last year's Bicentennial of the United Methodist Church was the frequency with which John Wesley's name was invoked, his career extolled as exemplary, with all his stock quotations trotted out to buttress preformed opinions, and yet how rarely it appeared that he had been lived with by those who revered him, how little his entire corpus had been probed and pondered.

When Lutherans speak of Luther, they either have his representative writings in view or the interpretive work of scholars who have mastered the Luther corpus firsthand. The same goes for most knowledgeable Presbyterians with regard to *The Institutes* (one thinks of the excellent work of The Calvin Society). Episcopalians are more often vague about their chief "doctor," Richard Hooker and his *Laws of Ecclesiastical Polity*. But their priests have usually been to school where they were given a soaking in Hooker and the Caroline divines for a while at least. Roman Catholic priests and theologians are usually knowledgeable enough about St. Thomas that it is a mite risky to misquote or distort him in their presence.

Methodists, by and large, have a multitude of mentors and

doctors, but largely on a happenstance basis, depending on which college, university, seminary or graduate school this person or that attended, when and with what major in which field of study. Rarely is Wesley chief among these tutors; generally, he is included only as an incidental figure (as a great man, an organizer, or evangelist, but not as a creative theologian or an important ecumenical resource). Wesley specialists are an endangered species, and the worst of this is that such an oddity causes less concern among Methodists than among other Christians, both of whom are more excited to save the whooping crane.

One of the things I came to realize in the course of the bicentennial, when I was forced to look more closely at American Methodist church history, was that this marginalization of Wesley in American Methodism is not recent and not accidental. Francis Asbury was not only a man with a mind of his own, but that mind was not much influenced by the more complicated nuances of Wesley's thought, partly because Asbury lacked Wesley's classical education, but also because he was much more a typical Middle England Nonconformist than an Anglican theologian shaped by the Eastern Fathers, with their subtler understandings of grace and free will.

And it is an interesting phenomenon that it was only two years ago that I discovered for myself what nobody had bothered to tell me (not Jesse Lee nor Freddy Norwood nor Charlie Ferguson, *et al.*): that Wesley died regarding Francis Asbury as having abandoned the connection between them. My colleague Professor Heitzenrater has a thesis that American Methodists, in 1808, consciously rejected Wesley's doctrinal authority as they already had rejected his administrative authority in 1786 (when they turned down his nomination of Whatcoat to the general superintendency). The chief evidence for this thesis, as many of you may know, was an action in the constitutional Conference of 1808, when a proposal was made vis-à-vis the First Restrictive Rule to stipulate in it a specific reference to Wesley's *Sermons* and *Notes*, and this was turned down by the Conference. I read this episode rather differently, putting more weight on the double reference to "our Articles of Religion" and to our (other) "present existing and established standards of doctrine." If Heitzenrater is right, the consequences will be awkward for the doctrinal commission of which he is vice chairman. But in any case, he has reinforced the point that American Methodism is much less Wesleyan than Asburian.

That is in itself a major clarification of the otherwise puzzling phenomenon, that we have always honored Father John and traipsed off to pay homage at his shrines in England (confused as most of them are), yet we have not studied him so carefully as we would have had to if we were to profit from him as our doctor and mentor in the faith.

Tonight I propose, as an exercise in filial piety and an adventure in Wesleyan theology, that we focus on a central theme in Wesley, grace and spirituality. My hope is that you will be interested in at least one way of looking at Wesley's axial theme of grace and some of its pneumatological outworkings, and this partly because the most notable achievement in the Roman Catholic-World Methodist Council bilaterals thus far was the discovery of so much common ground between us in pneumatology. But we are also in the early months of one of the most critical quadrennia that United Methodism has faced in a long time, with questions about doctrine and mission and ministry catching us sadly unprepared. Meanwhile, we are trying to staunch the hemorrhaging of the past two decades, and struggle with questions of morale and mission, with bleaker prospects than we had thought we had in my living memory, with more, and more portentous, changes on the way.

All through Wesley's career there were two antithetical conceptions of God's sovereign grace, one expressed in doctrines of election, irresistible grace, and the final perseverance of true believers; the other a semi-Pelagian notion of unfettered free will (mislabeled "Arminianism," which is a double misnomer, for Arminius himself was not semi-Pelagian and Wesley was not, strictly speaking, an Arminian).

The eighteenth-century reaction to the violence of the seventeenth century had been the willingness to purchase peace at the price of Christian convictions, to concede too much to the deists, the rationalists, the advocates of human autonomy. The temper of the times was latitudinarian; the level of Christian commitment was low; the phobia of the times was "enthusiasm." Pietism generated deep fears of a reenactment of something like the Civil

War and of the religious anarchy that had convulsed all of Britain (and Ireland) during the period of the so-called "Commonwealth." Better to put up with Restoration decadence than that again! The dominant doctrine of grace in the Church of England in the eighteenth century stressed the favor and blessing of God channeled through the church and her ministers, who claimed a virtual monopoly of the means of grace.

Wesley was a child of his time, but a succession of four successive conversions thrust him toward a new Christian conspectus and to a doctrine of grace as its organizing center. In 1725 he was converted from the conventional lightheartedness of an Oxford collegian to a "seriousness" before God and to a total commitment in his service. In 1727 he experienced a mystical illumination: a vision of God's surpassing glory (and of the consequent demands of holiness in the Christian life). In 1738 he had the "heartwarming" that we all know about: an unexpected experience of God's personal pardoning, reconciling and conquering grace, entirely inward and yet immediately turned outward. In 1739 he experienced the power of the Holy Spirit in and through his own ministry to men and women in misery and alienation that converted them to faith and the assurance of grace ("perceptible grace").

From then on for five decades he continued to teach and preach a rich and ample doctrine of grace and spirituality (with the consonant disciplines of Christian spirituality, construed as "growth in grace"). He sought to include the good essence of both the Catholic and Protestant traditions, as they were to be rediscovered in the Holy Scriptures and from the patristic tradition (chiefly Eastern).

Wesley was as staunch a Protestant as any other Anglican of his time, save in his refusal to exclude the Roman Catholics from the people of God. Indeed, you might want to read or reread his open "Letter to a Roman Catholic," where the shared core of doctrine between Methodists and Roman Catholics is itemized (including a profession of faith in the perpetual virginity of the Blessed Virgin Mary, an item that has astonished a few Methodists and Catholics who have noticed it).

For Wesley, grace is God's benevolence and mercy in all its ramifications, directed chiefly toward his human family, which stands with any other remedy in utter and total dependence upon that benevolence and mercy. Uncreated grace is manifest in creation, in Torah, in the vision of the prophets, and in all other revelations of God. It is of God's unmerited mercy that none of his human children has been left "without a witness" (the omnipresent Spirit, in whom we live and move and have our being). But grace was finally and fully revealed in Jesus Christ, whose life and death and triumph are the meritorious cause of our justification (instead of the formal cause, as the Calvinists insisted).

It is, as Rahner says, God's self-communication of unnecessitated love and mercy. But Wesley was more specific than Rahner as to the identity and agency of the self-communication. It is truly the Holy Spirit as active and intimate Self-Communicator. The Spirit bears witness with our spirits of God's reconciling pardon of our sins and of Christ's merits imparted as a transforming power, neither inherent nor infused (no *ante praevisa merita* here), but in the continuing imminent action of the Spirit. Here is a notion of an absolute divine initiative (all of grace is prevenient—in each and every good human action, from the first awakenings of the spiritual life to its highest reaches, but also never without some kind of human reaction, authentic and inauthentic, humanly freeing or self-defeating). Wesley took Galatians 5:25 very seriously: "all human beings live [*zomen*] in the Spirit as human, whether faithful or faithless. And this it is that enables believers to "walk" [*stroichomen*] in the Spirit (i.e., to be led of the Spirit)."

The Lutherans and Calvinists had taught that the human condition, apart from grace (what they called "natural man") was irretrievably hopeless. Wesley agreed with their conclusion, and disputed their premise:

> Yet this is no excuse for those who continue in sin, and lay blame upon their Maker by saying: "It is God only that must quicken us; for we cannot quicken our own souls." For allowing that all the souls of men are dead by nature, this excuses none, seeing there is no man that is in a state of mere nature; there is no man,

> unless he has quenched the Spirit, that is wholly void of the grace of God. No man living is entirely destitute of what is vulgarly called "natural conscience." But this is not natural; it is more properly termed "preventing grace". Every man has a greater or less measure of this, which waiteth not for the call of man. . . . So that no man sins because he has not grace, but because he does not use the grace which he hath.[1]

The key image in John Wesley's anthropology is the *imago Dei.* In sin, this image is not destroyed but disfigured. The effects of sin are less that they alienate God from us, but rather that they alienate us from him (and so also from ourselves). God was in Christ reconciling the world to himself; not reconciling himself to the world.

The younger Wesley wrote in 1735:

> The whole world is indeed, in its present state, only one great infirmary: all that are therein are sick of sin, and their one business there is to be healed. And for this very end the great Physician of souls is continually present with them, marking all the diseases of every soul and "giving medicines to heal its sickness."[2]

This theme of *therapeia psyches* continues and develops throughout his theological lifetime. But the young Wesley had added, "But as perfect holiness is not found on earth, so neither is perfect happiness: some remains of our disease will ever be felt, and some physic will be necessary to heal it."[3] Later he would come to believe that healing grace had no such limits (which is to say, he rejected the Lutheran doctrine of invincible concupiscence, epitomized in their slogan, *simul justus et peccator*). Instead, he taught that Christians may, and should be, perfected in love in this life—and expect so to be and "groan" for it.

The order of salvation, for Wesley, encompasses the entire span of the life of faith, which proceeds by stages toward its final end in glorification in the life of the world to come.

> . . . salvation begins with what is usually termed (and very properly) "preventing grace," including the first

> wish to please God, the first dawn of light concerning his will, and the first, slight transient convictions of having sinned against him. All these imply some tendency toward life, [i.e., freedom of the will to react to the indwelling Spirit] some degree of salvation, [a real] . . . beginning of a deliverance from a blind, unfeeling heart, quite insensible of God and the things of God.[4]

It should be added that this is not the only sense in which Wesley uses the phrase "preventing" or "prevenient" grace. As I said, all grace is prevenient in the sense that God's initiatives are always, and at every level, antecedent. Wesley coins the metaphor of the human soul as a "spiritual *sensorium*," designed in its creation to react to the Spirit's stimuli but latent and passive until such stimuli are appropriate and effectual. And when such stimuli do bestir us, we are free to react or resist. The Creator's graces (e.g., "natural laws" and physical processes) may not be resisted; the graces of the Holy Spirit may be. But they also may be accepted by the human *voluntas*, which is always being freed up by the Spirit's prevenient action.

I know several psychiatrists who are excited about this notion of freedom as an unfolding process. Such a view is not as subjectivist as it may seem to be, or has been interpreted by some in a narcissistic culture. Authentic spiritual experience is not self-originated; it is an experience of an actual reality over against ourselves even if also within ourselves. As Kant would put it (and did put it in Wesley's lifetime): "All truth arises in experience; it does not all arise from experience directly."

The Spirit may possess us, but always and only to his ends and purposes, which are spiritual and moral, through and through. Charisms that stir spiritual excitements without yielding the Spirit's harvest (Galatians 5:22—"Love, joy, peace, patience," and the like) are false charisms. Good works, apart from faith and grace, are not effectual in soul therapy (apart from faith, they fall into moralism). It is important to note, however, that Wesley expressly denied that good works apart from saving faith are *vitiae splendidae* (in Beza's glittering metaphor). The phrase has been attributed to St. Augustine, but I have not yet found it there. Article IX of the Thirty-nine Articles of the Church of England had spoken of "this infection of nature" that remains even in the regenerate. But Wesley would take it upon himself to revise this text in his abridgment of the Thirty-nine Articles, which he prepared for the Methodists in America.

His description of the order of salvation continues:

> Salvation is carried on by "convincing grace," usually in Scripture termed "repentance," which brings a larger measure of self-knowledge [or of our need for grace], and a farther deliverance from the heart of stone. Afterwards we experience the proper Christian salvation, whereby "through grace" we "are saved by faith," consisting of those two grand branches, justification and sanctification. By justification we are saved from the guilt of sin, and restored to the favour of God: By sanctification we are saved from the power and root of sin, and restored to the image of God. All experience, as well as Scripture, show this salvation [this restoration of the image, which is the human power to respond to God's initiatives] to be both instantaneous and gradual. It begins the moment we are justified, in the holy, humble, gentle, patient love of God and man [for Wesley, early and late, the essence of sanctification is the gift, power, and fruit of love—love to God above all else, and love to neighbor, viz., every child of God in all the world to whom we can be loving]. It gradually increases from that moment, as "a grain of mustard seed . . . but" gradually "puts forth large branches," and becomes a great tree; till in another instant the heart is cleansed from all sin, and filled with pure love to God and man. [Note Wesley consistently defines sin as the violation of known laws of God, which is to say, voluntary and deliberate.] But that love increases more and more, till we "grow up in all things into him that is our head," "till we attain the measure of the stature of the fullness of Christ."[5]

Here, we have grace characterized by a gamut of qualifiers: "preventing grace," "convincing grace," "justifying grace," "sanctifying grace." There are others: "accompanying grace," "the grace of assurance," "the grace of wisdom," "the grace of perseverance," "uncreated grace," "created grace." But always the constant meaning is that grace is sheer mercy, wholly gratuitous, a gift, a blessing. And the appropriate response to grace in any measure or mode is gratitude and graciousness.

In one place, Wesley coins a metaphor about the *ordo salutis* that I have not seen elsewhere (have you?): of porch, threshold (door), and living room. The porch of true religion is repentance, and repentance for John Wesley is not merely attrition or self-reproach nor contrition in the forensic sense. It is chiefly self-awareness: of one's distortions and disfigurements of the *imago Dei* (and therefore of one's true humanity). Its function, *metanoesis*, is to acknowledge one's need of healing by grace (rather than by justice or bare acquittal); to "hide pride from man" (as he puts it, quoting Job 33:17) and so prepare the heart and mind for a saving trust in God's pure, unbounded love, self-disclosed in Jesus Christ.

Justification is God's act of imputing the unmerited righteousness of Christ to a believing sinner and of imparting the righteousness of "a new creature in Christ." Justification is pardon, forgiveness, assurance and heart-cleansing. It is (as Wesley put it) what God does for us, in restoring a just relationship. And it is by faith alone as its only indispensable condition; there is no merit (previsioned, condign, congruent, whatever). It is sheer mercy, grace upon grace, an ineffable gift—to be received, accepted, twisted, and turned to its proper ends: hope and love.

Sanctification is the living space of true religion in which Christian life goes on growing up toward maturation, fullness, holiness, and happiness. Like all else, it is the work of the Holy Spirit: an eventful process in which grace and "the means of grace" work out their perfecting work. Sanctification is what God the Spirit does for us and with us and through us, insofar as we are responsive and faithful to the Spirit's prompting presence in our lives.

Classical Protestants had always had a problem with the linkage between faith and good works. They were rightly terrified of "works-righteousness." Wesley's concerns tilted the other way. His chief phobia was antinomianism: permissiveness, narcissism, faith without good works as fruitage. The grace of assurance and the grace of participation were correlates in one of his favorite biblical tags: "faith energized by love"—*fides caritate formata*.

Understood as radically given, and its agency as the liberating Holy Spirit (as the triune God's self-communicator), grace is interpreted as less a problem in speculative theology than it is as the energy and rule of the spiritual life. Grace is the energy of the contemplative spirit, and yet also of the loving actions prompted by the contemplations of God's pure, unbounded goodness.

Thus, spiritual formation and the processes of "growth in grace" are two perspectives on the same dynamic reality: The enhancement of the believer's participation in the divine love that is the essence of God's gracious providence (*metousia theou*). "All who desire the grace of God are to wait for it in the means which he hath ordained."[6]

The first of these ways is prayer: prayers of adoration, of thanksgiving, repentance, petition, and intercession—"prayer of every kind, public and private, and the blessings annexed thereto."[7] A second appointed means of waiting for grace is "in 'searching the Scriptures.'"[8] Wesley takes this as a command: ". . . let us know how a command can be more clearly expressed. . . . It is as peremptory as so many words can make it."[9] As an aside, he comments that Christians are not to neglect the Old Testament.

> Thirdly, all who desire an increase of the grace of God are to wait for it in partaking of the Lord's Supper. . . .
>
> . . . this is not a bare permission only, but a clear explicit command. . . .
>
> . . . the eating of that bread, and the drinking of that cup, the outward, visible means whereby God conveys unto our souls all that spiritual grace, that righteousness, and peace, and joy in the Holy Ghost, which were purchased by the body of Christ once broken and the blood of Christ once shed for us? Let all, therefore, who truly desire the grace of God, eat of that bread and drink of that cup.[10]

Wesley denounces the doctrine of spontaneity in desiring sacramental communion; it is an efficacious means of grace of which all Christians are commanded to avail themselves, not just "frequently" but, in a special sense "constantly" (as often as it is available), without excusing scruples about one's own moral "fitness" or that of the administrant.

Wesley's doctrine of sacramental presence was realistic but emphatically unanalytic: Christ is really and truly present in the Eucharist, but such a conviction required for him no explanatory theory. In Reason Calmly Considered, he tries to encourage Christians to be content with the mysterious words of institution themselves, without, however, falling into fideism or gullibility.

There are other means of grace and "spiritual formation": Christian conversation, the aid of good spiritual directors, the reading of "serious books," and methodical meditation. And since all the means of grace are aimed at holiness, it must be remembered that there is no holiness but social holiness, that one cannot grow in grace without disciplined self-oblations of love and service to others and most especially to Christ's poor. The way of holiness is the way of self-denial and cross-bearing—to the end always that the kingdom of God may come on earth and that his righteousness will be done in earth, as of course is the case in heaven.

> Yet as we find no command in Holy Writ for any particular order to be observed herein, so neither do the providence and the Spirit of God adhere to any, without variation: but the means into which different men are led, and in which they find the blessing of God, are varied, transposed, and combined together a thousand different ways. Yet still our wisdom is to follow the leadings of his providence and his Spirit; to be guided herein (more especially as to the means wherein we ourselves seek the grace of God) partly by his outward providence, giving us the opportunity of using sometime one means, sometimes another; partly by our experience, which it is whereby his free Spirit is pleased most to work in our heart. And in the mean-

time the sure and general rule for all who groan for the salvation of God is this—whenever opportunity serves, use all means which God has ordained. For who knows in which God will meet thee with the grace that bringeth salvation?"[11]

In another place Wesley speaks of spiritual maturity as the fullness of life:

> And now [prayer, and in pure intentions, the true believers] may properly be said to *live*: God having quickened them by his Spirit, he is alive to God through Jesus Christ . . . God is continually breathing, as it were, upon his soul [as in Genesis 2:7]; and his soul is breathing into God. Grace is descending into his heart, and prayer and praise ascending to heaven. And by this intercourse between God and man, this fellowship with the Father and the Son, as by a kind of spiritual respiration the life of God in the soul is sustained. . . .
>
> It consists of all heavenly affections and tempers mingled together. . . . It implies such a continual, thankful love to him . . . as makes it natural, in a manner necessary to us to love every child of man; as fill us with . . . "kindness, gentleness, long-suffering." It is such a love . . . as enables us to present our souls and bodies all we are and all we have, all our thoughts, words, and actions, a continual sacrifice to God, acceptable through Jesus Christ.[12]

Here then is a concept of God's gracious love and mercy that sees it as a truly personal self-communication offered to all by a gracious God "whose mercy is over all his works" (Psalm 145:9). Grace is as much a climate as it is an activity. It is love energizing human freedom without licensing it to self-indulgence or self-initiatives.

Such a view has its obvious deficiencies. To Roman Catholics and Anglicans, it may seem to minimize the encompassing presence of the church and its indispensable ministries. To Lutherans and Reformed, it may seem to fail to safeguard God's absolute sovereignty and leave the depths of the roots of sin in the heart unplumbed. To Protestant radicals, it seems to concede too much to the externals of worship and to stress too much the moral imperatives of the Law. It does, deliberately, reject violent revolution in favor of a conservative revolution that is forever transforming the structures of society in favor of humanity and humaneness. To Protestant liberals (mostly Pelagian), it concedes too much to God's sovereignty and not enough to human ability.

But even these problems may suggest something of its special genius. There is something here from each of the great traditions and also something that each tradition can learn. As such, it offers us an ecumenical perspective on the central theme in the order of salvation. Thus, at the very least, it is worth knowing about and reflecting upon, and I am grateful to you all for allowing me to speak of it as one who has learned more from it than he expected when he began to take Wesley seriously, as a theologian, some quarter of a century ago.

As the peroration of his thirteen sermons of "Our Lord's Sermon on the Mount," Wesley sums up his vision of the Christian life in grace. For all its quaintness it might be edifying for us to hear it as an authentic Wesleyan exhortation to us all:

> In a word, let thy religion be the religion of the heart. Let it lie in deep in thy inmost soul. . . . Be serious. . . . Let thy soul be filled with mildness, gentleness, patience, long-suffering towards all men, at the same time that all which is within thee is athirst for God, the living God; longing to awake after his likeness, and to be satisfied with it. Be thou a lover of God and of all mankind. In this spirit do and suffer all things. Thus show thy faith by thy works: thus "do the will of thy Father which is in heaven." And as sure as thou now walkest with God on earth, thou shalt reign with him in glory.[13]

Amen.

PART 3

Conference Occasions

Introduction

This sermon preached at conferences, defines the role of the laity—they "are the church visible in and to the world. [They] communicate the gospel, not chiefly by formal discourse, but by all the informal, indirect ways that illustrate their actual understanding of the gospel. . . . It is the *laos* (the people) who walk the Christian way in the world and so either convince the world that Christ is the way, the truth, the life, or leave it unbelieving. . . . The laos . . . bridge the gap between sanctuary and the sidewalk if it is ever bridged, between the pew and the office, home, school, factory, between the sacramental and the secular dimensions of existence."

This "does not mean any kind of lay control of the pulpit or the baptismal font or the Lord's Table—in the sacred ministry of sacred things, of Word, Sacrament, and church order. Your minister is . . . not your employee. . . . He is the representative in your midst of the whole church, the spokesman and agent of the church catholic within the church local. . . . It means putting our hearts and hands to work, together, to give the world a really persuasive, attractive, convincing sight of the people of God-in-live-action: a people drawn together . . . by their common love of God and their mutual obedience to his demand for a world fit for his children to live in. . . ."

In this sermon Albert Outler came off pro-laity and pro-clergy because both function in their respective roles as people of God, because he was pro-God's love. While Outler may have in strong terms condemned extremisms of laity and clergy, both loved bridge-builder Albert Outler.

SERMON 28

The Laity

> But you are a chosen race, a royal priesthood, a dedicated nation, and a people claimed by God for his own, to proclaim the triumphs of him who has called you out of darkness into his marvellous light. You are now the people of God, who once were not his people; outside his mercy once, you have now received his mercy (1 Peter 2:9-10, NEB).

It is interesting, and sometimes disconcerting, to realize when you look closely at Scripture and church history, how "minor" the role of the professional clergy has been, comparatively speaking, especially in the times of the church's crises and radical transitions. Always it has been crucial (as preparatory and supportive), but rarely has it been front and center when a crisis blows. It is a little like a coach: Once the game begins, he is still involved, but it's the players who have to get the job done, or else.

The Old Testament (certainly its first two-thirds) was edited with a distinct anti-clerical bias, with the prophets (who were not, of course, settled pastors or ecclesiastical leaders) cast as the "good guys" and with the priests and hierarchy as the "heavies." In the New Testament (until you get to the Pastorals) the same anticlerical trend persists. And even after the struggling new church gets under way, it is a full century before its clerical organization is fully stabilized and in control.

Thereafter, and in all the great revival movements and great outreaches, the role of the laity as a whole (and of outstanding laymen and laywomen in particular) has regularly been decisive. In the days of persecution (second and twentieth centuries) the honor rolls of martyrs always had their full complement of layfolk.

In the later days of revivals and reformations, the role and function of the laity were almost always decisive. Martin Luther was a clergyman, of sorts, but the Lutheran reformation was largely a lay phenomenon (a queer mixture of German populism and German princes). John Calvin was a layman all his life, a shining example of the lay theologian, the lay church reformer, the lay ecclesiastic who became competent, not only to represent the church in her secular witness, but to direct her policy and program-making processes.

John Wesley was a clergyman, of course, though rather more like Billy Graham than the General Conference delegates, who condemned Mr. Graham, had ever stopped to think! But Wesley's movement was, expressly and intentionally, a lay movement: lay preachers and teachers, lay witness and mission groups (personally controlled by John Wesley as their monarch and martinet, but so loosely that, for the most part, they were on their own). And, finally, most of the great revivals of Christianity in America have been led by clergymen, but actually manned by layfolk, as far as their follow-up and follow-through were concerned.

By the same token, whenever a church has been heavily clericalized, or strongly dominated by its hierarchy—or, conversely, when the laity have depended too heavily on their clerical hierarchy and bureaucrats for their mission and Christian self-understanding— the church's impact in and on the world has faltered more often than not and its effectiveness diminished. I could illustrate this by hours of historical documentation, but it may be enough just to point to the present malaise of organized Christianity (in all its mainstream examples): the failures of the contemporary church, in general. I do not speak as a pessimist or a cynic, but rather as a loving critic with a vision of what the church could and should be in our time.

This malaise and these failures are due, in large part at least, to a twin misconception:

1. That because the ordained clergy represent the church in some very special (and proper) sense (in their ministry of Word, Sacrament, and Order), they are, therefore, the church visible, in the church and in the world, in some special, unique way; and
2. That the proper role for truly loyal layfolk is to support the clergy in their role of being the church visible, while the disloyal laity do what they can to hobble and domesticate their overzealous clergy so as to produce a crop of tame cats or spiritual troubleshooters.

This is a profound confusion, on all sides, and the unraveling of it and the reweaving of its tangled strands into some sort of coherent doctrine of the people of God and their ordained and special ministries is one of the most puzzling and urgent of all the jobs we have before us in the United Methodist Church (or any other church that I know of, for that matter).

For if you were to ask the average minister, or layman, where to look for "the church," how to tell it when he sees it, how the church's mission in the world ought to be defined and executed, the typical answer, from a great many people (lay and clergy) would be: "the clergy," "the hierarchy," or at the least "lay leaders closely coached by the clergy" (with plays sent in from the bench, and often executed by the player-coach). And if someone were then to suggest that this is the wrong answer, the next, almost instinctive question might very well be: "Well, then, what else are the clergy good for?"

What is the real and essential distinction (in role or function) between the general priesthood of all believers, and the specially ordained ministers (members of the Annual Conference in full connection!) except, maybe, their formal education and the fact that many of them work full time at their jobs? We've had various commissions studying this problem for years, and we are still very far from clear, as a church, as to any truly necessary, essential distinction between laity and clergy—once we admit, as we do, that baptism and confirmation amount to the basic ordination to Christian witness, mission, and service.

For if the church is "the people of God," then the *laos* (the laity) are the church visible in and to the world. It is the laos who show the world what the church really is—not chiefly by their words but in their lives; and what the world sees of the *laos* is what it really believes the church is (and on this score, the world is right). It is the *laos* (the people) who communicate the gospel, not chiefly by formal discourse, but by all the informal, indirect ways that illustrate their actual understanding of the Gospel . . . their personal interpretation of Scripture, and of what Christian history they may know, and of their own personal Christian experiences: all in straightforward, credible language (and example). It is the *laos* (the people) who walk the Christian way in the world and so either convince the world that Christ is the way, the truth, the life, or leave it unbelieving. It is the *laos* (the people) who bridge the gap between sanctuary and the sidewalk if it is ever bridged, between the pew and the office, home, school, factory, between the sacramental and the secular dimensions of existence.

But all this depends on what kind of "people" they are, whose people they are, how well they understand their mission and servanthood and why, how truly they are God's people, how deeply and self-consciously and consistently they live and love and have their being in God's love and grace, and how really and truly their existences are understood as sacramental, i.e., as outward, visible, and tangible "signs" of God's inward and invisible grace and providence.

There are hundreds of voluntary associations in the world, many with admirable purposes and goals, many that are useful and rewarding to their members and to society at large. The church has no monopoly on political and economic wisdom, on prophetic vision and courage, on psychological and moral insight. But it is, for its own faithful at least, the only society with its conscious ground and end in God's love and righteous will; the only society wherein the neighbor is loved for God's sake, where persons are equal and cherished because they are equally cherished by God, where minorities have rights because they "are members one of another" in Christ's body, and for Christ's sake. The visible, tangible presence of the church in the world is not some sort of generalized goodwill nor a display of moral superiority, self-righteousness, or even what has all too often been called "lay theology" (half-digested Tillich or Barth or Harvey Cox—or whoever).

The church is effectively present in the world when Christian laymen and laywomen, who understand their Christian faith and its commitments, live out their lives in their worldly callings in the terms and feeling tones of their Christian commitments. These commitments begin with (1) their love of God above all else and of all else in God; (2) their love of neighbor in God and for Christ's sake; (3) their daily round of Christian self-criticism (sins acknowledged, repented, and forgiven); (4) their unwearied effort to make sense of the mysteries of evil and of good; (5) their gratitude for the occasional inrush of insight and uprush of joy; (6) their growing sense of serenity and stability as crises mount and the dark closes in; (7) their dauntless daring to turn the world upside down, for God's sake and for his kingdom's coming!

Give the world the sight of such a people—not heroes or geniuses or even tin-horn saints—but of dedicated, honest, and self-exposing witnesses to what God's love really means in and through their lives, and you have the church militant in the earth and missional: The real presence of Christ that can convince and convert the world. "If I be lifted up," said Jesus, "I will draw all men unto me" (John 12:32), and this is what it means for him to be "lifted up" and exhibited to the world he loved and for which he gave himself. And all of this is the work of the laity, for they are the church visible in the world. And the world will be converted to Christ, finally and fully and for real, by what they see of this church made visible, tangible, real by the people of God.

Now, if all this sounds to any of you—laity or clergy—as if it reduces the role and office of the ordained clergy to something not quite necessary or marginal, something less than sacred and indispensable, it is a sad sign of the profound confusion into which we have fallen. The persistent but heretical assumption that it is the clergy who are the church visible (in the church and in the world as well), and, consequently, that the laity's business is either to support the clergy as their representatives and spokesmen, or else to complain that this clergyman or that, or this group of clergymen or that, or even "the church" (usually clergy or clericalized laity) don't represent me (or us), don't speak for me (or us), etc. The other part of the same heresy, of course, is the clerics (or group of clerics) who act as if they were the church visible, audible and infallible (as in many of our General and Annual Conference resolutions, etc., etc.).

But surely it is obvious, or at least it has seemed obvious throughout Christian history, that the people of God cannot continue in their corporate life and mission in the world, or function validly and effectively, without sacral leadership, the special ministry of persons whose main office and function is the twofold one of helping the people of God to define and understand themselves as the people of God (with all that this presupposes and requires); and, second, to prepare God's people, in his sanctuary, for their mission in his *saeculum* (or world). For God's people is a sacral society, a community that lives and moves and has its being in the sacred mysteries of God's sovereignty, God's providence, God's relentless demand for love and justice in the world and in the sacred joys of worship, praise and thanksgiving, in the sacred moments of vision and ecstasy, the sacred excitements of courage in the face of danger, serenity in the face of death.

No sacral people can exist without sacral leaders, even though the sacral ministry has, of course, no intrinsic superiority in sanctity and holiness. All members of the *laos* are priests to one another (never to themselves alone), and all ordained clergy are, in this sense, also members of the church visible in the world.

But there is an ordained, set-apart ministry of Word, Sacrament, and Order that is different not merely in degree from that of the general priesthood. It is different in kind, and without such a ministry, adequately called, commissioned, and truly fruitful, the laity can never rightly exercise their ministry in the world, however earnest or strenuous. If ever there were a matter that is both/and and not either/or, it is this correlation and cooperation of laity and ministry that is an absolutely prime example. And it needs far more urgent and profound pondering than it has had in modern Christianity, in my time at least.

In any case, and with a wise and prescient instinct, the United Methodist Church is moving toward a lay-dominated church (however ill-advised some of its provisions for this may be, as they are in my judgment in our new so-called "Structure"). This is the clear meaning of the increase of lay representation in the Annual Conferences, in the Council on Ministries, in the boards and agencies, and in the enhanced roles of women, youth, and minorities in the policy-making processes of the church (always excepting the minority of the adult white male—the one remaining minority the church tends to exploit rather than truly care for). The Council on Ministries will now have one-third laymen, one-third laywomen, and one-third clergy, who may, of course, be male or female. Any way you look, the formal role of the clergy in program and policy making is being reduced.

The instinct for this, as I say, is sound, for if the laity are to exhibit the church before the world, they ought to be held responsible for the stance, posture, and image of the church in and toward that world. The clergy ought to be held responsible for the intellectual, spiritual, and ethical preparation of the laity (in large part, at least); but if the laity are really going to control program and policy making, then they must accept responsibility for this. And if they are not really going to control processes in which they have a clear majority of the votes, then we ought to admit openly that we are playing games in some very grave and serious matters.

All of this, though, raises the stark question as to whether our laity, by and large, are fully prepared to be the church visible in the world, to take full responsibility for the church's image in the world, before the unbelieving, disbelieving, misbelieving multitude. I do not mean whether they are academically proficient in biblical criticism and technical theology; this may or may not be necessary or important in the first instance. Rather, I want to know whether your Christian faith is clear, sound, personally real, and whether you can discuss it intelligibly with others so that it makes sense (to you and them), so that it is thoughtful, credible, with the ring of tested experience. You know as well as I do that laymen and women like this are few and far between. Nor do I ask whether you have any technical training in ethical analysis, but rather whether the reasons for your crucial value judgments are informed, thoughtful, credible as well as deeply felt at "gut level," as they now say. (This may be one of the causes of the epidemic of theological and ethical "colitis" that's going around!) I'm still spiritually depressed over the level and quality of the debates at the General Conference on social principles and structure, for they were, too often, examples of the same sort of simplistic, one-sided (often passionate) arguments, with the same obvious biases that one might expect in locker rooms or a precinct convention squabble. And there's no good in blinking at the fact that the laity are, for the most part, unprepared for the roles being thrust upon them!

All of which means that the most open, urgent, and momentous frontier in the United Methodist Church for the present and foreseeable future, is the renewal of the laity for their missional and leadership roles in the church they are becoming more and more responsible for. This does not mean just paying up, or hiring the clergy to be your religious spokesmen in and to the world. It most emphatically does not mean any kind of lay control of the pulpit or the baptismal font or the Lord's Table—in the sacred ministry of sacred things, of Word, Sacrament, and church order. Your minister is most emphatically not your employee or hireling. He is the representative in your midst of the whole church, the spokesman and agent of the church catholic within the church local (and you and he must both understand this unique relationship).

Your first duty is to seek and hear God's word in your minister's words to you (however unfamiliar his words may sound, according to your childhood training in Christian rhetoric). It's your job to seek and find God's grace proferred you in the minister's leadership of worship and his celebration of the sacraments (even if these may sometimes involve some fairly strange and ungraceful antics, according to your likes and prejudices).

You have a right to sound doctrine from your pulpits, edifying worship in your sanctuary, meaningful directions for your Christian witness and mission in the world. But your own personal feelings are not fully valid criteria for judging these matters, and your personal likes and dislikes are certainly not adequate norms in making your assessments. This is part of the point to our new statements on doctrine and social ethics: They offer guidelines by which you, and all Christians, can learn to analyze and form responsible judgments and policies, in addition to and in correction for your prejudices and personal biases. Nor are these statements infallible in themselves: They, too, must be tested against the revealed truth of Scripture, the wisdom of history, the inner light of conscience, and the calm objectivity of critical reason. Most of all, it means that professing Christians may differ vigorously in conscience and love, so long as they are brought and held together in their mutual commitments to God, in Christ, through the Holy Spirit.

This means some drastic changes in our traditional conceptions of what laymen/laywomen are and ought to be. It calls for deep, honest searching as to the reality and clarity of our Christian faith and profession, diligence in our probing of what this means and requires of us, vigorous self-discipline in prayer and reflection and self-directed Christian duty, bold initiatives in seeking and finding ways to make our Christian professions visible, audible, attractive, converting—in all your dealings with all God's children (and in every human, social circumstance where love and justice are at stake). It means putting our lives where our mouths are (for the pious types) or, alternatively, putting our mouths to useful work in explaining and communicating our real faith. Most of all, it means putting our hearts and hands to work, together, to give the world a really persuasive, attractive, convincing sight of the people-of-God-in-live-action: a people drawn and held together by their common love of God and their mutual obedience to his demand for a world fit for his children to live in, his command that love become the law of life, with joy and gladness as its chief hope and reward.

For if "you are truly a member of the Christian *laos*," as the man who wrote 1 Peter said:

> You have been born anew . . . through the living and enduring word of God. . . .This . . . is the word of the Gospel preached to you. . . . So come to him, our living Stone. . . . Come, and let yourselves be built, as living stones, into a spiritual temple, become a holy priesthood, to offer spiritual sacrifices [of your lives] acceptable to God through Jesus Christ. . . . [For] you are a chosen race [not by merit, genes, color or culture], a royal priesthood [not, remember, for yourselves, but for others] a dedicated nation [not for aggrandize-

ment but for service] . . . a people claimed by God for his own, to proclaim the triumphs [in life and death] of him who has called you out of darkness into his marvellous light. You are now the people of God, who once were not his people [scattered persons and rival groups]; outside his mercy once, you have now received his mercy (1:23-2:10 NEB).

And the God of all grace, who has called you into his eternal glory in Christ, will himself, after your brief suffering [your witness and service here], restore, establish, and strengthen you on a firm foundation [his kingdom]. [For] he holds dominion for ever and ever. Amen (1 Peter 5:10-11, NEB).

Peace to you all who belong to Christ! (1 Peter 5:14, NEB)

Introduction

This sermon, preached at the 1964 General Conference of the Methodist Church in Pittsburgh, Pennsylvania, admonished the institutional church to be faithful even as individuals are called to be faithful. Albert Outler said, "Some of you may know that my record as an apologist for the Establishment is a poor one. I was bred by parents who, separately and together, stood up to the tyranny of some of the really great ecclesiastical despots of an early happier day. Thus, I come honestly by my self-chosen role as 'an outsider.' I cannot bring myself to join in the chant 'we're doing fine; we're doing fine, etc." He added, "When did Methodists forget that the doctrine of the Fall and original sin applies to ecclesiastical institutions as well as men—and both to hierarchs and prophets?"

Outler said of his parents, "Mother and father were quite extraordinary people actually. Dad was this self-educated, wonderfully openhearted man. What I recall most clearly about him was the heartiness with which he moved through the world. Any and everywhere with people he was never obsequious. He grew up in the age of the tyrant bishops—Candler, Will Ainsworth. He was never obsequious to rich or eminent men and women. Never condescending either. Anybody was his friend by at least potentiality, and he moved among them with dignity."

As were his parents before him, Albert Outler was no apologist for the Establishment. He had a way of pointing his finger at ecclesiastical despots and saying, "Ye that do truly and earnestly repent . . . ."

SERMON 29

Our Fathers' Faith and Ours

Need I say more? Time is too short for me to tell the stories of Gideon, Barak, Samson, and Jephthah, of David and Samuel and the prophets. Through faith they overthrew kingdoms, established justice, saw God's promises fulfilled. They muzzled ravening lions, quenched the fury of fire, escaped death by the sword. Their weakness was turned to strength; they grew powerful in war, they put foreign armies to rout. Women received back their dead raised to life. Others were tortured to death, disdaining release, to win a better resurrection. Others, again, had to face jeers and flogging, even fetters and prison bars. They were stoned, they were sawn in two, they were put to the sword, they went about dressed in skins of sheep or goats, in poverty, distress, and misery. They were too good for a world like this. They were refugees in deserts and on the hills, hiding in caves and holes in the ground. These also, one and all, are commemorated for their faith; and yet they did not enter upon the promised inheritance, because, with us in mind,

God had made a better plan, that only in company with us should they reach their perfection.

And what of ourselves? With all these witnesses to faith around us like a cloud, we must throw off every encumbrance, every sin to which we cling, and run with resolution the race for which we are entered, our eyes fixed on Jesus, on whom faith depends from start to finish: Jesus; who, for the sake of the joy that lay ahead of him, endured the cross, making light of its disgrace, and has taken his seat at the right hand of the throne of God.

• • • • • • • • • • • • •

Remember where you stand: Not before the palpable, blazing fire of Sinai, with the darkness, gloom, and whirlwind, the trumpet-blast and the oracular voice, which they heard, and begged to hear no more; for they could not bear the command, "If even an animal touches the mountain, it must be stoned." So appalling was the sight, that Moses said, "I shudder with fear."

No, you stand before Mount Zion and the city of the living God, heavenly Jerusalem, before myriads of angels, the full concourse and assembly of the first-born citizens of heaven, and God the judge of all, and the spirits of good men made perfect, and Jesus the mediator of a new covenant, whose sprinkled blood has better things to tell than the blood of Abel. See that you do not refuse to hear the voice that speaks. Those who refused to hear the oracle speaking on earth found no escape; still less shall we escape if we refuse to hear the One who speaks from heaven. Then indeed his voice shook the earth, but now he has promised, "Yet once again I will shake not earth alone, but the heavens also." The words "once again" . . . imply that the shaking of these created things means their removal, and then what is not shaken will remain. The kingdom we are given is unshakable; let us therefore give thanks to God, and so worship him as he would be worshipped, with reverence and awe; for our God

> is a devouring fire (Hebrews 11:32-12:2; 12:18-29, NEB).

The passage read for us by Bishop Alton for our Scripture lesson comes from an ancient pep talk to demoralized Christians in the church's second generation after Pentecost. In the first generation, the gospel was preached in a setting of vivid apocalyptic expectations. God's great deed in Jesus Christ had ushered in a new aeon whose triumph was imminent and assured. This was good news indeed, (*evangelion*) real gospel—exciting as a showdown always is. Now, after a generation with no *parousia* in sight, many Christians were beginning to be impatient or discouraged that God had not intervened directly in the ambiguities of their existence in a world that had already outlived their calendar for it. This is not surprising. The optimists who strike for final solutions are often thwarted. Those who resent the adjustments that hope has to make with history are easily demoralized.

The Epistle to the Hebrews is an effort by an anonymous Christian sage to rally the flagging spirits of the brethren, by restating for them the gospel message; by recalling them to its mystery and wisdom; by exalting before them the Christ (our Elder Brother, High Priest, and Savior); by setting forth the ventures of Christian faith in their historical perspective. His conclusions, however, drawn from some very fancy theologizing, are thoroughly practical and personal:

> Since we have a great high priest, who is like us in every way, sin only excepted, who has passed through the heavens and opened up the way of life for us, let us therefore boldly approach the throne of our gracious God in the certain and sure confidence that we shall receive his grace and mercy in every time of need (4:14-16).

To know and count on this access to God's grace is good news for the fainthearted—then, now, or whenever. It is important to see how strongly our author emphasizes the connection between the past and the present, the children's faith and their fathers, between the heritage of the heroes of faith and the contemporary community of non-heroes. So closely are we joined to our fathers in the faith that they also have to depend on us for the outworkings of their dreams and visions, just as we must depend on them for the foundations on which we may build. It's up to us, so runs this argument, to see that what they lived and died for does not go for nought. Without us, their contributions cannot be "perfected." Here then is a clarion call to high-hearted, clear-eyed faith; a blunt challenge to the fainthearted and the fusspots of every age: "Fish or cut bait or go ashore; don't just stand there mumbling!"

Surely some of you, in this company, have already leaped ahead, down the meanderings of the people of God through time and space, to yet another mission to another demoralized church that began when

> two young clergymen, not very remarkable in any way, of middle age, having a tolerable measure of health (though rather weak than strong) began to call sinners to repentance! . . . God gave a signal blessing to their work. Many sinners were thoroughly convinced of sin and many truly converted to God. Their assistants increased, both in numbers and in the success of their labors. Some were learned; some were unlearned. Most of them were young; a few middle-aged. Some of them were weak; some, on the contrary, of remarkably strong understanding. But it pleased God to own them all, so that more and more brands were plucked out of the burning.[1]

In the beginning the chief mission of the Methodist societies was the renewal of Christian morale among men and women who already "belonged" to the Established Church, i.e., who had been baptized, confirmed, enrolled, etc. (What else do we mean by "belonging to the church," even now?) The Methodists had a horror of this nominal Christianity because they could see how cruelly it bored people, how sadly it deceived them, how tragically it distorted the Christian message from good news to good advice. Hence, they set out to call men to flee from the wrath to come (to repudiate their inauthentic existences) and "to continue to evidence their desire of salvation, by turning away from blatant evils, by busying themselves with the works of love and mercy, by availing themselves of the ordered use of the objective means of grace."[2] (I wish I knew how many of you recognized this as a paraphrase of our General Rules which we generally honor by ignoring.)

The Methodist Revival was significant because it gave the Gospel of Christ a new voice: good news to desperate people whose lives were otherwise an idiot's tale. To those who heard and believed the gospel, the Methodists did more: they gave them a new quality of comradeship that combined rigorous group therapy together with honest, warmhearted support. In these "societies," men and women found Christian guidance, Christian nurture, Christian ventures in righteousness (personal and social), and all of this under the lash of criticism and persecution that reminds us that Methodists were born for controversy—and have never been willing, when we knew what we were about, to settle for peace in place of justice.

All of this is to say that our fathers knew very well that the spring of Christian morale lies in faith, faith that expresses itself in grateful love to God and to all God's children, faith that in Cranmer's words, which Wesley made his own, is

> a true trust and confidence of the mercy of God through our Lord Jesus Christ and a steadfast hope of all good things at God's hand . . .; a confidence that though we should fall from him by sin, yet if we return to him by true repentance, he will forgive our offenses for his son's sake and make us inheritors of his everlasting Kingdom; that, in the meantime, he will be our protector and defender, and not withdraw his mercy finally from us, if we commit ourselves wholly unto him, hang only upon him and call upon him ready to obey and serve him. This is the true, living Christian faith, which is not in the mouth an outward profession only, but liveth and stirreth inwardly in the heart. And this faith is not without hope and trust in God nor without the love of God and of our neighbour, nor without the fear of God, nor without the desire to hear God's Word and

to follow the same in avoiding evil and gladly doing all good works.[3]

If something like this be true, then the Christian message is great good news, indeed—to twentieth-century men no less than to the first who ever heard it. Who thus trusts God, "a strong abode in heaven and earth possesses."[4]

It is only a tedious commonplace to say that modern man is demoralized. What is worse, we in the church are doubly demoralized because we, too, share the misgivings and anxieties of our fellows in the riven, writhing world; and, also, because we seem to have lost our confidence in our own unique business in that world; to see it that the Word of God is rightly preached, the sacraments duly administered, and scriptural holiness spread over these lands.

No matter how positive our thinking, however resolute our optimism, there's no blinking the fact that we are in an acute crisis of morale in the Methodist Church, a widespread faltering of faith in the relevance and efficacy of our elementary undertakings: evangelism, missions, education, social concerns, etc. And as a consequence, we are awash in a swirling tide of malcontentment: an atrabilious, stale condition in which so poor a novel as *The Stained Glass Jungle* gives aid and comfort to many a self-righteous cynic. All too many in the younger generation of our ministry are tragically estranged from their baffled and resentful elders, and this at the time when the first of the younger crop nurtured in the newer theological perspectives has begun to graduate into the upper levels of the ecclesiastical power structure.

From where I sit (or squirm) in a theological school, the most dismaying facet of this syndrome of demoralization is not the perennial ferment of maturing faith and vocational self-understanding. This is painful enough, but it can always be handled, one way and another, in a genuine community of authentic faith and grace. What dismays me is the rise and spread of what I would call *ecclesiastical hypochondria*, and I see this in many quarters among those who feel bound to proclaim the emancipation from ecclesiastical servitude.

To any church historian, the institutional church's lack of total relevance, in any of the crises she has thus far survived, is an old story—as is also the story of the church doing better in retrospect than prospect. But, nowadays, the discovery that the contemporary church is a good deal less than fully relevant, fully efficacious in the agonies and anomalies of our time, has produced violent spasms of misdoubt that the church is relevant at all.

To ease their pain, the disenchanted perfectionists give themselves over to the spiteful joys of making inventories of the church's foibles and failures. Such inventories come a dime a dozen: in sermons, essays, books, and speeches at the General Conference—all avowedly prophetic, all patently self-righteous! They range from the prophetic cynicism of Peter Berger, through pious petulance to the implacable bitterness of the typical headliner at student conferences, to the pathetic snobbery of the bright theolog who, fleeing from the intolerable ambiguities of the institutional church, falls finally, Ph.D. and all, into the academic slave market.

Just as with a hypochondriac who has trapped you into hearing his tale of woe, you marvel that he still has strength to speak, so also nowadays when our ecclesiastical breast-beaters are in full cry, I find myself looking about mournfully to view the ruins of the church that once must have been perfect (even though I know there never was such a thing in fact), a church that once must have ruled in righteousness over a docile, grateful society (another hangover from "Never-never Land"). They make me feel uneasy with their poignant slogan about our "post-Christian society," even though I know perfectly well that there never has been a truly Christian society for this one to be "post" to. But at least they set me pondering the ironies of hypochondriacs becoming hierarchs since it is an axiom that all hierarchs are hypocrites—an axiom to be matched by another: Hypochondria is faintly phony.

Some of you may know that my record as an apologist for the Establishment is a poor one. I was bred by parents who, separately and together, stood up to the tyranny of some of the really great ecclesiastical despots of an early happier day. Thus, I come honestly by my self-chosen role as "an outsider."

I cannot bring myself to join in the chant "we're doing fine; we're doing fine, etc."—or in the alternative shout: "Anathema to the critics, death to the rebels, to the boondocks with those who rock the boat." I leave to the unfathomable patience of God the blinkered sycophants, the hopelessly hopeful, those who confuse their cheerfulness with faith, their wishful thinking with hope, their servility with love. The plain fact is that the church in the modern world is in trouble, and we who are in the church are in trouble. Much of what our critics say is so, and we do not refute it by ignoring them or by excusing ourselves.

But healthy men in perplexity do not fall into frenzies of self-pity; brave men in danger do not end their liturgies with confessions of sin. The Christian who is honest enough to confess that the remembrance of his misdoings—and the misdoings of his church—is grievous to him and an intolerable burden does not therewith shuck that burden or fall back wearily after an orgy of remorse, especially vicarious remorse for the sins and shortcomings of "the power structure," as he may snidely call his elders and brethren in Israel.

If we are honest in the confession of our sins and the sins of our church, we ought then to believe that God is faithful and just to forgive us our sins and expect of us that we get on to the next question: What is there to be done; what can be done; how, when, for, and with whom, to what ends and by what means? At the very least, it's no good confusing the role of Amos of Tekoa with that of Don Quixote de la Mancha!

When did Methodists forget that the doctrine of the Fall and original sin applies to ecclesiastical institutions as well as men—and both to hierarchs and prophets? How did we come by this perverted perfectionism that assumes that the church could convert the world into Eden if only it hadn't sold out to Gehenna, if only we had Edenite laws and leaders? Are we really so cynical that we refuse to include the church in our doctrine of justification by faith alone—or to believe that she, too is *simul justa et peccatrix*—with sins to be repented of and remedied—and yet also the object of God's pardoning and enabling grace? Here is yet another of those places where pious exasperation would profit from historical perspective, not to mention the good that might come from a renewal of our evangelical understanding of the nature of the church.

Apparently, we have never really come to terms with the fact that "the people called Methodists" have become an established church without ever quite coming to theological terms with our origins as an evangelical society. Some of us, sometimes (the perfectionists), act as if we understood the rightful genius of Methodism to be that of the evangelical society—with its inbuilt puritanism. The rest of us seem to go on the assumption that it was our destiny to become an established church, with the blight of nominal Christianity that always bedevils an inclusivist institution. And, as if this residual tension between sect and church were not enough, we Methodists, in the course of the past century, have managed to cut ourselves off from our original traditions and ethos more decisively than any other major American denomination. The evidence for this is all over the place, but shows most visibly in the strange theological kaleidoscope that is contemporary Methodism. We can simply sniff at those who say that Methodists have no theology. The truth, no less disturbing, is that we have a hundred theologies, most of them borrowed!

The plain truth is that we run the theological gamut from blatant fundamentalism to bland unitarianism, from personalistic idealism to existentialism (which is not so far as some would suppose), from the old-fashioned and unrepentant liberals to the new-fangled liberals of the post-Bultmann school, from *The Upper Room* to *Christ Without Myth*. Every major theological vogue in Protestant thought in the last century has filled its quota of subscribers from amongst the Methodists. Then when its tide washed out, it remained as a residue somewhere in the Methodist amalgam.

Four years ago, the Episcopal Address made an interesting appeal for an exploratory study of our distinctive Wesleyan heritage and the possibility of some broadly conceived synthesis that might introduce some order into our doctrinal chaos. Of all the proposals in that great message that have gone unheeded *ad interim*, this one was the most assiduously ignored. And yet, if you ask what bedevils our ecumenical relations more than any other, save for an occasional absurdity like our demand that all Christendom define temperance as total abstinence (and this as the price for Christian unity), it is this: That Methodists are so wildly pluralistic, so passionately indifferent to historic Christianity.

Even this could be borne, and maybe made a virtue of, if only we were still intent upon the primordial enterprise for which God called us into existence, getting the Word of God rightly preached to all and heard by many, and the sacraments duly administered and received, with a table fenced by faith but not by class nor color. The only justification for our continued existence as a denomination would be something distinctive and effective about our passion that the gospel of pardon be proclaimed and accepted; the lordship of Christ announced and acknowledged; men made aware by sign, symbol, sacrament, and martyrdom that God in Christ is still reconciling the world to himself, sharing in our existence to the end that we might share in his; that sin, personal and corporate, be named for what it is; that Christ's atonement become the ground for man's doxology; that grace become the literal source and matrix of our living and dying; that the church be built up in and for the world.

Our fathers' faith was in the good God, the All-governing Father, in the gospel proclamation that, in Christ, the powers of sin and death have been broken "for us men and for our salvation."[5] They believed in the residence and the presidence of the Holy Spirit in the lives of the faithful. They abhorred the horrors of sin and of man's inhumanity to man so that they sobered the drunken; fought off human slavery; gave dignity to labor; and made thrift, industry, and sobriety truly practical virtues in a debauched society. They tried to integrate evangelical faith and evangelical living; they sought to provide effective nurture for the converted, significant community for the committed; they gave concrete meaning to the notions of holy living and holy dying. And if you say that this sort of gospel is not relevant to the modern mind, I can only wonder if you believe it, or something like it, to be true. If you take it for true, it is then only a problem in rhetoric to make it relevant.

Do you really think that modern man is not interested in, or able to hear, an honest word about faith as trust in God, a message about forgiveness as God's renewal of fellowship with those who will be honest with themselves and with him? Is it irrelevant, really, in a society starving for nonexploitative love, for men to bear witness to the strange freedom and courage that comes with our new life in God's grace, the new zeal for social revolution that comes from a Christian ethic of gratitude? Do you really think that, in a world stumbling through the valley of the shadow of the Bomb, there are not multitudes who would be challenged and changed by a passion to live in love and die in faith, struggling to understand how this commits them to responsible care for human culture and social righteousness?

Our fathers' faith reshaped history, not because they set out to reshape history but because they meant to haul men up short before the utter glory of God in judgment and mercy, to help them see their neighbors in a new light, and to devote themselves to creative but unostentatious service. This, or something like it, is what they meant by the preaching of the Word and administering the sacraments.

They were not fascinated, as we are, with the problems of communications and semantics. They were, however, obsessed with the truth and urgency of what they had to communicate. They had a message, a gospel; they had a commission; to save souls; they had a comradeship in disciplined Christian living; they had a sacramental passion that no man should miss out on hearing the gospel on their account, that no life go unloved.

Once upon a time, Methodism was Christianity in dead earnest. What more, what less, what else can we claim for our tradition, for our message, for our commission and comradeship, for our church? Can you imagine men with this faith and this ordination more than casually preoccupied with the church's failings and with the chores of institutional housekeeping? Would men with this spirit whine or rail or fawn? To put it around the other way, the same question in different terms, what could we hope for from a really sizable company of Methodists like this? I don't know exactly; but God knows I'd love to find out before I'm gathered hence! And where would there be a better place and time for something like this to be resolved than here and now, in these fateful days of this General Conference, where a great muddled church stands on trial not only before the un-understanding curiosity of the world but in a very real sense before the judgment bar of God?

Said the author of Hebrews to an earlier age and yet also to us:

> Remember where you stand: not before the palpable, blazing fire of Sinai, with the darkness, gloom, and whirlwind, the trumpet-blast and the oracular voice. . . . No, you stand before Mount Zion and the city of the living God . . . the full concourse and assembly of the first-born citizens of heaven, and God the judge of all, and the spirits of good men made perfect, and Jesus the mediator of our new covenant [with God], whose sprinkled blood has better things to tell than the blood of Abel. See that you do not refuse to hear the voice that speaks . . . The kingdom we are given [in the current shaking of the foundations] is unshakable; let us therefore give thanks to God, and so worship him as he would be worshipped, with reverence and awe; for our God is a devouring fire (Hebrews 12:18-19a; 22-25a; 28-29, NEB).

Let us pray:

> For the fellowship of this great Conference in which we are gathered; for the sense of thy presence confronting and directing us; for the heritage from our past and thy promised guidance into the uncertain future, we thank thee, O Lord.
>
> Accept us, yet once again, O most merciful Father, as we consecrate ourselves anew to thy service, so that thy Spirit may rule in our hearts by faith and our lives may be laid out in joyful witness to thy grace and glory, through Jesus Christ our Lord. Amen.

Introduction

This ordination sermon was preached at the 1964 Southwest Texas Conference meeting in San Antonio. While the situation caused the sermon to be directed toward the ordinands, by implication it was for the whole church. For only out of the whole church context does the ordination make sense.

Albert Outler's authority for this sermon is spelled out in the sermon: "The basic authority of the layman (ordained by his baptism-confirmation) is the authority of his own Christian experience. . . . Without this authority, any man is still playacting in his ministry. . . ." Outler spoke out of that experience: "The essential difference (the only distinctive one) between laity and clergy, in the Methodist tradition, is not that between an amateur and a pro, but between one who is priest in his home, neighborhood, office, and marketplace (always, however, in a private capacity) and one who is priest from the whole church to some segment of that church (and always in an ecclesial capacity)."

Dr. Outler accepted this authority from and to the whole church as experienced in the Wesleyan tradition. His final authority, Scripture, validated his own experience, and challenged his audience: "These, then, are your themes; urge them and argue them. And speak with authority. . . ." (Titus 2:15, NEB).

Albert Outler spoke with authority, an authority that took hold in his life even when he was not preaching. It was the authority given him (revealed in his expressed awareness of God's grace) that causes you to read these sermons to find out more about him. (This is true even if you read these sermons to find out why he agitates you!)

SERMON 30

"Take Thou Authority . . ."

(Ordination Sermon 1)

For your own part, what you say must be in keeping with wholesome doctrine. Let the older men know that they should be sober, high-principled, and temperate, sound in faith, in love and in endurance. The older women, similarly, should be reverent in their bearing, not scandal-mongers or slaves to strong drink; they must set a high standard, and school the younger women to be loving wives and mothers, temperate, chaste, and kind, busy at home, respecting the authority of their own husbands. Thus the Gospel will not be brought into disrepute.

Urge the younger men, similarly, to be temperate in all things, and set them a good example yourself. In your teaching, you must show integrity and high principle, and use wholesome speech to which none can take exception. This will shame any opponent, when he finds not a word to say to our discredit.

Tell slaves to respect their masters' authority in everything, and to comply with their demands without answering back; not to pilfer, but to show themselves

> strictly honest and trustworthy; for in all such ways they will add lustre to the doctrine of God our Saviour.
>
> For the grace of God has dawned upon the world with healing for all mankind; and by it we are disciplined to renounce godless ways and worldly desires, and to live a life of temperance, honesty, and godliness in the present age, looking forward to the happy fulfillment of our hopes when the splendor of our great God and Saviour Christ Jesus will appear. He it is who sacrificed himself for us, to set us free from all wickedness and to make us a pure people marked out for his own, eager to do good.
>
> These, then, are your themes; urge them and argue them. And speak with authority: let no one slight you (Titus 2:1-15, NEB).

Have you ever noticed how commonplace people take their commonplaces for granted; how readily they rely upon clichés; how disconcerted they are when pressed for clarity and cogency in their definitions and explanations?

This human trait was analyzed in one of the earliest Platonic dialogues, the *Euthyphro*. In this dialogue the old philosophic curmudgeon, *Socrates*, meets his cocky young neophyte, *Euthyphro*, one morning on the steps of the Athenian Court of Justice.

In the opening lines, it turns out that Euthyphro is there in order to press charges of impiety against his own father—wholly confident of being in the right (to say nothing of being self-righteous). This prompts Socrates to suppose that if Euthyphro understands impiety well enough to prosecute his own father, he must also understand what piety is (a notion Socrates avers he's never yet gotten quite straight). Euthyphro modestly agrees and thus is set up for Socrates' seemingly innocent question: "And what is piety?" Without hesitation or shame, Euthyphro answers, "Piety is doing what I am now doing. . . ." The remainder of the dialogue is devoted to the demonstration that Euthyphro had never really faced up to his clichés, had never really thought out his fine phrases, had never proved his fashionable jargon.

This habit of using language without quite knowing what it means—and therefore without really meaning it—is very strong in religious people in general, in clergy more especially, in theologs most especially. This is not, however, the time or place to go into that. What I would propose, instead, is that we focus on just one area of our habitual indifference to self-examination: What does it mean to be Methodist Christians and, within this murky area to aim at an even narrower issue, what is the Methodist understanding of ordination?

Here we are, about to witness and share in a great event; a uniquely solemn, climactic ceremonial—crucially significant in the lives of these ordinands, equally significant in the life of the church. Are we any clearer about what we are doing here than Euthyphro: "Ordination is what we are doing here tonight. Watch and you may catch on!" What is the order and office of the deacon? What will these men have when Bishop Galloway has finished with the service? What is the order and office of an elder, and what, if anything, is essentially different between an elder and a deacon—between elders and deacons and other members of the *laikos* of God?

If you have clear and adequate answers to these questions, please let me have them in writing and I'll see that they are duly transmitted to our new Committee for the Study of the Ministry. While waiting, however, I feel moved to comment on the grave confusion that is increasingly evident in the minds of Methodists in the face of such obvious queries about such familiar aspects of our Methodist ministerial polity.

The first comment is an obvious and ironic one. By law, we now allow laymen, deacons, and elders to do everything involved in the ministerial office, if their ministries are confined to a local congregation. What, then, is the difference between the ordained and the unordained? What is the difference indeed—when you get it down to the ecclesiological essentials—but a certain amount of formal education in a theological school? Does this mean that a Bachelor of Divinity degree is correlated, ecclesiologically, to ordination? But if this is the case, then what kind of doctrine of the church, ministry, and sacraments do we really have—or propose to have? Yet again, what is the real difference between a deacon and an elder—in our law or in our practice?

If, by now, you are impatient with such theoretical musings, and if you are saying to yourselves, "What does all this matter? What really counts is faith and the charism of the Holy Spirit in a man's heart and mouth," then you are pointing to yet another predicament in our Methodist ecclesiological self-understanding.

In 1960, as you know, the General Conference set up a Committee on the Study of the Ministry that was to report to the 1964 Conference. This report, as again you know, recommended the reduction of our traditionally two-ordered ministry to one order—the elder—together with the relegation of the term "deacon" to designate an office that might be exercised, upon occasion, by any baptized member of the church who is licensed to preach.

I do not intend here to dilate upon what seemed to me the glaring inadequacies of that report, or what I regard as the ineptness of its practical suggestions. This has been done with modesty and precision by Professor Dale Dunlap in a recent issue of *The Advocate*. My point is that when this report reached the Legislative Committee on the Ministry at Pittsburgh, the result was animated chaos: as ripe a disorder as ever I saw afflict a group of distinguished churchmen. The debate took a new turn every day—and sometimes more than one in 24 hours. When, finally, they grudgingly acknowledged the obvious, that they had, and could reach, no consensus among themselves in respect to an adequate doctrine of the ministry, it was with evident embarrassment that they remanded the whole question for further study to a new committee for another quadrennium.

Now, I've no disposition to interfere with the work of that new committee (may God have mercy on their souls), but there are a few things we might all hold in mind as we follow their work and participate in the church-wide debate that this whole topic requires. The first is that, sooner or later, we Methodists have got to come to terms with our double heritage and the various dyadic implications that that double heritage has for us. We began as an evangelical society within a branch of the church catholic. We have evolved into a separate denomination, autonomous, free (albeit inclined nowadays to gravitate toward a congregational polity, especially in our larger churches, toward a

Baptist view of the sacraments, and toward a pan-denominational view of ecumenism). Look through our *Discipline*— and through all our literature—and you'll see various anomalies: here of deposits from our inheritance from the Wesleyan societies; there the tokens of our role as a church (replete with a fully furnished ministry, duly administered sacraments, etc., etc.).

Membership in any duly constituted church turns on baptism and confirmation ("reception into full membership"). What, then, about that vivid declamation: "There is only one condition previously required of those who desire admission into these societies—a desire to flee from the wrath to come, to be saved from their sins"?[1] This is the original basis of the first Wesleyan society: a company of nominal Christians proposing to pool their forces in an attempt to respond to the Christian gospel in dead earnest.

Again, we have in every *Discipline*, the General Rules of our United Societies, which as you know every Methodist minister is obligated to read and expound annually in every congregation committed to his care.[2] Ahem. (*Discipline*, 1960, Para. 352.12.) Here is the societal element in our heritage, that wonderful fusion of the evangelical and the ethical in the Christian message that was so characteristic of Wesley—and once so characteristic of Methodists in general. On the other hand, we have our Articles of Religion, in which (in Article XIII) we are defined as "a congregation of faithful men in which the pure Word of God is preached, and the sacraments duly administered according to Christ's ordinance, in all those things that of necessity are requisite to the same"[3] (i.e., whatever it takes to get the pure Word preached and heard and the sacraments duly administered and received). Both belong in our Methodist heritage and community, but they are not the same things and they had best not be confused.

Again, we have an inherited doctrine of baptism (and confirmation, as the completion of the one initiatory sacrament) as the basic ordination of all Christians to the general priesthood—the essential priesthood of all believers, all witnesses, all teachers, all martyrs, etc. Baptism signs and seals a person into the *laos tou theou*— constitutes him as a layman (*laikos*)—the word also means a man of no distinction and still again in some passages: "a

Christian"! Within this general priesthood, however, is an especially selected and commissioned group of representative priests who, by immemorial tradition, both serve and serve *for* the general priesthood.

These men are chosen and designated by their representative gifts and graces (which should include education, but not exclusively) so that, in all their lives and actions, they are both disposed and qualified to act representatively—not of themselves, as disciples of some school or party, nor out of some vivid visceral enthusiasm, but as a representative of the whole of The Methodist Church, the entire segment of the people of God in this denomination. The essential difference (the only distinctive one) between laity and clergy, in the Methodist tradition, is not that between an amateur and a pro, but between one who is priest in his home, neighborhood, office, and marketplace (always, however, in a private capacity) and one who is a priest from the whole church to some segment of that church (and always in an ecclesial capacity).

Finally, we can see our heritage as a society in those wonderful interrogations propounded to those who are being received into full connection in the Annual Conference (originally as the personal assistants of Mr. Wesley himself):

> Have you faith in Christ?
> Are you going on to perfection?
> Do you expect to be made perfect in this life?
> Are you earnestly striving after it?[4]

Appropriate answers to these questions—which probe to the marrow of the Christian life of faith, discipline, and witness—qualify a man to be a Methodist preacher; and you will notice that they are widely and deliberately separated from the ordination rituals for deacons and elders. This corresponds to John Wesley's distinction (as, e.g., in his famous "Korah" sermon) between the "preacher" (the baptized-confirmed Christian with gifts and graces for preaching and pastoral care) and the "minister" (the ordained preacher, who has been duly authorized to act in and for the whole church, in the crucial acts that require and represent the whole church in action, i.e., in the sacraments).

The essential difference between the licensed preacher and the ordained elder does not pertain, primarily, to superior human qualities of any sort, nor to formal educational attainments or pretensions. It is not chiefly pragmatic (and this is where we tend to get confused, for, as Methodists, we would naturally prefer to solve all our problems pragmatically—as if we could). The real difference has to do with authority—by what right and with what basic authority does one act in and for the whole church?

The basic authority of the layman (ordained by his baptism-confirmation) is the authority of his own Christian experience, and that, as Methodists have always insisted, and rightly, is fundamental and prerequisite. Without this authority, any man is still playacting in his ministry—and may readily mislead the people and corrupt the church. But it is not enough. By itself, it is overly subjective and individualistic, too parochial and accidental, to constitute the final or full authority for the due administration of the sacraments. Baptism and the Lord's Supper are sacramental acts performed in, by, and for the local congregation, but the authority for their performance does not come from the local congregation. This authority comes from the whole church, understood as the whole church. It derives from the entirety of the Christian community both in space and time, the whole cloud of witnesses that surrounds every Christian congregation whenever it gathers to ask the Lord's blessing.

When the minister pronounces the words, "I baptize thee, in the Name of the Father, Son, and the Holy Spirit," he is not speaking for himself alone. This is no private transaction nor, primarily, a psychological event. When he presents the loaf and cup to the faithful in the Lord's Supper: "Take and eat, in remembrance," this is not a pallid bit of group therapy. These are representative acts, and their authority does not come, in the first and last analysis, from the charm and charisma of the minister, but from his representative character as the ordained and thus authorized agent of the whole body of Christ, the whole people of God.

Presently, at the crux of the ordinal for deacons, Bishop Galloway will say to each of these ordinands, "Take thou authority to execute the office of a deacon in the Church of God; in the name of the Father, and of the Son, and of the Holy Spirit. Amen."[5]

One tragically misunderstands these momentous words and this momentous event, if he regards either as perfunctory or magical. Humanly speaking, Bishop Galloway's personal authority cannot be transferred. Nor, for that matter, can the personal authority of these men—their powers, or charms, or influence—be thus enhanced by any such transference. But what is transferred is the right, the privilege and the obligation to be and to act as representative of the entire Methodist Church in every corporate ministerial function these men will ever hereafter perform.

This is not hocus-pocus, not mumbo-jumbo. But there might and ought to be a decisive change in your own self-understanding. Who am I? All too often this is a cant question, a narcissistic musing, as if the other narcissists and navel-gazers really cared about my identity. But it makes a difference if I can say, with Martin Luther, "I am a baptized Christian"; or, with John Wesley, "I am a representative of the whole church and, as such, I can regard the whole world as my parish."

Again, Bishop Galloway will say to the elders: "Take thou authority as an elder in the Church to preach the Word of God, and to administer the holy sacraments in the congregation. Amen."[6]

This will be an act by which you will henceforth identify yourself and be identified by others. It stipulates your real and rightful authority and it lays on you the undeclinable demand that you exercise your ecclesial authority, without selfish ambition on the one hand, and without false modesty or timidity on the other. Who am I? I am an ordained elder in The Methodist Church, and I stand before the world and before the mirror of my own self-understanding in that representative capacity. It is from the whole church that I received my ministerial authority; it is in the whole church that I exercise it; and it is only the church as a whole that can rightly judge my ministerial character—and that on grounds other than my personal popularity or lack of it.

Here is even more than the liberty of the Christian man. Here is the most fundamental freedom of them all: of the pulpit, font, and table. The Methodist minister is free lord of any and every congregation and subject to none (ecclesially speaking); the methodist minister is bound by his duty to the congregation to represent the whole church in their midst—and is, therefore, subject to everyone.

> For the grace of God has dawned upon the world with healing for all mankind; and by it we are disciplined to renounce godless ways and worldly desires, and to live a life of temperance, honesty, and godliness in the present age, looking forward to the happy fulfillment of our hope when the splendor of our great God and Saviour Christ Jesus will appear. He it is who sacrificed himself for us, to set us free from all wickedness and to make us a pure people marked out for his own, eager to do good.
>
> These, then, are your themes; urge them and argue them. And speak with authority: let no one slight you (Titus 2:11-15, NEB).

Make sure, though, that you distinguish between slights to your person and slights to your office, whether as members of the general priesthood or as members of the representative priesthood. Personal slights—as well as personal popularity—have to be dealt with with whatever grace and wit and courage you can muster, but never merely as self-consolation. But a slight to my office means a lack of respectful understanding of the essential nature of the church and its requisite ministry. Wherefore, let us seek always to act in the full consciousness of the authority we have received, never confusing it with our personal self-images, but neither allowing any unprotested indignity or denigration of the people of God.

We are, therefore, come to a great moment, to the real climax of this Conference. Tomorrow we shall know where you are to exercise your diverse ministries for the ensuing year. But now, already, tonight, if we really understand and share in what God is doing here in his church, in providing a representative ministry for his people—we could know what that ministry is and will be all about!

> Now in the presence of God, who gives life to all things, and of Jesus Christ, who himself made the same noble confession and gave his testimony to it before Pontius Pilate, I charge you to obey your orders irreproachably and without fault until our Lord

Jesus Christ appears. That appearance God will bring to pass in his own good time—God who in eternal felicity alone holds sway. He is King of kings and Lord of lords; he alone possesses immortality, dwelling in unapproachable light. No man has ever seen or ever can see him. To him be honor and might for ever! Amen (1 Timothy 6:13-16, NEB).

Introduction

On June 12, 1964, Albert Outler shared his faith with the Central Pennsylvania Conference, which met in Harrisburg, Pennsylvania. He put his experience of faith in these words: "Faith is not an end in itself, just as salvation is not an end in itself. Faith is a means to love, and the dynamic factor that relates faith to love—or matures faith into love—is human freedom acting in accordance with revelation and reason." Outler concluded his sermon with this challenge: "Let us see first what is first—the renewal of faith—the daily renewal of that faith in which we may live and work, in which we may suffer and grieve, in which we may grow old and die, in which we may face the slings and arrows of outrageous fortune and an unfriendly world that is not our home, but our mission territory."

How do you get this faith? Dr. Outler said in the spirit of the founder of Methodism: "Preach faith until you have it. And then because you have it, you will preach it. Or, as happened to John Wesley, preach faith until others have it and their faith will confirm your own."

In his post-retirement-retirement (he retired twice) days, Outler had more preaching engagements than he had during his heyday on the faculty. If he were preaching faith until he had it (and he was preaching it), he had a bundle of it to preach! Many who will read these sermons can confirm that his faith preaching brought that awareness alive in your souls. Maybe that is why he would light up when he saw you, greeted you, and loved you. Your faith brought alive by his faith reinforced his faith. He kept on preaching to others that faith he saw in you, that you got from him. He in return gained more, and others did too.

SERMON 31

Faith Renewed

There is still a vital point to that old wheeze about the college president who, when asked about how many students were in his college, answered, "About half of them."

This point got a new twist for me last fall in Vatican II, when they were debating the schema on the universal call to holiness to every Christian. There was much talk about the vocation of Christian laymen—both to witness and to sanctity—and not much was being said about the monastic orders and their place in this business of holiness.

Finally, the Master General of the Order of Preachers (the Dominicans) got up to redress the balance a bit. He reminded the bishops of the immense influence of monasticism and of the religious orders in the history of the church—and in the life of the church today. "Indeed," said he, "we seem to have overlooked the importance of the fact that nearly half of the Fathers of this Council are religious!"

It took me a full moment to untangle what that naturally meant to me, and what he intended by his use of "religious" as a noun—when we habitually use it as an adjective.

But a semantic confusion like this sets one to pondering. In one sense, all bishops are religious—look at their professions of faith. So are all our preachers: Remember that all of us have taken the vows of church membership. Besides, most of us have answered "yes" (or at least "uh-huh") to those startling interrogatories for admission into full connection:

> Are you going on to perfection?
>
> Do you expect to be made perfect in this life?[1]

All members of the church are religious, in this nominal sense—for they, too, are avowed believers and consciously dedicated servants and stewards of God.

Yet here is where our malaise and unease comes. All the religious people are not really religious. Or, at the very least, we do not manage to convey that impression in our actions as Christians. I have a great many acquaintances who frankly disavow conventional Christianity, who ignore or resist the claims of the church. One of them is my next-door neighbor who is convinced that "organized religion" is big business, with supernatural sanctions promised to suckers in place of normal dividends. Another is my left-wing liberal newspaper editor acquaintance (maybe you didn't know we had such a thing in Texas, but we do: *The Texas Observer*, a poor thing as a newspaper but full of courage and quixotism). This man says that anything that organized religion can do, enlightened humanism can do better. A third friend is a leader in our local NAACP—and he disturbs me most of all—for he argues that organized religion is chiefly an unintended bolster for the social status quo.

I can, and do, argue with these men—and others of my unbelieving colleagues in the academy and the world. But their basic charge still haunts me: Do we really believe what we say and sing and pray —in our private devotions, in our corporate liturgies, in the resolutions and pronouncements?

I hear a great many sermons, and I'm all too often quite clear as to what the preacher doesn't believe any more but not what he still believes. We are often clearer as to our humanitarian concerns than our awareness of and security in the mysterious grace of the living God. I hear a great deal about psychological self-understanding—and the gospel as insight—but not much that persuades me that these narcissists live in the heights and depth of the supernatural realities of God's self-revelation in Christ and in the whole order and round of creation.

I am one in heart and hand with those who join with the oppressed, the victims of human inhumanity; but I get an uneasy feeling all too often that the reasons and rootage of much of the social revolution is finally humanitarian. And, good as that is, I know enough of human history to know that this ideology is finally a great tyrant over the human spirit.

The renewal of the church depends upon the renewal of faith, and this means faith in God—the God and Father of our Lord Jesus Christ: Sovereign Creator, Encompassing Mystery, Inscrutable Judge, Incarnate Love, Resident Spirit; beyond any reach or management of man, beyond our power to wheedle or use, but the God who has come amongst us, "for us men and for our salvation."[2]

Christian faith is a vital relation to the supernatural—or eschatological if you like. Christian faith is faith in God, not about God. Christian faith is world-denying, in the sense that it designates this world and its value for what they are: transient, instrumental, finally trivial. Christian faith is ascetic, in the sense that it calls men from the immersions and distractions of the transient orders of existence and experience to the life of the Spirit, the life in the Spirit, to an ascetic disregard of all that does not serve as a means to spiritual fitness and the fullness of faith, which is love.

"We see on every side [said John Wesley in one of his greatest treatises, now largely unknown] either men of no religion at all or men of a lifeless, formal religion. We are grieved at the sight and should greatly rejoice if by any means we might convince some that there is a better religion . . . [,]no other than love: . . . the loving God with all our heart and soul and strength, as having first loved *us*, as the fountain of all the good we have received, and of all we ever hope to enjoy; and the loving every soul which God hath made . . . on earth, as our own soul."[3]

The means to this religion of love is faith, and here we come upon one of the really creative theological insights of John Wesley, which sets him off from both classical Protestantism and all sacerdotal forms of catholicism. Faith is not an end in itself, just as salvation is not an end in itself. Faith is a means to love, and the dynamic factor that relates faith to love—or matures faith into love—is human freedom acting in accordance with revelation and reason.

By the same token, God's sovereignty is not an end in itself, as the Lutherans and Calvinists tend to hold with their *soli gloria dei*. God's sovereignty is a means to divine grace. God is jealous of his sovereignty only in order to insure the final triumph of his love. Here, too, the freedom of God is his freedom, not to be sovereign, but to implement his love for creation, which is his "ultimate concern."

Faith, said John Wesley, is not a set of beliefs but a spiritual sensitivity to the encompassing mystery of God and the things of God. It is the spiritual sensorium of man, just as his neural organs and brain form his physical sensorium.

Faith is the eye of the soul, which gives it insight into the spiritual environment that is our natural home.

Faith is the ear of the soul, which hears the Word of God—of pardon, reconciliation, and commission.

Faith is the palate of the soul, which tastes and sees that God is gracious.

Faith is the feeling of the soul, which makes a man inwardly certain of the love of God shed abroad in his heart.

John Wesley said:

> "By this faith we are saved" from all uneasiness of mind, from the anguish of a wounded spirit, from discontent, from fear, and sorrow of heart, from that inexpressible listlessness and weariness, both of the world and of ourselves, which we had so helplessly labored under for many years, especially when we were out of the hurry of the world, and sunk into calm reflection. In this we find that love of God and of all mankind which we had elsewhere sought in vain. This we know and feel—and therefore cannot but declare—saves every one that partakes of it both from sin and misery, from every unhappy and every unholy temper.
>
> Soft peace she brings, wherever she arrives

She builds our quiet as she forms our lives;
Lays the rough paths of peevish nature even,
and opens in each breast a little heaven.
[Matthew Prior, "Charity," lines 5-8]

If you ask, "Why then have not all men this faith; all, at least, who conceive it to be so happy a thing? Why do they not believe immediately?"—we answer (on the Scripture hypothesis), "It is the gift of God" [Ephesians 2:8]. No man is able to work it in himself. It is a work of omnipotence. It requires no less power thus to quicken a dead soul than to raise a body that lies in the grave. It is a new creation; and none can create a soul anew but he who at first created the heavens and the earth.

May not your own experience teach you this? Can you give yourself this faith? Is it now in your power to see, or hear, or taste, or feel God? Have you already, or can you raise in yourself, any perception of God or of an invisible world? I suppose you do not deny that there is an invisible world: you will not charge it in poor old Hesiod to Christian prejudice of education when he says, in those well-known words,

Millions of spiritual creatures walk the earth
Unseen, whether we wake, or if we sleep.[4]

Now is there any power in your soul whereby you discern either these or him that created them? Or can all your wisdom and strength open an intercourse between yourself and the world of spirits? Is it in your power to burst the veil that is on your heart and let in the light of eternity? You know it is not. You not only do not but cannot (by your own strength) thus believe. The more you labour so to do, the more you will be convinced, "it is the gift of God."

It is the free gift of God, which he bestows not on those who are worthy of his favour, not on such as are previously holy, and so fit to be crowned with all the

> blessings of his goodness, but on the ungodly and unholy, on those who till that hour were fit only for everlasting destruction, those in whom was no good thing, and whose only plea was, "God, be merciful to me, a sinner" [Luke 18:13]. No merit, no goodness in man, precedes the forgiving love of God. His pardoning mercy supposes nothing in us but a sense of mere sin and misery; and to all who see, and feel, and own their wants, and their utter inability to remove them, God freely gives faith, for the sake of him "in whom he is always well pleased"[cf. Matthew 3:17; 12:18; 17:5; 2 Peter 1:17].
>
> This is a short, rude sketch of the doctrine we teach. These are our fundamental principles; and we spend our lives in confirming others herein, and in a behavior suitable to them.[5]

These words, these categories, these modes of conceptualization do not belong to the essence of the matter. It is the actuality of God's sovereign grace as the sole and utter hope and reliance of our hearts and mind and practice!

This actuality can be expressed in many rhetorical, philosophical, psychological modes. But faith is renewed as we sense the certainty that we are dealing with reality.

The renewal of the church depends on the renewal of faith, and this depends on at least three levels of renewal in our hearts and in our churches.

1. *A theological renewal.* I do not wish to overstress this, but no amount of spirituality is finally stable or effective unless it is rightly ordered in basic understanding. John Wesley's heart was strangely warmed at Aldersgate, but unless his doctrine had been basically sound by then, he might readily have lost himself in the maze of Moravian enthusiasm and antinomianism, as he very nearly did for a time. The renewal of our understanding and commitment to the Wesleyan theology would be a giant step to basic renewal otherwise.

2. *A liturgical renewal.* In the Roman Catholic experiment in reformation, the first and fundamental step was the reforma-

tion of their life of worship. God save us from liturgical fuss and feathers and grant us the grace to rediscover the simplicities and profundities of total devotion to God and neighbor in love.

3. *In corporate discipline.* Methodism is enacted faith—and this not on impulse or by rule but by corporate charismata. When Christian congregations covenant to love and discipline each other, strange and wonderful things happen.

4. *A renewal of conversions and the quest for holiness of heart and life.*

No established church has ever been renewed by itself or *in toto*. But church history is full of examples of renewals—none of them engineered, and no two by any one pattern or formulary.

In our time, our hope lies in our return to the awful, wonderful, glorious simplicities of the gospel: that God for Christ's sake has forgiven our sins—and will forgive them—and has, and will, set us free from the law of sin and death.

And this must be matched by the most sophisticated exegesis, the most agonizing hermeneutic, the most austere asceticism, the most adventurous commitments to difficult or diligent discipleship.

But it all comes down to the one utterly stark question: Are you certain of God's love and can you proclaim it certainly? Preach faith until you have it. And then because you have it, you will preach it.

Or, as happened to John Wesley, preach faith until others have it and their faith will confirm your own.

In all our "church work," in all our ecclesiastical business, in our ideological struggles, all our ecumenical handholdings, in all our doubts and fears and disabilities, let us see first what is first—the renewal of faith—the daily renewal of that faith in which we may live and work, in which we may suffer and grieve, in which we may grow old and die, in which we may face the slings and arrows of outrageous fortune and an unfriendly world that is not our home, but our mission territory.

Introduction

In relating the Methodist/Evangelical United Brethren uniting conference (Dallas, Texas, April 23, 1968) to the first Pentecost Albert Outler said, "Pentecost is rightly remembered as the day when the Christian church was launched on its career in history, for the world. . . . the analogy between that first Pentecost and this one could be edifying for us."

As to the style of the new church, he called for it "to be a church truly catholic, truly evangelical, truly reformed."

These sermons of Albert Outler clearly reveal that he was "catholic" to the core; that he was evangelical as he, like a broken record, repeats over and over: "Love as you are loved by God through Christ"; that he was, by his renewed nature, a reformer. When did anyone ever see him sit still, satisfied with the status quo, with being "average"?

When he mentioned that "the good is the enemy of the best," he reflected the early influence of his mother, viz., whatever Albert Outler did with his life, his mother would say, according to Albert, "Now did you do your very best?" Then Albert added, "And she would look mildly incredulous if I said I had!"

Since the uniting conference where this sermon was preached, the United Methodist Church has become a smaller unit, dwindling in souls; torn by the homosexual issue; threatened by special interest groups hammering out their own doctrinal statements, etc. We need to have another conference; this sermon needs to be preached again; this time the church needs to listen.

SERMON 32

Visions and Dreams

Fathers and Brethren and Sisters in Christ:

Here we are this morning, gathered from over the world and from all sorts and conditions of men, to celebrate a birthday, our birthday as The United Methodist Church. In just a few moments now, we shall join in a ceremony symbolizing our new covenant of unity and mutual growth together. The aura of every new-born thing is an aura of hope. And so it is with us today. We stand here on a threshold. A new horizon looms ahead.

In some ears, it may sound fantastic to relate this day to the first Pentecost as recorded in Acts 2—what with no rushing mighty wind, no tongues of fire, no glossolalia, etc. But actually, the lasting meaning of that Pentecost was its opening the way for others to follow.

> While the day of Pentecost was getting on, they [the disciples] were all together with one accord in one place. . . . And they were filled with the Holy Spirit and began to speak . . . as the Spirit gave them the power of utterance . . . about the great deeds of God (Acts 2:1, 4, 11).

This is, of course, an abridgment of the longer text, with the marvels omitted and also those two bits of local color that still intrigue me: the one where Peter denies that the disciples are drunk because it was too early in the morning (about the same time of day as now); and that other one about the 3000 new members added in one day. What a frustration it must have been for Peter to have all that happen, with no board to report it to!

Clearly, though, that first Pentecost was less significant for what happened then than for what came after. Pentecost was the day when the real work of the church began, when the Christian people accepted the agenda of their unfinished business in the world and began to get on with it. Those first Christians were not very well-furnished in terms of ecclesiastical apparatus. Their organization was shaky; their polity and discipline sketchy. Their theologians were in typical disagreement, and their most prominent lay leaders were Ananias and Sapphira!

Even so, that Pentecost was ever thereafter memorable as the church's birthday, as the day when Joel's prophecy was fulfilled, when the Holy Spirit would come and abide as God's governing presence in the midst of his people. This memory remained, even when the rushing mighty wind subsided to homiletical zephyrs, when glossolalia was relegated to the margins of Christian experience, when the tongues of fire gave way to controversy and conflict.

Pentecost is rightly remembered as the day when the Christian church was launched on its career in history, for the world. In every age, her performance has been scandalously short of her visions and dreams and her plain imperatives. And yet also in every age since that first Pentecost, it is the Christian church that has marked off the crucial difference between man's best hope and his genuine despair.

I know as well as anyone that this analogy between that first birthday and this one of ours does not apply foursquare. Our new church does not represent a radical break with our several past histories nor is there a comparable intention toward a radically new future. Even so, the analogy between that first Pentecost and this one could be edifying to us. This is the day when the real work of The United Methodist Church begins. It is a day when doors are opened that heretofore were closed, when new possibilities of reformation and renewal are literally "at hand."

The essence of the event is self-evident: it is the accomplished fact of The United Methodist Church. Where once, scarcely a generation ago, there were five churches, now there is one. Where once our differences kept us apart—with different languages and folkways—now they are overcome or at least contained within a larger circle of committed fellowship. We have been Christian brethren, after a fashion, for the better part of two centuries—but separated brethren. Now our memberships and ministries have been mingled without compromise or indignity; our separate traditions have been sublated and made one.

Obviously, no part of our venture in unity is really finished as yet. Our joy in this union ought to be tempered by our remembrance, in love, of those others of our Christian brethren, whom we acknowledge as such, and yet from whom we are still separated. Moreover, the various practical, domestic problems posed by our agenda in this conference loom large and exigent. It will not be a debonair fortnight; few of us are likely to be content with the outcome. Yet here we are and this is our birthday. Here we turn a new page in modern church history, and, just as smugness is excluded from our celebration, so also is cynicism.

Let us then ask ourselves what this fact of a new church makes possible. What will it take to turn this beginning into the reality of its promise and of our hopes? We can offer our ungrudging gratitude and honor to all those whose toil and tears, faith and fortitude have led us to this hour—so long as we are all clear that none of their laurels (and certainly none of ours) is for resting on. We have much to be grateful for, nothing to be complacent about. Our joy this day is foretaste: foretaste of a future that can be even more creative than we have yet dared to ask or think.

This means that, as we turn from our ceremony of beginnings to the tasks that follow, our foremost need is for a vivid sense of the church we have been called to be. By what norms shall we seek to transform our covenant into genuine *koinonia*? By what principles are we willing to be guided in the agonies of growth that lie ahead? To what heavenly vision are we prepared to be obedient in the difficult days and years that even the blithest optimist can foresee?

One thing is for sure: What has served till now as our *status quo ante* will simply not suffice for the upcoming future. For all its great merits, for all its saints and heroes, the standing order is now too nearly preoccupied with self-maintenance and survival. The world is in furious and agonizing turmoil, incomprehensible and unmanageable. The church is in radical crisis and in the throes of a profound demoralization at every level: of faith and order, life and work. In such times, business as usual simply will not get our business done. Our own past golden age (the nineteenth century), the heyday of pietism in a pre-urbanized society, has faded. Frontiersmen for tomorrow must be as dynamically adaptive to the new "new world" as our forefathers were in theirs.

There is, of course, a bit of glibness here, for the brute fact is that we have no clearly visible alternative to the *status quo* ready to hand, available merely for our choice and application. For all their advertisements, none of the new experiments in celebration of our own brave new world can honestly be hailed as the shape of things to come. Nor is it the case that any of our sister churches have had vouchsafed to them the blueprints for Zion's Ark, space-age model—though some (notably the Roman Catholics) have recently exposed themselves to more massive and more fruitful self-examination than we.

For freedom we have been set free from the outdated past. But it begins to look as if we have been condemned to freedom as well: Condemned to come up with something better than protests and complaints and self-righteous criticism of others; condemned to responsible prophecy, reform and renewal—or else to the fatal consequences of destructive discontent.

If, in this new church of ours, we are to avoid "the dinosaur syndrome" (with its zeal for furnishing later ages an abundance of fossils) or its opposite, "the Elijah complex" (with its self-pitying self-righteousness about our minority status), we must find our way forward in conscious concern for the continuum of the Christian tradition and history in which we stand with our forefathers; always aware of God's habit of linking the past and the future by means of the hopeful acts of men in decisive present moments like this one! We must learn to discipline our imaginations and inventions, not by our own constrictive biases but by

God's open-hearted mandates for his people, by patterns that will serve our common life in the body of Christ.

One version of the style of the new church that is to be has already been encapsulated in a phrase now familiar from the discussions of the Consultation on Church Union. It is a sort of motto that could qualify as a charter for authentic unity and effective mission: "We seek to be a church truly catholic, truly evangelical, truly reformed." These words themselves are obviously not new; COCU has no copyright on this motto. Its significance lies in its summation of three essential dimensions and concerns of any company of persons calling and professing themselves Christian. Each of the terms has had a varied history of interpretation and misinterpretation; each has been a fighting word at one time or another. It is only when all three are taken and held together—each blaming and explaining the other two—that we can recognize their relevance as goal points for the church we aspire to be: catholic and evangelical (both, not either/or); catholic, evangelical, and reformed—viz., with both catholic and evangelical concerns brought under perennial reassessment and re-formation in each successive new age.

One of the virtues of the motto is that it suggests a rich range of meanings, without specifying any single one of them as obligatory upon all. Certainly the interpretation I now propose makes no claim to finality. My only concern is to interest you in trying to understand its possible import for us in The United Methodist Church and in our efforts to shape her future during these next two weeks and the next two decades.

The basic meaning of the word "catholic" is "whole," "universal," "open." It reminds us that true unity not only allows for diversity, it requires it. "Catholic" has never rightly meant "uniform," "lockstep," "produced by template." It means "inclusive," a community in which all the members belong equally and by right of membership, in which all ministers share equally the basic office of representing the whole church, by right of ordination. It means "open," a community whose boundaries are set by the Christian essentials (the bare essentials at that) in which it is bad faith for anyone to deny full membership to any other save by the canons of faith in Christ and the Christian discipline that derives from that confession. This rules out all distinctions based on race, sex, class, and culture; and so also all distinctions based on partisan emphases on this doctrine or that, this form of worship or that, this pattern of polity or that. Here is the plain teaching of Wesley's sermon on "Catholic Spirit," a sermon we would do well to recall and to update in terms that might fit our own condition.

A church tormented and befuddled by racial strife is not yet truly catholic. A church that cannot manage her global tries without colonialism or autonomy is not yet truly catholic. A church that proudly (or humbly!) sets her own polity and folkways above those of other churches may be "united," but she is not yet truly catholic. A church that opens her sacraments to all other Christians, but is herself not yet eligible for sharing in the sacraments of some of the others, is not yet truly catholic. And if the main fault here lies, as we may think it does, with others fencing us from their sacraments, this does not alter the fact that we have rarely asked, with appropriate dignity, what is required of us, and them, for the valid mingling of our memberships, ministries, and sacraments. It is also true that the other churches are not fully catholic either—and this is the ecumenical tragedy. But if we are to join them in the search for a more inclusive, integral catholic fellowship in Christ, the least we can do is to commit ourselves to just such a fellowship in this new church of ours, and to open our hearts and minds to yet further bold venture in question of Christian unity.

But catholicity by itself is not enough. The church is called to mission, and her mission is both her message and the demonstration of that message in her corporate life. Her message is not herself either; it is her witness to the Christian evangel: to the scandal and folly of Christ incarnate, Christ crucified, Christ resurrected, Christ transforming human life and culture, Christ in the world, Christ for the world; Christ in us, our hope of glory! Thus, the church we are called to be must be truly evangelical, a church ablaze with a passion that God's gospel shall be preached and heard and responded to in faith and hope and love by all who can be reached and instructed and gathered into the fellowship of God's covenanted people.

The fullness of the gospel embraces all human concerns

everywhere and always, but the heart of the gospel is startlingly simple: That God loves you and me and all men with a very special love and that Jesus Christ is the sufficient proof of this love to every man who will receive and confess him as Savior and Lord. The gospel is the good news that it is God's love that pardons, heals, and reconciles; it is God's love that demands we be fully human; and it is God's love that opens up this possibility for us; it is God's love that can sanctify our memories and our hopes.

Yet this same gospel also reminds us, in every human circumstance, that our salvation comes from God's sheer unmerited favor. In no sense can it ever be earned or bought or wheedled. It does not come by any merit or demerit, by any good works or bad, by any claim that we can bring on our own behalf.

The word "evangelical" is concerned above all with the faith that receives the gospel wholeheartedly and in trust; it stresses faith as a gift from God, faith as man's basic response to God, faith as the mortal foe of all human pride, yet also faith as the loyal ally of all true human dignity. The church evangelical is, therefore, radically Christ-centered, disengaged from any final dependence on ecclesiastical apparatus of whatever sort, save only as it ministers to her central mission: That men may receive God's gift of saving grace in Christ and learn to live in the world in true communion with the Holy Spirit and with one another.

The church evangelical is a proclaiming church, but it is also a teaching church. Wesley often pointed out that the difference between his movement and the others—equally zealous in proclamation—was his provision of societies in which converts came to learn the meaning of the gospel in depth and in concrete life situations.

We Methodists and Evangelical United Brethren alike, by profession and fond memory, are grateful heirs of evangelical fathers and brethren. But we can scarcely boast of having fully claimed their legacy. A church falling behind in the race with an exploding and huddling population is not truly evangelical, despite its self-advertisements. A church that counts her evangelical harvest chiefly in terms of members added to the rolls is not truly evangelical. A church the vast majority of whose members do not really understand the great issues entailed by "the Protestant principle"—God's sovereignty, man's justification by faith alone, the witness of the Spirit, the life of grace, the authority of the Scripture as the prime source of divine revelation, etc.—such a church is not only not truly evangelical, it is, indeed, partaker in the greatest tragedy of modern Christianity: the abject failure of the teaching church.

Here we are, Christians by name and sign, organized to the teeth and involved in titanic labors of all sorts. Yet the generality of our people do not really know what the Christian faith purports, do not really believe in their hearts and minds what they profess with their lips, and, of those who do, only a few can give a rational accounting of it to themselves and others. The proof of this turns up in every great upheaval—doctrinal, moral, social.

The church evangelical must not be doctrinaire, but surely her people should be clear about the crucial priorities between God and man in the mystery of salvation and in the enterprise of our becoming fully human. Wesley and Asbury and Otterbein and Albright understood these priorities in their day and in their terms. Those days and those terms are not ours, but the same task remains: Of calling all men to the love of God above all else and of all else in God's Spirit.

Yet, even the best conceptions of catholicity and evangelical zeal sag out of shape as history moves the church along through time and change. The provisional becomes permanent, creative experiments from an early age become vested interests in a later one, the pragmatic warrant for a given polity becomes defensive and self-maintaining. What once was a sign of catholic spirit becomes a new sectarianism; what once was an authentic evangelical concern becomes calcified into theories about evangelism that do not get the whole gospel preached and heard and appropriated for life in the secular city.

And so the church, even as it seeks to be truly catholic and truly evangelical must also be truly reformed, constantly open to God's judgment upon the insidious idolatries of every successful venture, aware of the waning of every heyday, a church eager to be re-formed, re-newed: to have her spirit and power repristinated.

A church truly reformed is one that is open, intentionally and on principle, to creative change of every sort (in teaching, discipline, and administration)—not haphazard or reckless change, but not timid and grudging either. The church reformed lives by the Scriptures, for they alone provide a decisive appeal to the constitutive tradition of Christ without the dead hand of traditionalism; the Scriptures alone provide for radical, mandated change without the gusts and shallows of human ingenuity. Their authority does not rest upon their letter nor yet with any coterie interpretation, but upon the public sense of the texts and their original intentions, enriched by the wisdom of the teaching church through all the ages, sifted by the canons of critical reason and vital Christian experience in the modern world.

But the church reformed is also under the judgment of the future. The eschatological orientation of faith is forever demanding that the old be constantly reexamined and reconstituted—always with an eye to the urgent, the needful, the effective. The reforming spirit calls for self-examination without self-justification, self-criticism without self-loathing, creative discontent rooted in the conviction that the good is the enemy of the best.

It may seem to some a mite unseasonable to suggest that The United Methodist Church needs to take conscious, urgent thought of being or becoming truly reformed, just now! We are a church re-formed: what with our new plan and our newer report and with 10 more days to pull and haul away at these plans in discussion, amendment, and adoption. Surely this is enough for the present moment. Well, ye-s-s—in a way—but that's partly my point.

This plan and the report in the form in which they will stand when we adjourn will doubtless be the very best we can do, under all the circumstances, etc., etc. But for how long will that be good enough? The answer: Not much beyond the results being printed in the new *Discipline*.

Wherefore, now is the time, as at that first Pentecost, for young men to see visions and for old men to dream dreams, visions and dreams that ask more of the Methodist people than we have ever asked before, visions and dreams that offer a richer, fuller life for all God's people, visions and dreams that see this new church renewed yet again and again, not only in the Spirit but in her structures, functions, folkways.

This is not a proposal, not even indirectly, for any specific reform—yours or mine or anybody else's. It is, however, an open advocacy of the idea of reform and of the Protestant principle of *semper reformanda*. When more of us get accustomed to the notion that this new church of ours can be remade for yet more effective mission, for still more authentic democracy and local initiative, for still more efficient, adventurous leadership—and that all this can be done and should be done forthwith—then the pooled wisdom of our fellowship will surely be enabled to prove that rational, responsible change is a far more faithful pattern of obedience to Christ than the most devoted immobilism can ever be.

This, then, is our birthday—a day to celebrate, a day to remember, a day for our high hopes and renewed commitments. This is the day that the Lord has made. Let us really rejoice and be glad in it, glad for the new chance God now gives us: To be a church united in order to be uniting, a church repentant in order to be a church redemptive, a church cruciform in order to manifest God's triumphant agony for mankind,

> Till sons of men shall learn [his] love
> And follow where [his] feet have trod;
> Till glorious from thy heavens above,
> Shall come the city of our God![1]

Let us pray:

> O God of unchangeable power and eternal light, look favorably on thy whole church, that wonderful and sacred mystery; and, by the tranquil operation of thy perpetual providence, carry out the work of man's salvation; and let the whole world feel and see that things that were cast down are being raised up, that those things that had grown old are being made new, and that all things are returning to perfection, through him from whom they took their origin, even Jesus Christ our Lord.

Amen.

Introduction

This ordination sermon, preached at the New Mexico Annual Conference on May 29, 1975, uses the first person singular pronoun "I" as much as any sermon Albert Outler ever preached. He was a preacher preaching to laity, preachers, and preachers-to-be on the subject of ministry. The subject was too close to home for him not to preach in a witnessing manner. E.g., he says, "As an ordained minister in The United Methodist Church, I am finally obligated to my Christian conscience. . . . I am not my own. . . . As for my private behavior I am bound by my baptismal/confirmation vows that sealed me into God's *laos*."

He added, "I am, therefore, free to claim and update the Christian heritage . . . I was ordained in and by The Methodist Church; but the intent of that ordination was ecumenical. . . . Actually, my orders are now confined to The United Methodist Church and a few other churches that recognize them. But, in principle and intention, they are universal, which happens to be my own deepest ecumenical concern, not for myself alone, but for the ministry and the mission of the church universal. All of this, and much more, is the work of the Holy Spirit."

SERMON 33

The Holy Spirit in the Ministry

(Ordination Sermon 2)

I hope you are not allergic to a sizable reading from Ephesians, for scattered through three chapters are the basic texts for all I have to say tonight and all that we will be doing here today.

> Remember your [human] condition. . . . Your world [apart from faith] was a world without hope and without God. But now in union with Christ Jesus you who once were far off have been brought near through the shedding of Christ's blood. For he is himself our peace. Gentiles and Jews, he has made the two one, and in his own body of flesh and blood has broken down the enmity which stood like a dividing wall between them; for he annulled the law with its rules and regulations, so as to create out of the two a single new humanity in himself, thereby making peace. This was his purpose, to reconcile the two in a single body to God through the cross, on which he killed the enmity.
>
> So he came and proclaimed the good news: peace to you who were far off, and peace to those who were near by; for through him we both alike have

access to the Father in the one Spirit. Thus you are no longer aliens in a foreign land, but fellow-citizens with God's people, members of God's household. You are built upon the foundation laid by the apostles and prophets, and Christ Jesus himself is the foundation stone. In him the whole building is bonded together and grows into a holy temple in the Lord. In him you too are being built with all the rest into a spiritual dwelling for God.

• • • • • • • • • • • • •

In former generations this was not disclosed to the human race; but now it has been revealed by inspiration to his dedicated apostles and prophets, that through the gospel the Gentiles are joint heirs with the Jews, part of the same body, sharers together in the promise made in Christ Jesus. Such is the gospel of which I was made a minister, by God's gift, bestowed unmerited on me in the working of his power. To me, who am less than the least of all God's people, he has granted of his grace the privilege of proclaiming to the Gentiles the good news of the unfathomable riches of Christ, and of bringing to light how this hidden purpose was to be put into effect. It was hidden for long ages in God the creator of the universe, in order that now, through the church, the wisdom of God in all its varied forms might be made known to the rulers and authorities in the realms of heaven. This is in accord with his age-long purpose, which he achieved in Christ Jesus our Lord. In him we have access to God with freedom, in the confidence born of trust in him.

• • • • • • • • • • • • •

But each of us has been given his gift, his due portion of Christ's bounty. . . . And these were his gifts: some to be apostles, some prophets, some evangelists, some pastors and teachers, to equip God's people to work in his service, to the building up of the body of Christ. So shall we all at last attain to the unity inherent in our faith and our knowledge of the Son of God—to mature manhood, measured by nothing less than the full stat-

> ure of Christ. We are no longer to be children, tossed by the waves and whirled about by every fresh gust of teaching, dupes of crafty rogues and their deceitful schemes. No, let us speak the truth in love; so shall we fully grow up into Christ. He is the head, and on him the whole body depends. Bonded and knit together by every constituent joint, the whole frame grows through the due activity of each part, and builds itself up in love (Ephesians 2:11, 12b-22; 3:5-12; 4:7, 11-16, NEB).

If you want all this focused in a single sentence, I would suggest Ephesians 3:7, the apostle's claim that applies directly to tonight's ritual of ordination: "Of this gospel [of God's secret in Christ] I was made a minister, by God's gift, bestowed on me without any merit of my own, by the working of his power [of ordination]."

For me, as for most of us I would suppose, many things about an Annual Conference session we can take or leave—although we might differ as to just which is which. But, again for me (and I would hope for many of you) at least three high moments occur in any Annual Conference: (1) The acceptance of carefully selected and fully credentialed men and women into probation and ordination as deacons, (2) the reception of new ordinands into full connection and Conference membership, and (3) their subsequent ordination as elders.

There is also an earlier moment in the life of the church that we ought to make much more of than usually we do, viz., the very first licensing of a man or woman to preach, that event in which the inner call to a representative ministry in the church is first confirmed by the outer call that can come from the church and the church alone.

Self-appointed ministers are either authentic prophets whose contributions may be received in the church as extraordinary blessings or else as ordinary phonies. Neither the inner call nor the outer call by the church suffices by itself. It is when these two agree that we then have a true authorization to proceed to set that man or woman apart for the ordained, representative ministry in the church of Christ (as far as that may be agreeable in the church catholic and in The United Methodist Church as a whole, at the very least).

I stress this point because already a widespread confusion exists in our denomination as to the distinctive meaning of and justification for a set-apart, representative ordained ministry, in and through the Holy Spirit. The only part of the complex doctrine of the ministry that we seem to be agreed on is the so-called "general priesthood of all believers"—i.e., the parity of all believers, before God and each other, in their rights and obligations to serve as martyrs of Christ and servants to all God's children. Indeed, I'd be pleased if we took this theological point even more seriously than we do, viz., that it is the *laos* who are the church visible in the world, the church witnessing to the world, the church that the world sees and hears and is impressed by or else sees and ignores, no matter how eloquent and charismatic this or that ordained minister may be. Ask the average Methodist layman where to look for the church visible, and he will often say, "The clergy, of course; that's what we have them for." There they are, out front, visible and audible and sometimes highly self-conscious. They are leaders of the laity, substitutes for the laity, yet also sometimes (we think) employees of the laity, not to say hirelings.

But children of this world understand this self-deception better than we do; they are rarely deceived by it. They know, by a curious intuition (infused by the Holy Spirit in their unbelieving hearts) that, unless the *laos* provides an authentic witness to the Christian gospel (of liberation of heart, mind, and life), the clerical rhetoric and clerical presence count finally for very little. An unconverted church will never convert the world, no matter how evangelistic its clergy may be. An unreformed church will never reform the church, no matter how reformist its clergy are, or profess themselves to be.

The church is defined by mission, and that mission, in essence, is (1) witness to Christ and (2) service to his brothers and sisters. And this twin mission is carried forward (or else is left laggard) in the *saeculum* rather more by the laity whose witness is visible to the world at work and whose service is sacrificed, i.e., in the name and spirit of Jesus Christ.

But if all this is so, then why in the world do we need to

ordain men and women to a special ministry, as we are about to do here tonight, as the crown and climax of this session of this Annual Conference? It is a good question, a difficult question, and Methodists generally have not put in so much time pondering and probing it as they should. The result is very often much more ceremonial than evangelical; we all too often give very superficial answers to the questions as they are asked or to the larger question that they pose: Why have an ordained ministry at all? (1) We've always done it (which is not so: the Wesleyan Revival managed mostly with lay preachers for half a century). Or, (2) other churches do it (which is scarcely a decisive reason for us). Or (3), we need especially trained men and women to direct our congregations, lead our worship, preach and teach, and do at least a major share of the church's witnessing and service for us (which is to say, we need surrogates and substitutes whom we can employ in our own stead—and call them "full-time Christian workers"). There is a profound misunderstanding here, for every fully committed Christian is either a full-time Christian worker (even in his or her secular life and work) or else he or she is what Wesley called an "Almost Christian."

Actually, in the Christian tradition in general and in The United Methodist Church tradition in particular, there is an even more profound and valid answer to our question: "Why an ordained ministry?" This is what the General Conference Study Commission on the Ministry is struggling with right now. Their report will come before the General Conference next year, and it will probably involve an extensive rewrite of the chapter on "The Ministry" in the present *Discipline*. What I have to say tonight, therefore, is less an effort to scoop the Commission and the Conference than to involve you—all of you if possible: clergy, ordinands, laity, etc.—in a serious reflection upon the problem, a sort of personal analysis of your convictions about the ministry and where these convictions are open to further insights.

For this basic answer—my version of it at any rate—begins with the premise that various paired dimensions of the church get separated from each other all too easily: (1) the church secular (in the *saeculum*) and the church sacral (the church upreaching and inreaching for its divine, eternal mystery); or (2) the church local (here and now) and the church catholic (in space, time, and community); (3) the church deployed and the church deploying; (4) the church of the individual and small groups and the church as the whole people of God.

Now the laity—the church visible in the world—are, in general, secular, local, deployed, individualized or parochialized. And therefore by the same token, the *laos* needs a *cleros*—to be, again in general terms, the church sacral, catholic, deploying and above all, representative. It goes without saying that a representative, ordained minister is an individual member of the *laos*, from whose ranks he is called (*cleros*), and in this sense, he too is a member of the church visible in, to, and for the world.

It might help us to understand this better if we compared the ministry with its cognate professions, medicine and law, even if we wouldn't want to press the analogies too far. All intelligent people are interested in good health and know a fair amount about folk medicine, etc. In this sense, we're all healers ("the general priesthood of all healers"). Moreover, we know that licensed (ordained) healers are neither infallible nor omnicompetent, and we take it for granted that they are highly individualized persons in their private lives. But we know something else equally important—every good doctor is in some important sense a representative of his whole profession (which he honors as he acts representatively, in the best sense, or would dishonor if he disregarded or fell below the standards of his profession and its Hippocratic oath).

Likewise, we are all lawyers in a sense; we are the law visible in the world, since it is the law-abiding citizenry who make the rule of law work (if, as, and insofar as it ever does). But the good lawyer is one who is not on his own (however individualized his private life may be). By training and professional oath, he is a representative of the law and the rule of law. This is what we mean when we say that a lawyer is also "an officer of the court."

With some important qualifications, good ministers are no more private persons than doctors and lawyers (however individualized they are and ought to be). They are representatives of the church, and of the whole church—the church that stretches all the way back to its apostolic origins, that reaches all the way round the globe, that includes all sorts and conditions of humankind. They are "officers of the church," i.e., designated and authorized by the church (the whole church) to act representatively in all their official functions and responsibilities, and expected by the church always to be conscious of their representative role and responsibility. For the acknowledgment that they are truly qualified to act as public representatives of the universal church (and their authority to do so) is not theirs alone; it is the church's decision, through its delegated processes and persons.

These ordinands have, indeed, volunteered—they are here offering up their lives (the whole bit) to a special representative office and mission. But the confirmation of that offering, plus their authorization to exercise this public office "in the Church of God," is the action of the church. This, indeed, is the very essence of ordination. There is no magic here—but there is a mystery—and it is the mystery of the Holy Spirit's enduement of these persons with an office, with an ordination, with a spiritual afflatus that, if received and exercised consciously and conscientiously, will make them into effectual representatives, not of this congregation or that, this Conference or that—not even this denomination or that—but of the church universal, as large a part of the whole community of Christians in the world as may be willing (now or later) to recognize and acknowledge what we will have done here tonight.

As an ordained minister in The United Methodist Church, I am finally obligated to my Christian conscience, which is not just my feelings but is the final residue of informed analysis and responsible decision in the presence of the Holy Spirit and under his authority. And this is true of you, too (all of you). This means, amongst other things, that I have no right to appeal to my conscience against the church, in any private or subjective reaction, until and unless I have considered (fully and prayerfully) the implications of the decision in the light of my representative character and until I have reached an informed and responsible decision that I can be more truly representative of the whole church (its Scripture, tradition, Christian experience, and right reason) in and through a given decision or basic choice than in any other way.

I am not my own—I have not only been bought with the price of God's love in Christ (as all his children have), but I have long since committed my professional, representative career to the church and I am bound by vows to act in keeping with this office and ordination in all my public and official performances. As for my private behavior, I am bound by my baptismal/confirmation vows that sealed me into God's *laos*. And even when I fall short, or even betray those vows, that is what I have done, and I have no just cause to claim some subjective immunity from obligations I assumed as a free moral agent.

These ordinands (by their own profession) have been called inwardly, by the Holy Spirit in their hearts. They have also been called outwardly, by the Holy Spirit in the church. They have been examined, certified, elected to their orders by an authorized and delegated body of the church universal. Now, they are to be ordained to their respective ministries in the church and in the world by the Holy Spirit. Their subjective feelings are important; the official actions of the church are important. But all of them are contingent on a prior, present, and continuing action of the Holy Spirit who will, in fact, ordain them, if, that is, they are ordained validly and for real.

Now, if something like this is so, consider some of the practical consequences. One is that in the exercise of their ministerial office they are not, in the first instance, employees of the people they will serve nor hirelings of any given congregation nor the lackeys of any institution. They will be bound by their vows, but they will be freed by them, too. I am a free Methodist just because my first and final loyalties are not to any part or person within the Methodist establishment, but are to my ministerial calling, office, and ordination. I am not, at least in principle, bound by any of the current fads or fashions as they come and go—in theology, ethics, liturgy, or polity. I am, therefore, free to claim and update the Christian heritage as a whole and my Wesleyan heritage in particular. But I am bound to do any and all of this in as faithful and humble obedience to the Holy Spirit as my heart and mind can be kept opened to.

For another thing, I was ordained in and by The Methodist Church; but the intent of that ordination was ecumenical: "The Lord pour upon thee the Holy Spirit for the office and work of an elder in the Church of God, now committed unto thee by the authority of the Church of God"—so runs our official ordinal.

Actually, my orders are now confined to The United Methodist Church and a few other churches that recognize them. But, in principle and intention, they are universal, which happens to be my own deepest ecumenical concern, not for myself alone, but for the ministry and the mission of the church universal. All of this, and much more, is the work of the Holy Spirit.

Notice carefully, in the rituals for ordinations, how the questions are framed, what they presuppose, and what they imply—for now and henceforth. Indeed, I'd be deeply gratified if this sermon would prompt you—ordinands and the whole congregation here assembled— to attend to the text of the rituals with the profound seriousness they deserve (since almost every sentence has the weight of long reflection and not a little controversy behind it). Their language is quaint and some of it outmoded; but the issues are profound and urgent—and as relevant as tomorrow. For example,

> Do you trust that you are inwardly moved by the Holy Spirit to take upon you the office of the ministry in the Church of Christ? . . . [not The United Methodist Church mind you][1]

Are you, really—moved by the Holy Spirit?

Or, again, consider the first collect in the ordinal for elders:

> Almighty God . . . who by thy Holy Spirit hast appointed divers orders of ministers in thy Church [not ours, mind you!]. . . .[2]

And then, finally, after the episcopal interrogation and the ordinands' vows, all of us will join in one of the oldest prayer hymns in the Christian liturgy: *Veni, Creator Spiritus*:

Come, Holy Ghost, our souls inspire,
    And lighten with celestial fire;
Thou the anointing Spirit art,
    Who dost thy sevenfold gifts impart.

Thy blessed unction from above
    Is comfort, life, and fire of love;
Enable with perpetual light

The dullness of our blinded sight.

Anoint and cheer our soiled face
With the abundance of thy grace;
Keep far our foes; give peace at home;
Where thou art guide, no ill can come.

Teach us to know the Father, Son,
And thee, of both, to be but One;
That through the ages all along.
This, this may be our endless song.

Praise to thy eternal merit,
Father, Son, and Holy Spirit. Amen.

In your own strength (or even in yours and ours combined) all this rhetoric is preposterous, pretentious, or, alternatively, it may be just perfunctory (say any old thing in a ceremony, and then go on out afterward to do your own thing, regardless). This, however, is scandalous, in the literal, root meaning of "scandal," viz., an offence and obstacle to the honest faithful.

But if we have both a conviction about and an experience of the Holy Spirit in the ministry (as well as in the hearts of Christians, as well as in the upbuilding of the church, as well as in its mission in the world), then we really are in business, our Father's business. We experience the mystery of ministry in the grace of our Lord Jesus Christ, which is the love of God made manifest and effectual in the communion of the Holy Spirit.

Charles Wesley understood all of this, maybe even better than his brother John: this mystery of the Christian life in the Spirit, in all its dimensions. And one of his hymns that I have cherished greatly ever since it first helped me understand what my Christian experience was based on and what horizons opened out from that experience (and is one of my favorites for many other reasons as well):

Spirit of Faith, come down,
Reveal the things of God;
And make to us the Godhead known,
And witness with the blood.

’Tis thine the blood to apply
And gives us eyes to see,
Who did for every sinner die
Hath surely died for me.

No man can truly say
That Jesus is the Lord,
Unless thou take the veil away,
And breathe the living Word.
Then, only then, we feel
Our interest in his blood,
And cry, with joy unspeakable,
“Thou art my Lord, My God!”

O that the world might know
The all-atoning Lamb!
Spirit of faith, descend and show
The virtue of his name.
The grace which all may find,
The saving power, impart;
And testify to all mankind,
And speak in every heart.

Inspire the living faith,
Which whosoe’er receives
The witness in himself he hath,
And consciously believes;
The faith that conquers all,
And doth the mountain move,
And saves whoe’er on Jesus call,
And perfects them in love. Amen.

Introduction

On Monday night, June 7, 1976, the Northern New Jersey Annual Conference heard Albert Outler speak on the invention of America out of two great visions: "a covenant people of God" and "a social contract based on human rights—to life, liberty, pursuit of happiness, and what have you. The grievous flaw in both ideas . . . is that they were defined too narrowly. . . . Our original covenants and contracts did not include the native Americans or African blacks or (later) Roman Catholics and Jews.

"My real point is that if we understand the ideas that went into the invention of America, we could quite conceivably get on with the urgent business of reinventing America, " he continued.

"What's past is prologue . . . to a new future . . . a future into which Christ has already gone as the pioneer of our salvation and into which he calls us as his disciples."

We are now in the calendared future alluded to in this sermon back in 1976. America has not yet been reinvented according to the sermon's formula, which means that existentially we remain in the past. Albert Outler stood at the point position and shared with us what the One who stands at the Gate of the Years said to him: "Go out with your hand in God's hand, your life is his providence."

Albert Outler's greatest knowledge lay at this point. He knew that God's providence works. And ultimately that it is the only thing that does work.

SERMON 34

The Methodist Heritage in America

The Past as Prologue

It is a joy for me to be here—not to speak of the honor involved of sharing with you in this particular Conference session. Drew is one of my favorite places. I have so many good friends in the faculty and administration. And it is an honor and privilege to be associated with Bishop Taylor, for we also have many happy memories that we share together. Besides, I, too, am in the process of being retired (sort of) and am full of years and wisdom as to how one transfers from one rat race to another!

But I must admit to being warier (than I was) about this Bicentennial bit and whatever there is that properly may be said about our Methodist heritage over the past two centuries. In Portland, as a member of a General Conference Committee, I was set up as spokesman for a statement and a resolution that had been approved by the General Council on Ministries on Religion and Race. In it we had sought—carefully, we thought—to find the middle way between any nationalistic jingoism, on the one side, and from any national self-loathing on the other. And that wasn't easy.

One distinguished member of the committee wanted to mention, as a hypothetical possibility, that the American Revolution had been ill-advised: that the world just might be better off today if the British Commonwealth had not been disrupted. Others wanted to produce a litany for our national sins and wickedness, which we from time to time grievously have committed, by thought word and deed, against native Americans, blacks, Chicanos, etc. But when it was realized that such a litany would have to include the savage brutalities of "Reconstruction," of American anti-Semitism, American anti-Catholicism, Methodist complicity in the ravages of America's "Gothic's Age" (like the Vanderbilts, not to mention anybody closer home), it was decided to leave the idea of a litany alone.

One mischievous member wanted to mention that most American Methodists in 1776 had not been patriots but Tories, that Wesley himself had had the monumental impudence to denounce the Declaration of Independence, that Francis Asbury had spent the war in seclusion in the backwoods of Delaware, under constant surveillance and suspicion, etc. But that, too, was wisely vetoed.

The result was pretty pallid, except for the resolution that commended the Bicentennial to be celebrated in various ways—ecumenical, interreligious and international—and that we begin now to look toward 1984, when Methodists really can "point with pride" and all that. And we thought it was innocuous and celebrative. We were wrong; we were, in fact, ambushed, literally. And the same General Conference—of a so-called world church, mind you— that had, hours before, removed the names of all other countries except the United States of America from a list of nations offending against human freedom, approved a Bicentennial Statement that does, in fact, lift up some of our national sins and wickedness and blithely ignores all others. Consistency, as we often say, is the hobgoblin of little minds!

Besides, we've either had or will have enough Bicentennial hoopla of all sorts—with July Fourth still three weeks away. But a remarkable fact remains: We are about to celebrate (or bemoan) the two-hundredth year of what is by now the longest surviving example of representative national government on this globe, one of a tiny fraction of such governments in a world where tyrannies flourish and when the heady promises of political and economic liberation are only that—or worse.

National self-righteousness comes close to being an unpardonable sin; national self-loathing is a sure symptom of demoralization and decline. Patriotism is a mixed virtue, but woe betide that nation that fails to honor its heritage, that refuses to acknowledge its achievements and contributions to the cause of humanity.

What we seem to have forgotten is that America was born out of two traditions, both rooted in a longer, common heritage. One was the great Puritan heritage of covenant—written into our first truly American document, the Mayflower Compact, the idea of a community of people willingly subordinating individual interests and concerns to the common good, defined by just and wise laws, normed by the moral law in Holy Writ. It was, self-consciously, a covenant against selfishness and for altruism. The other tradition was deism—the Jeffersonian notion of inalienable rights and of Rousseau's vision of a "social contract," where private wills submit themselves, willingly, to the public will and the common good. Thus, the idea of "America" was invented out of these two great visions: "a covenant people of God" and "a social contract based on human rights—to life, liberty, pursuit of happiness, and what have you."

The grievous flaw in both ideas, in our American tradition, is that they were defined too narrowly (in terms of the WASP [White Anglo-Saxon Protestant] community that had invented America and thought they had a patent on it, in perpetuity). Our original covenants and contracts did not include the native Americans or African blacks or (later) Roman Catholics and Jews (especially those from central, southern, eastern Europe). Emma Lazarus' heart-rending offer of hospitality has always been somewhat qualified: Liberty's proud lamp beside her golden door has always been a little smoky and the golden door too often tarnished.

And yet—and it is this "and yet" that is the honest substance of this Bicentennial, which we ignore at our peril: This twinned vision of covenant and contract has guided a nation's growth, development, and contribution to world culture that cannot be equaled in human history, and is not likely to be matched by any alternative now in sight or in prospect.

American history, warts and all, may be laid alongside any other two centuries of any other national history in the world.

And the nation comes off with passing marks: In its passion for what the Continental Congress called "the sacred cause of liberty," in its overall successes in a heroic experiment of bringing at least partial unity out of an unprecedented ethnic diversity, in balancing out the rival claims of economic well-being and of ecology (rival because the premise of affluence is growth and the premise of ecology is equilibrium), in its fumbling efforts to be a responsible member of the family of nations (and fairly successful at it, overall, until lately). Americans who fail to acknowledge the overall positive value of these contributions are ill-prepared for the crises looming ahead of us.

The point to this rehearsal is not to boast, although a nation without self-respect deserves the fate that threatens this one. My real point is that if we understand the ideas that went into the invention of America, we could quite conceivably get on with the urgent business of reinventing America. For that is what I conceive our prime national agenda to be, now and for the foreseeable future. The alternative is—no Tricentennial.

What would be involved in any such reinvention of America? At least four main agenda items.

First, we will have to renegotiate the limits of our covenants and contracts and stretch them out 180 degrees. This is the good essence of what is labeled "liberation theology," and there are no good reasons why in any good covenant theology, all God's children are not welcome, by rights, into his covenanted community.

Second, we must rediscover that both "covenant" and "social contract" are moral concepts. They presuppose and demand a moral discipline that would preferably come as voluntary but that is imperative in any version of community and the public will. Charlotte Saikowski of the *Christian Science Monitor* has done a landmark journalistic survey called "After Permissiveness, What?" Her implied answer (mirroring a shifting consciousness all over the country) is "more moral sensitivity and moral self-discipline"—from fat to lean, from conspicuous expenditures to shared thrift and philanthropy, from decadence to decency, from antinomianism to self and social controls.

Third, America reinvented will have to reorder its priorities as between the rights claimed by the social-contract tradition, on the one hand, and the duties that are stressed in all covenant concepts of community. It's certainly not a question of either/or but whether anybody in any human society has rights without duties, and whether one's acknowledgment of his/her duties may not come closer to the notion of responsible citizenship (participatory democracy at its best) than any one-sided stress on rights. And here, even Jefferson and Lincoln agreed.

But, fourth, a reinvented America will have to recover the religious foundations of her moral covenants. For one of the things that we have proved beyond any doubt is that Adam Smith's "invisible hand" that gathers up various free enterprises based on "enlightened self-interest," is either mythical or palsied. We simply will not, as a nation, serve the common good at any real sacrifice to ourselves unless from some covenanted obligation to God and to his righteous rule in our nation and in the earth. The idea of the social contract was based on one or another assumption, of a natural altruism that surpasses self-interest or else of benevolent (if also coercive) governmental enforcement of the public interest. And now we know that both of these assumptions are false. We don't know, for sure, that covenanted service with our neighbor will work either. It's never been really tried in the nation as a whole, after 1820 or thereabouts. But it's the only alternative that I can see that might sustain the reinvented America for 1976 that might match the dreams and daring of 1776.

Now, the special application of this to this occasion is that the covenant idea of society belongs to Methodism, too—to our ideals and even to our Methodist performance at its best. For once the Methodists got rolling in the new America, they discovered that their understanding of Christian *mission* was remarkably close both to the ideals and realities of the American experience. Their disciplined liberty gave them a mobility and venturesomeness that matched the burgeoning national spirit and the opening westward frontiers.

The Methodist circuit riders ("friars on horseback," as Charles Ferguson calls them in his wonderful history of American Methodists titled *Organizing to Beat the Devil*) were men whose theology, however crude, was covenantal in essence and focused on conversion—i.e., the new creature in Christ, not just an improved version of *homo sapiens*.

Revivalism, which we did not invent but which we put to good use, was more than piety and crowd hysteria: It was (as Timothy Smith has shown) a powerful social force, serving the causes of social reforms as well as saving souls. The Methodists took readily to the idea of "a new Zion in the [American] wilderness" and struggled, more successfully than most, with their rival notions of "heart religion" and of higher education. Their polity of small "encounter groups" (shared by Asbury, Albright, Otterbein, et al.) provided the values of local initiative while their connectionalism saved them from the disadvantages of congregationalism. Their pietism fit very well with the low-church notions of the Protestant Radicals who flourished in America as they never had in Europe. Yet their Wesleyan heritage was strong enough for them to cherish the sacraments and a bobtailed Anglican liturgy. They were evangelical and obsessed with their mission to win the nation for Christ; they were catholic in their basic notions of universal redemption, free grace and holy living; they were reformed enough to be reformable, which is to say, open to wise and valid change.

There is a shadow side to this pragmatism. Methodists tended to fit somewhat too easily into their cultural environment—whatever that was—and especially as America turned more and more middle class. We made decisions based on pragmatic grounds—we said— when we were, in fact, imitating the current fads and fashions of some epoch. Even so, American Methodism is one of the better success stories in church history, which is not an extravagant boast.

But what is past is prologue (as Antonio commented to Sebastian in *The Tempest)*, and so we must ask, "Where does our heritage point to now and tomorrow?"

What, for example, is going to happen to a middle-class church as (it seems inevitable) the American middle class is increasingly macerated by the whipsaw of taxes and inflation (and governmental overhead)? What is going to happen to a church that has been predominantly WASP (White Anglo-Saxon Protestant) when WASP dominance continues to wane, as it has and as it will?

As we turn from any celebration that we can manage of our heritage, is there any doubt that any forecast of the future is sobering, at the very least (even the wild optimisms of Herman

Kahn)? No more physical frontiers—and now we know that space emigration is not a realistic safety valve for surplus population—or even for hardy adventurers. On this planet, the limits of growth are finally calculable and frighteningly finite. The social contracts that helped hold America (and other nations) together are falling apart, with no promising alternatives anywhere that I know of. One result of this is an obvious vacuum of leadership in our nation, our world, even our churches—because only communities can be led: gaggles and mobs generate chaos. This is why Washington resembles Bedlam more than the seat of a rational and competent government, why the United Nations has become a Lilliputian snakepit, why (in our own United Methodist Church) our vaunted new structures are working so poorly.

There are no easy answers to our present and future problems, but there are a few clear imperatives. We must, as Christians, reassess our notions of success and failure; we must redefine our goals and limits. Then, as means to these redefined goals and ends, we must recover the New Testament images of the church as the body of Christ, including and cherishing all its members as members one of another and not as a conglomerate of majorities, minorities, caucuses, and rotations.

We must remember the gospel of true human glory ("he who would be greatest among you, let him be your servant" Matthew 20:27). Too easily and often, we have asked the church to serve us—with fees paid or collected for services rendered. Now we must ask how we can serve the church (i.e., all our brothers and sisters in Christ) in new adventures in Christian discipleship, new initiatives in Christian social action (from Dallas to South Boston to the Sahel, to American labor councils and corporation board rooms). If our faith in Christ is authentic, this must show in our life witness, in the courage and joy that spring from grace-filled hearts, in sacrificial love and zestful ministry.

What's past is prologue, but to what? To a new future, that's what: to a future that is bound to be different, difficult, diminished— but a future into which Christ has already gone as the pioneer of our salvation and into which he calls us as his disciples. His gospel call is not to comfort, still less to self-pity or despair. We are not called to make peace with injustice anywhere in the world nor to survive at the cost of other peoples' aspirations. Christ calls us today, as he did others once in Galilee, to repentance (which is to say, to an admission of our radical need of God's grace and mercy), to faith (which is to say, to radical dependence on God's grace, in sunshine or shadow), to hope (which is to say, to an inner assurance of God's loving mercy and care) and to love (which is to say, to grateful outpouring of our gifts from God to others in his beloved community).

A new future is opening up before us all, a difficult future that has already begun to daunt most of our old-style progressives. In the Christian perspective, it matters less whether that future is hopeful or grim, but whether, having read off the shining record of our past, we are prepared to reenlist for yet another tour of duty in the upcoming future, to live and work and die by the faith that wrote the record and has yet more to write in history yet to come. Do we really believe that the amazing grace that has brought us safe thus far will go on leading us home—not on "flowery beds of ease" but through challenges that demand our utmost?

A new awareness (uneasy but finally hopeful) is seeping into the American consciousness—and elsewhere—that the age of affluence is drawing to its close, that WASP ascendancy is over, that our fashionable ego trips have gone nowhere, really, and have nowhere to go, really. Human happiness depends less on how we learn to manage our feelings or how we learn to exploit the infinite than upon our openness to God's grace, our obedience to his will for a fully human community.

For this is all that is left to us that we can really depend upon for joy and blessedness. Our only hope for meaningful life, for glory, happiness, and peace at the last still lies in that true humanity for all that Jesus Christ reveals to us; that he gained for us; that he is calling us into; that his life, death, and victory still stand as collateral for, in all our faithful endeavors to seek first his righteous rule in our hearts and in our lives with others.

> And I said to the man who stood at the gate of the
> years [like Bicentennials and such]:
> "Give me a light that I may tread safely into the unknown!"
> And he replied: "Go out into the darkness and put your

hand into the Hand of God.
That shall be better to you than light and safer than a known way."[1]

Is there, really, any better way to go?

Introduction

The distinction of an elder in the United Methodist Church as well as the elder's identity with the "priesthood of all believers" was clearly drawn in this sermon by Albert Outler at the June 3, 1981, ordination service of the Texas Annual Conference. In a nutshell he stated: "The *cleros* are a body of men and women who have heeded an inner call to live and work as full-time representatives of the church so as to enable the *laos* to be the church visible and attractive in the world. Ordination is the objective confirmation of that representative calling and its official authorization."

At the close of this sermon those present heard his voice choke with emotion as he came out with the words: "But if you and I and all of us, you on the verge of your ministry and I on the homestretch of mine, if we share in Wesley's conviction that the Holy Spirit is the ever-present power in our hearts and lives, if we rely on his power in the upbuilding of the church in the world . . . this will enable us all to share, humbly yet with real assurance, in the mysteries of that ministry into which you have been called and are being ordained. . . ." The Holy Spirit was the ever-present power in that moment as Albert Outler spoke and the audience listened and felt that Outler, too, was listening.

SERMON 35

The Paradox of Ordained Ministry

(Ordination Sermon 3)

It still strikes me as quite remarkable, after hundreds of Methodist Annual Conferences, that the service of ordination always seems something very special; it always has an atmosphere all its own. It's something like a commencement or an awards ceremony. It is, of course, very special for the families and personal friends of the ordinands. But there's something else involved, too. Here is a unique rite of passage, after years of preparation, into a lifelong career of sustained dedication. This is a hallowed hour. For me, in these later years, such services bring to mind old Simeon's *Nunc Dimittis*, "Now lettest thou thy servant depart in peace" (Luke 2:29). For here is the church entrusting its future ministerial leadership to younger, competent hands, and I find that hopeful.

Presently, Bishop Crutchfield, with his fellow elders, will lay hands upon these young men and women, and he will say to each of them, "Take thou authority. . . ." In this he will not be speaking for himself alone, but as a general superintendent of the entire United Methodist Church and for as much of the many other Christian bodies as recognize our Methodist orders. This, then, is a solemn occasion, and it never yet has palled on me, not even after all these repetitions over all these years.

Yet something of a paradox is here, too—a puzzle to ponder and reflect upon. For if there is one thing that all Methodists join in believing, it is the doctrine of "the priesthood of all believers." We may or may not practice it properly, but we believe it stoutly and we reject any and all theories of a sacerdotal priesthood claiming a monopoly on the means of grace. We may or may not know the text of Numbers 11:29, where Moses says, "Would that all the Lord's people were prophets, that the Lord would endue them all with his Spirit." But we find the idea congenial.

Nobody supposes that anything magical is about to happen here tonight. Ordination will not elevate these young men and women up to some higher level of moral or spiritual superiority, designate them as preachers and prophets, priests and pastors for hire or rent, in relief of the laity's responsibilities for their Christian witness and service. We understand, don't we, that all baptized/confirmed/converted Christians are "prophets"? They are prophets in the sense that they are seekers for and forthtellers of God's will and purpose.

We know that all Christians are priests, in the sense of being for others in their daily Christian disciplines. The priesthood of all believers has never meant that each of us is a priest to and for himself/herself (this is "privatism" and a heresy). Priesthood means being and acting on behalf of others, not to be ministered unto (or even to minister to oneself), but to minister and to give one's life (Matthew 20:28), freely, generously, out of heartfelt gratitude to God. But if this is the normal ministry and priesthood of all believers, of God's *laos*, why then do we need an ordained ministry, a *cleros*, separated and set apart by the acts in which we are all about to share tonight?

The same paradox can be put in yet another way. All baptized/confirmed/converted Christians are bound by public vows and impelled by the Holy Spirit to offer up themselves and all their powers to God as living sacrifices, dedicated to him and fit for his acceptance. This, as St. Paul reminds us, "is the worship which we, as reasonable creatures, should offer to God" (Romans 12:1). Moreover, considering the obligations that are entailed by any such dedication and service, we realize that nobody else can exercise this priesthood for us.

This, then, raises the question that still perplexes our church and other churches: If all the *laos* are prophets and witnesses, and if their obligations to God are to glorify and serve him, not only with their lips but in their lives, why then a *cleros*? Why a separate body of men and women entitled "ministers" or "clergy" or whatever? This is a perplexity that meets us at every turn in The United Methodist Church and still remains unclarified even in our official documents. I do not promise to clear it up in twenty minutes, but I do hope that all of us will take it for the challenge it is because confusion on this point has already wrought much havoc in our church and bids fair to create more.

Let's begin by trying to dispose of four popular misperceptions of the distinctive office and role of the ordained clergy.

1. *The first is that the clergy are a sort of elite corps with special privileges*, largely as bogus compensations for their self-chosen deprivations and also on account of their presumed "hot line to heaven." The clergy are elite, in the literal sense of having been carefully chosen, but they still belong to the *laos*. Moreover, their ministry must be more dedicated to the service of *laos* than to the promotion of themselves. There is, as I have had wonderful opportunities to know, a gracious fellowship amongst Methodist preachers, but it musn't become too cozy or enclosed. To be ordained is to be sent out among the people of God as servants and enablers.

2. *A second misconception is that the clergy are layfolk with a little extra education, liturgical know-how, pastoral skills, and fondness for the games ecclesiastics play.* I wish that parts of this were true; that they were better educated (and, indeed, they can become so if they have come to love learning and are committed to an ongoing life of inquiry). I hope they have a lively sense of ceremony and realize that "decency and order" in worship is itself a means of grace. But I'm more interested in their pastoral hearts than in their technical skills, for truly pastoral concerns will always find ways and means to nourish and to safeguard the flock of Christ.

3. *A third misconception, too often shared by preachers and people, is that the clergy are employees of a given congregation of folks who feel that since they are paying for the fiddle and the fiddler, they are entitled to call the tunes—and even to write the music.* A Methodist preacher is hedged about with many disciplinary duties and strictures, and there are elaborate provisions for checks and balances in the *Discipline* and the Methodist ethos. But one thing must be clear on all sides: No Methodist preacher is the hireling of his/her congregation. The lines of accountability run elsewhere and ultimately back to the authorization of the entire church and to the integrity of a minister's informed conscience. Ordination is the ground for the freedom of the Methodist pulpit, and while so sacred a freedom must not be abused, neither should it be reined in by the biases and crotchets of a local congregation. When I stand in a Methodist pulpit, I have a right to know that the full weight of the whole church is behind me so long as what I say there is rooted in Scripture, bolstered by tradition, made credible by reason and common sense, and given life and meaning by my own personal experience of God in Christ. And every member of The United Methodist Church *laos* ought to be glad to have it this way, for sure!

4. *Finally, it is sometimes supposed that the clergy are simply professional people with limited liabilities in their professional obligations and with unlimited freedom in their professional choices of schedules, agenda, or location.* To be ordained is to be enlisted in "Christ's militia," to be always on call, with a set of priorities in which the vocation of ministry always stands first. Nine-to-five (and twice on Sundays) will simply not get the job done, and if you aren't fully committed to full-time, lifelong service, you'd do better to ease out of it gracefully into some other career. Itinerancy no longer means frequent moving from circuit to circuit, but it still means what it always did to begin with: that Methodist ministers do not choose their places or types of service so much as they are deployed into them, as the appointitve powers deem best for the church at large. This is part of what ordination means, and your enlistment is not to this theater of operations or that, or for this hitch or that. In ordination you make yourself available to the most need, whatever and

wherever that is, and this is for the duration of your ministry (which is forever).

The representative ministry is, therefore, not the antithesis of the priesthood of all believers; it is the indispensable support system for that general ministry. Its uniqueness lies in its specific character as a representative ministry: a ministry that comes from the whole church to the local church, a ministry that links the church local with the church universal (in space and also in time), a ministry that links the proclamation of the gospel in this place with the original gospel and the universal gospel in every place. It is in this sense that the whole world is your parish.

The representative ministry is especially responsible for the Christian sacraments, since in these, Christians in any local church are linked to Christians everywhere, not ever forgetting that great cloud of witnesses before whom we now run the race set before us in our times. This is St. Paul's point in Ephesians: "Such is the gospel whereof I was made a minister, by God's unmerited gift, bestowed on me by the mighty working of his power" (3:7). To the others, called by the same mysterious providence to the ministry of the same gospel, he entreats them: "As God has called you, live up to your calling" (4:4, 11-16).

Let us now run through a series of four paired dimensions in this complex relationship between the general ministry and the ordained ministry. Such distinctions can easily be misconstrued, especially if you think of them in terms of either/or. But consider, for example, the difference between the laity as the church in the world and the clergy as the church trustee and steward of the means of grace. The laity are the church visible in the world (they are what the world really sees of the church and what it measures us by), the clergy are the designated trustees and stewards of the means of grace (not their possessors or manipulators, God forbid—but responsible for furnishing the people of God with every wherewithal for their effective mission in and service to the world).

Or again, consider the difference between the church local (all Christians in any given place) and the church catholic (since Pentecost and around the globe). Still a third pairing would be between the church deployed (Christians in action) and the church deploying (directing the action). And finally, there is a dialectic between the individual Christian (or Christians in small covenanted groups) and the entire people of God, set in the world to prepare it for God's coming kingdom.

Now the laity, generally speaking, are the church in the world, the church local, the church deployed and the church in mission. They need, as a complement and for guidance, a leadership that represents the church sacral, the church catholic, the church connectional, the church ecumenical. These men and women about to be ordained here are not thereby being withdrawn from God's *laos*; they are being made more fully representative of that *laos* understood in its totality. And this is why, in every one of their public and official actions, clergy must understand themselves as representatives and not as ecclesiastical entrepreneurs, each free to do his or her own thing.

We have a partial analogy for this in the representative character of licensed physicians, of members of the state bar, of members of the teaching profession. There is something like a medical *laos* in the sense that all people are responsible for their health and the health of the community (and we are going to have to become more and more responsible in this area). You don't have to be a licensed M.D. to be intensely health-conscious and actually competent in many ways on many levels. Moreover, as we know, the "ordained" healers are not themselves infallible nor omnicompetent. They help us get well or stay well. What matters is that the good physician is both an individual in his/her own right and yet also a representative of the healing arts and community. And the very best physicians are those who are always on call whenever really needed.

Likewise, there is a *laos* of lawyers in the sense that all citizens amount to the law made visible in the world, since it is a law-abiding citizenry that makes the law work even as well as it does. We do not hire a lawyer to obey the law in our stead, or to help us to evade it. What we need is for him/her to represent the law to us and to the court. This is why lawyers are designated as "officers of the court."

Finally, we are all learners and teachers and in that sense, no different from our teachers. But we need representatives of the life of learning; they symbolize and effectuate the *laos* of learning. This is how we measure their quality: How well does this teacher or that represent the life of learning to the rest of us?

So it is, given some crucial qualifications, with the ordained clergy. The very essence of ordination is its conscientious designation of qualified persons as representatives of the whole church. The *cleros* are a body of men and women who have heeded an inner call to live and work as full-time representatives of the church so as to enable the *laos* to be the church visible and attractive in the world. Ordination is the objective confirmation of that representative calling and its official authorization.

The clergy are not holier-than-thou; the call to holiness is universal. They are not the only prophets around; "would that all God's people were prophets" (Numbers 11:29). This is why Wesley endorsed lay preaching, understanding it as the general form that prophecy properly takes. But these young men and women do have special responsibilities to which they are or will be vowed, from henceforth and forever. One is the responsibility for being well-furnished for their ministries, well-informed, and professionally trustworthy. They are also responsible for being effective evangelists, pastors, and teachers of the gospel of grace (for understanding that gospel and for its effective communication and praxis). They are responsible for being available and responsive to every victim on every one of life's Jericho roads. They dast not pass casually by on the other side! They are responsible for being truly personal and personable, yet also for being fully a conscientious professional. Ordained persons do not cease being themselves, but they have covenanted not to confound their crotchets with their callings.

There is no magic here, but there is a mystery—the mystery of the Holy Spirit's enduement of these ordinands with an afflatus that will, if consciously received and conscientiously exercised, turn them into representative ministers, not of this congregation or that, but of our entire denomination and also of as many other Christian bodies as now recognize our Methodist orders. Their first duty is to The United Methodist Church; their wider duties are to the church ecumenical, but their final obligation will always be to their informed, responsible, and representative Christian consciences. This means that their personal decisions will have to be deep-rooted in the framework of Scripture, tradition, reason, and common sense. For only then will their personal experience be trustworthy and representative.

Ordination, then, is the conferring of our office; it is a confirmation of a divine calling and sending. This is why in some churches it is said that ordination brands a person with "an indelible character." We have no such doctrine in our tradition, but whenever I think of the good ministers I have known who have given themselves in devoted ministry for decades, I see something that is no longer superficial nor artificial, if it ever was. The ministry is not a mask to put on and take off; it is a total commitment to a sacred task bolstered by a divine gift.

Now, let me speak, in closing, to you who are about to be ordained. Few, if any, of you were called like St. Paul, but each of you, I trust, is here with the stable inward conviction that you are truly called to this representative ministry into which you are about to be ordained. For now, finally, you will be outwardly vested with an ecclesial authority that will avail you little unless it really is the outward and visible signing of what is already true inside your hearts and wills. You have been examined, certified, elected; and you will be welcomed into what I can certify to you as one of the most remarkable comradeships in all the world. You are about to be bound by solemn vows, yet also freed by them. You are free persons in the liberty with which Christ has freed us all, only do not use your freedom to license or self-advantage. You are not bound to any reigning fashion—in the church or in the world. You are free to claim your heritage and to update it. But you are bound to do all of this in as faithful and humble obedience to the Holy Spirit as your best impulses lead you to, for it will be the Spirit who will ordain you in spirit and in truth.

You are being ordained into the ministry of the church universal: "The Lord pour upon thee the Holy Spirit for the office and work of an elder in the church of God . . ."[1] (no reference here to The United Methodist Church or this Annual Conference). Indeed, at every crucial point the ritual will invoke the Holy Spirit as your divine authority and agent, now and for all your future ministries. This is why I suggest that you listen carefully to the language of these rituals and see how much they mean of what you mean by your vocation. Even John Cosin's translation of that beautiful old Latin hymn (*Veni, Creator Spiritus*) will not seem so quaint if you realize that it is the Holy Spirit who has led you here and will lead you from here into all the joys and satisfactions of what can be a wonderful and deeply rewarding career:

> Come, Holy Ghost, our souls inspire,
> And lighten with celestial fire;
> Thou the anointing Spirit art,
> Who dost thy sevenfold gifts impart.
>
> Thy blessed unction from above
> Is comfort, life and fire of love. . . .

Is it any wonder that John Wesley was fascinated by the metaphors of light and fire or that our United Methodist Church logo is the paired flame and cross?

In ourselves, or on our own, all this rhetoric is a mite preposterous, and if you have been thinking of your ordination as a rigamarole leading to a job that you can fashion to your liking, then the ceremony can be nothing more than perfunctory and maybe even scandalous—in the literal sense of words and gestures understood in so cynical a way as to offend sensitive souls. For remember, your congregations will still be full of people who will take your ordination as a sign they can trust you to minister to them in Christ's name (and not your own) and in the Spirit's power (and not your own). Woe to him or her who offends one of these little ones.

But if you and I and all of us, you on the verge of your ministry and I on the homestretch of mine, if we share in Wesley's conviction that the Holy Spirit is the ever-present power in our hearts and lives, if we rely on his power in the upbuilding of the church in the world (through the witness and service of those whom we will have furnished for their mission), then you really will be crossing a new frontier; and the church of God will be gaining new resources for its total mission. This will enable us all to share, humbly yet with real assurance, in the mysteries of that ministry into which you have been called and are being ordained—to be representative ministers of the grace of our Lord Jesus Christ, which is the love of God made manifest and effectual in and by the power of the Holy Spirit. For which may God's richest blessings be and abide upon you always. Amen.

Introduction

On June 8, 1983, at Wesleyan College in Macon, Georgia, Albert Outler preached the ordination sermon at the South Georgia Annual Conference. There was, indeed, some nostalgia expressed in the opening statements. (There had to be: Fifty-five years before that occasion he was ordained deacon in that Conference.) The interesting aspect of this nostalgia was not only to see his old friends (probably few "old" friends were there from his peer group of ordinands), but to recall his own calling and ordination to be a special representative for Christ and his church in the world.

In these Sermons on Several Occasions you can see some of the events in Albert Outler's life from the verge of his ministry, through the fifty-five years of ministry, into the twilight zone of his life. You can see that the Holy Spirit controlled his destiny beyond any human manipulation.

As his end closed in on him, Albert Outler conserved energy for the uncompleted tasks already begun and talked in terms of passing the mantle onto others.

But the church did not let him rest. In his last days the phone rang, mail came, hands rapped on the door, and voices cried out, "You must help write a new Doctrinal Statement to guide the next General Conference" (1988). He wondered out loud, "How can I do all these things that demand so much time and energy of an old man?" He asked the question while knowing the answer: "By God's ever-present power in our hearts and lives, the Holy Spirit." The power of this faith gave Albert Outler a brighter twilight zone—according to the view of the church.

SERMON 36

The Church's Real Business

(Ordination Sermon 4)

I can't begin to tell you how special an occasion this is for me—to be back in South Georgia; back here in Macon, where being an associate of Mulberry Street was my last full-time pastoral assignment—one of Mrs. Outler's and my happiest memories; back at Wesleyan College, where my two sisters went to school and where I went to Pastors' School in the summer; back in this Annual Conference where my father ministered for so long and so well; back to an ordination service that follows my own deacon's ordination in this same Conference by fifty-five years—a quite incredible five decades. It is a delight to be here among you, a great honor to be in your Conference, and I thank you from the bottom of my heart for your hospitality and interest.

I know very well, of course, what your main interest in this Conference session will be, and it is not the formal sessions of Bible study in the mornings and the sermons at night. But, after all, you will need interludes between ballotings and their reportings, which are homiletical and exegetical descants on church politics. And who better for such interludes and descants than a tired old veteran whose interest in the church is as deep and earnest as ever, but whose concern for who is where on the ecclesiastical pyramid has dwindled down to nearly nothing? I know something of the great troubling issues that will confront the next General Conference that threaten to spoil its mood for a proper celebration of our Bicentennial. I remember my involvements in a half-dozen earlier conferences and their problems, each truly new set of problems as ominous as the last. I have watched the church's survival through the disorders of all these years (disorders in the world, disorders in the church), and I still face the future (your future, that is) with confidence and hope. "'Tis grace hath brought [us] safe thus far, / And grace will lead us [on]."[1]—home, too, as I know full well.

It is fitting that this ordination service comes so early in the Conference, for in it we are defining a vital aspect of the church's real business, and we will be entrusting our future ministerial leadership into younger, eager, competent hands. Even an old academic curmudgeon finds this exciting, after all these years and after a full hundred annual conferences.

In a few minutes now (and it may seem longer to you than to me) Bishop McDavid will lay hands on these young men and women and will, in the name of Christ and as an authorized superintendent of the entire United Methodist Church, bestow upon them the authority of the designated representative ministry in the church of Christ. "Take thou authority,"[2] he will say to each and every one. Notice that he will not be acting on his own. As a general superintendent of the entire United Methodist Church, he will act for the whole denomination and for the entire larger Christian community as well. But what will all this mean to you, and to the rest of us, for you to take this authority thus bestowed and to go out from here to exercise it in your varied appointed tasks?

Nothing magical is about to happen. These young men and women are not about to be removed from the priesthood of all believers, or set up on a pedestal of moral or spiritual superiority. But why, then, their ordination, why then a *cleros*, differentiated in any significant way from the *laos* who are, after all, the church visible in the world?

Let's begin an answer by disposing of four popular misconceptions about the clergy as a special group of ministries within the general ministry. In the first place, they are not an elite corps with special privileges because of some presumed hotline to heaven. They are a chosen group—but chosen for particular roles in leadership and responsibility in the stimulus and guidance of the *laos* in their lives and ministries in the world. Their greatness in this special ministry will be measured, as Jesus told the first apostles, by their preeminence in service. "I am amongst you as one who serves" (Luke 22:27). This was his prescription for the church's apostles and prophets, then and now (John 13:15-17).

By the same token, though, ordination to the representative ministry is not a trick of changing laymen or laywomen into something different by dressing them up in clerical orders, and costumes and licensing them to "play church" in public! I am presupposing that they have the requisite skills and preparation for their leadership roles. But what matters more is whether they see themselves as more than preachers (layfolk can preach, and ought to), more than liturgists (layfolk have liturgical talents, too). What matters most is their sense of calling to be designated and authorized representatives—of Christ in the first and last instance, but then more specifically of The United Methodist Church in her mission and ministry in the world.

A third and ominous misconception is that in this ordination and reception into Conference membership (on trial or in full connection) these men and women are being designated as "pastors for rent or lease," "prophets for hire," as employees of this congregation or that, who, since they pay the fiddler, feel themselves entitled to call the tune and sometimes even write the music.

Ordained United Methodist ministers are not the hireling of any congregation. When they stand in United Methodist pulpits or elsewhere, they are, or ought to be, assured of the backing of the whole church whose representatives they are so long as they faithfully represent that church with convictions rooted in Scripture, nourished by tradition, bolstered by reason and common sense, and expressive of a lively personal experience of God in Christ. And every United Methodist ought to be glad to have a minister like this. It is, indeed, the congregation's right to have such ministers, and it is their duty to respect them on these grounds and not on any other, such as a "charming personality."

There is a fourth misconception that I think I see more and more in the newer generations of clergy and in our seminaries, a notion that betrays a great tradition. It is the image, borrowed from the world, that the ordained minister is yet another professional with a nine-to-five job, in which one gets paid for services rendered and who otherwise has an untrammeled personal life to lead. To such people, the connectional and appointive system unique to Methodism may mean only a way of getting ahead in the church in a fashion similar to the way one might work up to the top in a corporation or a secular business. This is a profound and self-defeating misunderstanding. The ordained clergy are Christ's militia, enlisted for the duration, on call, available for duty and need, day in and day out, with their personal lives subsidiary to their ministerial vocation. They are Christ's deputy shepherds, prepared to give their lives for his sheep! If this prospect seems unappealing to you, it should raise an honest question about the validity of your calling, and there are quiet and graceful exits provided for all those who want out, or who ought to want out, of a ministry that asks too much, namely your all.

Ordination, then, is the calling out and the setting apart of an authorized representative ministry of The United Methodist Church in and for the Christian laity at large. The clergy are the indispensable support system for the whole church to carry forward her mission in the world. The unique character of a United Methodist minister lies in this special function, of linking the universal church to the local church, that links the proclamation of the gospel in this place with the original gospel (as recorded in Scripture) and with the universal gospel (as manifest in the ecumenical witness around the world and in all the churches). Anything less than this is inadequate; anything more is a tilt toward arrogance or distortion.

This local representative of the church catholic is responsible for the specifically universal ministrations of the gospel in the local church, "the Word rightly preached, the sacraments duly administered and order faithfully administered"[3] (always in the name of Christ and always as a conscientious deputy of The United Methodist Church, never just on one's own). This was St. Paul's point in Ephesians: This is the gospel "whereof I was made a minister by God's unmerited grace, bestowed on me by the mighty working of his power" (3:7). In the same spirit he could exhort us, "As God has called you, so then live up to your calling!"(4:1).

This does not make of a Methodist minister a great oddity in our society, where we have other men and women who are ordained to their special vocations and professions. Come to think of it, the idea applies to other professions, or ought to. We who are not physicians constitute a medical *laos* who need "ordained" physicians to aid us in our responsibilities for our own health and the health of the community. Thus, we are having nowadays more and more emphasis on preventive medicine, which does not mean less dependence upon our physicians; it means a clearer view of their distinctive roles as representative of the healers' guild. By analogy, the people of God are dependent upon their representative ministers, not to do their ministries of witness and service for them but to aid them in making these ministries more faithful (to Scripture, tradition, reason, and Christian experience), and also more fruitful (in reconciling the world to God).

This same analogy holds true between the *laos* of public justice and our lawyers. The lawyer whose main concern is personal success is not going to help us very much, which is why we have so grave a crisis of confidence nowadays in the legal profession. Likewise in learning—being literate and well-informed is everybody's business. But we also need official and authorized representatives of the community of learning as symbols and agents for our sakes. Ordained teachers and professors do not learn for us; they help us to learn for ourselves.

These young men and women here tonight are about to be vowed to a special set of responsibilities, from henceforth and forever. One is the responsibility of being well-furnished, well-informed, trustworthy, and, in this sense, representative of the whole church's wisdom and vision. They are also to become responsible for the church's evangelism—her outreach, ingathering and upbuilding. To them is committed the ministry of the gospel of grace, and the responsibility for seeing that this gospel is understood and communicated. They will be responsible for being available and helpful to every victim on every Jericho road; they must not excuse themselves because they are already late for a committee meeting in Jericho! They are responsible for being truly personable, and yet also and always fully and conscientiously professional. The ordained minister has not ceased being himself/herself; but he/she has covenanted not to confound a set of personal crotchets or enthusiasms with their ministerial callings.

There is no magic here, but there is mystery. It is the mystery of the Holy Spirit's enduement of these ordinands with an afflatus that will, if gracefully received and conscientiously exercised, turn them into representative ministers in and for the whole church, not of this congregation or that but for the entire United Methodist Church, anywhere and everywhere—and for as many other Christians and other human beings as may acknowledge their ministerial orders and standing. Their first duty is to their own denomination, which includes a reliable understanding of our Wesleyan heritage and our distinctive Methodist mission. But their wider duties are to the church ecumenical, and their final duty will always be to God's own work and will as this is revealed in Christ and understood by an informed and representative Christian conscience. This means, among other things, that their ministerial acts must not be merely personal, subjective, or impulsive. They must be deep-rooted in our fourfold guidelines (Scripture, tradition, Christian experience, and common sense), for only then can our personal experience become objective and therefore trustworthy to others.

Ordination, then, is the solemn conferring of an office; it is the church's act of confirming a calling and of sending men and women out into their life of mission. This is why, in some churches, they speak of ordination as conferring "an indelible character" upon a person. We have no such doctrine in our tradition, yet I can think of many good ministers grown old in the service of God and his people who have seemed to me to have taken on a character that could never be easily erased. The ordained ministry is not a role to be put on or taken off at will. It is a total commitment to a sacred task, bolstered by divine gifts and graces.

Now, in closing, I would like to speak more directly to you who are about to be ordained. My guess is that few of you have had a Damascus Road experience, maybe not even an Aldersgate experience yet (John Wesley had been ordained for ten long years before that happened to him). But each of you, I trust, is here with a stable inward conviction that you are truly called to this representative ministry of which we have been speaking.

Now, at long last, you are to be vested outwardly with an ecclesial authority that will avail you little unless it represents an inner reality of heart and will. You have been examined, certified, graduated, elected; and now you will be welcomed into what I can certify is a wondrous fellowship. You are about to bind yourselves by solemn vows, yet you are also about to be freed by those very same commitments. Already you are free persons in the liberty with which Christ has freed us all; only now you must be especially careful not to use your freedom to any license of self-indulgence. You are not bound to any reigning fashion, in the church or in the world, yet you are not at liberty merely to cultivate your own oddities. You will be free to claim your large, rich heritage from the whole of the Christian past and to update it. But you are also bound to do all this in faithful and humble obedience to the Holy Spirit, for, as the words of the ritual make abundantly clear, it will be the Holy Spirit who will be ordaining you, in spirit and in truth.

Note well that you are being ordained into the ministry of the church universal: "The Lord pour upon thee the Holy Spirit for the office and work of an elder in the Church of God."[4] There is not the slightest mention of The United Methodist Church in the entire ordinal. Every crucial reference is to the Holy Spirit as your divine authority and upholder, now and in all your ministries. It will, therefore, serve you well to heed the language of these old rituals carefully and see how they translate into your sense of calling and commitment and how they challenge that sense.

At the heart of the ordinal for elder there is a quaint old Latin hymn that echoes an ancient and profound theme, *Veni, Creator Spiritus*. You ought to ponder John Cosin's fairly literal translation of it a hundred years before Charles Wesley wrote a poetic paraphrase:

> Come, Holy Ghost, our souls inspire,
> And lighten with celestial fire;
> Thou the anointing Spirit art,
> Who dost thy sevenfold gifts impart.

Thy blessed unction from above
Is comfort, life, and fire and love. . . .

In any case it will help if you realize that it is the Holy Spirit who has led you here; it is the Holy Spirit who will lead you from here into all the joys and satisfactions of what all of us pray will be a wondrously rewarding career. And it will help if you remember how fascinated John Wesley was with the Holy Spirit's symbols of light and fire, which is why the current logo of our United Methodist Church is the paired flame and cross.

In yourselves, and on your own, the tasks you are undertaking are impossible. If you are thinking that you are taking on a job that you can fashion to your liking or if you see the ecclesiastical world as an oyster for you to shuck, then this ritual will sound more like rigamarole than reality. At best, it will be perfunctory and, at the worst, scandalous—in the literal sense of highflown words construed so cynically as to offend sensitive souls. For you must never forget how many people in your congregations will take your ministerial character as a sign that they can trust you to minister to them in Christ's name and in the Spirit's power (not your own). Woe to him or her who offends one of those "little ones" by imposing merely private tastes and passing fads on them! Woe!

Here we are together tonight—you on the verge of your ministry and I in the twilight of mine. And yet if we share together Wesley's conviction that the Holy Spirit is God's ever-present power in our hearts and lives, and if we truly rely upon his power in our efforts to upbuild the church and to serve the world, then you will be crossing a new frontier, and the church will be gaining welcome new resources for her total mission. Given such a conviction, you will be enabled to share, humbly but with rock-steady assurance, in the mysteries of the ministry in which you are now to be ordained, representatives of the grace of our Lord and Savior Jesus Christ, which is the love of God made manifest and effectual, in and by the power of the Holy Spirit. In which high calling may God's richest blessings rest upon you now and abide with you always. Amen.

Introduction

At Baltimore's Lovely Lane United Methodist Church, where a Christmas Conference in 1784 organized the Methodist Episcopal Church in America, Dr. Albert Outler preached this Bicentennial sermon on Sunday, May 6, 1984, while the General Conference was in session. People sat in chairs placed in aisles and immediately before the pulpit; they stood along the walls of the sanctuary; and those who couldn't get in crammed the doorways and peered into windows.

Albert Outler was comfortable in pulpit-preaching situations such as this. His discomfiture showed when he returned to the Conference. He had been to too many conferences to put much faith in them. He had seen conferences self-destruct.

Ever since the 1984 General Conference Albert Outler had been exercised over the big pushes by neo-Calvinist evangelicals to remake the Doctrinal Statement into some form of narrow legalism and by liberal social ethicists to dilute the doctrinal statement into an antinomian "gospel." He saw these efforts as diversions from a responsible freedom in the Spirit, which is essential to evangelical and social reform.

To stem the tide of radical doctrinal onslaught that could become the law of the church, Outler did what he could do best: He preached salvation by grace (all eight Wesleyan expressions of it) through the works of the Holy Spirit, grounded in Scripture, attested to by tradition, reasonable to the mind and heart, and experienced to be the truth. If Albert Outler were alive to preach this sermon just prior to the vote to be taken on doctrinal matters at the next General Conference, the outcome of the vote would be more nearly right in the Wesleyan sense. His spirit will be there. Someone will speak the concern of this Lovely Lane sermon. . . . And you never know what may happen at a United Methodist General Conference.

SERMON 37

Empowered To Witness

(Acts 1:4-8)

We are together here this morning (members of this congregation and Methodists from other parts of the world) to share in a special heritage at a special moment and in a very special place. This Sunday is a time "between the times": the midpoint of our Bicentennial year, the midpoint in this Bicentennial General Conference, the midpoint between a world epoch that is fading and a new one emerging. Thus far the General Conference has been largely preoccupied with celebrations and maneuverings. Now come the times of hazard, of shortened debates and of hard decisions (and, as all old-timers know, with less time for deliberation than will be needed and with more decisions than can be made wisely in the time allotted).

We have had the achievements of the two centuries past rehearsed and have been made aware of the formidable challenges that lie ahead in Century Three. We are proud and thankful for Methodism's history of service to the gospel of Christ. Yet, deep down, we also have this uneasy awareness of a certain loss of momentum in our church and in her mission, a certain malaise in her esprit and morale, a shift from a consensual mood (which Wesley called "catholic spirit") to an adversarial mood, in which, after each close vote, the winners cheer for themselves and the losers sulk. There are, thank God, many churches across the country and across the globe that are alive and life-giving, but they are too readily thought of as exceptional. We even make the feeble boast that our overall losses last year were less than previously. Time was when we pointed to our statistics of burgeoning growth as proof of God's special favor. Now we have shifted to the logic of Gideon's band. Now it is fashionable to argue that it is quality that really counts. We have altered our self-image from that of a church on the march to that of a church in a mode of maintenance.

The world about us grows more and more foreboding. The political processes on which we placed so much reliance seem more and more decrepit and ineffectual. Shrewd observers speak more and more frankly of "the decline of Western influence in the world." The Western dogmas of progress and human perfectibility are no longer devoutly believed or believable. The shadow of the mushroom cloud grows darker. After two centuries of success in an atmosphere of triumphalism, we must now recollect that historic Christianity, in all its branches, has had a long history of surmounting successive institutional and cultural crises and that its prime confidence never has been in the teeter-totter of optimism and pessimism, but in the invincible sovereignty of God's grace and providence and in the constant action of the Holy Spirit in upholding the church and empowering her in mission, in good times and bad.

This is the point to our text and its place in the first chapter of Christian church history: "The Acts of the Apostles." It is the risen Lord's first promise to his befuddled disciples facing a perplexing future: "After the enduement of the Holy Spirit [and, presumably, because of it], you will receive power, and will then become my 'martyrs' [my witnesses]: in Jerusalem, Judea, and Samaria, and away to the ends of the earth" (1:8). This, I hope, will remind some of you of John Wesley's paraphrase of this same text, in his *Explanatory Notes*:[1] "Ye shall be empowered to witness to My gospel, both by your preaching and suffering" (which is to say, by "martyrdom" in both senses of the term: living by the gospel and suffering for the gospel).

This, as we know, was the secret of Christianity's survival

and growth, in the first age, and ever since: men and women empowered to witness, not on their own and not just to each other, but exclaiming to the world that "Jesus Christ is Lord and Savior (of the whole human family) to the glory of God the Father." This has also been the secret of every reinvigoration of the body of Christ ever since, and never more so than in the Evangelical Revival of the Wesleys and in American Methodism. What real power we have had is spiritual power. This is Wesley's point in another of his "notes," on Luke 1:35—

> The Power of God was put forth by the Holy Ghost, as the immediate divine agent in this work; and so He exerted the power of the Highest as His own power, who, together with the Father and the Son, is the Most High God.[2]

At the heart of the true Methodist heritage there has always been a robust doctrine of the Trinity!

On this special Sunday, we are well enough aware of the myriad issues confronting the General Conference and the church and the world, and you will understand my temptation to editorialize on at least a few of them. "Keep back thy servant, Lord, from presumptions; let them not have dominion over me" (Psalm 19:13)—even as I recall Wesley's wry reference to the medieval Spanish king who opined that had he been present at the creation, he would have had some very helpful suggestions to make.

The point is that tensions fester in the legislative committees, and disruptive proposals still hang in the balance. There is, therefore, a natural tendency to suppose that United Methodism's fate and future are about to be decided by what happens between now and Friday. So it is, in a very important sense. But not finally and here we must be clear. Our real empowerment for effective witness still will come from its only valid source: the Holy Spirit in our hearts and lives and in the church at large. The larger end we have in view, therefore, is not just legislation but empowerment for witness—the proclamation and the exclamation of gospel, its manifestations in our sacrificial love.

We should not underestimate the decisive role of general conferences and other great occasions, but we need not overestimate them either. It may be useful to remember how many ostensibly "great occasions" have actually been stultified by their consequences. The formal authority of an ecclesiastical body and its actions is never decisive in and of itself. "Councils," quoted Wesley, "may err, and have erred."[3] Authority comes from God, through the consensus of the truly faithful, as they are guided by the Holy Spirit, by Holy Scripture, and by the Christian tradition. Ask not, then, how this conference fares. Ask rather whether it will itself be refreshed by the Spirit and will help renew the church with fresh hope and vigor for fruitful Christian mission.

Take, for example, the so-called First Council of Constantinople of 381. Formally speaking, it was irregular and not truly ecumenical. And yet it came up with a constructive resolution of the formidable Arian crisis, and it gave us the best of all the ancient creeds (the one commonly called "Nicene"). By contrast, 60 years later, the Second Council of Ephesus was formally correct and proper. Yet its results were nullified by the lack of reception of its decisions by the Christian community at large.

We Methodists might well be reminded of the British Conference of 1784 (six months before our Christmas Conference over here), when Wesley confronted his preachers with a new plan for their constitution. His scheme was a bone of contention and there was sharp contention in the Conference. It is interesting, therefore, to check out Wesley's reference to its last day, August 3d: "Our conference concluded in much love, to the great disappointment of all." So may we also hope and pray for a similar outcome, come Friday!

Even the Christmas Conference, large as it looms today, was a minor affair at the time and made only a slight impression, not to mention the bad example it set for later Methodist Conferences: "We were in great haste," wrote Asbury in his *Journal*, "and did much business in a little time."[4] But what momentous business it was and what splendid consequences it made possible!

The Centennial Conference of 1884 was a splendid registry of an exuberant self-confidence, but not all of it was well-founded. And so the story might go on.

Thus, this Bicentennial Conference and all else this year will have to be judged, not by this vote or that, but on whether or not what is now a dispirited church becomes an inspirited one, enlivened for her urgent tasks.

The first Methodist century saw a great evangelical conquest of the demographic frontiers of the new nation, even as it also saw many tragic schisms and separations. Our second century has seen massive cultural transformations, along with unprecedented transitions in doctrine and ethos, e.g., the triumph of Enlightenment perspectives in theology, the spread of the Social Gospel, the rise of new theories of Christian education and spiritual development, the rising dominance of emotive ethics and utopian eschatologies. Now, as we enter Century Three, it is increasingly plain that nineteenth-century conservatism and twentieth-century liberalism are both spent forces. The former never really understood the richness of Wesley's doctrine of grace; the latter never really grasped his doctrine of sin and sanctification. Wesley had ransacked the Christian tradition to come up with a creative and powerful understanding of sin and grace, of justification and sanctification; and we must go and do likewise. Until Ephesians 2:8 is restored to the heart of our message—"we are saved by grace through faith"—the power of our witness will continue to be enfeebled.

Wesley's teaching about the Holy Spirit, and also the sources of that teaching, in Scripture and tradition, could be newly instructive and relevant for us. It certainly has been at the heart of past Methodist renewals whenever they have come. Christian existence is life in, with, and under the Spirit, whose indwelling presence is the divine energy that is the ground of our human spirituality. It is the Spirit's prevenient grace that is the divine initiative in human hearts. The Spirit is God within us, witnessing to the grace of assurance of sins forgiven as well as to love, not as a means, but as the end of faith and hope. It is the Spirit "who completes the work of Christ by placing himself as the innermost reality in each human being" (Evdokimov). Incidentally, this is one of the great themes of the early Eastern fathers, from whom Wesley learned so much; it is still the essence of Eastern Orthodoxy, from which we, too, have so much to learn.

It is the Holy Spirit who represents Jesus Christ as Lord to each new age and culture. It is the Holy Spirit who empowers his faithful followers to faithful discipleship in word and life. This was the secret of Methodist outreach in Century One, of Methodism's prophetic courage and vision in Century Two. It will be the open secret of refreshment and renewed vitality in Century Three.

The Spirit-Wind is blowing across the world in our time and in places that one might have thought unlikely—Indonesia, Korea, Africa, even here at home (on college campuses and even in some churches). In more places than before, there are growing aspirations for truly human life beyond wretchedness and apathy, aspirations for Christian experience in live earnest. But remember that "aspiration" is a cousin-word to "spirituality." There are also growing hungers for inspiration in and for life abundant. But, again, "inspiration" is also a cousin-word for "spirituality." This, then, is our hope: refreshment for a jaded church by the power of the Spirit representing the risen Christ who makes all things new. Gerard Manly Hopkins was right:

> There lives the dearest freshness
> deep down things . . .
> Because the Holy Ghost over
> the bent
> world broods . . . with Ah!
> bright wings.[5]

In the worlds that have been and in the new world unfolding, the Christian power of authentic witness will come less from human ingenuity than from hearts, minds, and lives open to the leadings of the Spirit; less from mutual exhortation than from the recognition that it is his work in the world to lead men and women into the fullness of their true humanity in Jesus Christ.

It is in this sense that our hopes and prayers for the Bicentennial General Conference must be for its willingness to be led of the Spirit and not to confuse emotive rhetoric and trendy ideologies with the Spirit's leadings. We are not talking about subjective piety here but about the objective, operative gifts of the Spirit (especially the gift of "discernment of spirits"). We are talking about the objective, manifold fruit of the Spirit (especially love, joy, and peace and the rest of that laundry list of Christian virtues in Galatians 5:22). Let these be the tests of judgment, of every speech and every vote.

Our prayer is that nothing be done to dispirit the faithful, nothing to comfort the artisans of schism; and let us not forget that Wesley defined schism not only as divisions between groups but rather more often as alienations and bitterness within the soul of the church itself. Here is where Wesley's ideas of "catholic spirit" and "schism" might alter the mood and atmosphere of our churches and of the General Conference.

The horizons of the future are already opening up beyond this Conference: toward a future that God is still holding open for his human family, whom he will never abandon and yet will never coerce. What will matter most in that future is the recovery of our monomania in mission—the mission of human salvation in all its fullness for all the peoples in all the world. This is a gospel beyond class and ideology to dignity and true "liberation," beyond race and sex to true community, beyond adversarial theologies of all sorts toward justice, righteousness, and the Rule of Grace.

The distinctive design of "The people called Methodists," it was once widely agreed, was "to reform the nation (to restore its morale and *esprit*) and to spread Scriptural holiness (the love of God and neighbor) over these lands."[6] Here is a task that demands the best and the most of us all, for it means a truly renewed kind of evangelism, truly renewed conceptions of Christian growth and maturation, renewed commitments to Christian social action ("social holiness" as Wesley called it, "since Scripture knows no other kind") by preaching and suffering and living and caring and turning the upside-down world right side up again. This task of spreading scriptural holiness remains as our task, to be helped or hindered by general conferences and by our boards and agencies, but not preempted by any of them. The United Methodist Church exists to manifest the power of the Spirit and not the other way round.

This wonderful old church in which we are worshiping today, with its lilting name and all its indelible memories, is "The Mother Church" of American Methodism. Our presence here is a token of our appreciation of a wondrously rich heritage, yet also a sign of our commitments to a new future in which our hungers and hopes for another Great Awakening may find at least the beginnings of their satisfactions.

The men who came to Baltimore 200 years ago were empowered to witness; so may we still be. They were evangelists; so should we be. They had a vision of a New Zion in the wilderness; our vision must be of Zion in a new wilderness—a modern humanity in dire disorder. From Baltimore their witness to the gospel spread to the uttermost parts of the earth, and that now has brought us back to Baltimore once again for a new beginning.

But all truly new beginnings are spiritual; they come from inspirited churches, enlivened and enlivening. It is not for us to know (or try to control) the final ends of history. We are commissioned to help shape them. The end of it all is the Father's business. It is enough for us, says our text, to open our hearts and minds to the inspirations of the Holy Spirit, that we may be empowered to give word and life and winsomeness to the true gospel of Christ, to our nearest neighbors, and on out to the uttermost human frontier. So may it be here in these next few days and in the years that stretch out beyond. So may it be with all the people called Methodists everywhere in all the world. So may it be with God's people in every place and every future, secure, as we all may be, in the unfailing Providence of God.

Let us pray:

> O God of unchangeable power and eternal light, look graciously upon thy whole church, that wonderful and sacred mystery; and by the tranquil operation of thy perpetual providence, carry out the work of our salvation. And let the whole world feel and see that things that were cast down are being raised up, and things that had grown old are being made new, and that all things are returning to perfection through him from whom they took their origin, even Jesus Christ our Lord. In the name of Jesus and in the power of the Paraclete. Amen.

Introduction

Albert Outler preached this sermon at the Texas Annual Conference on May 28, 1984, in response to the investiture of one million dollars given to Southern Methodist University by the Texas Conference that established the Albert C. Outler Chair in Wesley Studies. He reminded his audience that "the United Methodist Church has no precedent for a dogmatic creed or confession. United Methodists ought not to have any of the current theological trends imposed on them, as official. Nor am I suggesting the mere resuscitation of Wesley's rhetoric and polemics. . . . But we do need to learn Wesley's special ways of fruitful Christian reflection: of living in the biblical world until biblical perspectives become familiar and applicable in contemporary life, in all its varied cultural contexts."

The manner in which Outler handled this honor reflected the way he received comments about himself. He may have asked you (if you were a preacher whose judgment he respected) how his sermon came across. If you answered by heaping praise on him, you would have failed. If you answered in reference to his content, to audience participation, to what his message said to you, he would have given you an A. He was more nearly satisfied when he was assured the message came through adequately. He would have preferred to hear a good argument from you on a point in the sermon than a mountain of praise that rested on the quicksand of ignorance.

Outler sharply differed with Richard Heitzenrater's interpretation of the second clause of the First Restrictive Rule. The irony is that Heitzenrater at the time served as professor of the Albert C. Outler Chair in Wesley studies. And that was all right with Albert Outler—not that Heitzenrater was right but that he was thinking about the problem.

SERMON 38

Our Wesleyan Heritage and Our Doctrinal Future

I still have another beatitude to propose to you: Blessed is the man who finds himself caught up in a great and good cause and, in its pursuit, finds such stalwart friends and allies as your incomparable Bishop Crutchfield and Bill Scales and Bob Parrott and the Crismans and all the host of wonderful folks here in this great Conference!

It is a joy and a delight and I cannot begin to tell you how deeply grateful I am for what you have done and for all that you have made possible. My life has been filled to overflowing with all sorts of unexpected and unmerited blessings (so that when I speak of justification by grace, I truly know whereof I speak). But none of all these splendid happenings has made me more confident of the long-term future than your act, as a Conference, of endowing the chair and program at Southern Methodist University.

We do not yet know how much this uncommon vision and generosity of yours may mean for the future of theological education in The United Methodist Church and in the ecumenical community. It reminds us all of what annual conferences can do, and it might very well serve as a pioneering example to others across the jurisdiction and the church. It goes without saying that I am pleased to have my name associated with the venture, but what matters much more is the assurance of an ongoing, developing project that will bear fruit in many ways (some predictable, some not now foreseeable). It is a magnificent thing that you have done.

But let me fall back on an old teacher's prerogative and remind you of a new development in The United Methodist Church's near future that needs to be linked with your project so that you can see how timely your venture has been and will continue to be. As you know, one of the five new commissions authorized by the Bicentennial General Conference is one that is directed to review and revise the present statement in our *Discipline* on "Doctrine and Doctrinal Standards." The fact of these new commissions reflects a deep-running ferment of theological interest, and portends a more conscious and official concentration on Methodist doctrine and teaching than we will have ever had in American Methodist history.

There is no way now that Methodist leaders (academic, clerical, and lay) can avoid being drawn back to the very first two questions asked in Wesley's first Methodist conference, in 1744: "What to teach" and "How to teach." Nor will this dialogue be confined any longer to the so-called "upper circles." The reports of these five commissions (and the doctrinal one, especially) will concern not only the next General Conference (1988) but all of the rest of you who may be around then.

The outcome will be an alteration in the theological climate of United Methodism in many different ways, for better or for worse, and into the going future. For if, as I foresee, any one of these reports should trigger either one or both of the first two Restrictive Rules in our Constitution, all of you would be directly involved straightaway. For then there will be ensuing debates and votes in all the annual conferences throughout the church.

The question asks itself irresistibly: are United Methodists prepared for such a spate and spasm of doctrinal reflection and debate—and the controversies that may thus be stirred? If the obvious answer is "No, not really" (and this ought to be obvious to anyone who heard the debates at Baltimore or who reads the *United Methodist Reporter* with any regularity), then an urgent imperative follows: "*Now* is the time for all good Methodists to come to the aid of their church—in the hope that what might otherwise be disruptive may actually be turned into a positive development."

As you know, early Methodists were intensely concerned with the core doctrines of Christianity, focusing especially on the central issue of salvation by faith. They were, accordingly, deeply involved in debate and controversy. Doctrinal questions dominated the early conferences: one could reconstruct a full-orbed summary of Methodist doctrine from the *Minutes* of the annual conferences from 1744 to 1765. In American Methodism, from 1784 to 1816, selected doctrinal tracts were included in each *Discipline*. Moreover, their doctrinal consensus was so strong that in 1808 they had already stipulated that:

> The [delegated] General Conference shall not revoke, alter, or change our *Articles of Religion* [which meanwhile had been moved forward in the *Discipline* from Wesley's placement of them as appendices), or establish any new standards or rules of doctrine contrary to our present existing and established standards of doctrine.[1]

This is our famous First Restrictive Rule. It has never been altered, and no constitutional amendment under its restrictions has ever been passed, viz., a two-thirds majority of a general conference and a three-fourths majority of all the members of the annual conferences present and "voting." The phrase "our present existing and established standards of doctrine" referred to the provision of Wesley's Model Deed of 1763, viz., Wesley's *Explanatory Notes* (1754) and the 44 published sermons in his *Sermons on Several Occasions*, 1746-60. Thus, the Articles of Religion, the *Notes*, the *Sermons*, and the General Rules (covered by the Fifth Restrictive Rule) were the elements in "our present existing and established standards of doctrine." They still are, historically and legally.

Because the doctrinal consensus in American Methodism was so solid in Century One; and because of the difficulties of amendment, they never have been challenged (even when they were, in effect, being ignored in Methodist pulpits and the classrooms). Indeed, in the Centennial Conference in Baltimore in 1884, Dr. J. B. MacFerrin was cheered when he declaimed:

> Mr. Chairman:
>
> We have not come here to legislate, or to make suggestions with regards to, new creeds. Some say it is time for the creeds of the churches to be remodelled. Well, that may do for some peoples' creeds but not for ours. Our creed is like the New Testament—finished! Woe betide the man who takes anything out of it or puts anything into it. Justification by Faith, the Witness of the Spirit, Sanctification of Heart and Life: these are the grand peculiarities of Methodism. Let them be preserved forever![2]

The irony here, of course, was that the winds of doctrinal changes were already blowing so that within the next half-century, the official standards of doctrine still stood intact, but the theological climate had been drastically changed. The result was a sort of quiet agreement that we would avoid anything that threatened our official doctrinal equilibrium. Indeed, in 1968 we were so wary of official doctrinal controversy that we simply juxtaposed the Evangelical United Brethren *Confession of Faith* alongside the Methodist Articles of Religion, declaring specifically (even if not quite accurately) that:

> The Evangelical United Brethren Confession, The Articles of Religion and the Wesleyan "standards" [i.e., the *Notes* and *Sermons*] are thus deemed congruent if not identical in their doctrinal perspectives and not in conflict.[3]

Nevertheless, the 1968 Conference adopted a proposal for what was originally labeled a "creedal commission." This was mandated to produce a "new Methodist creed" to displace the Articles and the Confession. This was finally amended to provide for "A Commission on Doctrine and Doctrinal Standards," which, over the course of four strenuous years, came up with our current Part II of the *Discipline*: "Doctrine and Doctrinal Statements and The General Rules."

In the process, the statement was submitted to the Judicial Council for its declaratory judgment as to whether or not it brought the First, Second, or Fifth Restrictive Rules into operation. Their opinion: it did not. Even so, the Commission's report was adopted by an incredible majority on a count vote of signed ballots: 925 yeas to 17 nays.

Early on, however, there were complaints from various partisans of single-issue theologies that their concerns had not been fully met. There were murmurings from the liberals that the statement was too conservative, and snorts from the right wing about its outright avowal of doctrinal pluralism, not only as a fact of life in The United Methodist Church but, more importantly, as an avowed Wesleyan principle. What we had had in mind, of course, was something like Wesley's quite characteristic avowal in "The Character of a Methodist" (1742):

> The *distinguishing marks* of a Methodist are not his [theological] *opinions* of any sort. [Elsewhere he would define "opinions" as diverse theological interpretations—this formulation of Christology or that, this theory of atonement or that, this or that ecclesiology; even the famous "Five Points of Calvinism," were "opinions"!] [A Methodist's] assenting to this or that scheme of religion, his embracing any particular set of notions, his espousing the judgment of one man or of another, are all quite wide of the point. Whosoever therefore imagines that a Methodist is a man of such and such an *opinion*, is grossly ignorant . . . he mistakes the truth. . . . We believe, indeed, that "all Scripture is given by the inspiration of God"; and herein we are distinguished from Jews, Turks, and infidels. We believe this written Word of God to be the *only and the sufficient* rule both of Christian faith and practice; and herein we are fundamentally distinguished from those of the Romish Church. We believe Christ to be the Eternal Supreme God; and herein are we distinguished from the Socinians and Arians. But as to all opinions which do not strike at the root of Christianity, we [Methodists] "think and let think."[4]

This is not a solitary utterance; it is repeated a dozen times elsewhere in the corpus, and the contrary is never even hinted at. And if you wonder what, then, are the distinguishing marks of a Methodist, you can read the whole tract in Volume VIII of the Jackson edition, pp. 340-47 [but see note 4 above]. Indeed, this is the sort of homework that I would urge because you are the men and women who are going to have to debate this issue of pluralism before the quadrennium is over and especially at its end. And if you are ill-prepared for it, the debate will be merely confused. The assignment should also include such things as Wesley's great sermon on "Catholic Spirit."[5]

But there are many Methodists who put more store by their particular doctrinal opinions than Wesley did. We have a growing number of doctrinal zealots (right and left) who are bent on imposing a theological monopoly on the church, in accordance with "the truth" as they see it. They won the day in Baltimore. And now we shall see what happens, and the 1988 General Conference will have to sit as a grand jury to pass judgment on the commission's findings; And whether, as I said earlier, the commission's report triggers either the First or the Second Restrictive Rules (or both) and even the Fifth (not to say embroiled). The sooner we begin to prepare for such a prospect, the more hopeful we may be of a responsible dialogue (as contrasted with emotive rhetoric and voting from the viscera).

None of the members of the Doctrinal Commission of 1968-1972 regarded our report as final and fixed. In the report itself we urged continued development within the fourfold guidelines of "the Wesleyan Quadrilateral." In this sense, we welcome the new commission, although I myself think it would have been far wiser to have put the chief responsibility for such an enterprise into the hands of the Council of Bishops as our chief pastors and teachers so that the whole venture could have been more continuous and cumulative. Now, however, we have to go with what we have and use the occasion and the process as fruitfully as possible. This is why I appeal to you, as one of the bellwether conferences in the whole church, to enlist yourselves at one level or another in the enterprise of theology in the Wesleyan spirit, and in the transformations it might achieve in turning a declining church around and set it on the march again!

The church does not live by doctrine alone, but neither can it grow and spread without a sound and lively doctrinal consensus. If the new doctrinal commission can move us toward such a consensus about the basics of Christian beliefs, we and the world will all be the better for it. If not, the General Conference of 1988 would do well to receive the report as a sign of progress and continue the process for yet another quadrennium, preferably in the hands of the Council of Bishops. The United Methodist Church has no precedent for a dogmatic creed or confession. United Methodists ought not to have any of the current theological trends imposed on them, as official. Nor am I suggesting the mere resuscitation of Wesley's rhetoric and polemics. Wesley's texts cannot merely be repeated as if they were magic mantras; he would be the first to scorn such idolatry.

But we do need to learn Wesley's special ways of fruitful Christian reflection: of living in the biblical world until biblical perspectives become familiar and applicable in contemporary life, in all its varied cultural contexts. We need to salvage from the Christian past those nuggets of Christian truth, insight, and wisdom that have survived the dross of theological controversy. We need to bring our best use of objective reason to bear upon the reinterpretation of traditional formulations so as to enhance their appeal to men and women of reason and religion (i.e., to the spiritual hungers in all humans).

The gospel needs credible explanations as well as proclamation and not just argumentative rationalizations. But always there must also be the spiritual energy of the heart assured by faith, sustained by hope, inflamed by love. The gospel must be exclaimed; it must be witnessed to with power in Christian life and work and sacrificial service. The gospel can (and should) be made theatrical by proclamation and liturgy; it must be made dramatic and converting by the power of Christian example: intense, sustained, and life-altering. It must be carried out into the world, to the wretched of the earth—with a view to their reconciliation to God and their restoration to full human status in the human community. This was the nub of Wesley's notion of the

Christian mission: faith, hope, and love in outreach—convicting, converting, and transforming human existence, personal and social.

What has come home to me more and more as I have read Wesley over the years is the difference between his own theological opinions (many of which are still interesting but no longer relevant) and his understanding of the vital core of Christian truth, which is still valid. He had opinions about almost everything, from astronomy to medicine and theology; his curiosity was lively and wide-ranging. And he did not always live by that slogan of his, "to think and let think."

But always, at least from 1738 onwards, he had a vivid focused vision of Christian existence that he refused to cast in creedal form but that he kept alive and refreshed. The single term that sums it all up was grace: God's free, unearned, unmerited mercy and favor, his pure, unbounded love, revealed incarnate in Jesus Christ, continued in present power through the Holy Spirit, and offered freely to all of every age and station, who "earnestly repent of [their] sins and are in love and charity with [their] neighbors and intend to lead a new life, following the commandments of God, and walking from henceforth in his holy ways."[6]

Grace, for Wesley, is God's cosmic beneficence. Creation is not a mere artifact nor a self-enclosed universe. It is, rather, a work of grace. The crown of creation is the human family, with its stamp of the image and similitude of God himself—the special gift of awareness of God, our specifically human capacity to react to God's initiatives. This is what "*pre*venience" means. God acts and this enables us to act, in specifically human ways. We can act humanly because God has made us "for himself" and as unique individuals, in *his* image. But grace, as God's beneficence, only begins with creation and the image. It continues as the climate of our secret life from the first dawnings of spiritual consciousness, on throughout the drama of life's tragic dialectic between faith and unfaith, all along the way of our earthly pilgrimage, unto our re-creation in the life of the world to come!

I would feel a lot easier about the future of Methodist doctrine if I could foresee even a vague consensus forming around the basic core of Wesley's vision of Christian existence, as an order of salvation that convicts, justifies, reconciles, matures, and sanctifies the believer, through grace. If we were disposed to live in the atmosphere of Scripture as our basic frame of reference, we could differ in our theological opinions. We could maintain our diverse theological opinions in creative tension. What would matter would be an agreement in our understanding of the Wesleyan view of "the general sense of Scripture," viz., the basic "narrative" of the stages of Christian existence: of formation (the image of God in finite creatures), of deformation (the spoliation of the divine image and its displacement by prideful self-interest), of reformation (God's initiative in Jesus Christ to reconcile and renew, to remake us new creatures in Christ), and of restoration of the divine image, which is the essence and end of salvation (as Wesley makes plain repeatedly). This is less a particular theological position than it is a basic perspective. It is a perspective that was never formulated in a single form of words. There are three dozen summaries of the gospel in the Wesley corpus, and no two of them are verbally identical. There is a lesson here for us to heed.

And yet each summation presupposes the sovereignty of grace, the omnipresence of grace, the sufficiency of grace, the uniqueness of Christ as the incarnation of uncreated grace, and of the Holy Spirit as the divine agent of all created and operative grace in human life and human affairs. If we understood that the kingdom of God and *his* righteousness is a rule of grace, in life and society and in the long reaches of time and eternity, we could withstand the winds and tumults of doctrinal confusion, and still find the insight and energy for effective evangelism, authentic nurture, and effective social action.

Some such shared theological perspective—biblical, traditional, rational, experiential—is the task of the clergy as pastors and teachers of the church. The editorial, theological, and liturgical opinions of the clergy are always of some passing interest to the people of God. But what really matters is that the clergy should teach the people of God what the Scriptures and the church have to teach them, and to do this in a credible, reasonable form that sparkles with the signs of vital experience. The greatest sorrow of my life is the realization that, after four decades of life and work in theological seminaries, I have to recognize that the theological confusion and trendiness of contemporary clergy is worse than when I started, and there is no way to excuse myself from some responsibility in this impoverishment.

But in the Methodist tradition, it is the laity and not the clergy who are the church visible in the world. The laity are the church, winsome and attractive, or else the church dull and unimpressive, or else (though God forbid) the church ridiculous and sometimes even repulsive. If the world is to be won for Christ, it will be by the grace of God and the empowered witness of the *laos* (which, of course, includes the clergy but only as an important subspecies). The doctrinal future of Methodism, humanly speaking and barring miracles, lies in the hands of the Methodist laity. After all, you have half the votes, and if, four years from now, you have a doctrinal amendment swirling through the annual conferences, there will be a doctrinal crisis with which you had better be able to cope, or else.

The Texas Conference, with exceptional foresight and generosity has established a chair and program in Wesley Studies. You have honored me in the process, and I am deeply grateful for the honor. But I know all too well how readily such honors are forgotten, whereas assured good causes live on and on.

Already, your initiative has given rise to Laity Week at Southern Methodist University, and now there is a Center for Methodist Historical Studies in which some of you are already interested and in which all of you may be involved. Already, you have had theological colloquies throughout your Conference. It occurs to me, therefore, that room could be found in your future calendar for seminars in Wesley Studies, in local congregations and in your districts. What if there were a scheduled lecture in each Annual Conference on the Wesleyan heritage and its contemporary relevance? What if the Council of Bishops undertook to prepare a magisterial letter on the topic "our present existing and established standards of doctrine," with a view to clarifying such issues for both clergy and laity alike? What if our church literature were to reflect more concern with the Wesleyan distinction between core consensus and theological rivalries?

And if some of you groan at an old teacher's piling on so much homework, let me assure you that I understand at least some of the bafflement and frustration that you may feel. Wesley is hard to read, especially without notes and context and updating. For years my friendly students have complained to me that Wesley's sermons made for deadly reading. How on earth, they asked, did such dull sermons have such effects when we find them so hard to follow or even to finish? This, of course, is why we have found it so much easier to make Wesley a cult hero and to reverence his relics than to study his writings in requisite depth so as to let his remarkable message come to be our own. But persevere! Never mind the eighteenth-century rhetoric and argument. Look for the aphorism, for the nuggets, for those flashing summations of the gospel, for the interesting sidelights that illuminate Wesley's central vision. Ask less for entertainment than for instruction. Ask less for "wow!" than for "Ah, so!"

And remember two main points, above the others. One applies more especially to our evangelicals; the other is more pertinent to the trendy partisans of "new," single-issue causes. The first point is that orthodoxy and true religion are by no means the same thing. Wesley distinguishes them clearly in his *Plain Account of the People Called Methodists*, of 1748:

> The points we [Methodists] chiefly insist upon are four: First, the *orthodoxy*, or *right opinions*, is at best but a very slender *part* of religion, if it can be allowed to be any part of it at all; that neither does religion consist in *negatives*, in bare harmlessness of any kind; nor merely in *externals*, in doing good or using the means of grace, in works of piety (so called) or of charity; that it is nothing short of or different from "the mind that was in Christ," "the image of God" stamped upon the heart, inward "righteousness" attended with the "peace" of God and "joy in the Holy Ghost". Secondly, that the only way under heaven to this religion is to "repent, and believe the gospel", or (as the Apostle words it) "repentance towards God, and faith in our Lord Jesus Christ." Thirdly, that by this faith, "he that worketh not, but believeth on him that justifieth the ungodly." is "justified freely by his grace, through the redemption which is in Jesus Christ." And, lastly, that "being justified by faith," we taste [here on earth] the

> heaven to which we are going; we are holy and happy; we tread down sin and fear, and "sit in heavenly places with Christ Jesus."[7]

Why will people who believe and experience such things go on to insist upon dogmatic orthodox formulations? My guess is that come 1988, they will rue the day that they rejected the hard-won pluralism of 1972.

But Wesley also had a warning word to Methodists in the nominal majority: It comes from his fear of a "declension of religion" such as we ourselves have seen over the past three decades. In 1786, he wrote out this concern in his *Thoughts Upon Methodism*:

> 1. I am not afraid that the people called Methodists should ever cease to exist either in Europe or America. But I am afraid lest they should only exist as a dead sect, having the form of religion without the power. And this undoubtedly will be the case unless they hold fast both the doctrine, spirit, and discipline with which they first set out.
> 2. What was their fundamental doctrine? That the Bible is the whole and sole rule both of Christian faith and practice. Hence they learned: (1) That religion is an inward principle; that it is no other than the mind that was in Christ; or in other words, the renewal of the soul after the image of God, in righteousness and true holiness. (2) That this can never be wrought in us (by any of our own efforts) but by the power of the Holy Ghost. (3) That we receive this and every other blessing merely [through grace] for the sake of Christ; and (4) that whosoever hath the mind that was in Christ, the same is our brother, and sister, and mother.[8]
>
> (Check out the next five sections for yourself!)

From this short sketch any man of understanding may easily discern Methodism by a few prudential regulations. The essence of it is holiness of heart and life: the circumstantials all point to this. As long as they are joined together in the people called Methodists, no weapon formed against them shall prosper. But if ever the circumstantials are despised, the essential will soon be lost. And if ever the essential parts should evaporate, what remains will be dung and dross.

United Methodists have a choice, and it can no longer be avoided or temporized. We can continue in our ways of struggle between outmoded rivalries and narrow majorities, along with fragmentations that lead to "schism in the Methodist soul," or we can attempt in real earnest to graft new human sensitivities onto the still living rootstock of our Wesleyan heritage and find the refreshment that will give us a new lease on life in Christ Jesus.

We cannot wait for a doctrinal commission to do this for us; it is our job and it has already begun. To the splendid project you have launched at Southern Methodist University, you must add your own initiatives, your own discoveries, your own commitments to the tasks of evangelism, nurture, and social action that go with holiness of heart and life. God bless you for what you have done and for all that may follow from it. And may he grant you the wisdom and energy to cope with the challenges and opportunities in the opening future. So may his Holy Spirit light up a truly promising way into your third century. Amen.

Introduction

At the Central Texas Annual Conference ordination service on June 5, 1984, Albert Outler preached this sermon. He made a strong call for open communication between the seminary and the church "out there," and emphasized that the seminary educates those who are led by the Holy Spirit to become appointed representatives of the church.

This conviction led Albert Outler from Yale to Perkins School of Theology. At Yale he had to "jump the fence" between the seminary and the church every time he left and returned. In an effort to break down this fence, he took a church his last three years at Yale. He said, "I took a church in Wallingford, a little silversmithing town fifteen miles northeast of New Haven, and lived in the parsonage at Wallingford and taught at the divinity school. I had a remarkable experience because, in Wallingford, the leading church was the Congregational, the next was the Episcopalian, the next was the Baptist, and the fourth was the Methodist."

High on the agenda of Albert Outler, as he and Merrimon Cuninggim began the new era for Perkins School of Theology in 1951, was to begin a wedding between the seminary and the church. That tradition continued in the form of interns working in local churches, hospitals, etc. Less than the best of health in his later years prevented Dr. Outler from going out and preaching in churches as much as he once did. But when he did go, he did not have to jump a fence. With wit he would say, "My jumping days are over."

SERMON 39

"Take Thou Authority. . ."

(Ordination Sermon 5)

I have two texts tonight and they are from the Ritual of Ordination in which we shall presently join, where Bishop Russell will say to the ordinands here, "Take thou authority to execute the office of a deacon in the Church of God . . ." and then "Take thou authority as an elder in the Church of God, to preach the Word of God and to administer the holy Sacraments in the congregation." Together they suggest (rightly) that the distinctive thing in the act of ordination is the conferring and receiving of authority.

What is about to happen is that you who are ordinands are to receive an authority that you do not how have, and the rest of us are to be reminded of the authority that United Methodist clergy have and that United Methodist laity do not have. I realize, of course, how shocking such a notion will sound to some and how confusing to others. Indeed, some of us saw a thousand United Methodist big shots (General Conference delegates) wallowing in just such a confusion on these very same points, viz., the differences, if any, between the priesthood of all believers, on the one hand, and an ordained ministry on the other. And in this case, the specific differences between a deacon and an elder. The confusion is pathetic. But the logic of the United Methodist ritual is quite clear. What would be the point of asking you to receive an authority that you already have? Baptized, confirmed Christian believers are already entitled to preach and prophesy and, *in extremis*, to baptize, and maybe even to administer Holy Communion. Something additional is about to be conferred and the act ought to be deeply meaningful to us all and not just to these ordinands.

It is, therefore, important to consider the nature of the authority of the ministerial office (diaconal, presbyterial, episcopal) that sets the ordained ministry apart from the general priesthood. There is a narrow middle way here between an exaggeration of ministerial authority on the one side and its reduction to mere function on the other. What on earth, pray tell, is this alleged authority the ordained clergy have that the general priesthood has not? It had better be something important, and it had better be understood, else our devout belief in the dogma of equality may be affronted (and our ordained clergy encouraged to misunderstand their distinctive roles and responsibilities).

We all know preachers who claim too much authority or the wrong kind. We also know preachers who claim too little. No wonder, in these cases, the laity react ambivalently. So let's begin with a laundry list of what kinds of authority Bishop Russell will not be conferring on these ordinands or that the rest of the clergy here do not have either.

1. ***It is nothing magical or mystical.*** The bishop will not be casting a spell nor making these men and women more pious or more spiritual than they are already. I have never known a congregation in which the piety and spirituality of some of the laity did not equal or exceed the piety and spirituality of their minister. This is not to disparage spirituality. God be praised for all devout preachers. But let us not deceive ourselves; their spirituality is not superior, if and when it is, because of their ordination.

2. ***Ministerial authority is not moral.*** God be praised for all men and women of moral integrity in the ministry (without it all else is lost or undermined). But even so, there are men and women of equal integrity in the pews and the community—or ought to be. This, then, is not the basis of the distinctive authority you are about to receive and thereafter to exercise for the rest of your life.

3. ***It is not intellectual.*** There will be no raising the I.Q. of these ordinands by the imposition of hands. That did not happen even when you were handed your Master of Theology diplomas. You will soon learn, as if you did not already know, that there are also highly intelligent men and women out there in the pews—and might be more if the Methodist Church did not have so strong an anti-intellectualist tradition.

4. ***Ministerial authority is not even professional.*** Here are the clergy, certified Masters of Theology, many of them doctors in the church. They are authorized to teach (Bible, church history, theology and ethics, and politics and culture), to lead the people of God in liturgy (and to discourage them from memorizing anything so that it could be used devoutly without a text because they know that next Sunday, or in another church, it will be different). They are prepared (sort of) to counsel and to lead in community service and in Christian social action.

Many churchfolk are prepared to be impressed by these outward signs of professional expertise. And in our processes of screening candidates for the ministry we often stress professional degrees almost as much as we do "gifts, graces, and fruits," even though we managed without them for a century and a half out of two. It ought to go without saying that I would be the last man here tonight to decry professional training for our Methodist clergy. It is only that I wish so earnestly that our "Masters of Theology" were that—really the experts they are certified to be. Even if they were, however, that would not be the basis of their distinctive authority as deacons and elders in the church of God.

5. ***And finally, despite all appearances to the contrary, the proper authority exercised by Methodist ministry does not depend, on principle at least, upon that old reliable, "personality"***—by which we usually mean an attractive combination of charming manners, smooth talk, and charisma. These are, for all too many of us, our stock-in-trade. What is worse, many of our people are glad to have it so. I have, in my lifetime, known many

a man who understood his shepherding role more as that of piping to his flock than of feeding and safeguarding them. I have known many a congregation that was content if they could count on a weekly solo performance of high quality.

God be praised for all charismatic preachers (especially those with the gifts listed in 1 Corinthians 12:7-10) and for all eloquent and winsome men and women. But the ministry has no monopoly on personality. "Would to God," said Moses, "that all God's people were prophets, that the Lord would pour out his Spirit upon them all" (Numbers 11:29). And in any congregation on a given Sunday morning there are truly outstanding lay men and women (or would be if the church had done her mission well).

Well, if our proper and valid authority as deacons and elders in the church of God does not derive from one or another or all of the above, what sort of authority can we be talking about? What is it that Bishop Russell has to give that you can receive and use in good faith to good effect?

The answer, validated by Scripture and tradition, is simple and clear, but we have so far forgotten it that it will sound strange and new in many ears, which ought to help us understand the current confusion in which we Methodists stand vis-à-vis the ministerial office. It is this: These ordinands are about to receive, as many of the rest of us have already received (whether or not we have used it rightly) the authority to be and to act representatively, which is to say, as appointed representatives of as large a fraction of the whole church of God as may now recognize their credentials to do so. It will be the authority to serve as envoys of the church catholic in and with the church local and *vice versa,* as liaison agents between this congregation or that and the entire *koinonia* of Christ. The people of God, says 1 Peter 2:9, are "a chosen generation, a royal priesthood, a holy nation, a peculiar people." But not every member of this royal priesthood is called to represent the whole of it as a delegated, ordained ambassador. Every Christian is a representative of Christ in and to the world, but not as an officially accountable deputy of the church's official doctrine praxis. The ordained minister is not a parrot nor a maverick nor a private pontiff.

And so the church, through its elected and accountable officers, selects and calls qualified men and women, who themselves also feel called to be and to act as deputies, envoys, agents, emissaries, ambassadors, representatives of the church universal to the church local. Moreover, they are to do all of this day in, day out, in all their public actions, with the church's backing and with her delegated authority. As our chief pastor and general superintendent, Bishop Russell has the authority to convey this sort of authority to you. And you, by virtue of your election by this Conference, are qualified to receive it. This is what will be happening, beneath and beyond all ceremony and symbolism. But unless you understand this and respond in good faith, what you receive will be negligible.

In this ordination, then, you are taking it upon yourselves to be and to act in and from and for the church universal, in and for and to the church local—and the other way around, too. You are undertaking to stand for the whole church in the local congregation and wherever else you may be. You are undertaking to speak responsibly for the whole church, which means that you must know and agree in some valid measure with the consensus of the Christian faithful. The words you preach are not to be your words alone, but the church's word as witness to authentic interpretations of the Word of God. The sacraments that you administer are not to be your own ritual devisings, but the sacraments of Christ delivered into the church's care and keeping.

Your role in the congregation and community is not that of projecting your own image, but the church's reality, the image of the servant-ministry to which you have been ordained. And this will be the measure of your greatness, your "success." "For the Son of Man came not to be ministered to but to minister [to serve] and to give His life as an outpouring" (Matthew 20:28). In this role of the church's representative, all your gifts and graces will be useful and fruitful: your vivid sense of the Sacred and of your participation in the divine nature and sharing this great mystery with others, your moral character, your intellectual concerns, your professional expertise, and, of course, your personality. You will, certainly, be more effectively representative if you are as charming as you can be, as eloquent as you can be, and as impressive as you can be, all for the sake of the cause you are representing, in the congregation and in the world.

Ordained men and women are, therefore, vowed to a special set of responsibilities, in and for the whole church. They are responsible for traditioning (which is to say, passing on) the church's mission in and to the world, of standing in a long and honorable succession and seeing to it that the Christian heritage is not lost and that the Christian future is not stultified. They are responsible for the church's vision of herself as outreaching, ingathering, and upbuilding. They are responsible for being available on every Jericho road, and it will never do to plead a committee meeting in Jericho as an excuse!

An ordained minister need never cease being himself/herself, but those ordained must be ever mindful of their covenant—the covenant that is about to be reenacted here tonight—and so avoid all confusions between their personal crochets and their ministerial callings. There is, as we have said, nothing magical going on here; but there is a mystery. These persons are about to be changed from their places and roles in the general priesthood to the role and functions of the representative ministry in the church of God. It is a mystery of the Holy Spirit's enduement of the ordained minister to the status and role of envoy, of delegate—of representative. Representative, mind you, of the Church of God (there is not a single word about The United Methodist Church or the Central Texas Conference in the entire ritual). This business of being and acting representatively is not just for now and then—on show and for occasions—but always and everywhere. Ordained ministers have made a total commitment to a lifelong sacred task in which they are upheld by divine grace and power.

My guess would be that few of the ordinands here tonight have had a Damascus Road experience—maybe not even an "Aldersgate experience." But I do hope, earnestly, that each of you comes to this altar with a stable, inward conviction that you are truly called and disposed toward something like the representative ministry of which we have been speaking. You are about to bind yourselves by solemn vows, yet you will also be freed by those same commitments, freed from the status of being the employee of any local congregation, freed from arbitrary authority in the church or out of it. For in your actions as the whole church's responsible envoy, you have the whole church behind you.

Note well that you are being ordained into the ministry of the church universal: "The Lord pour upon thee the Holy Spirit for the office and work of an elder in the Church of God . . ."[1] Every crucial reference in the ritual is to the action of the Holy Spirit as your divine authority and upholder. It is the Holy Spirit who has led you here; it is the Holy Spirit who will lead you from here into all the joys and satisfactions of what all of us pray will be wondrously fruitful careers.

In yourselves and on your own, the tasks of the representative ministry are impossible. This is why, for those who try to make it on their own, their ministries become perfunctory or else self-centered. Our only trustworthy reliance is in the Holy Spirit, with whom our risen Lord has promised to empower you with the power of witness and service—close at home and nearby, yet also on out and out to the ends of the earth.

Here we are together tonight, you on the verge of your ordained ministry and I in the twilight of mine. Yet if we and our Methodist brethren and sisters share John Wesley's conviction that the Holy Spirit is God's ever-present power in our hearts, if we truly trust in his power in our efforts to upbuild the church and to transform the kingdoms of this world into the kingdom of God and of his Christ, then you can receive a decisive authority to be and act for the whole church as her envoy and representative, and not to abuse or neglect your role and function. The church will then be the gainer as it welcomes you into such a ministry for its future.

The British Methodists have continued a tradition in their conferences that I am sorry we Americans have lost. For the closing of each annual session, as they are heading forth with renewed commitments to their representative tasks, they turn together to one of Charles Wesley's greatest hymns and sing it as they do few others. Since you will not be doing this at the adjournment of this session of your conferences (not as a tradition at least), it occurred to me that we might all be edified by sharing in it now as a shared statement about the Spirit's life and power in the general priesthood of all believers.

For those who are now about to receive their authority for their ministry, for all of us, there is a reminder of our real authority in all things Christian in the hymn "Captain of Israel's Host":

Captain of Israel's host, and guide
of all who seek the land above,
Beneath thy shadow we abide,
The cloud of thy protecting love:
Our strength, thy grace; our rule, thy Word;
Our end, the glory of the Lord.

By thine unerring Spirit led,
We shall not in the desert stray.
We shall not full direction need,
Nor miss our providential way;
As far from danger as from fear.
While love, Almight Love, is near.

Introduction

Albert Outler preached this sermon at the 1985 Pacific and Southwest Annual Conference. The core of truth around which it is built lies in the following threefold charter of the church in the Gospels: the Great Confession of Peter (Matthew 16:16), the Great Commission (Matthew 28:19-20), and the Great Commandment (John 15:12). "These three, then, form the charter of the church: Personal religion, Social religion, and Communal religion." In some ways the church fails in one or more of these areas at all times. At this point Albert Outler turns prophet and acknowledges his precarious position: "When the historian and analyst turns prophet, he is skating on thin ice. But we ought, because we must live in it."

Outler skated on thin ice when he preached this sermon, and continued to skate on thin ice. His skirmishes within the larger Christian community (i.e., the Second Vatican Council, ecumenical councils, United Methodist boards and agencies, the United Methodist Council of Bishops, etc.) gave him moments on the thinnest of ice. And every now and then some would have you think he went under. But after awhile he would come huffin' and puffin' and saying something like he said in this sermon: "Never has any power of earth or hell been able to extinguish the divine fire of faith which the church has always cherished. . . ." Thus said Albert Outler, the historian/analyst, and the ice-skating prophet.

SERMON 40

The Church: Nature and Task

The word "church" has various meanings for different people, but almost always it is too narrow: a building or organization in my hometown; the Methodist denomination; Protestantism. We rarely think of the church as that community or brotherhood of men and women in Jesus Christ, stretching in an unbroken line over nineteen centuries and providing the only possible basis for productive Christian fellowship. And yet the Christian church (and here we are talking about the actual, visible, historical church) has never been perfect; it has always been (compare 2 Corinthians and on down), in one way or another, a failure.

There is another, and still more important sense, in which the church has never completely failed; and there has never been a time when it was not the greatest potential source of blessing in human society.

But, in this first approach, we need to have a candid and thoughtful look at the limitations and shortcomings of the church in order that we may have a critical and yet loyal perspective from which to evaluate its possibilities and promise.

The church has failed and is failing because:

1. ***Its constituency tends to regard it as a hospital rather***

than a headquarters. Its members act as though they are patients to be cared for rather than as active agents, ready to be directed into constructive service. Thus the energies and vitality of the church are dissipated by this self-centered attitude.

2. ***It has, because of its divisiveness and individualism, tended to be a cafeteria rather than a family table.*** We pick and choose according to our individual preferences and prejudices; our interest and loyalty blow hot or cold, depending on whether we like this person or that feature about the church. We do not think of ourselves as "members one of another," as any good family will inevitably do.
3. ***The church's ideal and message have tended to be a coat of shellac, rather than an infusion of creosote.*** It is too easily taken for granted that the ideals, demands, and values of the Christian varnish are to be accepted as veneer rather than as life-and-society transforming.
4. ***The church has been more like a flight of butterflies than a hive of bees;*** pleasant and attractive but aimless and individualistic rather than united and unselfish, devoting the effort of the individual to the welfare of the community.

It is easy to criticize and to find fault with the church. It is easy to be destructive. But for the Christian, the rule is that you may be as critical as you are loyal.

The church is not merely a human society; its origins, its nature, its significance, and its destiny are grounded in its relation to the divine, to an act of God in history (the coming of Jesus the Christ), and to the continuing power of God's Holy Spirit in the life of human society. The charter or constitution of the church, therefore, is not to be found in expediency, but in faith. Let us find the threefold charter of the church in the Gospels:

1. ***The Great Confession*** of Peter (Matthew 16:16). On the rock of Peter's faith, devotion, and spiritual insight, Jesus proposes to found his church. This is the pillar of personal religion.
2. ***The Great Commission*** (Matthew 28:19-20). "Teach them

to observe all things whatsoever I have commanded you," i.e., the teachings of Jesus. This is the pillar of social religion.

3. ***The Great Commandment*** (John 15:12). "That ye love one another as I have loved you." This is the pillar of brotherhood, of communal religion.

These three, then, form the charter of the church: Personal religion, Social religion, Communal religion.

The most immediate challenge to the church is that it waken to its own lack of self-consciousness or awareness of its nature and its task. To do this, we shall need to form small groups or cells dedicated to the cultivation, in devotional and intellectual fellowship, of a new and more vital insight into the nature and responsibility of the modern Christian community. To this end, study groups should be organized to read and discuss the major and most practical issues. I should like to suggest a brief bibliography for you to choose from:

George Stewart, *The Church* (A Hazen Book)
R. N. Flew, *Jesus and His Church* (Abingdon)
Georgia Harkness, *The Faith by Which the Church Lives*
Walter W. Horton, *Can Christianity Save Civilization?*
C. C. Morrison, *What Is Christianity?*

For the major topics of discussion, I should like to suggest the following very complex but crucial problems:

1. The individual and the church
2. The church and the world
3. The church and the state
4. Denominationalism
5. The church as an agency of social change

These are times of swift change and in such periods only those spiritually prepared and socially alert are able to catch and, in part, influence these vast forces of change. We need to include, at one and the same time, the best in the past, the most courageous and loving in the present, and the most constructive and far-seeing truths and values for the future.

The challenge to the modern church is this: Can it change to meet the needs of this day and generation without at the same time fatally cutting its tie with the past and thus forfeiting its heritage of truth and power?

When the historian and analyst turns prophet, he is skating on thin ice. But we ought, because we must live in it, to turn our inquiry toward the prospects for Christianity and the Christian church in these dark days that surely lie ahead. As we do so, we should carry Jesus' continuing promise to his disciples: "Lo, I am with you always, even unto the end of history" (Matthew 28:20).

Christianity is not, primarily, a code of ethics or a pattern of conversion, but the continuing and continuously renewed life of the Risen Christ in the community and fellowship of men and women who have met and been overmastered by the Spirit and truth of Jesus the Savior. Christianity is a "Gospel," the gospel of continually renewed life and power within the beloved community of God.

The church began its life in dark days. It had a single working formula:

1. God will bring in his kingdom in his own good time and way—hence, patience and hope.
2. Christians must press on toward that kingdom with all their moral and intellectual might and main.

Thus the church ventured forth. In many periods of its life, it was tested and tried as by fire. In those times, the nominal or "sunshine Christians" fell away, and the church was reduced in numbers but was renewed in power. But never has any power of earth or hell been able to extinguish the divine fire of faith that the church has always cherished even if it has not always exemplified it.

As we look about us, we see a mighty conflict of ideologies that will, in any case, profoundly affect the conditions in which the church of tomorrow will live. We must be prepared to face increasing tension between the church and the demands and claims of the state, and it may be that many nominal church members will drop by the wayside. The machinery of the institutions involved will probably suffer dreadfully, and we must be prepared to endure much that would sound fantastic if predicted today.

But the church will live. There will be a faithful and intelligently loyal remnant who will preserve her truth and her power. And within the fellowship of her common life will be the unconquerable spirit of the Galilean who has promised us, "Lo, I am with you always, even unto the end of history."

Introduction

In this message to members of the John Wesley Theological Institute, February 9-11, 1986, Outler addressed the universal problem of social injustice. At the outset one sensed that he had jumped into the fray of social injustices, not on any particular side of rational arguments, but with a conviction that there was a better way to get at them than the usual form of consequentialism ethics ("good" ends seem to justify any means to achieve "good" ends or relieve intolerable despair). That conviction was grounded in the great biblical theme that all social injustices with their associated human indignities were an affront to the righteousness and compassion of God. This biblical theme included not only God's reaction, but also his action—the Rule of Grace, an alternative to the options of submission and violence. The grace of God bestowing human gratitude to human service, "personal holiness" (love of God) bonding with "social holiness" (love of neighbor).

That is how a conservative revolution is run. And nobody gets any thanks for it, save God. Indeed, neighborly love inspired by grace leads not toward Utopia but to Golgotha.

Outler was involved in the cause of social justice even as he delivered this message. He called for a revolution because the status quo was humanly intolerable. He revealed by his demeanor that nonviolence did not mean inaction. It meant the action of grace, freely received and freely given in a faith energized by love.

This discourse ended with Outler saying, "My confidence has returned that the Rule of Grace is worth living and working and dying for. . . . This is the assurance of which John Wesley so often spoke, in which he lived and died."

SERMON 41

How to Run a Conservative Revolution and Get No Thanks for It

I speak this morning with some diffidence and a lively sense of ambivalence, for two very good reasons. For one thing, we turn now from history (where I feel more or less at home) to editorializing (where I feel less confident, whether you will be able to tell it or not).

I also have an uncomfortable sense of venturing into the crossfire between liberals and conservatives and thus appearing to single-minded men and women like the fabled chameleon on the Scotch plaid. It makes sense to me to feel at home with Tom Fox (on the Catholic left) and with Ed Robb on the Protestant right, and I feel equally free to speak my mind to each. They, in their turn, for whatever reasons, are willing to have it so. I could, of course, multiply such instances. But these movements of mine across battle lines offends many of my liberal friends who demand that I choose up sides and stand flatfooted on one or the other. I leave them unjudged, but in my case this would be illiberal and partisan. Thus, I have had to reconcile myself to their reproaches rather than forfeit my devotion to one of the essential features of ecumenical dialogue: "the integration of the good essences in each of two or more opposing sides" (*integratio oppositorum*).

Such an apologetic preface is pertinent just now because I am about to speak of John Wesley's views of social, economic, and political justice and of human well-being—thus also of his struggle to set and keep the two Great Commandments in their proper order. This, as we all know, is a controverted topic. There are those who see Wesley's social views as reactionary, as having hindered a pro-Marxist revolution in British society, from monarchy to socialism. And there are those who see this as a good thing, while others see it as a bad thing.

Still others see him as a prime influence, among others, in a conservative, nonviolent revolution that helped create a new social conscience among the English poor and artisan classes, that promoted the so-called "Reformation of Manners" that aided Britain's escape from the worst-case scenarios of the Industrial Revolution. This, I aim to argue, contributed in a limited but still positive way to the conservative revolution that set nineteenth-century Britain somewhat apart from Europe in general (and America) on such points as slavery, the criminal justice system, and a pervasive sense of law and order (a phrase once usable in a positive sense).

In the contemporary world, we are at the end of that older era (as Paul Tillich and Reinhold Niebuhr reminded us a half century ago) in which change could be welcomed because it could be trusted to aid the onward and upward surge of humanity (the splendid new dogma of Progress). Older ones among you can remember having read the Romantic poets in college; in my time no one would have escaped the bracing optimisms of Tennyson and Browning ("T & B" it was called in the better colleges) and other hopeful seers of the human prospect.

Progress seemed obvious and self-evident; we have the residues of those convictions in our hymn books to this day. There is, for example, that dithyramb to utopia by John Addington Symonds, "These things shall be: a loftier race / Than e're the world hath known shall rise. . . ."[1] In the year I was born, Ozora Davis wrote about "the day of dawning brotherhood" that was breaking "on our eager eyes, / And human hatreds flee before the radiant eastern skies"[2] Moreover, at the time, it seemed credible and inspiring! Now, however, the phrase "radiant eastern skies" is bound to remind us of Teheran, Baghdad, Moscow, Beirut, Athens, Rome, and Chicago! That you should smile at such quaint ironies can be taken as a measure of the radical alterations in cultural climate that have occurred in our century; more precisely, for many, in the last two decades, despite the Spenglers and Niebuhrs who forecast them so long ago that they seemed implausible in those old days.

Basic change is feared and resisted by those who are doing well enough to suspect that their prospects will be put at risk by an altered future. Change is welcomed and assisted by those who stand to gain thereby: by those who foresee utopia, or alternatively, by those in despair so deep as to believe that any future is bound to be better than their present.

We know a good deal about the history of radical despair. Those of you who have read Umberto Eco's *The Name of the Rose* will have been reminded of how unsettling the radical eschatology of the "spiritual radicals" (like Joachim of Fiori) had been in the High Middle Ages. (You could have learned this in seminary, but I can tell you sadly how few of my students were ready to appreciate that much ancient lore when I was dispensing it, again back in the old days.)

We have already spoken of John Wesley's horror of the revolutionary violence of the godly radicals, of the seventeenth-century Puritans and the "Independents," the "Levellers," the "Ranters," the "Fifth Monarchy Men," the "Muggletonians," and the like. Given this mindset, it was all the more remarkable that Wesley was not a reactionary, as his father had been along with other such irreconcilables as Henry Sacheverell and Bishop Atterbury.

The point here is that radical revolutionaries (from Spartacus to St. Simon and Marx and Castro and Daniel Ortega) are readily seduced by one or another form of the ethics of consequentialism. Good ends (or, alternatively, intolerable oppression) suffice to justify in their minds whatever means that may be designed to achieve their good ends in view or to relieve the intolerable despair. And so it came to be taken for granted that catastrophe is an acceptable interim in any passage from the intolerable present to utopia yet to be. A golden age of "peace with justice" will come cheap at almost any price. To be sure, some eggs will have to be broken in the making of any good omelette. And this is why Lesik Kolakevsky could say in all sincerity, that "mankind must be driven into paradise, by force if necessary."[3]

Indeed, in the dialectic of radical revolution, there is a moral necessity for a dictatorship dedicated to the proletariat in order for the dictatorship of the proletariat to be achieved. There must be a liquidation of the bourgeoisie, and this is the exciting task and privilege of the intelligentsia (those divinely ordained patrons, as they see themselves, of the "proles"). This was one of Orwell's points in *1984*. St. Simon's "*New Christianity*" projected a social order in which individuals can rightfully be subordinated to the common good by the experts (i.e., those who are morally and intellectually qualified to define the common good and to enforce it). This, he thought, was the lesson taught by Plato in *The Republic*. Consequentialism would become the linchpin of the Marxist ethic (as Steven Luke has shown in *Marxism and Morality*). Auguste Comte could believe that the bourgeoisie would be persuaded to accept their liquidation freely at the hands of a benevolent intelligentsia.

I can find no references to Kolakevsky in the literature of the American social gospel and very little about St. Simon; this is odd, for their logic is nearly alike even though their moral ambiances were so different. Now, in our time, the consequentialism of Karl Marx has a vigorous new vogue among a wide range of Christian intellectuals, along with a working majority of secular humanists as well.

But what if, in all this, retributive justice and distributive justice manage to get confused and collapsed together? What is the net gain in the system of canine justice when one underdog achieves the status of top dog, for the time being; and then, in the corruptions generated by power, distorts the utopian visions that had been generated by his erstwhile deprivations? What if the result of violent revolution is not much more than a rotation of leaders within the wolf pack?

Humankind has suffered at least as much from the Robespierres and Khomeinis of this world as it has from the Machiavellis and the Hobbeses. But where is it written that submission and violence are the only options before us? Some gain is surely registered when oppression, of any kind, is relieved. But what if another oppression is then set in place, often as difficult to overthrow? Are we forever victims of that "fourth law" of Michael Murphy: "Those on top of any heap tend to prefer it that way"?

I speak with some experience of this dangerous group psychology of "victimization." I grew up in the psychological climate of a conquered province, which is to say, a region conquered and plundered by men with whose grandsons I am now at peace and in fellowship. This means that I have the remains of archetypal Southern prejudices still lodged in my unconscious, along with other *fomes peccati* of original sin, not yet purged by grace doing its perfect work. But at least it helps me understand, without condoning any of it, the paranoid atmospheres in Northern Ireland, in the State of Israel, among the PLO and the Hezbollah. And this much I can tell you: Victimization generates *revanchisme* at least as readily as it does a thirst for justice. And this throws some light on the persistence of so loathsome a thing as racism in regions where slavery once poisoned the moral wells. Where it fails me is in my efforts to understand racism in other parts of our country where slavery was never either law or custom.

When I was young, a Harvard historian named Crane Brinton tried to explain the ambivalences of radical revolution in a weighty little book entitled *The Anatomy of Revolution*. He was denounced for it by the (then) new breed of self-styled "social engineers." He reminded us that "the will to power," which is to say, the impulse to push others around, is, as the saintly Nietzsche had insisted, "the very energy of life itself"!

As a historian and political philosopher, Brinton concluded that radical revolutions tend regularly to cannibalize their children—or at the least to betray them. For example, the papal triumph at Canossa did not benefit the papacy; its true beneficiaries were the feudal lords and emperors of the time. On the other side, the imperial coup at Anagni, when the bullies of Philip the Fair mugged the arrogant Boniface VIII, did not benefit the empire, really. Instead, the bonus went to the partisans of nationalism who proceeded to bring medieval Europe to the brink of ruin so that Luther could defy both pope and emperor and still die in bed. The beneficiaries of the French Revolution were not the socially sensitive priests who helped get it launched nor even the zealots who saw themselves forced to the bloody tactics of "The Terror." Rather, it was Napoleon and his marshals, and after them, the "*petit bourgeoisie francais*." Russian Communism has done well by the members of the Party but poorly by the Russian proletariat. Even the American Revolution, nobly conceived as it was and on the whole conservative, left slavery unchallenged and the subordination of women and the genocide of native Americans, along with a set of plutocratic values that dominated all classes and that still flourishes mightily.

I am not defending human oppression in any of its forms, nor any *status quo ante revolutionem*. Every *status quo* slides quickly enough into one or another form of corruption or oppression. This is why all utopian *con*structions invite their *de*construction.

The point at issue, however, and it runs deep into the heart of any probing of human sin and malaise, is whether *deconstruction* and *reconstruction* can ever be managed rationally and without blind vengeance? What does it take for radical revolution to contribute positively to what Kenneth Boulding likes to call "human betterment"? Such a question exposes ambivalence in such phenomena on at least three levels:

1. The outcome of extensive violence is literally unpredictable. But can this ever be a valid justification for leaving the wretched of the earth to suffer their fate passively? What do they have to lose?
2. The powerful are loath to relinquish their power to the powerless or even to share it. But how can power be wrested from despots by nonviolent resistance and/or moral suasion? Political history suggests that altruism is more of a luxury than a primal social instinct.
3. Are utopian visions ever realistic? Or can we conclude from their history, from Rousseau to Elaine Scarry (*The Body in Pain*), that the very notion of Utopia is an elemental form of human fantasizing? If so, can Christians ever distinguish between their eschatological vision of the reign of God and his righteousness, on this earth, and secular utopianism in any of its modalities?

Any simple answer to any one of these dilemmas is facile and irresponsible. And a panacea of them all together is simplistic on its face.

Yet one of the plainest of the great biblical themes of social justice is that human indignity, of whatever sort, is an affront to the righteousness and compassion of God. Those who take injustice for granted are victims of still another illusion. Hobbes thought he was simply stating the facts with his famous aphorism about human life being "solitary, poor, nasty, brutish—and short." But was it ever intended to be so? Can any Christian ever be content to have it so? For any humans anywhere? Freud thought it a "scientific hypothesis" that "civilization" bred "discontents" and that these erupted, from time to time, in disharmony and violence. But must we concede him any such hypothesis? If not, what are the alternatives and what are their terms?

The radicals cut through these Gordian knots with the sword of righteous indignation: Impose the good, by violence if need be, and evil, overthrown, will wither. The conservative, always in danger of moral paralysis, believes that if evil is restrained by violence, the good will flourish on its own. There may be, though, at least one more alternative: The conversion of what de Tocqueville called "the habits of the heart," which can move the privileged and resourceful to self-oblation (as persons and classes) in their service of God's reign and his righteousness, here and now, on earth. For de Tocqueville, it was *noblesse oblige.* For post-feudal Christians, it was more nearly the imperatives of grace and gratitude, the grace of God bestirring human gratitude to human service.

But the problems of "man's inhumanity to man" become insoluble when God is invoked as committed to one side or another, against all the others. If God is for the poor, does that also mean that he hates those of us who are not poor? It is pretty brazen for us to claim that it is enough for us to be "poor in spirit" or that *we* can "identify with the poor" convincingly. What is this but moral confusion—with the worst traits of the Pharisee and the publican combined? This confusion is an ancient one, and the brothers Wesley were involved in it.

They were born and bred Tories. Their parents before them had each, separately and before they married, renounced their Nonconformist birthrights and had converted to Anglicanism, chiefly because of their common horror of social disorder, which was always associated in their minds with the old Puritan theocracy. There are many British Methodists who would prefer to identify the Wesleys as Puritans because of their obvious devotion to certain Puritan traditions of spirituality, conscience, and the work ethic. But to Samuel Wesley and Susanna Annesley—and to their children—Puritanism also meant violence (to the greater glory of God, of course). The Puritans, they thought, had plunged Britain into a tragic Civil War. They had justified a king's beheading on theological grounds, and then had unleashed a bedlam of religious and social anarchy that left the country demoralized, literally, for a full century and more. As John Wilson has reminded us in his *Pulpit in Parliament,* the Puritans had mingled church and state in new patterns, but none of them much better than Laud and Stafford at their worst. The horror of this tragic disorder lay embedded in John Wesley's consciousness and shaped his views of Christian social action.

This points to the kernel of truth in the otherwise perverse misinterpretations of Wesley as a reactionary. This is what led the Marxist revisionary historians like Eric Hobsbawn and W. P. Thompson to pitch onto the thesis of Élie Halévy about Methodist conservatism and then to argue that Wesley, by helping to throttle the revolutionary spirit of the 1780s and 1790s, had thereby prevented the triumph of democracy then and there. This thesis had had its earlier analogue in Christopher Hill's sparkling and learned arguments to the effect that democracy could have come to England in the 1640s and '50s, had Cromwell not crushed the egalitarian spirit of the Levellers and their kind.

All of which is astonishing and misleading. Fernand Blaudel (a better historian than Thompson and as good as Hill) has shown how far England had moved beyond all theories of divine right monarchy by the death of Queen Anne (1714), and how different the cause of political and social history in eighteenth-century England had been from that of France during the same period. The English Crown had been cropped by Parliament in 1688; an Act of Religious Toleration had changed the ecclesiastical climate. And the Whigs had come into an unchallenged ascendancy from 1714 to 1760 (a fact that the Wesleys deplored). All this had allowed a mercantile middle class to develop, which in turn, gave rise to a Hanoverian prosperity that gave us Georgian architecture and much else now commonplace as "modern." In France, the feudal despotism had gone unrelieved, so that a cataclysmic break had been made "inevitable."

Wesley and the Methodists, therefore, did not "save England from the French Revolution"; they helped prepare England for the Industrial Revolution and for the Reformation of Manners that made nineteenth-century Britain into one of the less inhumane countries in the world (far less inhumane than nineteenth-century North America).

Wesley's Methodism helped promote the nonviolent abolition of slavery in 1807 and 1820. With Quakers and Anglican evangelicals, they pushed forward in prison reform, child labor laws, and the trade union movement (many of the shop stewards in British "Labour" were Methodist class leaders). The Methodists even promoted a Puritan view of the family, and an ethic of thrift, industry, and sobriety, which we have been taught to denigrate as "Victorian." Ironically, nowadays, we are having it explained to us that the Japanese analogue to this Puritan ethic accounts for their economic ascendency over us!

We have also been taught to applaud the rise of the social gospel in England and America, and to claim great credit for Methodism's role in it. We are entitled to all the credit anyone will give us, now that we are facing so very different a prospect after two World Wars, and with a Cold War still fraying the nerves and conscience of the world and spreading dread around the globe. We need the comforts of a triumphant past as we view the return of brutalism in so many parts of the world, the descent of America into moral chaos, the apparent impotence of our churches and our prophetic rhetoric against racism, sexism, ageism, and the inhumanities of communism and pan-capitalism.

But comparing the track records of the radicals (from John Wilkes to Robespierre "the Incorruptible" to Karl Marx, et al.) with those of the socially concerned conservatives (from Wesley and Wilberforce and the Seventh Earl of Shaftesbury), it is at least arguable that nonviolent change has been as effectual in its benefits to humanity as the more spectacular uprisings of the oppressed. At least, the case is clear in any comparison of Britain and France from 1750 to 1850. In 1848, when liberal revolutions broke out in every country in Europe, the one in England was the only one that strengthened the hand of the liberals.

This is not to claim that Wesley should be labeled a great political reformer. For, odd as it seems now, his commitments to social reform never prompted him even to reach for the handles of political power (in church or state) when, conceivably, he might have; and, clearly, we have come to think of this reaching for power as our opportunity and obligation.

Wesley's opposition to the American Revolution was ridiculous, even if you demythologize that revolution so as to see it as a side effect of a larger war between Britain, on the one side, and France and Spain on the other. Wesley's chosen role was the conversion of men and women, not only to "faith" but to altered lifestyles that put them into the world without becoming of it. His opposition to "drams and spirits" was less a political crusade than a moral one. He did not practice total abstinence, but he knew then what we have finally learned the hard way (but not from him, alas) that alcoholism is a disease and that intemperance of any sort is a sin.

The essence of his "social gospel"—the ground of his "conservative revolution"—was what he called "social holiness" (love of neighbor) and he would insist that personal holiness (love of God) is fake except when bonded to its twin. "The Bible," said he, "knows nothing of a solitary religion."[4]

The essence of neighborly love, for Wesley, was threefold. First, the Christian life is a life of liberty under God, with no other allegiance as rival or peer. Moreover, liberty on any other term cannot be saved from license. Secondly, every human life is a gift from God and bears the signature of God's vocation in it. Later, Albrecht Ritschl would speak of grace as *Gabe und Aufgabe,* a gift and a task. The gift is from God and always prevenient; the task is to make of this world a fit habitation for God's human family. The third essential element in neighborly love is, therefore, a profound reverence for the sacredness of every human life, whose worth and dignity are endued from above, deserving of sincere respect, as if on that ground alone.

The validation of this sacralized status of human life (by contrast with any sentimentalism whatever) is in God's self-disclosure in Jesus and in Jesus' focus on God's kingdom and his righteousness. One of God's self-revelations in Jesus is that, though "he is no respecter of persons," neither is his grace and mercy measured out by merit. Every person's worth is an estimate of God and not from any of us. This is the deepest root of the *theologia crucis,* for neighborly love inspired by grace leads not toward Utopia but to Golgotha (as it did for Jesus).

The sufficient motive for a revolutionary ethic, then, cannot be righteous indignation. Nothing less than the faith that is energized by love (*fides caritate formata*, Galatians 5:6) will uphold the Christian in his/her witness in a hostile world.

This rules out utilitarianism and consequentialism. What all social change must aim at, if it is to be called Christian, is the image of God in every person, which marks off his/her individual "character," a special identity within the equality of unequals, under grace. This is not the sort of fake egalitarianism that some of us seem to find so exhilarating. It is instead the sort of equality that one sees in a good family, where nobody is equal, actually, and yet where everybody belongs, not least of all the weakest.

Wesley was deeply committed to this ethic of self-oblation. He loved the poor, as we all do, or say we do; this is now a prescribed refrain in prophetic rhetoric. But Wesley lived among the poor (as our prophets seldom do); he shared their enforced deprivations voluntarily; he spoke of them lovingly as *Christi pauperes;* he distributed to them the sizable fortune that passed through his hands during his lifetime. All the while, he also moved easily among "the middling sort" and was even welcome in the Huntingdon mansion in Cavendish Square and the drawing rooms of Lady Glenorchy, to whom he was "chaplain" for a time. There is no psychohistorical explanation for this; he was not all that convivial and he was easily irritated by the presumptions of the affluent. But he honestly respected the sacral dignity of every person, not as a matter of merit, but as a manifestation of grace. He had a theological alternative to Kant's humanitarian maxim: "Take care to treat humanity always as an end and never as a means only." Wesley's ran thus: "Take care to treat all persons, known and unknown, always in terms of grace and gratitude, and never just utility."

It is a moral distortion to claim one's dignity on the basis of birth or merit, or to accord dignity to others on any such terms. This had been the flaw in classical and feudal ethics. It set honor and humility over against each other as antitheses, and this is why Jesus' definition of "greatness" as preeminence in service (Mark 9:35) never caught on. It was too radical a reversal of the commonplace acceptance of pecking orders, castes, and classes (as in our church, our civil state, and in the Marxist societies).

Wesley had learned this biblical notion of greatness (dignity as grace-filled service) from the archetypal Christian tradition, which he saw caricatured by pompous men and women claiming to be servants of the servants of God and still preserved in our ecclesiastical and academic pecking orders. And an ethic in which the essential imperative is for men and women to recognize, enhance, and defend the dignity and rights of every other human being (regardless of worldly worth or status) and to do so out of gratitude to God and love of neighbor, *coram Deo;* this sort of ethical commitment is social and global, and revolutionary into the bargain.

Wesley never supposed that this sort of society could be legislated or imposed by coercion. Law, he thought, had the negative power to restrain and punish evil and thus was indispensable. In that sense, he and the Methodists were bold to put politics into the pulpit, specifically against vice and crime. But for the positive aims of the gospel, which were personal *and* social without distinction, they looked to moral suasion and to the defense of human dignity as God's will (indeed, as a prerequisite of salvation). Thus, an energetic moralism was taprooted onto an evangelical premise. Frequently, Wesley would disparage his own *General Rules* unless they were obeyed from evangelical motives: "It is . . . expected of all who continue [in a Methodist society] that they should continue to evidence their desire of salvation. First, By doing no harm . . . . Secondly, By doing good . . . . [and] Thirdly, By attending upon all the ordinances of God . . . ."[5]

This is a revolutionary ethic for Christians who have escaped the superego of customary morality and self-serving politics. It carries with it an immunity from cultural fads and fancies—and from being bought or sold by popular hucksters of "success." The Christian whose self-respect is oriented toward God's image within and whose respect for others is oriented toward that image within them can be as self-assured as they are humble without self-disparagement. The Christian sense of self, *coram Deo,* is a safeguard against selfishness or its transformations in the various forms of class or caste consciousness. Ours is a world that encourages self-advertisements: a world of strokes and put-downs, of victimizations and narcissism, and finally of violence—sometimes justified as being in defense of "justice," *humanly defined* (and therefore, partial and self-interested).

The Christian revolution, as Wesley envisaged it, starts at a different point: that justice is what God wills for any and all his children, which is to say, their God-given humanity. In himself and his ministry, there was this strange and fruitful mix of Tory socialism and Radical Protestantism. He translated the old feudal rule of honor (and its obligations) into the still older Rule of Grace: "Freely ye have received, freely give" (Matthew 10:8).

Wesley favored a separation of church and state because he abhorred the Constantinian bargain. But he would also have deplored the tendency of our secular judiciary (or any other) to set any other limits to the free exercise of religion than a necessary restraint of some clear and present danger to the public good (not just some other rival religion or some other secular prejudice). Wesley was part Tory but also a born Leveller. Methodists have always had this weird tradition of democracy and parliamentary procedure within an authoritarian leadership. It used to work fairly well (compared to other polities). Now, however, it is not working well at all—at least not where our leaders confound their power with their spiritual authority and where the church is structured so that its visible unity has come to be obscured or ineffectual.

The evangelicals and the social gospel prophets set up a tragically false antithesis when the evangelicals lay their wagers on social reform as an automatic consequence of faith, and the prophets bet on faith as a bolster to social action regarded as an end in itself. The confusions fostered by such false disjunctions have been endless and are still wreaking their havoc among us.

Evangelicals advocate a humane social order (at home and abroad) without risking much of their own in its implementation. Liberals advocate a humane social order (at home and abroad), yet also with minimum risk to their own creature comforts. The radicals then cry, "A plague on both their houses," because of their all-too-obvious compromises that hold us hostage to what the world (for us, the ecclesiastical or academic worlds) can give us or take away from us.

I, for one, feel deeply the sorrows (and the embarrassment) of that godly man in Matthew 19:16-30, Mark 10:17-31 and Luke 18:18-30 and in the apocryphal Gospel of the Nazarene 16, (cited by Origen in his Commentary on Matthew 19:16-30) who could not bear to part with his possessions in order to follow Jesus (*nuda nudam Christum sequere*). I have not found the heroic virtue to deny myself much nor am I comforted by those bald-faced rationalizations dredged up by the final redactors of the Gospels (about those who deny themselves here below being recompensed in heaven). But then there are our own comfortable prophets who hire themselves out to afflict the [other] comfortable people, i.e., the bourgeois majority in The United Methodist Church. By the same token, the moral indignations of other revolutionaries would edify me more, and prompt more than my attrition, if their "preferential options for the poor" included a preferential option to be poor themselves. This is why Dom Helder Camorra of Recife was able to drive me nearer to repentance than any of our home-grown heroes who commute to 475 Riverside Drive from comfortable suburbs or city condos.

The Methodist Revolution, as Bernard Semmel has shown, was less a crusade to capture political power by men and women convinced of their superior righteousness than an experiment in dignified living in a world that had confused dignity with status and power. Men and women living and working together in a God-given assurance of their worth to him, in this world and the next, are as close to the biblical conception of justice as we are apt to know. And if this is also linked with prophetic contests against any sort of affront to such human dignity or its callous violation, then we have a social *gospel.* The paradigm for this social gospel (on the personal level) is in Galatians 5; on the collective level, its paradigm is hidden somewhere in the cryptography of the Apocalypse. And if such patterns of social transformation be scorned as unrealistic by utopians who also believe in tooth fairies or as opiates for the miserable or as a slave mentality, let those who do so go on then to explain to the rest of us how it is that their ideologies are not amphetamines to the jaded or hallucinogens for secular zealots. A Christian revolutionary is apt to believe that the *Magnificat* has served humanity more humanely than *The Communist Manifesto*!

Does any radical revolution that you know about strike closer home to "the root of all [social] evil" than Wesley's "rules" for "the use of money," and has it ever struck you as odd that St. Paul and St. Karl agreed on the point of greed as the primal social sin? Wesley's rules were three: (1) social responsibility in the acquisition of property, capital or the means of production; (2) self-denial in one's stewardship of riches of every sort; and (3) the renunciation of all surplus accumulation.[6] This Christian image of the Christian life was compounded by his rule of neighborliness: (1) my "conveniences" must give way to my neighbor's "necessaries"; (2) my "necessaries" must be shared with my neighbor's "extremities"[7] (and "my neighbor" must be defined as anyone of God's other creatures whose need is anywhere within the range of my loving care—or yours). Do you know of any professed "option for the poor" that went further than this or that has been ignored more cavalierly by its professors?

In American Methodism, this revolutionary ethic was made normative for the circuit riders by its incarnation in Francis Asbury. This made its mark on early Methodists, including its passions for temperance and abolition (save in the South, and even there among those anti-slavery freeholders to whom most historians have turned a blind eye). But in the fateful transitions of nineteenth-century Methodists from a folk religion to a bourgeois church (and it interests me that our contemporary Methodist radicals speak of this as *embourgeoisment*, which seems pretty fancy), the Methodist ideals of personal stewardship continued to be extolled as much as ever, even as we came more and more to rely upon the secular state to protect the helpless from degradation (what Wesley called "extremities").

What an irony that we should have such a heritage of conservative revolution, more radical than Malthus (who counseled acquiesence in human misery), than Adam Smith (with his faith in altruism that was at least as naïve as Wesley's faith that grace can conquer greed), than Marx (whose idealism has soured into cynicism, wherever it has been tried)—and that we should still prefer the charades of prophetic rhetoric and politicized theology. We extol the virtues of divestment in South Africa and on valid grounds. But who will speak a word for a more radical divestment: of affluence in The United Methodist Church at large?

Alasdair MacIntyre (in *Beyond Virtue*) has traced for us the bankruptcy of contemporary ethics, but all he can come up with, finally, is a backward glance at Benedictine monasticism. Richard Fox (in his comprehensive and yet strangely uncomprehending biography of Reinhold Niebuhr) has allowed us to see how it was a gospel of paradox that tamed a glib young cynic. The coterie theologians of our time strike at our complacencies and lay guilt trips on us of various sorts—for which we would be more grateful if they were not so partisan and so tolerant of the other instrumentalities of injustice that also oppress God's family, along with American capitalism. The prophet Amos began with the iniquities of the other unjust nations before he got around to Israel—but with a fiery indignation against them all. It is still an instructive "gradual" of prophetic denunciation.

We live in a world awash with misery, discontent, and violence. Most of us have supplanted Evensong with nightly vigils before The Tube with its diurnal litanies of tragedy and human folly. The wretched of the earth are angry and vengeful. Those of us who have settled on our lees try to expunge our guilt by recourse to vicarious prophets and to editorializing preachers. If ever a revolution was called for, this is the fullness of time for it. The status quo (here and everywhere else I know) is humanly intolerable.

But we had better choose our revolutionary leaders with great care, not for their ideals so much as for their taproots in the power of grace that really can humanize. The young Hegel had a noble vision of a harmonious human community governed by reason and rational beings. What came of it was a chilling rationalism embodied in the Prussian state. The young Marx was passionately devoted to the salvation of the proletariat from its dehumanization. What came of it was a socialist empire in which the human cause has not been enhanced by much. God save us from all prophets and panaceas: from the Rousseaus of this world or the Saint-Simons or the Stockmans—so well-intentioned and yet so harmful. God grant us Christian activists who serve God and humanity not only with their lips but in their lives, by giving up their perks and profits to aid Christ's poor.

What is crucial in all human crusades is their priorities, whether or not the First Commandment is first and the Second is never minimized by being second. We need to know whether our prophet believes that God has a favored fraction of the human family, or loves what he has made in all its diversity and ambivalences. In the permanent Christian revolution faith comes first and is aimed at hope and love; but love is always aimed at the restoration of God's image in the whole family. And love, as Wesley would say, is very different from sentimentality. In this connection, it is important nowadays to ask a crusader if he/she sees God taking sides against any of his creatures except in defense of the whole family.

This is one of the crucial differences between radical and conservative. The great wickedness of the "Christian" crusades in the twelfth-fourteenth centuries and the Moslem crusades in our own times is their shared thesis that God hates some groups or classes because of their group and class identifications.

That God plays favorites is clear enough in the biblical narratives. But apart from some barbarities, which Wesley set aside as "not fit for the mouths of a Christian congregation," the narrative itself is about God's uplifting of the poor and his judgment against all perpetrators of injustice and inhumanity. God does have an option for the poor, and also another option for their oppressors if they turn from their wicked ways, repent, and submit to his Rule of Grace (what else is that Jonah bit about?).

God must be outraged with America. For three transgressions of Kennedy and Johnson, for four of Nixon and Reagan, yes! But is God as complacent as American liberals are with Marxist despotisms? God hated the old regime in France. Was he more content with the Paris Commune and Napoleon? Nowadays, God may very well be on the side of the Southern hemisphere and against Yankee imperialism (I grew up in a climate in which something like this was said; and in those circumstances, it came to seem blasphemous to me). Whatever became of the God whose judgments are impartial, whose mercies are over *all* his works?

Radical revolutionaries seem to believe in a sort of politicized double predestination that even Calvin would have rejected out of hand since he knew very well that politicians are better judges of self-interest than of the common good (and, of course, he understood this of church politicians as well). But for the ideologue, nothing is too good for the politically elect and nothing too bad for the politically damned. Colonialism was an abomination before God and humanity. Is injustice in a post-colonial regime not also to be judged by an everlasting Torah (and not just in Haiti or the Philippines)?

In his rejections of double predestination in soteriology, Wesley implicitly affirmed a political creed of universal redemption by nonviolent means, which is never to say inaction. To prophesy against oppressors is not to wish them ill; it is to resist their oppressions by moral means and to call them to repentance and amendment of life. John XXIII had never seen a live Methodist before the last year of a long life. But in *Pacem in Terris,* he had already given eloquent voice to the vision of a conservative revolution that Wesley had seen two centuries before and that Methodists in general are the poorer for never having seen to this day: That "peace on earth" requires even-handed justice, firm resistance to injustice in all its forms and not just an endless shuffling amongst pecking orders and the brutal rotations of top dogs and underdogs.

It belongs to Wesley's notion of revolution for "the justified and regenerate" to seek perfection in this life and never to settle for pie in the sky. This means struggle. It means costly involvement in political, economic, and social conflict without undue reliance on their efficacy; "thou shalt have no other gods before me," saith the God of Sinai. The cost of any such struggle will be blood, the blood of Christian martyrs in the New Testament sense of witnesses to the lordship of Christ, whatever the cost. I hold no brief for "Onward Christian Soldiers" (though I seem to lack at least some of the prejudices that will exclude it from our new hymn book). What I would like, though, would be a comparatively rousing hymn for Christian martyrs, worthy of its theme.

I wish, and pray (even work a little) for a nonviolent revolution on humanity's behalf, even though I do not see one looming on the near horizon. "Lord, I believe; help thou my unbelief"! But I can see some of its martyrs, and I do not minimize the symbol of having the birthday of Martin Luther King, Jr., accepted as a national holiday. I was heartened to hear of John Paul II's applause for Gandhi's *satyagraha*. Nor is it insignificant that this same pope is, or so I hear, about to endorse (with some cautions) the Brazilian bishops' version of liberation theology. None of this, nor any of the other current Christian heroics, is likely to overthrow the despots and the bloodsuckers in our time (my time, at least). But there are many signs, here and there, of the only kind of revolution that could reward its revolutionaries with something more human making than the macabre sport of dancing on the skulls of *kulaks* and *campesinos*.

Eschatology is a tricky business. It is not for us "to know the times and seasons which God has kept within his own control" (Acts 1:7). Frustrating as this seems to those of us who prefer to see our ends before we risk our primal commitments, there is, however, a clue here as to what it could mean, even now, if we took the Ascension seriously and turned to the power of the Spirit as our true reliance in our callings as witnesses to Christ, wherever we are and also to the ends of the earth.

Ad interim, God's kingdom can be served and his righteousness taken as our norm and translated into the rule of grace against all principalities and powers that thwart the real and full humanity of God's children. For surely one of the victories of those principalities and powers is in their fostering of a blind faith in the humane outcome of inhumane means that humans have chosen to consecrate, either to God (as their warlord) or to "humanity" (as their idol). Would not our willingness to let grace do its daily work, through our lived-out answers to our verbal petitions that God's kingdom shall come and that his will shall be done on earth, change the texture and the feel of our life together? Would this not alter the contours of our social ethics and worldly involvements?

Even at the end of the evening news I keep on being reminded that something like this is the sort of conservative revolution (or at least the vision of one) to which John Wesley tried to commit us. And then, because such a vision is so nearly consonant with grace's great venture—the renewal of the *imago Dei* in our souls and all others—my faith gets refreshed. By Compline time (or my evening prayers), my confidence has returned that the Rule of Grace is worth living and working and dying for. That, for any given day or night, ought to be enough. And it is! This is the assurance of which John Wesley so often spoke, in which he lived and died; and for every gift of it in our lives and work, all thanks and praise to God be given. Amen.

Introduction

This sermon was given at Lake Junaluska on July 10, 1988, on the occasion of "World Methodist Sunday— a 250th Anniversary." The following note was attached to the manuscript: "As usual, I cannot judge of its worth or merit but in it I've tried to say what I could about the special virtues of our Wesleyan heritage, on the points of mission and of 'the world' as 'our parish' (or 'neighborhood'), and my apprehensions about the weakening sense of that tradition in contemporary Methodism. For good or ill, it belongs in your files, and I figured that I might as well send it on 'as is' rather than have it typed once more."

Typical Outler! He never knew when he completed an address whether he got his message over to his audience or not. This was the case every time he spoke. He felt totally inadequate to judge whether what he said "took" or not. He never doubted what he had to say, but he questioned whether he got that message over to his audience.

On this occasion, as with others, he rang the bell again. One can hear that ringing from the manuscript in these concluding words: "This, my beloved brothers and sisters, is a valid version of the glad tidings of salvation. And if so, we, too, are still commissioned to proclaim them to all who will hear us, anywhere and everywhere in our world parish, our world neighborhood, in the name of the Father and of the Son and of the Holy Spirit! Amen."

SERMON 42

World Methodism's World Parish — Then and Now

It goes with being "Methodist" that "World Methodism Sunday" should mean many different things to different groups of Methodists over the world. This particular year, however, may be special because, as I suspect, all of us share a common concern: an appropriate commemoration of the 250th anniversary of our beginnings. We should have more than a moment in time in mind ("about a quarter before nine o'clock," May 24, 1738); we need to recollect and reappropriate that whole climactic year in John Wesley's spiritual life and ministry that stretched from sometime in February of 1738 to sometime in June of 1739. At its beginning, the most we can see is a dejected man in psychological and spiritual turmoil. By its end, we see a religious leader with a stable, zealous faith orientation that would guide and uphold him and the Evangelical Revival for the rest of a long and fruitful career. The pivot of the year (by no means its sum, however) was May 24, 1738.

So far, so good. Surely, both the historians and the Methodist people agree on this much of the complex story. There are those who have made too much of "Aldersgate," and there are those who continue to disparage its significance. What would Methodism be without its extremists?

But what more, and what now, is to be said about Methodist beginnings that is not tediously threadbare or outrageously novel? By now, everyone of you has been through one or more commemorations of the Aldersgate event—in England, in our Annual Conferences, in our home churches. What has it meant to focus yet once again on this decisive slice of Christian church history? What has happened to "the people called Methodists" as they look ahead into a future about which the only certitude is that it will be no mere extrapolation of that to which we are more or less accustomed? Pondering such questions it occurred to me that, for this special day in this special company, we might focus less on Aldersgate by itself, and more on the biblical vision that guided those beginnings and the horizons toward which we have been pointed if, as, and when we have been faithful to that vision. Accordingly, as a way of giving you enough stout pegs on which to hang your thoughts, it occurred to me to offer you not one but a full quartet of texts, each familiar to all of you and yet each quite remarkable in its own right.

Two of them are from the Holy Scriptures and two are from John Wesley (not, of course, as "Scripture," but as a reminder of Wesley's habitual way of thinking and speaking biblically). My aim, of course, is to show that these four texts belong together, and how much more they have to tell us when taken together than when any of them stands alone.

Thus first, we turn to what we already know as "The Great Commission": i.e., the ending of Saint Matthew's Gospel. Surely, none of you requires yet another contexting of it:

> Jesus said to his disciples [and to all disciples in whatever future]: "Complete authority [*exousia*, not *dynamis*] in heaven and on earth has been committed me [to depute to you, on my terms]. Go, therefore, and make disciples among all the *ethne* [not "nations" in any modern sense; but all ethnic and cultural groups whatever], baptizing them in the name of the Father and of the Son and of the Holy Spirit, and teaching them to be faithful to all that I have commanded you to be. And rest assured of this: I will be with you in

your mission always, until the very end of time (Matthew 28:18-20).

Our second text is a parallel to the first; I call it "The Grand Deployment." It appears in the preface of the Acts of the Apostles—both as a warning from the Risen Lord to the still bewildered disciples against their presumption and also as a commissioning of them in a mission that would involve a traditioning of the gospel from generation to generation:

> It is not your business to know all about calendars and great moments (the Father has kept all these under his own authority [*exousia*]). But you are about to receive a special power [*dynamis*], when the Holy Spirit comes upon you [*epelthòntos*, not *baptìsmos*]. Then inspirited, you are to bear witness to me in Jerusalem and around in Judea and Samaria, and away to the ends of the earth (Acts 1:7-8).

Here is the double horizon of missions: here at home and "away to the ends of the earth." You begin to see the whole world from wherever you are.

Our third text, from Wesley, is the inevitable passage that all Methodists know, at least by the hearing of the ear. I presume to quote it to you with a few omissions that most of you will spot and understand, and to add a brief addition from the *Journal* account that is sometimes omitted:

> About a quarter before nine [and how like Wesley to insert a reading from clock time into such a timeless moment!] while [Luther] was describing the change which God works in the heart through faith in Christ, I felt my heart strangely warmed. I felt that I did trust in Christ [not merely hope or assent, anymore], Christ alone for salvation, and an assurance was given me [notice the verbs in their passive voice!] that he had taken away *my* sins, even *mine*, and saved *me* from the law of sin and death.
>
> [Forthwith] I began to pray with all my might for those who had in a more especial manner despitefully

> used me and persecuted me. I then testified openly to all there what I now first felt in my heart.[1]

With great respect to all the divergent interpretations of this classic passage, I venture to suggest to you that there is no single way to get it right. Wherefore, given the strictures of our time, I beg leave to run through a brief listing of a few salient points and leave whatever questions they generate open for further pondering, while we move on to the larger question of its consequences in Wesley's career:

1. Wesley's entry for May 24, 1738, is the longest and most deeply introspective passage in the *Journal*, a sign of its importance in his mind; but note how literally unexpected the crucial events in the whole account seem to have been. There is little here that was self-induced!
2. Note Wesley's odd phrase about his heart being "strangely warmed." This reminds us that he was a man of tightly reined emotions, so different from so many Methodists, long since grown accustomed to warmed hearts as a vivid norm of true religion. Indeed Methodist services without "rousements" (of one sort or another) are often judged as somehow deficient.
3. Again, note the Christocentric focus of the whole experience. What Wesley claims to have understood for "the first time" is the wholly unmerited grace of Christ alone.
4. But note the twin emphasis here in the pneumatological premise of Wesley's experience of "sins forgiven" ("an assurance given to me"—by the Holy Spirit, of course). This looks toward a deepening awareness of the interdependent roles of Christ and the Spirit in the mystery of God's self-revelations.
5. Notice Wesley's response to this peak experience: forgiving the trespasses of others as a fruitage of assurance of his own sins forgiven.
6. Finally, note his first public action: an open witness, rather than a clutching of his feelings to himself.

This open testimony to others suggests a linkage with the

final text that we will need today; it is the familiar passage about the world being Wesley's parish, a motto that has been used to justify more denominational triumphalism than Wesley ever had in mind. The slogan appears concurrently in letters by John Wesley and George Whitefield, and this raises the question about a possible common source. Wesley's letter was not addressed to James Hervey (as Telford supposed) but perhaps to John Clayton (as Frank Baker has conjectured). What is clear, however, is Wesley's conviction about a Christian's authorized outreach as a witness to Christ. By whose authority and license is a Christian licensed to evangelize? Within what territorial bounds? In Wesley's time, in the Church of England, these questions had a fairly simple answer in Canon Law. Since then, however, it has come to be more and more ambiguous. Nowhere in contemporary world Methodism has the term "parish" had a clear and operative meaning. Moreover, there is a silent conspiracy to ignore the plain fact that Wesley's claim to a lawful freedom to preach when and where he chose would not be tolerated nowadays by any set of Methodist authorities anymore readily than they were by the Church of England. At any rate, here is the claim as Wesley expressed it to a law-observant friend who approved Wesley's message but was distressed by his reckless methods:

> I look upon *all the world as my parish;* thus far I mean, that in whatever part of it I am [as in Acts 1:8-9], I judge it meet, right, and my bounden duty, to declare unto all that are willing to hear [all *ethnoi*, as in Matthew 28] the glad tidings of salvation. This is the work which I know God has called me to and sure I am that his blessing attends it. Great encouragement have I therefore to be faithful in fulfilling the work he hath given me to do.[2]

The issue here is age-old: the clash between what Wesley's own church meant by "parish" and his splendid, pre-Constantinian vision of Christianity's mission as worldwide and unbounded (as in Matthew 28 and Acts 10) to declare "the glad tidings of salvation" to any and all, "away to the ends of the earth." The lexical basis for such a vision is an old use of a special sense of *paroikia* (and its numerous cognates) as "a neighborhood." A neighborhood is not a place where all are alike, but where strangers may live together as friends. Thus, Wesley's idea of a world parish is a startling extension of human togetherness—of Christians living anywhere as in the world but nowhere as of the world, as defined by secular values alone.

Wesley was historian enough to regard the survival of Christianity through its successive "worlds" as a providential phenomenon. He knew how insignificant it had been in its beginnings and how it had been carried by faithful and heroic traditioners to the ends of the earth. He had a fondness for the itinerant friars and preachers of the late Middle Ages and he had understood his ordination as Fellow of Lincoln College as a special license to preach anywhere (*ius praedicandi ubique*). Now that he had finally got the meaning of "heart religion" into clearer perspective, his urge was all the more imperative to witness wherever to whomever would heed him, with or without episcopal appointment or the approval of a Board of Ordained Ministry.

I, for one, cannot imagine a Methodist Annual Conference that would admit John Wesley into full connection—and only a few to which he might even have applied. But I still think that he would have agreed on these four texts that we have reviewed as setting forth a valid set of evangelical imperatives and challenges to Methodists anywhere and in every age. It is still meet, right, and our bounden duty as Methodists to take the whole world for our parish and thus to follow wherever the way is opened (by God, that is, and not by ecclesiastical directives) to declare to any and all who will listen the glad tidings of salvation. This includes the double duty of knowing what those glad tidings are and of proclaiming them not only with our lips but in our lives.

By any measure you can name, this is a breathtaking vision of the Christian mission and of Methodism's place in it. God's design for the whole world is that it should be a neighborhood in which Christians are especially ordained to act as neighbors to all their neighbors--whomever, wherever. Moreover, when you consider what the image of "neighbor" meant to Wesley in his larger sense of salvation (how, in his vision of Scriptural holiness, the second half of holiness was always "neighborly love"), you can perceive something truly distinctive. The outreach of Christian witness, initiated by the Holy Spirit and in his power, reaches from here to everywhere: the world as a neighborhood for Christ. Here is the vital link with another conviction of Wesley's: God's especial purpose in raising up the Methodist people (i.e., to spread scriptural holiness over the land) always included the love of God and of neighborhood— always together and always in that order. Here, then, our texts converge: go into all the world and to all *ethnoi*; witness to Jesus Christ as Lord and Savior within the whole human neighborhood, away to the ends of the earth.

The traditioning of Christianity, as Wesley knew very well, had always depended, in all ages and different circumstances, upon the winsome witness of Christians as neighbors, deeply imbued with the outgoing spirit of neighborly love (among themselves and toward all others). Christian words and Christian ways are both essential in the showing forth of Christ. And, of course, they work better together than alone.

This, then, is the larger context in which John Wesley saw the world as his parish in 1739. But it was more constricted than he had any way of knowing. It was very British, Euro-centered, colonialist, Tory. But he saw humanity as a community of neighbors, and there were no limits in principle to his global vision. What are the limits to ours?

"Aldersgate" was less an affair of Wesley's feelings than of his pneumatological understanding; what came of it was a new, steady assurance of the witness of the Holy Spirit in his heart and life, with an inbuilt moral imperative to get on with his ministry even as its unexpected events unfolded, whether his heart was warmed or heavy.

The emotional uprush of May 24 was not repeated; it was scarcely mentioned again, except by implication. In its wake, Wesley visited the Moravian heartland and failed to impress them favorably; they failed to inspire him or to edify him as he had hoped. Months after Aldersgate he was still subject to spiritual lapses. On October 14, 1738, he complains of lacking "that joy in the Holy Ghost"[3] that he supposed was normative; the next evening, he is "doubtful of [his] own [spiritual] state."[4] On December 16, he recalls "reflections" he'd had on October 14 "on the state of his own soul": "I have more pleasure in eating and drinking and in the company of those I love, than I have in God."[5] Still, on January 4, 1739, he continues in the toils of an incurved emotivism: "And I feel this moment I do not love God; which therefore I know because I feel it."[6] From this, he concludes (he repeats it three times over): "I am not a Christian"[7]—and all of this after Aldersgate.

What matters, of course, is that, despite this preoccupation with his feelings, Wesley never faltered in his actual commitments, reoriented as they were now by his assurance from the indwelling Holy Spirit of God's upholding grace in his life. He did not feel like going to Bristol in March 1739 (it was, as a matter of fact, decided by the casting of lots). He did not feel like venturing into the streets and fields to preach. Guided by feelings alone, or by the counsel of at least some of his well-meaning friends (including his two brothers), John Wesley could have had a heroic ministry; it might also have been no better than self-righteous and ineffectual. We Methodists have often been confused about the radical difference between pious subjectivity and the inner witness of the Holy Spirit. We have preferred the comfortings of our Dr. Feelgood to the classical doctrine of the objective indwelling presence of the Spirit.

What kept Wesley going and what made his ministry so effective was his steady awareness of the Spirit's supernal witness to the buoyancy of unmerited grace. What happened at Aldersgate was a fresh nuancing of trust in the Spirit's empowerment. As at Aldersgate, it was not joy or high spirits that came first, but salvation "from the law of sin and death" (Romans 8:2). The fruit of the Spirit was not ecstasy but the impulse to do "the works of love and mercy" (as in Galatians 5:22-23). With and without high spirits, Wesley continued his walking in the Spirit (as in Galatians 5:25). This is to be seen in his ungrudging diligence, in his calm decisions to cast his lot among Christ's poor and disadvantaged, in his blithe disregard for fashion and fame—and canon law! One can see it in his redefinitions of social justice in and for the circumstances of his time, in his loyalty to sound doctrine even while expressing his scorn for theological controversy, in his intolerance of intolerance, in his balanced stress on faith and good works.

My clearest impression of Wesley after 1739 (with lapses, to be sure) is of his stable sense of "upheldness" that depended less upon his feelings than on his willingness to be led by the Spirit's objective guidance. If this sounds odd, it may tell you something about your pneumatology and your sense of the Spirit's "real presence."

It ought to go without saying that Wesley's world parish and ours are literally worlds apart. We have not yet done a very good job of sorting out their fascinating parallels and disparities (and now I suspect that it will take another generation after mine to rescript Methodism's future). Wesley's world parish had an expansionist future. It stood on the verge of two centuries of colonial expansion and industrial and political revolution. New ideas of progress were being racheted up to the status of dogma. Old utopianisms were being transformed into political or psychological programs (by such Enlightenment heroes as Adam Smith, Karl Marx, Friedrich Nietzsche and others). It is striking to see how eagerly Wesley stood with the "moderns" where he could, except on the one nonnegotiable point of their confidence in the human capacity to achieve the human destiny.

Methodism's world parish nowadays has seen the grand utopias soar and fade. Now you face a global future that will not be an extension of the accustomed past, and it will not be easy to cope with—geopolitically, culturally, or spiritually.

John Wesley was not what our men and women of public affairs would call "a man of public affairs." But he knew that both Mammon and Superman were false gods, and he said so. He was, in many ways, a romantic, but he did know that anthropocentrism in any of its myriad forms (some of them disguised as "religion") is idolatrous and, in the nature of the case, self-deluding. Moreover, he understood how classical Christianity had faced and survived many a previous crisis of cultural change (each with its clutter of confusions) and that, in every case, the gospel's identity and continuity had been maintained far less by human genius than by the church's faithfulness.

This faithfulness from the beginning had been deep-rooted in Scripture and tradition (*not* the multiple "traditions of men"). Note how naturally Wesley speaks of "Scripture and Primitive Christianity," for he understood that Scripture comes to each new generation with its own challenges of interpretation (of "hearing the doctors and asking them questions," Luke 2:46). The church has always been willing to be tested by the norms of rationality but has never conceded any prior rights to reason apart from revelation. Above all, true Christian faithfulness has been radiated by fire and light by the continuous indwelling of the Spirit.

Methodists seem never to have wondered why Wesley refused even to try to formulate the entire compass of Christian beliefs, why he never provided his people with a systematic theology, why he quietly omitted the article "On the Creeds" from that peculiar abridgment of his of the Thirty-nine Articles. Evidently, he thought he saw a better way to the truth that makes us free—"the truth as it is in Christ Jesus," spoken in love and manifested in life. This was the way of witness, in words and lives, of the truth as it is in Christ Jesus understood and applied existentially.

Later Methodists, by contrast to their Founder, have tended to be memorialists in mentality and ethos, as if the commemorations of events had some magic power in themselves to reenact them. As man and boy I have participated in more memorials than I can remember. Mostly, though, they have tended to honor the form of some great occasion or another more than they succeeded in renewing its original power. The reason for this is instructive, which is to say that every "real presence" is effected, in its actual occurrence, by a prevenient action of the Holy Spirit and not by some theatrical re-presentation. Any part of the past, therefore, is reenacted as a new event when the Holy Spirit "comes upon us." This is why the *epiclesis* is always so crucial in every truly sacramental action. Thus it was at Pentecost; thus it was with Saint Augustine in the Milanese garden, with Luther on October 31, 1517, with Wesley at Aldersgate.

Halford Luccock, great Methodist preacher and great teacher of preachers, had his own wry way of commenting on how "natural" it is to mistake a sign for the thing signified. One of his favorite illustrations of this resorted to church steeples! Roman Catholics and Anglicans, he would point out, favored crosses on their steeple tips—tokens of their reverence for the Holy Cross and, sometimes, as proxies for not having to bear their own. Congregationalists (and he taught in a school founded by them) often favored weather vanes, to signify their democratic sensibilities to the shifting winds of opinion. The Methodists (his father, as you may know, was a Methodist bishop) often preferred lightning rods, in remembrance of the fact that they had already been struck and against the odd chance that it might happen again!

The "real presence" of Aldersgate and its actual power cannot, therefore, be recovered by mere recollection, however solemn. Such experiences come when they come and are better prepared for by opening our hearts to the Spirit's spontaneities than by any ritual or recollection. Aldersgate is really renewed, this year or whenever, as faithful hearts are opened by the Spirit's assurance of pardon and grace as a fresh and free gift. What has to happen is that we truly hear the word of Romans 8:14-17a, that we are God's heirs and Christ's joint-heirs, "if so be we suffer with him now, that we may also be glorified together."

The Aldersgate event could not be reconstructed if that single classic text in the *Journal* had somehow been lost. But the doctrine of "life in the Spirit" needs no reconstruction; it needs only the sort of attention that it has, alas, not had. You can find Wesley's version of it in many a sermon ("On the Witness of the Spirit," I and II: "The Marks of the New Birth," "The Great Privilege of Those That Are Born of God," plus a half dozen of those later sermons (1780-1790) that Wesley scholars seem to have conspired to ignore. The imprint of Aldersgate, then and now, means much more than a warmed heart. It can be seen in every vivid instance of the sheer gratuity of God's grace. Aldersgate stands for a Christian's awareness of what God is doing for us and in us and through us that we can never do on our own. It is a perpetual reminder of that mysterious project of salvation itself, i.e., the restoration of the divine image in our souls. This is the shared premise of all Wesley has to say about the divine prevenience and the religious response, in which personal attitudes and actions are changed, remotivated, reoriented toward holiness (i.e., love of God, love of neighbor).

Wesley had a way of pointing to the reality behind the biblical metaphors for "Spirit" in action: terms like "breath," "wind," "fire," "light." He spoke easily of "God's breathing into us and of our breathing into him by a kind of spiritual inspiration and aspiration." He distilled these into a single striking phrase, "spiritual respiration." I would love to know where this came from—or was it an original coinage?

There is a special brand of "will mysticism" here, in which the emphasis is not at all on "absorption into the divine" but very much on human participation in what is God's active Rule of Grace. In it, love of God and love of neighbor are dynamically interactive; it involves a cluster of great perennial themes in classical Christianity:

1. Adoration ("Lost in wonder, love and praise").[8]
2. Commitment to Jesus' coming kingdom ("Jesus shall reign where'er the sun /Doth his successive journeys run").[9]
3. Upheldness ("Our strength, thy grace; our rule, thy Word; Our end, the glory of the Lord").[10]

Here, finally, we can see our texts converge: the whole gospel in and for all the *ethnoi* (every truly human diversity); a gospel to and for the people in both the Lucan sense (6:20) and the Matthean (5:6); a gospel for all but the proud and those who seek good human ends by evil means. Wesley understood this whole gospel as systolic-diastolic balancing of personal and social holiness. He even talked about voluntary divestiture of all surplus accumulation, only to have the Methodist people turn a stone-deaf ear to him. He turned away from the ecclesiastical politics that had neutered his own church, only to have his successors two centuries later fall in love with secular politics all over again (as one can see in Methodist preoccupation with polity and politics).

"World Methodism" began as Christianity itself had begun: an obscure movement in a remote corner of the world. In each case, the prospects for survival were scant. Thence, it spread from homelands to far lands, "away to the ends of the earth." In crisis after crisis, Methodism has been remarkably adaptive, but often at the cost of excessive diversity and fragmentation. Once upon a time we could speak of "pluralism" in its dictionary sense of "diversity." But the term was given a bad name and is currently under an interdict by The United Methodist Church Council of Bishops; in the Episcopal Address (1988) Bishop Tuell pronounced "the last rites" for "pluralism." What bishops inter, let theologians not presume to exhume. But radical diversities remain, nonetheless. And in the new world that is looming ahead as our parish, Methodists will need a good deal more than wisdom and courage "for the living of these days." The eighteenth century will serve us no longer as paradigm; still less the nineteenth or the first eight decades of the twentieth. The most nearly adequate vision for Methodism in its third centenary would be an imaginative mix of apostolic Christianity and the best of ecumenical church history, across the centuries and across the chasms.

One of the truly urgent requirements for a revival of primitive and ecumenical Christianity would be a recovery of the truly trinitarian doctrine of the Holy Spirit—concerned with the dynamic fusion of true spirituality and Christian social action that finds an apostolic harmony between faith and good works. Our holiness and Pentecostal brethren and sisters have often stopped short of Wesley's full-orbed pneumatology, settling for what amounts to "a unitarianism of the Third Person." Our crusaders for social justice have developed a secularized spirituality, settling for a moralism that presumes to enlist the Spirit in aid of their own agenda. The irony of this situation is that what comes from our resounding good causes has, thus far, been ineffectual.

We are assembled here in triumphant celebration. World Methodists have much to be proud of and grateful for—but also with much to repent of (what we have known to do and have left undone). Men and women in whose lives the power of pardon and grace has broken the power of sin and death cannot be content with talk and prayers about the kingdom of God and *his* righteousness, especially in churches where "like-mindedness" includes racism, sexism, ageism, what have you! We must discover the actual opportunities of sacrificed love in a bewildered and disorderly world. Let us continue to pray for the gift of warmed hearts; let us realize that the real answer to that prayer will be inspirited lives.

The Great Commission sends us out to all. The Grand Deployment demands that our witness be faithful and honest, "away to the ends of the earth." Aldersgate was Wesley's way of experiencing sheer grace and his crucial realization that the Holy Spirit is the Giver of grace. Finally, the scope of a faithful witness is to the whole world envisaged as a neighborhood in which neighbors are neighborly because they are sisters and brothers in God's single human family. "The neighbor," said Wesley, "is every child of God" (whomever, wherever) to whom we can be of any aid and comfort. Methodism's special message is only a variation on the oldest and most truly ecumenical message of all: that God's costliest gift to the whole world was aimed, not at its condemnation (just as that might be), but its salvation, by grace through faith—"not of ourselves; grace is the gift of God" (Ephesians 2:8). A vivid sense of this assurance would amount to a real reenactment of Aldersgate, an experience of its real presence.

World Methodist Sunday, Anno Domini 1988, finds us Methodists and Christians of every sort at a momentous juncture in church history—on the threshold of a future that is in God's hands but that we can spoil by inattention or disobedience. In such a time between the times, the continuance of our zealousness in business as usual (even with redoubled efforts) is simply another way of playing ostrich. Already such zeal reflects the law of diminishing returns. Why else would we hear boasts from Annual Conferences about having "lost fewer this year than last"? Already, the semi-Pelagianism that has always been in our heritage has turned into Pelagianism proper, while our latent Montanism, in other quarters, grows less and less relevant in a postliberal age.

From time to time, we hear nostalgic noises about getting back to the Wesleys to help renew our heritage. But if we should ever get that far, we would have to look further backward, into the heritage of the Wesleys. It would commit us to the search for a consensus on the apostolic faith that would transcend our denominational factions. Nothing less will sustain a Christian unity beyond mere amiability or compromise. Then, and only then, would we be prepared to move beyond our outmoded patterns of our accustomed polity, theological methodology, liturgical fads and fashions. They worked fairly well until thirty years ago, but now they seem more and more quaint, less and less effectual. The fundamentalist-modernist controversy was exciting when I was young; its contemporary confusions have become boring to the young.

We are moving into a future in which reliable road signs have not yet been set up beside history's meandering way. The odds in favor of a world Methodist tricentennial worth commemorating depend on our seeking and finding new ways to honor Jude 9 ("The Lord rebuke you") and on our renewing our loyalties to Scripture and tradition, in which reason will have to be recovered from rationalization, when "Christian experience" will have to be more self-critical than emotional. But much will survive; much will be renewed and it will all center on the earliest Christian confession, that "Jesus Christ is Lord, to the glory of God the Father" (Philippians 2:11)!

The later Wesley was curiously ambivalent about the movement that he had been led to guide. He took great satisfaction from the great deeds of God that he had witnessed and participated in. But he became increasingly disenchanted with its flaws and failures (as we can see, for example in his 1787 sermon "On God's Vineyard"). We have, therefore, good precedent for our loyal criticism to the shortfallings of contemporary Methodist establishments, just as Wesley was a loyal critic within the Anglican Church. His antidote to disenchantment was not to turn to something new. Always, it was a reemphasis upon "heart religion" ("the old religion," "the religion of the Bible"). Given the heart of the gospel, Christians have lived well through many a strange twist and turn of church history. The Spirit's lamp has been dampened only when the Christian disciplines have been relaxed or when Christian leaders have been preoccupied with maintenance more than mission.

In his old age, Wesley reflected more and more on the genius of Methodism and on its uncertain future. In 1777, he took advantage in one of his proudest moments to remind his people of the heart of the matter, their hope for a usable future—with never a word about polity, but an exhortation to authentic spirituality.

The occasion was the laying of the cornerstone of that neat new chapel on City Road, which was to replace the hulk of the Foundery, which had served him as headquarters for nearly 40 years. He understood well enough that the Methodists were going to have real trouble with their problems of organization and polity after he was gone (as indeed they did). He had seen Methodism still flourishing long after the first generation of the Revival. He foresaw a lagging of zeal in mission without perennial renewals. Even so, he was enthusiastic about this new chapel and what it might come to mean. Most of us know the place now as a shrine (after successive restorations). But what should the patriarch say to the faithful who crowded into the still-unfinished building out of a pouring rain? Words of remembrance, of course. Words of heightened expectations, yes. But no words about new programs. In a significant way he turned back to the spirit of Aldersgate, with no reference to the event itself.

What seemed to him to matter most for Methodists in their new future was a new birth of the faith with which their forebears had set out. And if I may be so bold as to say so, here on the eve of a Jurisdictional Conference, this is still what matters most in any Methodist future. And so, in remembrance and fresh commitment, I propose that we borrow Wesley's peroration from that old sermon for our own, now and in whatever future God is holding open for world Methodism. Notice, as you listen, how intensely personal each word was to those people back then, and still may be to us:

> Examine your conscience before God. Are *you* an happy partaker of this scriptural, this truly primitive religion [just described]? Are you a witness of the religion of love? Are you a lover of God and all mankind? . . . Whosoever thou art whose heart is herein as my heart, give me thine hand. Come and let us magnify the Lord together, and labour to promote his kingdom on earth . . . Let our whole soul pant after a general revival of pure religion [to grow and to spread] . . . [Let us pray for] the restoration of the image of God . . . in every child of man. Then let us endeavour to promote . . . this scriptural, primitive religion . . . let us provoke all men [and women], not to enmity and contention, but to love and to good works; always remembering those deep words (God engrave them on all our hearts!), "God is love; and he that dwelleth in love dwelleth in God, and God in him."[11]

This, my beloved brothers and sisters, is a valid version of the glad tidings of salvation. And if so, we, too, are still commissioned to proclaim them to all who will hear us, anywhere and everywhere in our world parish, our world neighborhood in the name of the Father and of the Son and of the Holy Spirit! Amen.

Introduction

When Albert Outler prepared these last lectures in this book, he was thinking about those matters that concerned him the most. In those latter days there was a deep sense of his own finitude. He felt his end was near.

What he said in this lecture, given at Lake Junaluska at the evening service on July 10, 1988, wrapped up his thoughts about greatness, a subject that threaded all other subjects he spoke on. He asked, "How do you measure greatness among Christians?" And then showed that the answer does not come from archons ("big shots") of the world, those who exert pecking-order power over others. Quite the contrary with Christians. He said with biblical grounding, "Whoever would be greatest among Christians is to be the most gracious and most helpful servant of all."

In his lectures Albert Outler did something few theologians have learned to do: he communicated. He made sense. He made you feel that it was his fault if you did not understand what he was saying. He could speak from the highest level on the ladder of abstraction, sprinkle his thoughts with a dose of Latin phrases, and make you feel that you understood. He communicated himself. He was the message.

In the case of this message, the people heard it loudly and clearly as they heard *him*. He did not try to lord it over them, did not hanker to show them his greatness. He delivered his soul. And they got the *message*.

SERMON 43

The Measure of Greatness

One of the stranger things in "that strange world within the Bible" (Barth's parallel to Wesley's phrase, "the general tenor of the Bible as a whole") is the biblical notion of divine sovereignty and its mirrored image in the providential history of humanity. There is no question, anywhere, about the fact. God is God and he is One; beside him there is no other. "And God said, 'Let there be light,' and there was Light," Big Bang or however. But in Job's case there were all those arguments topped off with a whirlwind and only then did Job come around to the main point. "Then Job answered the Lord, 'I know that thou canst do all things and that no purpose of thine can be thwarted," (42:1-2). He was not saying that God's purposes are irresistible but that they cannot finally be thwarted (the Hebrew root here denotes "pruning"). God's sovereignty is nowhere in doubt anywhere in Scripture. What is excluded are notions of a Divine Tyrant or Cosmic Computer.

This is strange talk. Elsewhere, in the shadows of ancient mythology there looms the ominous figures of Fate and Chance, Necessity and Happenstance, Good Fortune and Bad Luck. Only in the biblical account, along with the various stresses on the regularities in the natural order and, by contrast, the lurches of human history, the final controls are not arbitrary power; they lie within the complex of moral imperatives that the Bible speaks of as *Torah* (God's will, God's rule of righteousness). Nothing supersedes God's moral law, and nothing contrary to it ever succeeds, finally. Human history is overlaid with tracings of this divine moral order. It is, however, the last lesson that humans seem prepared to learn from history, and, typically, they have insisted on learning it the hard way. The checkered process of learning this lesson is the "plot" of biblical history.

Pagan reflections about Fate and Fortune as dominant forces in human affairs are replaced in Scripture with an understanding of the primal tragedy of human pride, which generates the sort of ontological anxiety that leads to folly and overreach. These anxieties have been acted out in one form or another of the Dominance-Submission Syndrome. The irony here, however, is that in any of its many forms, this syndrome distorts the *humanum* from God's original design for it. The biblical narrative begins with a family of creatures in a divine experiment who would freely and lovingly share in the Creator's peaceable kingdom of righteousness, but always and only as creatures, never exempted from creaturely limitations, never given to gain some sort of advantage over our fellows, to hack at the cosmic odds.

Thus the Genesis story. And before that, similar scenarios about primal pride appear in stories from Ugarit, Ebla, and from the ancient world in general. Later, it will become St. Augustine's story: about infant jealousies, adolescent mischiefs, adults in turmoil, "the two cities" (love of self vs. the love of God). It is the age-old story of war and peace, the grim sagas of ruthless, even if also futile, struggles for preeminence, fame, or glory. Its basic formula appears with variations, from ancient tyrants down to our times and all epochs in between.

This thirst for preeminence, professed or concealed, has resulted down through the whole of history in a profound ambivalence in human affairs. We are made to be fully human, which means humane at the very least. Our inhumanity to others thwarts our own humanity. History's pages are stuffed with injustices committed by humans against humans and suffered by humans at the hands of other humans. The human bid for superhuman power generates familiar theme and variations. We begin with aboriginal patterns: pecking orders and pyramids of dominance and submission (as if this were the real stuff of history). If somebody wins, somebody loses. To be somebody means to push somebody else around (and the more one has to push around, or who have to say "Please," the merrier). This is all too familiar a scheme of things. In it, "success" and "greatness" are measured and valued by what we could call "The Centurion's Complex" (from Matthew 8). "Greatness" is here defined by the principles of rank or status and arbitrary control.

Thus, the evidence from ancient times to this morning's newspaper is that the ideal of human achievement has been dominance, or, as Orwell and Camus have put it more recently, "the power to humiliate at least some others with impunity." This secular ideal of mundane greatness was reenforced by appeals to the divine right of kings and by vivid comparisons between the splendors of earthly courts and the Great Court of Heaven. Everyone was to understand his place in the pecking order or social pyramid and to keep it, cheerfully or at least contentedly.

Note well, moreover, that in any of the various pecking orders, servants are always far down on the totem pole. All ancient terms for "servant" suggest lowliness and menial status. This is why those strange metaphors of the Suffering Servant in Second Isaiah confront us with such astounding force (or would, if we were sensitive).

Such connotations of servanthood (and of God himself as Servant) have provided theologians with many a headache; we prefer our theoretical reflections to be neater and more rigorous than the Bible ever allows for. If God is truly sovereign, then it follows that his will is at least as irresistible as that of a great earthly potentate whose whims meant life or death. No servant images in those perspectives, save as metaphors for mudsills. But the biblical narrative tells us differently. It excludes both alternatives of external sovereignty, absolute or limited. (And where does that leave us?) Absolute sovereignty implies the heavenly tyrant, but theologies of limited sovereignty lead straight into the quicksands of ontological anxiety. Pity the poor theologian who is asked to make sense of all this—and tries to do so in a "systematic" theology.

Thus it had been from time immemorial. Thus it was in the world into which Jesus came. The Roman Empire was already in its time of troubles. Here was Jesus in an obscure corner of one of its conquered provinces that had been deeply radicalized by violent men whose religious zeal was political, and whose violent aims were kept ablaze by their religious fanaticism. Indeed, the shadows of the forthcoming holocaust of A.D. 70 were already limned against history's skyline by rebellions and crosses and other signs of the Rule of Brute Power.

Into such a chaos, "Jesus came preaching: 'the kingdom of heaven is at hand' [or 'in your very midst']" (Matthew 4:17). He spoke of a divine kingdom of peace and righteousness that could be ignored or rejected, in word and deed, but never really or finally thwarted. Here is the biblical paradox in its essence, and Jesus confronted his disciples with it in the central petition of the model prayer he gave them: "Thy will be done on earth, as it is in heaven" (Matthew 6:10). Here is the biblical vision of true sovereignty and of authentic human responsibility integrated in God's set design for human history.

For what sense would it make to pray God that his will be done on earth if already that will were irresistible in all respects? Does not the Lord God Almighty, maker of heaven and earth and of all things visible and invisible, already know what we need and provide for all? Yet here is a biblical scenario about God (not a god, mind you), in which God's will has not been done on earth as it is in heaven, since Adam and Eve opted out of God's rule in favor of their own self-rule!

The story line in the biblical history is not at all simple, but some things in it stand out clearly. The universe is not a divine gesture of sheer power or whimsy; the biblical vision is of a creation generated by God's love of being, goodness, and beauty; more specifically, as a sign of his compelling interest in having a community of creatures whose human potential was deliberately ambivalent. They could be truly godlike (the core of truth in the first temptation (Genesis 3:1-5). Or they could try to drape themselves with mantlings of divinity and so fall into self-delusion.

John Wesley was very clear on this point of sovereign grace and human freedom, in an age when it was an apple of discord (and long had been). But he refocused the question and helped set it in a more positive light. His claim was that the distinguishing mark of the human was not intelligence or arbitrary freedom. It was, rather, "our singular capacity for God,"[1] our God-given powers to participate, as finite creatures, in God's creative purposes. Wesley's anthropology is a series of variations on the theme of the human created in the image of God; of sin as the ruination of that image; of salvation as the restoration of that image in holiness, wholeness, and glory. He could see a gracious patience in God's holiness.

In the natural order, God's will is done on earth as it is in heaven. Thus, as we come to know more and more about this natural order (still without knowing very much for sure), the more awesome the mystery of nature becomes. Increasingly, it is being seen as a fascinating dynamism of chaos and randomness that is nevertheless formed with enough determinate regularities that the whole is orchestrated into something analyzable and so nearly predictable that empirical science is possible and technology can flourish, even if also within some very unsettling limits of radical uncertainty.

In a different key, the biblical images of God consistently reflect a vivid awareness of God's majesty and glory: dominion, power, beauty, and awe-ful wonder. The Bible (and especially the Psalms) is a book of praises ("Praise to the Lord, the Almighty, the king of Creation!").[2] It exalts God's wisdom, power and might. God reigns without a successful rival. "The God of Hosts is with us, the God of Jacob is our refuge" (46:7). "He is the king of glory" (24:10). In this vein, Isaiah's vision (6:1-4) can be recognized as typical: The Lord upon his throne, high and lifted up, with seraphim and cherubim in attendant reverence and adoration: "Holy, holy, holy, is the Lord of hosts; the whole earth is full of his glory." The triumphant visions of the Revelation round out the canon and crown all the other images of benign sovereignty.

This makes it all the more remarkable that the same Bible's providential history of the same human family unfolds, nonetheless, with so tragic a plot and so glorious a vision. The course of high religion in human history never has run smooth. In Genesis it gets off to a bad start and lurches from one misadventure to another, always with the same basic formula. God is in charge of the human project; his strange kingdom of righteousness is forever. Yet it is resisted by his chosen people, and it seemed to have ended on a Roman cross. But in this tragedy of tragedies—Jesus' passion, death, and resurrection— God shattered the power of brute power; he "broke the law of sin and death" (Romans 8:2). Contrary to all our accustomed thoughts about sovereignty, God has chosen to rule "the world with truth and grace."[3] In many more ways than one, he is determined to make "the nations prove/The glories of his righteousness,/And wonders of his love."[4]

True faith can grasp this and depends upon it. To the "wise in this world" (1 Corinthians 3:18, KJV), it is nearly incomprehensible. The disciples make their obtuseness plain by their reactions to Jesus' parables. In all the parables, God's sovereignty is taken for granted, though it is nowhere thought of as arbitrary or whimsical. God's kingdom is "at hand" [or "among us"], but it cannot be exploited or corrupted, save at the peril of human souls being tragically self-deluded. There is a strange kind of greatness here that was glimpsed by Sydney Lanier in his simile about the shy, self-effacing marsh hen that confidently builds her nest and flies "in the greatness of God."[5] There is the more dramatic image in the Apocalypse of the Lamb of God both as Victim and Victor in the same eschatological drama. The pathways of history are strewn with monuments to the pomp and circumstance of that world once typically recognized as great. But we know better. The real landmarks of history have been set, verily, by the saints and heroes of the Spirit.

The age-old story of secular history is the story of the rule of the archons of this world ("archon" is the New Testament term for a big shot). It is still our accustomed way of sizing up a situation. In current pop culture, Bruce Springsteen is "The Boss." Ross Perot is a real archon in the business world. You have your lists of archons and I have mine. We take it for granted that in every human collective, some one (or group) is archon, and the rest of the group are supposed to adjust themselves to the ways things are run or else fall afoul of the powers that be.

The biblical history of human destiny is so different that, even as well as we know it, in general we still find it hard to take it seriously as an integrated view of human existence. There are its strange beginnings, with a wandering Aramean (Genesis 12:1-5), called to set out on a special mission to God knows where. The narrative unfolds to include his descendants and their misadventures (and, by implication, it always keeps coming down even to us). They, like we, found it unwelcome to learn that their divine election was not to self-serving power but to sacrificial servanthood. What is worse, here is a lesson not yet learned by later generations. What God seems to have had in mind was a people who would serve the human family as models and teachers of true humaneness (the love of God and the love of neighbor). What his people (including us, of course) have actually preferred is some role in which they (and we) could be archons.

The Psalms mock the kings of the earth. Why, then, did the kings prefer their own sycophants? None of the biblical prophets was an archon in his day; interesting, isn't it, that not a single court prophet (archons in their time) is in the canon? Since then, however, the biblical prophets get themselves quoted by our archons in synagogues and church, in justification of their opinions. This is why Micah 6 is so radical. But why do we hear it so much more often quoted in high places than we see it observed?

> **Question:** And what does the Lord require of us?
> **Answer:** To do justly, to love mercy, and to walk humbly before God (v. 8).

But you cannot sincerely say "Amen" to this until you have pondered that phrase, "walk humbly"!

The highest peaks in the great massif of biblical prophecy are those extraordinary Servant Poems in the so-called "Second Isaiah" (40-61). There we can find the deepest insights into the divine mystery until we come to Jesus himself. Indeed, we find Jesus quoting Isaiah at the outset of his own public ministry (Luke 4:16-21), identifying himself with God's anointed servant. This correlation is at the heart of the gospel: the Lord God, self-manifested as Servant, whose servanthood, though suffering, was not demeaning but redeeming! The fourth Gospel adds another arresting symbolic act (John 13), with its story of Jesus' preparing the disciples for their mission, after his imminent departure from among them.

> Well aware that the father had entrusted everything to him, and that he had come from God and was going to God, Jesus rose from the table, laid aside his garments and taking a towel, tied it round him. Then he poured water into a basin and began to wash his disciples' feet and to wipe them with a towel (vv. 3-5).

Now, what do you suppose ever happened to this instance of an explicit action and "ordinance" of Jesus, comparable to Matthew 26:26-29; Mark 14:22-25; and Luke 22:14-20?

> I have here set you an example; you are to do for others as I have done for you (v. 15).

All this, and more, lies behind that fascinating cluster of accounts about the sons of Zebedee and their pious campaign for high office in Christ's coming kingdom (in Matthew 20:20-28; Mark 10:35-45 and Luke 22:24-27). It is obviously the same story but none of these texts is an exact replica of either of the other two and this suggests that the incident was widely remembered among different early Christian communities who, in their oral traditions, altered some of its details even while preserving its essence.

There are several interesting problems here: why does Matthew have the mother of James and John serving as their campaign manager? Were the other disciples jealous because they, too, were equally ambitious, or because they were truly humble? We could even update these same questions on the eve of a Jurisdictional Conference and add a few new ones. What kind of a spin would this incident have gotten in *The United Methodist Reporter*, if they had been there?

Through it all, of course, the central issue is clear enough and precisely the same in all three versions: How do you measure greatness among Christians, individuals, or groups? Those who sit at the table and are served; or those who bring the trays, do the serving, and wash the dishes? The question still arises, and Jesus' answer remains the same. Twenty-five years ago, this point about serving tables came home to me more forcibly than ever before when, during the Second Vatican Council, some of us were being entertained at lunch by friars of the convent of Saint Francis of

Assisi; suddenly I realized that one of the waiters serving us was the prior himself!

Each of our texts of this story has Jesus commenting on how the archons of the world love to lord it over their inferiors. The Lucan version, however, has an ironic twist. Here the archons are anxious to have their inferiors applaud their "leadership"; they love to be praised as "benefactors." We know about that too, don't we?

Thus, the punch line in the stories strikes an exposed nerve: "But it shall not be so among you" (Luke 22:26)—nor, presumably, among your successors either. The pecking order among Christians is to be turned upside down, which is to say, abolished. Whoever would be greatest among Christians is to be the most gracious and most helpful servant of all. Here is a stark reversal of conventional values. All the Greek and Latin terms for "humility" are pejorative. So also their synonyms: "abjectness," "self-abasement," and their cognates. By contrast, the Christian notion of an unpretentious servant, whose quiet self-confidence is based upon his or her unmerited, God-given dignity (one's real worth), was a radically new concept in interpersonal relationships. It is an awkward one, too. How can a proud man be humble?

Time was, as the older ones of us remember, when modesty and a humble demeanor were normative amongst well-bred folk in their public behavior, despite all the false modesty and fake humility that underlay their outward demeanor. It was simply bad form to advertise one's own self, or to toot one's own horn solo. One simply did not boast to others, or spike a touchdown football in life's end zones. There was even a code that encouraged men and women to let other people praise us if there was to be praise. This tended to inhibit egotism, or at least to keep our egos under wraps. Of course we knew several variants on Coleridge's phrase about pride aping humility.[6] Some of us knew the story of the Benedictine who claimed he could out-humble any other monk in the monastery. Even so, there was a certain ethos of modesty among most well-mannered people. Such folk were brought up not to preen themselves in public, not to scramble for their places in the sun—in sum, not to brag.

Now, however (or so the current wisdom runs), all this self-depreciation is unhealthful and harmful. Loving your neighbor as your own self has come to mean that self-love is the right beginning point. Seek first your own self-esteem and various luscious fruits of fame and recognition will be added on. An inferiority complex is a dreadful malady, to be cured by strokes and self-affirmations of one sort and another. He who tooteth not his own horn risks deafness by silence!

I do not presume to contradict my psychotherapist colleagues (clerical and otherwise) who preach and practice the gospel of self-esteem. But we are still allowed to wonder aloud if all these outspoken self-advertisements have really raised the level of emotional health, social passion, or real caring in human affairs (here or elsewhere in the world). So far as I can see, pride paraded (whether naked or scantily clad) has not yet improved the humane textures of either secular or ecclesiastical politics so much as we were assured it would. Where two or three egotists are gathered together, especially in the name of candid self-seeking, it only bodes ill for church and civil state.

The gospel story abideth still. Jesus saw the paradox of greatness and servanthood in a very different light than we have grown accustomed to, especially in our "psychological society." I know people who think that Jesus should have had courses in self-assertiveness training, that his public relations staff was poor. Nietzsche despised Christianity as "a slave morality" and pointed to the Beatitudes as a case in point. What healthy mind, he asked, can take their priorities seriously, especially with the one about "the poor in spirit" heading the list of the blessed? The more radical reading in Luke is even worse. Or, again, why should the "meek" inherit the earth except in six-foot plots? The meek we know cannot even get the floor at a church meeting; they have this air of being ineffectual among our high and our mighty. We have learned much, of course, about being cool and clever. There was, as you will remember, that airline that went too far in its arrogance with its slogan: "When you have got it, flaunt it." Sad to say, they went bankrupt. But egotism still has a fall-back rule: "if you have got it, make sure that it does not go unnoticed"!

Now, I know as well as anyone the futility of such moralistic musings—and, better than anyone here, the impropriety of any criticisms of mine of "the high and mighty" in our midst, or even of those who aspire to great heights. Who am I to talk like this? My own career, as some of you know, has been graciously spared any major executive responsibility (in the church or in the academy). Thus, I have good friends who gently chide me, and rightly, for my obvious lack of compassion for the sons of Zebedee and their current avatars.

But our texts still stand, and so does their definition of "greatness" in those same paradoxical terms of preeminence in service. But do not forget the other point that they also have in view. Jesus was very clear that the good servant has no call to feel "abject" or "self-abased." There was none of this in his case nor even in great saints like Francis. "Gentle Jesus, meek and mild"[7] is a false image unless it is balanced off by the immense dignity that came from his utter self-assurance of God's bestowal of his status as "my beloved son, on whom my favor rests" (Matthew 3:17). The Christian meek are not lacking a strange but unmistakable dignity. They are quietly assured of their rightful worth in the world, and they know that it comes from the sovereign grace in which they live, from the sovereign Spirit with whom they walk. This is the point to the social gospel as proclaimed in *The Magnificato* (Luke 1:46-55), and why Christians in the great traditions include this splendid psalm in their daily rituals. It is an early sampling of feminist theology at its best.

We are like the ancients in our shared horror of the image of lowliness. It was a daring project for Christians to try teaching the pagans (and some of their fellow-Christians, too) that heaven is not to be stormed by force or bravura. The Christians found it all too easy to learn from the world the advantages of self-assertion, the "high" that comes from clout and status. We, too, still call Alexander "The Great," even though we know that Alexander's teacher, Aristotle, was far greater a servant to mankind. Marcus Aurelius was an emperor, Epictetus was a slave; but who was the greater and why? Tiberius' order to Pontius Pilate had been, "Keep down disorder!" Jesus' word to Peter was different: "Feed my sheep" (not fleece them, mind you, but feed them). "Find your joy in being their servant."

What this adds up to is that Jesus' notions of greatness were a world away from all the conventional alternatives: either of self-abasement or self-promotion. His vocation, and ours, was not to be ministered unto but to minister, and to do this in the dignity that comes from God and with an ennobling passion that God's will may be done on earth as his people are truly served, in their real needs.

In this tradition of greatness-in-service, we Methodists still have to learn much from what John Wesley had learned from Jesus. It is much more important than our preoccupations with his warmed heart (or ours) and from the eminence that he reflects on us as our patriarch. From childhood, Wesley was a rigorist, but that did not make him an effectual servant. He could in later life speak of his having had "the faith of a servant" but even his performance as a servant in Oxford and Georgia was not very humble. What he finally learned is what we still need to learn: The spirit of servanthood is a gift of the Spirit, and it must be so received and put to good use by us—"in the Spirit." The self-conscious servant, trying to become great by being self-consciously humble is a pious fraud.

Wesley's real usefulness as a servant began when, as he says, he suffered himself "to become more vile"[8] and to go out into the fields to proclaim the glad tidings of salvation, to those marginal people in Kingswood. He then moved from a bourgeois setting in central London to live among other marginal people in their urban equivalent of an urban slum in the shattered ruins of the Foundery in Upper Moorsfield. His greatness and his service grew together; they reinforced each other as he set out to evangelize his world parish (without episcopal appointment), as he went about serving human needs, and without customary rewards.

In all of this, however, he was a person of great dignity, with a self-respect that he insisted on, especially in the midst of the mighty. He was a greatly gifted man, but my guess is that this would have gone for naught had it not been for his passion for service and his nearly total lack of earthly ambition. I have often had this irreverent fantasy: What a wonderful irony to have a whacking great banner as backdrop for some great gathering of Methodist movers and shakers, with its motto taken from Wesley's note on Luke 22:26: "But ye are to be benefactors to mankind, not by governing, but by serving."

We know, of course, how eagerly this notion of servanthood

has had its lip service among Christian archons. One of the papal titles is "servant of the servants of God," and we have heard the same phrase in Methodist high places. A familiar Methodist euphemism for a promotion is about someone who "has entered into a new field of larger service." Yet with all the hypocrisy and cant that piled up, history has left us an instructive honor roll. Why else would Pilate ever have been remembered but for his uncomprehending encounter with Jesus (who was, at the time the least well-known of all the chief actors in the drama of Luke 23:2-5). There have been giants on the earth in every age; their fame has been fickle. For example, in the thirteenth century, Emperor Frederick II enjoyed his popular title, *stupor mundi* ("the wonder of the world"). But how now does the great Frederick rank with that lean ascetic from Assisi named Francis Bernadone or that rotund philosopher from Aquino named Thomas? Who was the greater benefactor to mankind in the sixteenth century: Charles V (who "saved" Europe from the Turks) or Martin Luther (who saved the *sola gratia* from the papists)? Or, who remembers now, how in the eighteenth century Bishop Warburton so greatly overshadowed the brothers Wesley?

In our time, we, too, know how our archons love to lord it over the rest of us (in the *saeculum*, in the *academia*, and in the *ecclesia*) and how they love to be admired for their "leadership" (which often amounts mostly to moving people around like chess pieces, from this job to that). Greatness is still imaged as a ladder, signified by rank, status and clout. On such ladders, those on top have the best view. There is even a proverb to this effect, the so-called "Moebius Theorem": "It is only the lead dog in a dogsled team that gets much of a change of scenery."

But our texts still say what they said before. The Suffering Servant remains as the crucial symbol both in Isaiah and also in the Synoptics (cf. Philippians 2:5-11). The image of the Humble Servant radiates the fourth Gospel as an inner light. True greatness lives unadvertised in the unnamed hosts of men and women who believe that what is sovereign in God is his grace and whose lives are lived in and by the rule of that grace, persons more than content to squander their gifts and talents on gracious service without trying to compute their rightful compensation or to claim it. Greatness is an aura in faithful souls who trust God to gather up all their oblations into an enduring treasure for all the saints, and to comfort them with a wry sense of humor, even as the sand castles of their careers crumble in the tides of history.

It is not for us to reckon up the final tallies. It is for us to be found faithful in our callings, hoping for no more, but no less than "Well done, good and faithful servant; enter into the joy of thy Lord" (Matthew 25:21). Whoever among us hankers to be great, let him or her accept these terms and measures of true greatness in the way and spirit of the Son of Man, who came not to be served but to serve and to give his life" (Matthew 20:28). All this may sound strange and unnatural in a society like ours and in a church like ours. But it is also very biblical—and very true!

Let us pray:

> O Jesus, we "have promised to serve thee to the end; be thou forever near us, our Master and our friend."[9] We pray thee, therefore—in the greatness of thy ministry, as an obscure and humble teacher, in the noble tragedy of thy Passion, in the glorious victory of thy resurrection and ascension—to reveal in our experience a fulfillment of that messianic promise that forever upholds grace and power, even in a world that is forever getting them in the wrong order. So also send thy Spirit among us: "to kindle a flame of sacred love,"[10] to stir up our ambitions to serve rather than to be served, to respect dignity in ourselves and in others of what thou hast made in us and hast made us to become, here and hereafter. Let us, then, even now, begin to enter into thy joy and into thy Rule of Grace. Thus, by thy grace, give us "grace to follow [thee, our] Master and [our] friend"[11] in whose name and spirit we pray. Amen.

Introduction

This is the last lecture/sermon given by Albert Outler. Appropriately it happened at one of his favorite places, Lake Junaluska, July 3, 1989. The reader would receive an added blessing by listening to a tape recording of the event. While the manuscript allows you to chew on particular thoughts that grab attention, the audio puts you in the middle of an orchestration of sounds between Outler and his United Methodist Church Historical Society Convocation audience: audience laughter, triggered by typical Outlerian wit and humor, well-placed stillness and silence during an emotional final five minutes, and an ovation at the end that went on and on and on. All this vindicates Outler's thesis: He shared his faith in a manner that the audience will never forget. They unwittingly became a part of the traditionary process he talked about in his presentation. But to his chagrin some fell from that experience of grace and returned to their old Pelagian ways of developing a confessionary United Methodist Church—of giving United Methodists something to which they can give mental assent in order to know salvation. That battle rages on.

But for Albert Outler this exercise was his best and his last. While behind the podium for this last discourse, Outler was alive with verve and vigor. But when it was over, he was through. With drained physical and mental energies he said, "It's time to hang 'em up." On September 1, 1989, he died.

But thanks to him and to the Wesleys before him and to the Anglicans before them and to the church before them and to the New Testament church, in spite of what the United Methodist *Discipline* might say, the traditionary United Methodist Church lives on in our faith experienced and shared by grace.

SERMON 44

Through a Glass Darkly: Memories, Forebodings and Faith

The aging Wesley, modestly as he thought, regarded the Methodist Revival as unique among God's great works.

> [The Methodists] increased to hundreds, to thousands, to myriads, still pursuing their one point, real religion, the love of God and man ruling all their tempers, and words, and actions. Now I will be bold to say such an event as this, considered in all its circumstances, has not been seen upon earth before, since the time that St. John went to Abraham's bosom.[1]

American Methodists (and United Methodists later) took to this "more-upbeat-than-thou" outlook like ducks to water. They still like "prophetic utterances" but prefer moralistic denunciations of social ills they deplore over indictments of their own hypocrisies. Radical critics of Methodist polity have not had a happy history, from O'Kelly to Maclin. But optimists disappointed can turn fierce critics. The most unsparing denunciation of Methodists that I know appears in Wesley's sermon "On God's Vineyard." This came about four months later than the sermon just quoted (you must look it up, for it goes on and on). He speaks of flaws among the Methodists, on whom God had poured such special blessings:

> . . . prejudice, evil surmising, censoriousness, judging, and condemning one another—all totally subversive of that brotherly love which is the very badge of the Christian profession; without which, whosoever liveth is counted dead before God. It brought forth . . . every evil word and work—all direful fruits, not of the Holy Spirit, but of the bottomless pit!
>
> It brought forth self-indulgences of every kind. . . . It brought [forth] such base, grovelling affections, such deep earthly-mindedness as that of the poor heathens. . . .[2]

All of us know the Methodist story as one of phenomenal success, from Aldersgate to whenever in the twentieth century that you can detect the tilt from a Methodism upward and outward bound toward a United Methodism curved back upon itself, with less stress on mission than on maintenance. I learned this success story in my parsonage home, even as I was also realizing that my maverick WASP father and my Huguenot mother were not being carried to the skies on Methodist beds of ease. I could, and I did, become a credentialed church historian with no requirement to do more than tuck a few stereotypes about Methodism into my professional kit bag. One reason for joining you in the Convocation is to lend whatever encouragement an old man can to younger United Methodist church historians as they learn how to balance their loyalties to general church history, ecumenical church history, and denominational church history.

In my own case, my concerns for this balance were generated almost by accident. My own first General Conference (in 1956) split the traditional Methodist linkage between ordination and eucharistic celebration (the ostensible rationale for what had been done in 1784). The next two General Conferences were bores (except for the painful memories of their obvious bewilderment in the face of ungraceful revolts by the youth groups and the blacks, who had suffered the outrages of the Central Jurisdiction and the hypocrisies of a self-styled "inclusive church"). Besides, so much more exciting things were happening elsewhere: in the dialogues between theologians and psychotherapists, in the ecumenical world (from Lund to Montreal, from Evanston to New Delhi, and above all, there were the connections with Vatican II), and in two projects aimed at reconnecting a shallow-rooted Protestantism with its classical fibrous-root system: *The Library of Christian Classics* and *A Library of Protestant Thought*.

It was out of this latter project that came the impulse for John Wesley to have a volume of his own. This, in turn, had something to do with the attempt to do for Wesley what was being done better by Reformed Christians for Calvin and by Lutherans for Luther. I would be the last man alive to sing small whatever progress that has been made in Wesley Studies across the past three decades. Given the circumstances, it has been impressive, at least to some. I am entitled, however, to notice how soft a thud was given off when the new edition of Wesley's *Sermons* hit the United Methodist waterbed.

The half chapter of United Methodist church history that I know well enough at first hand to qualify as eye-witness focuses on United Methodism's fitful concern with doctrine and doctrinal standards over the past three decades. For me, this concern began with a collaboration with Bishop William C. Martin on his Episcopal Address to the Methodist General Conference of 1960. The heart of that address was an attempted summation of essential and distinctive Methodist doctrines. It was approved by the Council of Bishops and reasonably well received at Denver. But it planted the seed of illusion in my mind that such a reception reflected a latent doctrinal concern among United Methodists.

It has, therefore, taken me much too long to learn that Methodists will vote for almost any kind of doctrinal statement provided that (1) it is not emotively offensive, and (2) that it promises to avoid or ease doctrinal contention. United Methodists love to argue generally, and do it with verve, but not when doctrine is the issue. At the Christmas Conference (1784) Wesley's notional abridgment of the Thirty-nine Articles was received without demurrer, even on the point of his excision of the Anglican Article VII, "Of the Creeds." From 1808 to 1968, the Articles (minimally doctrinal, explicitly anti-Calvinist and anti-papal), and the General Rules stood constitutionally protected in the *Discipline*, devoid of official interpretation. The consequence has been an invariant form of doctrine along with a widely variant development of doctrinal teaching. It is the fact that the majority of interpreters of The First Restrictive Rule (from Abel Stevens to Professors Oden and Cushman) have taken that rule in its ordinary rhetorical sense, as a compound sentence with two conjunctive clauses; the first stipulating the Articles, the second denoting Wesley's *Sermons* and *Notes* (at the least) as "our present existing and established standards of doctrine" ("present" as of 1808). This interpretation was carried over to The Plan of Union and thence into the doctrinal statements of 1968. (In 1972 the Judicial Council mooted the issue with its decision that all doctrinal statements in the United Methodist *Discipline*, save only the Articles, *Confession*, and *Rules*, are legislative matter, subject to continue in force or apathy until acted upon by some subsequent General Conference.)

This left us in 1968, or so we thought, with Articles, *Sermons* and *Notes*, *Confession of Faith*, and *General Rules* as the corpus of "our present, existing and established standards of doctrine." These were fixed forms of doctrine (requiring "religious assent"); they bore up a considerable clog of irreconcilable interpretations on points theological, ethical, and political. Methodism has been the most fissiparous of all the mainline American traditions; the least disturbed about the diversity of the doctrinal premises of its teachers.

We are now forbidden, by episcopal mandate, to use the P-word ("pluralism") with reference to *diversities* among United Methodists. (When asked by a United Methodist bishop if Free Methodists were really free, Bishop Paul Ellis of the Free Methodists quipped, "Free Methodists are at least as free as United Methodists are united!") The announced reasons for this episcopal interdiction were embarrassingly unsophisticated: The chief one being a perceived equivalence of "pluralism" and "indifferentism." (This is, of course, a lexical mistake and a logical eccentricity.)

The 1972 Statement had made an explicit but not emphatic distinction between "pluralism" and "indifferentism"; we had realized that such a distinction was crucial, but had assumed that it was also commonplace, taken for granted. This was a fatal mistake. The distinction was promptly ignored by professional theologians as readily as by corporate lawyers. Now I finally know why. The majority of United Methodists *are* doctrinally indifferent; they may not know what Jude 3 means but they know what they like. Give them normative articles from which the historic creeds have been deliberately excised, and they go on using those unauthorized creeds or new creeds or none. Give them an article on "Birth Sin" and they construe or misconstrue this in Pelagian terms more psychological or traditional than biblical.

In 1972 they voted to include Wesley's *Sermons* and *Notes* as "our present existing and established standards of doctrine." In 1988, they designated these same *Sermons* and *Notes* as "models of exposition." The 1972 statement was deliberately designed to include United Methodist evangelicals and other groups (with their doctrinal premises) into the intradenominational debate about United Methodist doctrine and theology (to accept, only for purposes of debate, the ill-informed distinction currently in force between *doctrina* and *theologoumena*). Ironically enough, it was the evangelicals who promptly pounced on the P-word as an obstacle to what they also wanted: political clout. Now, we are shut of the P-word, and the evangelicals are still distanced from the switches of power.

Some of us had seen the Christian future in the utopias of the 1960s and early 1970s, at Woodstock, in black power, feminism, the peace movement, the death of God, liberation. There were others of us who had seen glimpses of the Christian future at New Delhi (1961), in Montreal (1963), and in the Second Vatican (1962-1965). Some of us (in Faith and Order) had worked for a decade on the recovery of still-usable insights from old debates on Christology, liturgy and, most curiously, on tradition (a pneumatological view of the crucial tasks of Christian "traditioning," in the literal sense of 1 Corinthians 11:23). It was not quite coincidental that these ecumenical explorations had led me to the brothers Wesley, not as Methodists but as "evangelical catholics." Salvaged from the Methodist stereotypes, by choice and in method, the Wesleys were Christian traditioners, one through singable poetry, the other with preachable prose. They were pietists but not scholastics. And they abhorred innovation, except in the re-presentation of the faith already traditioned to the saints. This discovery (if that turns out to be what it was) led me into an absorbing indoor sport, the aim of which was to "find" that *ephapax pistis* in Wesley and through Wesley's sermons. The prize has been a rich banquet of head and heart, however inadequately I may have served it up to others.

Moreover, the United Methodist quadrennium of 1968-1972, was contexted in the turmoil of the still uncomprehended upheavals in the spheres of religion and secular culture, e.g., *The Unraveling of America* (Allen Matusow), *Coming Apart* (William O'Neill), *The Destructive Generation* (Collins and Horowitz), *The Present Age* (Robert Nisbet). Those two decades were exciting and soul-searching in ways now hard to explain or reenact. For some of us, the overall gradient in American churches and secular institutions has been downhill.

In 1968-1972, however, it looked for all the world like an authentic *Kairos*: a world in turmoil and deep demoralization, with every index of social well-being pointing downward into an abyss of permissiveness and decadence. But here, "for the facing of this hour,"[3] was a new United Methodist Church—big, brawny, muscular, sentimental, self-confident, eager for "the living of these days."[4] No matter that the structures of the United Methodist Church had been jury-rigged by corporate lawyers and church bureaucrats concerned with optimum power flowing up and down the organizational plumbing. United Methodists are pragmatists, "can-do people" who keep what works and let what doesn't fall of its own weight. Never mind our cross-eyed *Discipline*, in which the responsibility for "planning the temporal and spiritual interests of the entire church" is mandated to the Council of Bishops and the "doing" of these plans left to the United Methodist curia. "Everybody" understood that the real center of gravity in the *Discipline* is not in Part I, but in Part IV and specifically Chapter 5.

I have known the first three presidents of the Council of Secretaries; I count them friends and can vouch for their dedication, probity, and personal modesty. And yet I have heard each of them speak openly of their settled conviction that the presidency of their curial Council was (and was designed to be) coequal with the presidency of the Council of Bishops. The wonder, then, is not that a polity with such radical anomalies wired into it has not worked well, but that it is still working as well as it is.

What mattered most for me, however, was that the new church was to have an unprecedented thing: a statement on *Doctrine and Doctrinal Standards*, and a revised statement of social principles. This will seem merely a personal crotchet unless you remember that in 1968 this sort of project seemed both desirable and possible. That year marked a sort of high-water mark of ecumenical progress—in Rome, Geneva, in The United Methodist Church. Among the United Methodists, John Wesley seemed to be regaining theological stature, less as eponymous patriarch and more as a conduit back to Methodist origins and into the far richer resources of the larger Christian tradition itself. The notion of "our common history as Christians" (hooted at in Lund, 1952) was increasingly received as meaningful. The elusive idea of "The Christian tradition," over against the plural "traditions of men," was helping to get us beyond the old dichotomies, e.g., Scripture vs. "tradition" (understood always as "human traditions"). Finally, but by no means least, United Methodism was becoming less WASPish, less chauvinist, less bourgeois, less nationalistic. We had declared ourselves an inclusive church, and room had to be made in it for a plurality of partisan groups who still called and professed themselves *United* Methodists. We were not, then or now, inclusive, nor any of all those other good things such as "united." But we were groaning so to be!

Time would fail us even to encapsulate the story of our dreamings. It would, moreover, be nugatory now, since the 1972 Statement has now been relegated to the special limbo prepared for recent past events. But there may be some historical relevance in a few retrospective comments on what we thought we were doing in 1968-1972.

The drafters of the Plan of Union (headed by Charles Parlin) had agreed early on not to touch with a ten-foot pole any of the doctrinal questions raised by the union, save only to certify that the Methodist Articles and Rules and the Evangelical United Brethren Confession were to be "deemed congruent if not identical in their doctrinal perspective and not in conflict." "Congruent if not identical" was a valid statement and as far as I was willing to go. But Mr. Parlin insisted on adding the last phrase, which was and is now not quite true. He spoke of "legal reasons," the avoidance of "doctrinal niceties," etc.

Then came the first surprise for me: the generality of the delegates in Dallas seemed to take it for granted that what the new church needed was a new creed or, at the least, a new "Confession of Faith." They seemed to assume that United Methodism was another confessional tradition, like the Lutherans, Reformed, and Baptist Christians and despite Wesley's pointed rejection of "confessionalism" in any of its conventional meanings. He spoke emphatically of "saving faith" (fiduciary faith, "assurance," what the scholastics had spoken of as *fidas qua creditur*). He has many summaries of the soteriological heart of the gospel, but always in language varied enough to avoid even the appearance of a set formula (i.e., an invariant form of words requiring assent; he was over-emphatic in his denigrations of "orthodoxy": *fides quae creditur*).

For days in Dallas (and even after) one heard the phrase "the new Creedal Commission." It took a bit of doing even to keep open the issue of a "traditionary community" (such as the early church had been and such as some of us believe Wesley had in mind). But it was managed, and we emerged as the Commission on Doctrine and Doctrinal Standards (CDDS). There was, however, enough of a divided mind in the commission itself that we experimented with creed making and confession formulating in our first four sessions. And then a Wesleyan consensus about Jude 3 seemed to emerge. The least that this still means is that the Statement of 1972 was not meant to be a confession. It was meant to aid the traditionary process that had served the Wesleys and other Anglicans before them and the undivided church before that. We intended this to be a pointer to the common core of biblical faith (nowhere formularized in Holy Writ), and to set this into a revisable context of *theologoumena*, along with methodological comments by the way. All but the core was deliberately left open to an ongoing process of dialogue, revision, unfolding development. And even with respect to the core, the way was left open to "more light yet to shine forth from God's Holy Word."

We deliberately took Wesley's motto about thinking and letting think in the way we thought he meant it (and Meldenius before him) with respect to opinions that do not strike at the heart of Christianity (including all opinions calling for more assent). For Wesley deplored all dependence on bare assent to all doctrinal statements, including orthodoxy. Faith in faith, yes, but *fides qua*, and even more urgently faith in faith energized by love (*fides per caritatem opertur*).

We were hoping to help guide a new church on its pilgrim's way toward a convergence in authentic community with all God's people, in God's unfolding future and looming parousia. It was (as I realize now) a quixotic venture and, of course, foredoomed in an ecclesiastical enterprise modeled after a corporate conglomerate. We failed to articulate and communicate our visions. The venture foundered in shallow seas where winds of doctrine shift and blow, in more ways than one.

The Methodists in 1964-1968 were sensitive to the anomaly of having two formal doctrinal statements and two Restrictive Rules about doctrine. There was a push to drop the Methodist Articles and to keep the EUB Confession as more ample in its own right. In the special session of 1967, a motion to this effect was narrowly defeated. In the debate, the Articles were roundly criticized as inadequate and antiecumenical. One delegate observed that John Wesley had rested more of his own doctrinal weight on the Edwardian *Homilies* than on the Thirty-nine Articles. His conclusion was that, given the Wesley *Sermons* and *Notes*, we could dispense with the Articles with no great loss.

Later in the early stages of the CDDS project, after we had broken several lances on a couple of new creeds and one new confession, a subcommittee, co-chaired by Harold DeWolf and Bruce Behney, brought in a special report on the Articles. On the basis of a sizable bill of particulars the subcommittee proposed that the Articles be dropped, and that the *Confession*, *Sermons* and *Notes*, and *Rules* stand as our officially acknowledged foundation documents. Everybody understood that this would trigger the First Restrictive Rule, but the committee argued that the gain would outweigh the risk; they even thought the General Conference would buy it.

The argument persuaded a sizable majority of the commission and the recommendation to delete was entered on our minutes. The chair was horrified, despite his long-held judgment that the Thirty-nine Articles were the least edifying of all the major sixteenth-century formularies and that Wesley's *ad hoc* abridgment of them was one of his less helpful editorial exercises. But what we assumed was that, even without the Articles, United Methodists would still have Wesley's *Sermons* and *Notes*, despite the fact that we knew then about the Ward motion and had examined the arguments that had since been brought forward. What did not cross our minds was that an established historical conjecture, backed by a consistent consensus of its interpreters (from Stevens to Oden to Cushman) could be supplanted by another historical conjecture (based on what still seems to me a forced exegesis of the data and absent of any traditionary support that appears in the primary texts or eyewitnesses).

The DeWolf-Behney proposal was later reconsidered and thus the way was opened to our present new situation, in which the question of the historical referents of the First Rule is now more densely ambiguous than ever before. A footnote: In the special 1970 General Conference's debate on our "Interim Report," Harold Bosley asked whether the commission had even dared to contemplate dropping the Articles altogether. They are "excess baggage," he said, "that we don't really need to take along into the future!" I mention this less to reopen the question than to stress the drastic veer that has happened in what had been a sort of exegetical continuity.

Stuck with the Articles, the CDDS had then to do something about their antiecumenical tone and temper, especially after the cordial reception accorded the World Methodist Church delegation by the Romans at the Vatican Council (two out of the three original trio were United Methodists). What happened was an attempted recontextualization of the offending Articles and an ecumenical reformulation of the current United Methodist self-understanding of them. This was drafted as an address from The United Methodist Church as church to the Roman Catholic Church as church, seeking a more truly mutual understanding between Roman Catholics and the United Methodists.

The General Conference of 1970 approved this with what I took to be some enthusiasm. There was a ceremony in the Vatican; there were some ticklish discussions. The upshot was a directive from Pope Paul VI to Cardinal Villot to respond favorably to the United Methodist Church as church. Bishop James Malone came to Atlanta in 1972 to present Rome's friendly message to The United Methodist Church and some of us thought it a historic moment. The generality of United Methodists, preoccupied with restructure and with current social action issues, sat on their hands. The matter was then explained by one of the most obscure footnotes in a *Discipline* full of obscure footnotes. The Romans concluded that they had been gulled by a good idea that was, however, a non-starter.

The CDDS had plunged into another quixotism, that was also more my fault than anyone else's. All my professional life I had lived with the curious history of Anglican-Roman, Anglican-Protestant dialogue about *essentia* and *adiaphora*. The Anglicans were a traditionary tradition, not a confessional one, and John Wesley had been, as he thought, a faithful Church of England man. Thus, the Chicago-Lambeth Quadrilaterals and the Malines Conversations were important milestones in my ecumenical initiation into the mysteries of Christian disunity and unity. The analogue between the phrase "Lambeth Quadrilateral" and the phrase "Wesleyan Quadrilateral" seemed natural enough, but I was dumb enough to underestimate the number of literal-minded people who would construe it in geometrical terms and draw the unintended inference that this downgraded the primacy of Scripture. And this was of a piece with my failure to imagine professional colleagues confounding "pluralism" and "indifferentism" and then trying to make something sinister out of it. It was a fault; it was a grievous fault, and grievously have I suffered from it.

Three major issues confronted the first regular General Conference of the new church in 1972: (1) the restructuring of the original jury rigging of 1968; (2) a new "Statement of Social Principles"; (3) the first official statement about doctrine and doctrinal standards in American Methodist Church history to be proposed to a General Conference for a signed ballot. If you stop to remember, American society and the world around us were coming unglued. But the burning issue in Atlanta was polity. Not ecclesiology, mind you, but "administrative order." Charles Parlin's Plan of 1968 was discarded, and a new one (crafted by another corporation lawyer, Leonard Slutz) set in its place. It was even worse conceived than Parlin's (and I'm on record as having said so on the Conference floor so that none of this is 20-20 hindsight). But the Conference thought it could not tarry for something better.

The Social Principles statement was dealt with with similar exigency. The original report (predictably left-leaning, especially in the areas of human sexuality and politics) was at risk of rejection. It had to be rewritten on the spot by the legislative committee under dire pressures, with results that can be defended only as being better than they might have been, which is a story deserving of its own vignette. By contrast, the Doctrinal Statement (circulated in printed form in advance) was presented late one morning, with lunch as a deterrent to extended debate. The debate was concluded in 17 minutes, and the Report approved by 925 Ayes and 17 Nays (one of these was Mr. Slutz's; another from a Filipino delegate, another by the Good News delegate, still a fourth by the delegate from British Methodism). All of the omens seemed auspicious! It was a great moment and too many of us were swept up into a false euphoria.

The commission had urged the Conference to provide some sort of meaningful follow-up, with a view to an ongoing process of cumulative development and quadrennial revision. This would have been consonant with our notion of a traditionary church. Next to nothing of this sort happened. Our wisest critic, Professor Cushman, found it distressingly imprecise and vulnerable to misinterpretation; he turned out to be right. By and large, it just sat there. In 1976, Professor Cushman petitioned the General Conference for it to revert to its older form of an uninterpreted text of foundation documents, with all historical and theological excursus omitted. That would have shattered the dream of that new church in quest of cumulative doctrinal consensus. But now, with that dream faded, one can see the exasperated wisdom embedded in Cushman's proposal.

One of our concerns, which had to do with what Professor Wainwright now snidely speaks of as "the glorification of 'pluralism' in which the 1972 Statement indulged itself," was to make room in the United Methodist Church for our self-styled evangelicals! However explained, the fact remained (still remains) that those people have been distanced from both our power cells and our seminary faculties in The Methodist Church and The United Methodist Church for as long as I can remember. For example, in the early sixties, the Perkins faculty vetoed its dean's nomination of Timothy Smith as assistant professor of American church history. For his consolation, Smith had to go on to a tenured post at Minnesota and thereafter at John Hopkins (he is currently the president of the American Society of Church Historians). All this compounded the irony that it was a group of evangelicals who promptly pounced on the term "pluralism" and helped damn both the term and its positive connotations by equating it with indifferentism. Other evangelicals, as I am happy to record, have joined in the general cause of a Wesley renaissance in imaginative and generous ways. Thus, no one takes more satisfaction than I in the fact that a Wesley Fellow, of A Foundation for Theological Education, has just been granted tenure at Yale.

The 1972 Statement was designed quite deliberately for further development. We also proposed that the Council of Bishops take up more vigorously their traditional responsibility as teachers in the church. Appeals went out to seminaries (despite our memories of earlier fiascoes) for conciliar collaborations in and between their faculties. This was utterly crucial to the process of real reception in the new church of the ecclesiological vision that we had tried to descry. Its promulgation had been so hearty that I had been blinded to the reality of its decisive *non*-reception.

And so the old Quixote was taken aback at Baltimore when the General Conference, celebrating our Bicentennial, moved to mandate not a revised doctrinal statement, but a brand new one, and then, as if to emphasize their yen for innovation, rejected a supporting motion to place the project under the guidance and supervision of the Council of Bishops. It was a portentous development, the end of which none of us can yet foresee. The image that sticks in my mind is of a tall ship with large sails unfurled to doctrinal winds, listing from side to side for want of ballast. What had seemed a *kairos* has now become another incident in a meandering story.

The hour is late and, in any case, I am disqualified from the panel of judges in the critical evaluation of the new Statement. But I am an *amicus curiae*, and beg your indulgence for four comments half-descriptive, half-evaluative. First, it is a statement with very real merits of its own. Second, the original text was worked over to its advantage in the legislative committee at St. Louis in what was a truly edifying instance of "conciliar theology" (the UMC could learn some very fruitful lessons here). Third, its public reception in its first year has been relatively quiet, with no announcements thus far of plans for a constructive follow-up. Of the six written evaluations that I have seen, four (all from Duke) find for the new statement. The other two (one from the United Methodist left, the other from United Methodism's ecumenical vanguard) intone their requiems for the old Statement in very different keys. No non-Methodist, to my knowledge, has yet weighed in on either side.

My fourth comment has to do with how new the new Statement is (for all its unacknowledged borrowings from the old). This is in two ways: In the first place, it commits The United Methodist Church to a basic shift from its "traditionary" stance that it had accepted in 1972 (by a 99 percent majority) around to the status of a "confessional church" (this by a majority of 95 percent). In the second place, despite its admiring view of Wesley, it formally uncouples the traditional pairing of the Articles and Rules from the *Sermons* and *Notes* as equally normative. This leaves the exegesis of the second clause of the First Restrictive Rule radically unclear. Whatever 1988 did or did not do, it did not settle the now famous debate between Professor Heitzenrater on the one side and Professor Oden (and now Professor Cushman) on the other. And wherever we may stand in this *Auseinandersetzung*, we all have to start with the striking fact that the highest human authority in the United Methodist Church has, within the span of 16 years, voted for two opposed interpretations of its First Restrictive Rule (basing its judgment in each case on historical conjecture). Moreover, the majorities in each case were greater than on any other contested issue in living memory.

What *is* the canonical state of doctrinal norms in The United

Methodist Church at the present time? I frankly do not know—after several readings of the current *Discipline* (and the *Daily Christian Advocate* for 1988); after personal correspondence (and visits by phone) with two good friends, Tom Oden and Richard Heitzenrater; and after having run the relevant documents by a couple of canon lawyers for review. *Ad litteris*, it would seem that our only constitutionally protected doctrinal "statements" are the Articles, *Confession*, and *Rules*. The *Sermons* and *Notes* (plus other documents) are stipulated as exemplary "models of exposition." The force of contrary agreements, implied in The Plan of Union of 1968, had expired with the automatic deletion of Article VII in Section III of the 1968 Constitution (its expiration had already been scheduled in 1986). Some of us regard this a grievous distortion of Methodist tradition, tied as that had been to the intent and spirit of the Model Deed (1763) and the "Large [American] Minutes" of 1773 and 1784. This, however, is now irrelevant. What *is* relevant is the resultant uncertainty as to the legal referents of the First Restrictive Rule.

On some days I find this worrisome. But the grace of constructive remembrance prompts the rueful thought that it may be yet another instance of much ado about not very much. We may now have the form of a confessional church, with not one but *two* "confessions," not identical but not yet in open conflict. Compared to the really great evangelical confessions (e.g., cf. Schaff, Vol. III) the United Methodist Articles are a deficient statement of normative Christian teaching (e.g., in Christology, pneumatology, and symbolics). The Articles plus the *Sermons* and *Notes* complemented each other. Now, for the time being, we are stuck with *sola Articula*, with a set of United Methodist *theologoumena* that allows for the same degree of diversity that we had before, before the P-word was interdicted.

But, as they say in Australia, "Not to Worry." The United Methodist Church *is* a traditionary church, whatever any current *Discipline* may say, and the *Sermons* and *Notes* will continue to exercise as much or as little influence on United Methodist doctrinal self-understanding as if we knew precisely what the First Restrictive Rule really means. The earthly remains of the last United Methodist theologian decisively influenced by official stipulations in the *Discipline*, against his/her convictions based otherwise, lie somewhere in an unmarked grave.

Our current doctrinal confusions do not arise from latitudinarian statements. They come from the breakdown in our effectual traditioning of the living classical Christian tradition in the Methodist teaching ministry over the past century (the traditionary process worked wonderfully well during the first century).

A revivified UMC will depend then, in large part, on a renovated process of traditioning the biblical *fides qua creditur* (faith as trust, "lived faith"), faith from those who have it conveyed to those who seek it by the Holy Spirit, who is the divine witness in every gift of faith. We know now that Wesley was actually wrong with all those sniffs of his about "orthodoxy," i.e., true teachings proposed for mental assent (*fides quae creditur*). Methodism has experimented with orthodoxy, heterodoxy, and heresy (Pelagianism in particular); and orthodoxy is still better by far than its alternatives, even if still inefficacious by itself alone. No one has ever been saved by mere assent, even to true statements. Still and all, salvation by grace through faith is a better doctrine than salvation by moral rectitude, in whatever guise. The experience of faith is also more valid than the experience of self-righteousness. The Scripture way of salvation is more valid (and more interesting) than self-realization by whatever formulae (New Age psychology and wisdom from the East notwithstanding). Scriptural holiness is more radical than pietism or moralism. And moralistic editorials (from whatever viewpoint) are not sermons, even when delivered from pulpits and decked out with Scripture.

A trinitarian doctrine of the Holy Spirit would do us all more good than the pneumatological smog we have to breathe nowadays, both in charismatic and liberal congregations. Last Pentecost Sunday, in a lively United Methodist Church, we were invited to pray, collectively, to "Almighty God, who shares your loving kindness through the Father, Son, and Holy Spirit, that we may experience the blessings of your divine nature and live within the boundaries of your Providence." What is more, the people I asked about so startling a form of words emphasized that their focus had been on the pious intent of the prayer and not its words.

We know how hard it is nowadays to get through a service of worship without being asked to reflect on God's gender and psychology, as if Article I (or the Shema, Deuteronomy 6:4) had never been written. Sometimes one may wonder if we are being tempted to become idolators (i.e., worshipers of a pictured god) of a higher order?

There was a healthy debate in 1988 about the primacy of Scripture. The United Methodist future will be brighter if, as, or when liturgy, preaching, ethos, and esprit in United Methodist churches become more biblical in the saving faith in which we live and love and work and go on our way into death and toward the life of the world to come.

There is a rising consciousness among United Methodists of being a church in crisis. Bishops sound the tocsin; bureaucrats ratchet up their rationalizations. Bishop Wilke follows an alarming book, *And Are We Yet Alive?*, with a hopeful book of *Signs and Wonders*. There are said to be minishments of confidence even in the seminaries. But as the Pelagian rhetoric of our moralism goes up, our membership figures ease down by a little, year after year, along with other indices as well.

It is, I know, a mite tiresome to keep citing that old chestnut of Wesley's about Methodism's prospects (as of 1786):

> I am not afraid that the people called Methodists should ever cease to exist either in Europe or America. But I am afraid lest they should only exist as a dead sect, having the form of religion without the power.[5]

The rest of this short four-page "Thought" goes downhill after that, and ends with "a few prudential regulations" (yet also with a few flashes of light in the gloaming). We have all read so many various prescriptions to fill out Wesley's subjunctive preface that I am loathe to add another. But it is the case that Methodism survived Wesley and his far lesser epigones, even if not so well as we have been told by our triumphalists. And United Methodism may well survive the parlous state into which it seems now to be miring like a dinosaur in a cretaceous swamp. For despair is not a Christian option, and providential history can be counted on to serve, not one scenario but many, yet God's gracious purposes and human responses that are consonant with them. St. Paul put this in its right perspective:

> Hard-pressed on every side, we are never hemmed in; bewildered, we are never at our wits' end; disappointed we are never abandoned to our fate. . . . Whatever the case, our eyes are fixed, not on things to be seen, but on the things unseen, for the visible passes away, whereas the realm of the unseen [metahistory in the power of the prevenient Spirit] endures eternally . . . Therefore, we never lose confidence. (2 Corinthians 4:8-9a, 18, 5:6).

The wisest historian I have ever known well taught us to look for the paradoxes in church history and the metahistory in which all human history is set. Given the Spirit's prevenience, he would say:

> The purpose of a historical understanding is not so much to detect the divine action in history as to understand the human actions in the bewildering variety and confusion in which they appear to a human observer.[6]

Father Georges Florovsky had been an eyewitness to the end of Tsarist Russia, the savagery of Leninism; he did not live to see the new ambivalence in a world where neither communism nor capitalism is serving the human cause very well. But he never did a whit less of what he could because of adverse prospects, never a whit less because of brighter ones. Christians do not work to bring in the kingdom; rather they are called to be alert and ready for its appearing.

The human prospect was not reassuring when Wesley lay dying in that little room in the house on City Road in early March of 1791. The prospective for the Methodist future was even less assured. His had been a strange life in a strange time: incredible achievements laced with nagging frustrations. What remained clear and steady to the end was his deepest motive: "I'll praise my Maker while I've breath; And when my voice is lost in death, Praise shall employ my nobler powers"[7]; and his steadfast conviction: "The best of all is, God is with us."

Thus, for those of you engaged in the continued perplexities of church historians who have to balance off realism and sober hope, whether in wider or more local spheres, you must resist the seductions of despair over what looks like a declining church in a declining age. You might even take heart and courage from Herbert Butterfield's hard-worn serenity (he was himself a great historian and a Methodist nurtured in a great tradition):

> Hold fast to Christ, and as for the rest, hang loose, while doing all you can to honour his Name and the Christian cause.[8]

Amen.

Endnotes

Sermon 1—*The Meaning of Sacrifice*

1 Cecil Frances Alexander, "There Is a Green Hill Far Away," stanza 5.

Sermon 2—*The Power To Love*

1 *Rudyard Kipling's Verse,* inclusive ed., 1885-1918 (Garden City, N.Y.: Doubleday, Page, 1919), 504.

2 Cecil Frances Alexander, "There Is a Green Hill Far Away," stanza 5.

Sermon 4—*The Ecumenical Road Ahead*

1 The Third Assembly of the World Council of Churches, *The New Delhi Report* (New York: Association Press, 1962), 116.

Sermon 5—*Buildup to a Letdown?*

1 The Third Assembly of the World Council of Churches, *The New Delhi Report* (New York: Association Report, 1962), 116.

Sermon 9—*The Paths of Glory*

1 Thomas Gray, "Elegy Written in a Country Church Yard," stanza 9.

Sermon 10—*Pilate's Plight*

1 *The Works of John Wesley,* vol. 1, Sermons I, 1-33, ed. Albert C. Outler; Sermon 14, "The Repentance of Believers" (Nashville, Abingdon, 1984), 343.

2 William Bryan Forbush, *Foxe's Book of Martyrs* (Philadelphia: Universal Book and Bible House, 1926), 9.

Sermon 11—*Methodist Pluralism*

1 *The Works of John Wesley,* vol. 1, Sermons I, 1-33, ed. Albert C. Outler; Sermon 7, "The Way to the Kingdom" (Nashville: Abingdon, 1984), 220-21.

2 *The Book of Discipline of the United Methodist Church, 1984* (Nashville: 1984, The United Methodist Publishing House), 78-85, para. 69.

Sermon 12—*Biblical Primitivism in Early American Methodism*

1 *The Letters of the Rev. John Wesley, A.M.*, ed. John Telford, 8 vols. (London: Epworth, 1931), 7:239.

2 *The Book of Discipline of the United Methodist Church, 1972* (Nashville: The United Methodist Publishing House, 1972), 56, para. 69.

3 *The Works of John Wesley,* vol. 3, *Sermons 71-114,* ed. Albert C. Outler; Sermon 74, "Of the Church" (Nashville: Abingdon, 1986), 50-51.

4 Richard Watson, *Sermons and Sketches of Sermons;* Sermon 21, "The Influence of Revealed Truth Upon a Nation" (New York: Phillips and Hunt, n.d.) 2:473-81. Cf. also pp. 107, 179, 369.

5 Nathan Bangs, *An Original Church of Christ; or A Scriptural Vindication of the Orders and Powers of the Ministry of The Methodist Episcopal Church* (n.p., 1837), 10-11.

6 *Ibid.*, 9.

7 *Ibid.*, 11.

8 Thomas Brooks, *Works*, 4:374.

9 Bangs, *Original Church,* 381-82.

10 Richard Abbey, *An Inquiry Into the Ecclesiastical Constitution, the Origin and the Character of the Church of Christ and the Gospel Ministry* (n.p., n.d.), 33.

11 *Ibid.*, 80.

12 *Ibid.*, 112-13.

13 Richard Watson, *Theological Institutes* (Nashville: Southern Methodist Publishing House, 1860), 683.

14 Thomas Campbell, *Declaration and Address,* 1809.

Sermon 14—*Women, War, and Liberal Education*

1 Wendell L. Willkie, "Education Determines Civilization," *Vital Speeches of the Day* 9 (February 15, 1943).

2 *Ibid.*; 262.

Sermon 16—*"Unite the Pair So Long Disjoined"*

1 *The Work of John Wesley,* vol. 18, *Journals and Diaries I* (1735-38); eds. W. Reginald Ward and Richard P. Heitzenrater (Nashville: Abingdon, 1988), 249-50. (Journal entry for May 24, 1738).

2 *Ibid.*, 250.

3 *Ibid.*

4 From *A Collection of Hymns for the Use of the People Called Methodists* (London: Wesleyan Conference Office, n.d.), 442-43.

Sermon 18—*Blessed Are the Peacemakers*

1 James Russell Lowell, "The Present Crisis."

Sermon 19—*The Constraints of Love*

1 *W. B. Yeats: The Poems,* ed. Richard J. Finnerman (New York: Macmillan, 1983), line 3.

2 Hal David, "What the World Needs Now," (Blue Seas Music, 1965).

Sermon 21—*And So What Have You Done for Me Lately?*

1 Eric Hoffer, *The Temper of Our Times* (New York: Harper and Row, 1967), 93.

2 *Ibid.*, 99-100.

3 *Rubáiyát of Omar Khayyám,* ed., Edward Fitzgerald (New York: Illustrated Editions Co., 1934), 55.

4 Leon Harris, *Biography of Godfrey Lowell Cabot* (New York: Athenium, 1967), xiii-xiv.

Sermon 24—*The Mission Fair*

1 Reginald Heber, "From Greenland's Icy Mountains," stanza 1.

2 Ozora A. Davis, "At Length There Dawns the Glorious Day," stanza 1.

3 John Oxenham, "In Christ There is No East or West," stanza 1.

Sermon 25—*No Abiding City*

1 Katharine Lee Bates, "America the Beautiful."

Sermon 27—*Wesleyan Spirituality*

1 *The Works of John Wesley,* vol. 3, Sermons III, 71-114, ed. Albert C. Outler; Sermon 85, "On Working Out Our Own Salvation" (Nashville; Abingdon, 1986), 207.

2 *Ibid.*, 533, Sermon 109, "The Trouble and Rest of Good Men."

3 *Ibid.*, 534

4 *Ibid.*, 203, "On Working Out Our Own Salvation."

5 *Ibid.*, 204

6 *The Works of John Wesley,* vol. 1, Sermons I, 1-33, ed. Albert C. Outler; Sermon 16, "The Means of Grace" (Nashville: Abingdon, 1984), 384.

7 *Ibid.*, 386.

8 *Ibid.*

9 *Ibid.*, 387.

10 *Ibid.*, 389-90.

11 *Ibid.*, 395.

12 *The Works of John Wesley,* vol. 2, Sermons II, 34-70, ed. Albert C. Outler; Sermon 45, "The New Birth" (Nashville: Abingdon, 1985), 193-94.

13 *Works,* 1:698. Sermon 33, "Upon Our Lord's Sermon on the Mount, Discourse the Thirteenth."

Sermon 29—*Our Fathers' Faith and Ours*

1 Albert C. Outler, *Library of Protestant Thought* (New York: Oxford Univ. Press, 1964), 109ff.

2 *The Works of John Wesley,* vol. 9, *The Methodist Societies: History, Nature, and Design,* ed. Rupert E. Davies, "The Nature, Design, and General Rules of the United Societies in London Bristol, Kingswood, and Newcastle Upon Tyne (1743)." (Nashville, Abingdon. 1989), 69-73.

3 Outler, *Library of Protestant Thought,* 130.

4 *Lutheran Book of Worship* (Minneapolis: Augsburg, 1978), 450.

5 The Nicene Creed.

Sermon 30—*"Take Thou Authority . . ." (Ordination Sermon 1)*

1 *The Work of John Wesley,* vol. 9, *The Methodist Societies: History, Nature, and Design,* ed. Rupert E. Davies, "The Nature, Design, and General Rules of the United Societies in London, Bristol, Kingswood, and New Castle Upon Tyne (1743)" (Nashville: Abingdon, 1989), 70.

2 *Doctrines and Discipline of the Methodist Church 1960* (Nashville: The Methodist Publishing House, 1960), p. 140, para. 352.12.

3 Article XIII, *The Book of Discipline of The United Methodist Church 1968* (Nashville: The United Methodist Publishing House, 1968), 40.

4 *Ibid.*, 122, para. 334.

5 *The Book of Worship for Church and Home* (Nashville: The Methodist Publishing House, 1964), 46.

6 *Ibid.*, 52.

Sermon 31—*Faith Renewed*

1 *The Book of Discipline of The United Methodist Church 1968* (Nashville: The United Methodist Publishing House, 1968), 122.

2 The Nicene Creed.

3 *The Works of John Wesley,* vol. 11, *The Appeals to Men of Reason and Religion and Certain Related Open Letters,* ed. Gerald R. Cragg; "An Earnest Appeal to Men of Reason and Religion" (Oxford: Clarendon, 1975), 45. This vol. is now published by Abingdon.

4 Cf. Note 2 in *Ibid.*, 48.

5 *Ibid.*, 47-49.

Sermon 32 —*Visions and Dreams*

1 Frank Mason North, "Where Cross the Crowded Ways of Life," stanza 6.

Sermon 33—*The Holy Spirit in the Ministry* (Ordination Sermon 2)

1 *The Book of Worship for Church and Home* (Nashville: The Methodist Publishing House, 1964), 52.

2 *Ibid.,45*

Sermon 34—*The Methodist Heritage in America: The Past as Prologue*

1 M. Louise Haskins, "The Gate of the Year," in *Masterpieces of Religious Verse,* ed. James Dalton Morrison (New York and London: Harper and Brothers, 1948), no. 287.

Sermon 35—*The Paradox of Ordained Ministry* (Ordination Sermon 3)

1 *The Book of Worship for Church and Home* (Nashville: The Methodist Publishing House, 1964), 52.

2 *Veni, Creator Spiritus.*

Sermon 36—*The Church's Real Business* (Ordination Sermon 4)

1 John Newton, "Amazing Grace, How Sweet the Sound," Stanza 3.

2 *The Book of Worship for Church and Home* (Nashville: The Methodist Publishing House, 1964), 52.

3 *The Book of Discipline of The United Methodist Church 1968* (Nashville: The United Methodist Publishing House, 1968), 109-10.

4 *The Book of Worship,* 52.

Sermon 37—*Empowered To Witness*

1 John Wesley, *Explanatory Notes Upon the New Testament* (London: Epworth, 1948), 394.

2 *Ibid.*, 203.

3 *The Works of John Wesley,* vol. 18, *Journals and Diaries I* (1735-1738), eds. W. Reginald Ward and Richard P. Heitzenrater (Nashville: Abingdon, 1988), 171. (Journal entry for September 13, 1736). John Wesley was quoting Article XXI of the Thirty-Nine Articles, "On the Authority of General Councils."

4 *The Journal and Letters of Francis Asbury,* eds. Elmer T. Clark, J. Manning Potts, Jacob S. Payton, 3 vols. (London: Epworth: Nashville: Abingdon, 1958), 1:476.

5 *Poems of Gerard Manley Hopkins,* ed. Robert Bridges, 2d ed. (London: Oxford Univ. Press, 1931),

6 From the *Large Minutes* of 1789. Cf. *The Works of John Wesley,* 1:85, note 70.

Sermon 38—*Our Wesleyan Heritage and Our Doctrinal Future*

1 *The Doctrines and Discipline of The Methodist Church 1956* (Nashville: The Methodist Publishing House, 1956), 12, para. 9.1.

2 H. K. Carroll, W. P. Harrison, and J. H. Bayliss, *Proceedings, Sermon Essays, and Addresses of the Centennial Methodist Conference Held in Mt. Vernon Place Methodist Episcopal Church* (Nashville: Southern Methodist Publishing House, 1885), 33.

3 *Report of The Theological Study Commission on Doctrine and Doctrinal Standards,* Albert C. Outler, Chairman, 1968, p. 17.

4 *The Works of John Wesley,* vol. 9, *The Methodist Societies: History, Nature, and Design,* ed. Rupert E. Davies "The Character of a Methodist" (Nashville: Abingdon, 1989), 33f.

5 See *The Works of John Wesley,* vol. 2, "Catholic Spirit," 81-95.

6 From the "Invitation" of the Ritual for Holy Communion.

7 *Works*, 9:254f.

8 *Ibid.*, 527.

Sermon 39—*"Take Thou Authority"*. . . (Ordination Sermon 5)

1 *The Book of Worship for Church and Home* (Nashville: The Methodist Publishing House, 1964), 52.

Sermon 41—*How to Run a Conservative Revolution and Get No Thanks for It*

1 J. Addington Symonds "These Things Shall Be," stanza 1.

2 Ozora S. Davis, "At Length There Dawns the Glorious Day," stanza 1.

3 The source of this quotation has not been traced.

4 On August 17, 1764, J.W. wrote Lady Maxwell, "I am no great friend to solitary Christianity," *The Letters of the Rev. John Wesley, A.M.*, ed. John Telford, 8 vols. (London: Epworth, 1931), 4:261.

5 *The Works of John Wesley,* vol. 9, *The Methodist Societies: History, Nature, and Design,* ed. Rupert E. Davies; "A Plain

Account of the People Called Methodists" (Nashville: Abingdon, 1989), 257.

6 *The Works of John Wesley,* vol. 2, *Sermons II, 34-70,* ed. Albert C. Outler; Sermon 50, "The Use of Money" (Nashville: Abingdon, 1985), 268. Cf. also *Works* 9:530, "Thoughts Upon Methodism."

7 *The Works of John Wesley,* vol. 1, *Sermons I, 1-33,* ed. Albert C. Outler; Sermon 98, "On Visiting the Sick" (Nashville: Abingdon, 1984), 394.

Sermon 42—*World Methodism's World Parish—Then and Now*

1 *The Works of John Wesley,* vol. 18, *Journals and Diaries I (1735-1738);* eds. W. Reginald Ward and Richard P. Heitzenrater (Nashville: Abingdon, 1988), 249-50. (Journal entry for May 24, 1738).

2 *The Works of John Wesley,* vol. 19, *Journals and Diaries II (1738-1743),* eds. W. Reginald Ward and Richard P. Heitzenrater (Nashville: Abingdon, 1990), 67. (Journal entry for June 11, 1739).

3 *Ibid.*, 19. (Journal entry for October 14, 1738).

4 *Ibid.*, 20. (Journal entry for October 15, 1738).

5 *Ibid.*, 27. (Journal entry for December 16, 1738).

6 *Ibid.*, 30. (Journal entry for January 4, 1739).

7 *Ibid.*, 31.

8 Charles Wesley, "Love Divine, All Loves Excelling."

9 Isaac Watts, "Jesus Shall Reign."

10 Charles Wesley, "Captain of Israel's Host."

11 *The Works of John Wesley,* vol. 3, *Sermons 71-114,* ed. Albert E. Outler; Sermon 112, "On Laying the Foundation of the New Chapel" (Nashville: Abingdon, 1986), 592.

Sermon 43—*The Measure of Greatness*

1 Cf. *The Works of John Wesley,* vol. 2, *Sermons II,* 437-50, ed. Albert C. Outler; Sermon 60, "The General Deliverance."

2 Joachin Neader, trans. Catherine Winkworth.

3 Isaac Watts, "Joy to the World."

4 *Ibid.*

5 Sidney Lanier, "The Marshes of Glynn," IV 7.

6 Samuel Taylor Coleridge, "The Devil's Thought," stanza 6. "And the Devil Did Grin, For His Darling Sin/Is Pride That Apes Humility."

7 Charles Wesley.

8 *The Works of John Wesley,* vol. 19, *Journals and Diaries II (1738-1743),* eds. W. Reginald Ward and Richard P. Heitzenrater (Nashville: Abingdon, 1990), 46. (Journal entry for March 21, 1739).

9 John E. Bode, "O Jesus, I Have Promised."

10 Isaac Watts, "Come Holy Spirit, Heavenly Dove."

11 John E. Bode, "O Jesus, I Have Promised."

Sermon 44—*Through A Glass Darkly: Memories, Forebodings and Faith.*

1 *The Works of John Wesley,* vol. 3, Sermons 71-114, ed. Albert C. Outler; Sermon 102, "Of Former Times" (Nashville: Abingdon, 1986), 453.

2 *Ibid.*, 515. Sermon 107, "On God's Vineyard"

3 Harry Emerson Fosdick, "God of Grace and God of Glory," stanza 1.

4 *Ibid.*, stanza 2.

5 *The Works of John Wesley,* vol. 9, *The Methodist Societies: History, Nature, and Design,* ed. Rupert E. Davies, "Thoughts Upon Methodism" (Nashville: Abingdon, 1989), 527.

6 Father Florovsky in Tsarist Russia.

7 Isaac Watts, "I'll Praise My Maker While I've Breath."

8 H. Herbert Butterfield, *Christianity and History* (New York: Scribner's, 1950), 146. ". . . the Principle: Hold to Christ, and for the rest be totally uncommitted."

Index

A

D

E

F

G

H

I

J

K

L

M

N

O

P

Q

R

S

T

U

V

W

Y

Z